Yes! I have my

HUTCH

CHARLOTTE BREESE

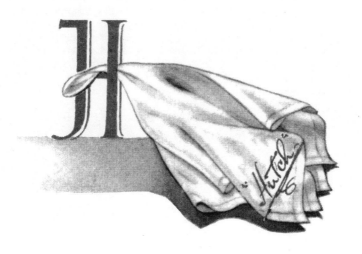

BLOOMSBURY

Grateful acknowledgement is made to the following for the use of their photographs: 4, Driggs Collection/Magnum; 9, Cliché Seeberger Frères/Arch. Phot./© CNMHS, Paris; 8, The Cole Porter Collection, the Yale Collection of the Literature of the American Musical Theatre, Historical Sound Recordings, Yale Music Library, and the Cole Porter Musical and Literary Property Trusts; 10–13, 15, 33, 34, 39, 47, 48–50, The Hulton Getty Picture Collection; 16, 20–22, 27, The Mander and Mitchenson Theatre Collection; 42, Sheffield Newspapers Ltd; 38, BFI Stills © Carlton International Media Ltd; 58, The Fairfax Photo Library; 53, PA News; 56, Nick Brown; remaining photographs courtesy of the Hutch Collection.

Grateful acknowledgement is made to Warner/Chappell and IMP for permission to reproduce lines from the songs 'Dance dance dance little lady' and 'I travel alone' by Noël Coward; 'High Hat' by George Gershwin and 'Love for Sale' by Cole Porter; to the BBC Written Archives Centre for permission to reproduce BBC in-house correspondence; to Peters Fraser & Dunlop for permission to quote from Evelyn Waugh's *Diaries*; to Redwood Music Ltd for permission to quote from 'They Didn't Believe Me', words by Michael Elder Rourke, and from 'You Try Somebody Else', words by Buddy DeSylva, Lou Brown and Ray Henderson; to Laura McKenna for permission to quote from 'Too Many Martinis' by Anne de Nys; to Boosey & Hawkes Music Publishers Ltd for permission to quote from 'These Foolish Things' by Strachey/ Maschwitz, copyright
© 1936 by Lafleur Music Ltd.

First published 1999

Bloomsbury Publishing Plc, 38 Soho Square, London WIV 5DF

A CIP catalogue record for this book
is available from the British Library

ISBN 0 7475 4596 0

10 9 8 7 6 5 4 3 2 1

Typeset by Hewer Text Ltd, Edinburgh
Printed by Clays Ltd, St Ives plc

For my marvellous parents – Dick and Miriam Odgers

CONTENTS

ILLUSTRATIONS

ACKNOWLEDGEMENTS

I would like to thank my children – Olivia, Cecily, Josephine and Tabitha – for their indulgence; my sister Clare for her support and my brother James for his practical help; Irfan Husain and his family for their love, hospitality and encouragement; Peter Breese for his generosity. I am also most grateful to Hugh Bredin for his enthusiasm, patience and expertise, and to Liz Calder, Alexandra Pringle and Ingrid von Essen.

My friends and extended family helped a lot: Diny Shepherd-Cross, Hasan Askari, Sarah Tillie, Bubli Brar, Jane Broadley, Diana Alderson, Edward Synge, Jane Angus, Willa Walker, Ivor and Katerina Porter, Charles Swift, Tom Stacey, Jean Letts, Vicky Wilson, Jane Willoughby, Renu Chopra, Alice Lewes, Phoebe Anne Magee, Fiona Hassard, Celia Campbell, Peter Johnson, Kay Hargreaves, Barry and Anne Nation, Robin Melville, David Sheppard, David West-Russell, Davina Campbell-Golding, Syra Vahidy.

I am most grateful to James Moore for the time and trouble he has taken over years to supply me with Hutch's music, and to him for the discography he has created for this book. Hugh Palmer has also helped us both with musical details. Stephen Bourne has been similarly helpful with information about films. Val Wilmer has been most generous with interviews, information and introductions. Principal variety and theatrical sources have included Philip Hindin, Tom Eggerdon, Patrick Newley and Ned Sherrin, who have painstakingly corrected my errors. David Heneker, Bill Pilkington and Harold Berens contributed ubiquitously. To Hutch's lovers, friends and children I owe the greatest debt of thanks.

I have not made distinctions between living and dead informants – though I can't keep track of them, I lose them weekly and miss them sorely. I have used titles erratically, when their owners seemed inseparable from them. The list is not exhaustive, others appear in the notes and I apologise to anyone that I have omitted.

Hutch in Grenada: especially Ray Smith of St George's, also Alfred De Bellotte, Linlessa Leid, Joan Bain, Daura MacEachrane, Ziffi Duprey, Olive Butler, Jeri Allen, Maud Thomas, Eugene Rose, Elma Belizaire, Molly McIntyre, Flora Coard, Sydney Mitchell, Ches Gibbs, Stressman and Everett Thomas, Sylvia Renwick, Leonard Copeland, H. J. Hughes, Alister Hughes, Jill Shepherd, Joseph Benjamin, Georgie Gibbs, Willie Redhead, Jean Thelander, Ossie Gibbs.

Hutch in Harlem: principally Gabrielle, Alison Rae, Phoebe Magee and Steve Ross; also Mavis and Marissa Fleming, Harvey Sands, Marjorie Phillibert, Lamuel Stanislaus, Henry Copeland, Brian Rust, Chris Clarke, Val Wilmer, Howard Rye, Stanley Black, Reg Varney, Simon Becker, Bobby Short, Laura Chinn.

Hutch in Europe: particularly Alison Harris; also Brodrick Haldane, Princess Torlonia, Chris Ellis, Jim Tucker, Elizabeth Welch, Frank Hooper, Ted Morgan, Princess Sita of Kapurthala, Lawrence Pratt.

Hutch in the twenties: specially David Herbert; also Gerry Moore, Joan Vyvyan, Sir Peter Saunders, Michael Thornton, Norman Quilliam, Harry Gold, Dame Barbara Cartland, Philip Buchel, Norman Hackforth, Micky Migdoll, Tony Wheeler, Frank Squires, Don Johnson, Noel Browne, Artemis Cooper, John Morgan, Mary Hildersley, Nigel Pemberton, Allanah Harper, Lady Alexandra Metcalfe, Elizabeth Longford, Jimmy Perry, Sir Steven Runciman, Roland Philipps, Anthony Powell, Peter Quennell, Sir Harold Acton, Graham Payn, Sir John Mills, Dame Peggy Ashcroft, Gwenol Heneker, Barbara Young Pullman, Bruce Kellner, Harvey Sands, Ossie Gibbs, Derek Cheek, Anne Chisholm, Bertice Reading, Derek Jacobi, Vivian Ellis, Richard Murdoch, Paul Tanqueray, Catherine Courtenay, Charles Sweeny, Jeff Green, Ernie Wise, Hubert Gregg, John Gardiner, Sheridan Morley, Tiny Winters.

Hutch in the thirties: Richard Baerlein, Stephane Grappelli, Stanley Black, Sydney Lipton, Ivor Crosthwaite, Jack Bentley, Lady d'Avigdor Goldsmid, Geoff Tansley, Grace Kennedy, Reg Varney, Ben Warriss, Len Lowe, Alan Clare, George Elrick, Adelaide Hall, Arthur Prothero, Jim Casey, Betty Middlebrook, Tessie O'Shea, Richard Hough, Catherine Courtenay, Tom

Corbett, Sir Lionel Thompson, Johnny Riscoe, Sandy Forbes, Chili Bouchier, Louis Benjamin, Gordon Blackie, Alan Dell, Mrs B. B. Goodwin, Bobby Jay, Wendy Tonkinson, Nat Temple, Dave Kaye, Leslie Berens, Judy Shirley, Evelyn Laye, Cavan O'Connor, Peter Elliott, Lew Lane, Roy Hudd, Betty Turner, Cyril Fletcher, Beryl Reid, Doris Hare, Mike Craig, Charlie Chester, Adrian Morgan, Mrs Gordon Crier, Joe Daniels, Joe Deniz, John East, Jonathan James Moore, Ken Pye.

Hutch in the war: specially Jess Pilling; also Wally Ridley, Brian Johnston, Mairi Craven, George Wiebencer, Michael Pointon, Violet Davies, Judy Campbell, Joyce Brazell, Marjorie Lipscomb, Phyllis Rounce, Stephen Williams, Stewart Morris, Jean Boht, Leslie Perowne, Robert Nesbitt, Henry Tiarks, Bill Cotton, Joan Skillington, Dan Gillies, Barry Band.

Hutch in the 1950s: particularly Patrick Baring, John Hurst, Eqbal Ahmed; also Russ Conway, Nicholas Parsons, Sydney Shaw, Tom Corbett, J. Swindells, Glyn Roberts, Lord Kimberley, Jean Abbott, Harold Fielding, Lord Foley, Johnny Dankworth, Lew Lane, Sydney Grace, Terry Miller, Leslie Berens, Chris Hutchinson, Pat Hamshere, Mike Duke, Michael Bentine, Eric Braun, John Marven, Clare Bloom, Roy Oakeshott, Johnny Wise, Sylvia Garnsey, Julian and Miranda Tennant, Sir Lionel Thompson, Peter Charlesworth, Richard Parker, Roger Longrigg, Wolf Mankowitz, John Gardiner, Susan Morris, Lance Percival, Danny La Rue, Christopher Moorsom, Peter Noble, Beryl Bryden, David Firmin, Robert Gibbons, David Brown, Bertice Reading, Michael Pointon, Duke of Bedford, Anne de Nys, Dick Emery, Nell Dunn, Miriam Field, Mitch Raper, Cardew Robinson, John Hurst, Teddy, Babs and Joyce Beverly, Margaret, Duchess of Argyll, Charlie Drake, Richard Stilgoe, Sibylle Bedford.

Hutch in India: specially Bubli Brar, Pearson Surita and Vina Lindsay; also Robert Sykes of the British Council, Dan Gillies, Peter and Lilian Sarter, Lawrence Pratt, Russi Mody, Silloo Mody, Ellis Joshua, Tim Carter, B. M. Khaitan, Henry Burdwan, Danny Burdwan, Bootchi Das, Bob Wright, Khaddu Mama, the Rajmata of Jaipur, Hubbie and Munmun, Peter Heneker and Mehtab.

Hutch in the 1960s: particularly Pat Hamshere; also Frank Duffy, Nigel Dempster, Joy Gillespie, Sir John Hannam, Peter Cox, Larry Adler, Michael Thornton, Peter Sasdy, Tom Webster, Sandy Wilson, Keith Salberg, Maggie Christiansen, Colin Brown,

Charles Chaperlin, John Chilton, Bill Shand Kydd, Mark Sykes, Robert Woods, George Glenton, Annie Ross, Bishop Mervyn Stockwood.

Hutch in Nairobi: particularly Peter Colmore, also Deborah Marvin, Alan Bobbe, Lakhia, Micky Migdoll, Joan Vyvyan, Harry Winfield, Bob Charm, Pamela Kikumi, Ruriq Ronski, Jeri Allen, Mteze Tuma, Charles Markham, Javed Ali Khan.

Chapter One

A West Indian Upbringing
1900–1916

Grenadians are bloody show-offs and bloody snobs.

C. Bernard Gibbs, Grenadian

G renada is a beautiful island with towering green mountains, racing streams and waterfalls, lakes, long beaches of soft white sand and lush tropical foliage. Bougainvillaea and flamboyants flourish and there are many varieties of cactus. Sugar apples, papayas and limes are abundant. Throw a seed on the ground, say the Grenadians, and it sprouts instantly. The scent of spice rides on the breeze and clings to the skin long after. Grenada used to be known as the Isle of Spice, as the only spice-producing island in the western hemisphere.

By the nineteenth century there were sugar-cane plantations, coffee, cotton, cocoa and a little indigo. These products and rum were exported to the UK. Most of the inhabitants were French and had been given political rights and religious freedom. Some 83 per cent of all landholdings were less than five acres. This preponderance of peasant landowners is characteristic of Grenada and one of its biggest assets. These people carefully saved their earnings and educated their children at the best schools they could afford. Their descendants occupy positions of importance in Grenada today, unlike most of the other islands, where a distinct division persists between the wealthy landowners and the poor labourers. Prosperous white planters had children by house slaves in the early days. These children were often sent to school in England and then returned, creating an educated, wealthy class of local people.

The Hutchinsons came from Skye in the Western Isles of Scotland. They were first mentioned in 1747, in association with the Macdonald clan, and have strong links with Guyana. However, it was from Barbados that George Washington Hutchinson came with his brother to Grenada some time before 1880. As he was keen to fit in, George modified his accent but never quite shook off traces of his Barbadian origins. Shortly after he arrived, he started a long relationship with Annabella, a girl of some local standing. She bore him two sons, Leon in 1880 and George in 1882. Oddly, although George is identified as father against their names in the parish register, their mother is not named. As George was only nineteen and very poor when Leon was born, the boy was mostly raised by a French family friend, Mrs Miles. But he brought up his younger son, who was darker-skinned and dimmer than Leon, rather haphazardly by himself.

By 1889, George had registered as a merchant, and set up as a hatter and importer of cloth in the main street of Gouyave, a little fishing village on the west coast of the island – Gworve to older, educated Grenadians, Gwarve to everyone else. Although the grander people of the town were too snobbish to allow him to be more than a peripheral figure, George was still a respected and popular member of the community. His imported hats attracted fashion-conscious people throughout Grenada, and he enjoyed dealing with his suppliers in Europe and North America. Until his mid-fifties, he was a useful batsman and wicket-keeper in the village cricket team; and, although not on the church council, he regularly played the organ and was regarded as trustworthy enough to collect glebe rents.

George was known as Hutch, Hutch the Hatter and, possibly because he was dark-skinned and rather colour-conscious, Passmore. Given the need to marry well and, in particular, the high premium on fair skins, in 1899 George married Marianne Simm Turnbull. Her father, a Scotsman called Alexander Turnbull, had owned a beautiful estate at Grand Roy, Gouyave, and Marianne was rich enough in her own right to stay at home and not to work. She was intelligent and strong-willed, and, although hardly more educated than her husband, could speak both English and French. Yet, in spite of all those advantages, Marianne had remained on the shelf until she married at forty. She was nine years older than George.

George's first child with Marianne was born on 7 March 1900, delivered by Dr Dunbar Hughes, who was also his godfather when the baby was christened Leslie Arthur Julien two months later.

Many Grenadians were called Julien, after the leader of an uprising against the British in 1795. Slaves had first been brought to Grenada by the Spanish in 1503, drawn mainly from the Ibo and Yoruba peoples of Nigeria. Slavery was not abolished in the UK until 1833, and slaves in Grenada were then freed after a four-year apprenticeship. When Leslie later claimed that he had French, Spanish, English, Carib-Indian and African blood, he omitted two strains, the Maltese-Portuguese and the East Indian. Within the same family there are often great variations of skin, eye and hair colours, and great significance is attached to these. The temperament of the average Grenadian has been described by one of them as 'a mixture of English discipline, French joie de vivre, the indolence of the negro . . . and the independence of the land-owner'.[1]

George and Marianne's second child, Ivan Washington, arrived in 1902. The family lived in a large rented house in a poor area two minutes' walk from the Anglican school in the Charlottetown area of Gouyave, bordering the beach at Duncanstown. Also living there were two adopted boys who were vaguely related to the family. One, Earl Duprey, was the same age as the Hutchinson boys, but the other, Herbie Hyacinth, was at least thirty years older. They were essentially servants answerable to George, who, as head of the household, gave them bed, board, clothes, schooling and training in various duties in exchange for their labour. If not the 'outside children' of some family member, they were, like George's eldest son Leon, the sons of parents who could no longer afford to keep them. Both boys were treated well, and remained happy and loyal members of the family. At that time in Grenada, as in many other parts of the world, including Britain, only very poor families did without menial help as there was a huge surplus of labour, and salaries and the cost of living were very low.

The household was completed by two of George's unmarried sisters, Miss Carrie and Miss Georgie. Everyone had their own bedroom in the rambling, dilapidated house, and there was an outside bathroom. Another sister, Rose, was married to Marianne's brother Walter, known as Watty, and they lived in an adjoining house. They had a daughter called Wyomi, or Omi, who was fifteen years older than Leslie. Watty Turnbull was the district postmaster and a government warden; Rose taught sewing at the primary school. As Watty and Rose were better off than George and Marianne, Watty paid many of the expenses of bringing up Leslie, Ivan and Leon. These arrangements were conducted openly, and Leslie greatly resented everyone knowing just how much he was indebted to his uncle.

As a child, Leslie respected and admired his father. George Hutchinson was strict with his boys and insisted that they must be hard-working, obedient, responsible and clean-living with no bad language or drunkenness. Even before Leslie could walk, George taught him to swim, along with Ivan and their friends. Later, he taught them to fish with a spear and with their hands. Although they were always welcome to play at home, Leslie and his friends preferred to have fun outside, especially on the beach, where he used to collect shells.

Gouyave is a drowsy little port with a main street running parallel to the beach where fishermen with small boats and big nets bring in their catches. On 29 June (the feast of saints Peter and Paul) the Fisherman's Birthday Festival has long been held there and involves the blessing of nets and boats followed by dancing, feasting and boat races. The town's weathered red-roof houses along the sea wall are dominated by the Anglican and Catholic churches behind them. Gouyave is also the centre of the nutmeg and mace industry, for both are produced from a single fruit and have a powerful smell, as do the cocoa beans which ferment in vats near the beach.

When he was eight, Marianne sent Leslie to have piano lessons with Emily Arthur, a canon's daughter from a well-off family. She taught Leslie social skills and gave him his first intimation of how he might use his talents to become rich and famous. Through her, and later through the governor's wife in St George's, Leslie came to 'learn the white man'; even as a boy, he realised that his future progress would depend on pleasing whites.

Leslie and two other presentable boys were chosen to act as

ballboys at tennis parties at the local big house. While they enjoyed watching the rich at play, they took exception to being treated as inferiors when the hosts were the parents of school friends who often stole apples from the Hutchinsons' garden.

Leslie was adored by his mother, who revelled in his high spirits, even when he and his friends taunted her brother by shouting 'Watty Bubu' ('Monkey Face') at him as he sat working at the window next door. Watty and Omi were both remarkably plain. Marianne was thrilled that her elder son was all that her husband was not: startlingly handsome, fair-skinned, talented, clever, funny and, thanks to her love and encouragement, delighted with himself. She was very ambitious for Leslie, and wanted everything good in the world to drop into his lap.

Leslie was Emily Arthur's star pupil, and worked hard at St John's primary school down the road from home. He was taught history, geography, arithmetic, religious knowledge, agriculture, hygiene and taking dictation; and, as a member of the scholarship class, he also learned mental arithmetic and to read at a rate of 100 words a minute. His school day comprised five hours of lessons with a break for lunch, then playtime. There were no organised games, but there were twice-weekly drill parades in the churchyard with the pupils carrying broom handles. Hutch's cousin Wyomi was a pupil-teacher. A devious, intimidating woman over six foot tall, she was often the ringleader in any mischief. The headmaster, Rupert S. Hewitt, was a dedicated, decent, humourless man whose air of pompous authority made little impact on his unruly school. His log describes outrageous behaviour in a precariously genteel style:

> 1910. Miss Turnbull was not in her place this morning and sent no excuse. If these young ladies were employed in a store, they could not coolly absent themselves from duty and send the lame excuse that they had gone to service. When people are employed, their duty takes precedence over all other things. As a result of her absence, the working of the school was hindered.

> 1911. The Reverend Canon Arthur, manager of the school, investigated a complaint against Miss Turnbull (whom he had, incredibly, promoted). Ada Stewart removed her daughter Alice

from the school because Miss Wyomi Turnbull had knocked the child's head against the wall, causing the child to be sick.

1912. Miss Turnbull sent me a message telling me to go to the devil. She was suspended and made to sweep the school much against her will . . . I have again directed all female teachers to leave their crochet work at home. It is utterly impossible for them to attend to their duties and at the same time have their eyes riveted. When crochet is being knitted, schoolwork is done in a slipshod fashion and the discipline of the classes goes to the dogs.

George Hutchinson was the usual organist at the dank Anglican church in Gouyave. Like the chorus girl in a backstage musical who steps in when the star twists her ankle, the twelve-year-old Leslie took over one Sunday when his father was sick. He had practised on the old harmonium at home, and knew the service backwards. So, although his feet barely reached the pedals, he played with great poise, never once glancing at his hands. When the service was over, he gracefully acknowledged the compliments of the parishioners. Some of them hid their smiles: Leslie had always been encouraged to show off.

Ten years later, in 1922, George Hutchinson would disrupt the Sunday service by retching in spasms and mopping himself with a large, white handkerchief. He vainly tried to staunch the blood which splashed vividly over the ivory keys. As they helped him out, the parishioners hid the disgust they felt because consumption was a disease of the poor and meant certain death. By then Leslie was no longer there to replace him.

In September 1912, the headmaster recorded that Leslie had won a scholarship to the Grenada Boys' Secondary School in the capital, St George's. Although the award was limited to just one Grenadian boy a year, the distinction was more of a tribute to the premium the Hutchinson family put on education than to Leslie's innate ability. This is confirmed by the fact that in 1916 his less clever younger brother Ivan also won the scholarship, taking two years longer over it than Leslie. If the boys had been any darker and the family any poorer and without past evidence of strong white genes, they would not have had a hope of gaining the award; apart from anything else, they would have been far too busy with menial chores such as fetching water and tending the family goat. Although St George's is only 12 miles from Gouyave, there was virtually no transport, and so Leslie had to be a boarder; as a result, he was so cut off from home, he might almost have gone overseas. For his father, Leslie's achievement was the vindication of many sacrifices; Marianne too was proud but sad to see him go.

The coast road south to St George's winds past soaring mountains, old plantation houses and valleys covered with banana and breadfruit trees, palms, bamboo and tropical flowers and spices. St George's is a charming harbour town which straddles a promontory with steep hills and very narrow roads which climb from the lagoon. Inter-island vessels and wooden schooners and skiffs load and unload. Mellow bricks, red tiles and wrought-iron balconies of the colonial Georgian buildings frame the splendid views. For generations every Saturday farmers, fruit growers, hat makers and spice dryers have come to spread their wares across wooden stalls or on the cobblestones. One vendor makes rotis, another stirs a fragrant oil-down (a local stew) and the smell of cinnamon and clove hangs in the warm air. Close by, the long sweep of Grand Anse beach stretches as far as the eye can see.

The first motorbike arrived on the island in 1904 and a Stanley steam car soon after. Before 1914 there were only half a dozen cars in Grenada, but 200 by the end of 1919. Leslie would have used the beautifully decorated buses (which still survive), each with its name painted on the back – 'Why Worry', 'Have Faith' and 'Mystery de Luxe'. They were trucks that had been converted into buses by a superstructure of open benches with posts at each end supporting a roof. A canvas blind was rolled down when it rained.

The Grenada Boys' Secondary School was founded in 1885 by planters for their children. It provided a classical education roughly on a par with an English grammar school, and was, at first, fee-paying. However, the year before Hutch joined, it was taken over by the government and became free. It had seventy-two boys, and the headmaster was a Welshman, D. Hedog Jones. As a scholarship boy, Leslie went into a higher form than normal pupils. One of the top ten students, he moved up the school rapidly, often at the rate of a form a term, and shone at all his studies, including, of course, music. He boarded with a distant relative, Mrs Nellie La Barrie, up a winding cobbled street near the school. She took good care of him, and was much impressed by his ability to hear a piece of music just once and then play it immediately by ear.

Later in life, Leslie said that he had played opening bat for the school eleven, and was keen to become a professional cricketer but had to set this ambition aside to study for his Cambridge exams. None of his contemporaries can recall his sporting skills but, whatever the truth, cricket became an abiding passion. A further characteristic, his outstanding clarity of diction, was also acquired at this time. Fifty years later, Leslie attributed this to the inspiration of his English teacher who gave him the part of Portia because everyone wanted to hear him declaim the set-piece speech 'The quality of mercy is not strained'.

Another lifelong enthusiasm got off to a poor start, however. When Leslie was fourteen, his father visited him and swept him off to a brothel. Thirty years later, Leslie told a girlfriend that the encounter had frightened and distressed him. It is probable that, in being forced into an experience before he was ready for it, he lost something more important than he gained – his childhood innocence.

Home for the holidays in Gouyave, Leslie was increasingly unpopular with the locals. They compared him unfavourably with his brother Ivan, who was less clever but polite and friendly. By contrast, Leslie dressed sharply and put on airs. 'He was fussy and standoffish,' remembered one contemporary. 'He thought himself superior with his new friends at the school away. You would think he was a white man, because he always behaved as though he was top of the social ladder and you were at the bottom.'[2] His old friends resented this selfish boy, now big, broad and good-looking, loudly practising his singing and piano, and clearly showing that he had grown out of his birthplace.

Leslie took his Cambridge exams, roughly the equivalent of A levels, in his third year, in the autumn of 1915. On leaving school, he became a government clerk. As a holder of the Cambridge Certificate, he qualified for the relatively high wage of £5 a month; otherwise he might have been paid as little as £1. It was the sort of safe, steady job that another man might have been happy to pursue until retirement, but Leslie was holding out for better things. Meanwhile, together with other young men ambitious to get off the island and study abroad, he gave concerts in St George's. The choir was directed by a very musical shop-owner, Clem Thompson, and the catholic repertoire embraced popular classics, musicals and, at Christmas, Handel's *Messiah*. Leslie played by ear and improvised and, like the other aspiring boys, saved his share of the takings for travel expenses.

His plans materialised sooner than he had hoped. In the summer of 1916, a girl who had been at his primary school in Gouyave sold him a ticket to New York because she had fallen in love and no longer wanted to leave Grenada. For Leslie, as for most ambitious West Indians, the USA was the place to go. Although 2,300 miles away, it was only half as distant as Europe, where in any case war was raging. Moreover, unlike the UK, the USA did not openly bar immigrants on the grounds of colour. Whatever they did, the immigrants were always described by their families back in Grenada as 'getting on well in New York'. Those who failed never returned. Nor did some of those who succeeded.

Later, Leslie said that, even before he left school, it was his father's idea that he should study to be a doctor. 'I didn't know what I wanted to be. I just wanted to roam about a bit first.' Leslie's godfather, Dr Dunbar Hughes, had long urged George to encourage Leslie to study medicine. He also offered to contribute to expenses. George asked his eldest son, Leon, then thirty and hoping to be a dentist, to escort Leslie; to study alongside him at Meharry Medical College in Nashville, Tennessee; and to send back regular progress reports on himself and his half-brother. He also paid for their fares and their studies, and gave them each a small allowance. Ivan was to join them later. Adding to Leslie's funds were, possibly, the governor's wife in St George's – some thought Leslie had caught her eye – and certainly Uncle Watty, who had scooped the Panama sweepstake and given all his nephews a generous share of his windfall. This money was vital as the USA made each immigrant produce 'show money' to prove they could survive there; the amount requested was substantial, and was occasionally passed back down the queue.

So Leslie left the island. His parents had given him the best possible education, together with the resources and confidence to succeed. Their prayers and high hopes went with him. None of them knew they would never see each other again.

After he had gone, the family rarely heard from Leslie. But, when he finally made some, he sent money to his father's sister Miss Carrie, and later to his cousin Wyomi.

The Grenadians kept track of Leslie Hutchinson's career. In 1929, school friends wanted to see him at the London Palladium but, with standing room at ten shillings each, could not afford to do so. A local politician, Theophilus Albert Marryshow, did see Hutch perform in London, and was shocked to find both Edwina Mountbatten and Ivor Novello paying court to him in his dressing room. When Marryshow returned to Grenada, he reported on Leslie in great detail, and the islanders started to buy his records. They also heard him on the radio, including a live performance in a Silver Jubilee broadcast in 1935 which was programmed for a time when West Indians would be awake. On it, Hutch said, 'I hope people are listening in Grenada where I come from. I haven't got any relations left there, but I've still got property in Grenada and I know quite a lot of people.'[3]

When Hutch visited Trinidad in 1937, everyone in Grenada thought he would then proceed to his island home which was only an overnight trip away by boat. People prepared a special reception for him and, when he did not show up, were disappointed and angry. In fact Hutch did come to Grenada but he came swiftly and secretly to avoid all publicity. He saw a cousin of his father's, Gordon Hutchinson, and gave him two of his records. He went to tea with Canon MacEachrane, the successor of Canon Arthur, in Gouyave and played the piano for him and his family. He then slipped away as quietly as he came. He may well have wished to avoid meeting Wyomi; but, that formidable and predatory cousin aside, all those who had been close to him were dead. Anyway, his home was now in Europe.

For all that, the Grenadians were, and still are, pleased that a local boy did so well.

Chapter Two

Harlem Stride
1916–1924

If you're white, you're right; if you're brown, stick around; if you're black, stay back!

Folk saying

A fter a short and enjoyable journey from Grenada, Leslie's ship, the SS *Mayaro*, docked in New York harbour on 6 September 1916. Leslie and Leon were logged by the immigration authorities as, respectively, a sixteen-year-old clerk, five foot ten inches high, and a thirty-year-old stenographer of six foot two. They were met by a family friend[1] and went straight on to Nashville.

Meharry College was one of the few places in America where black people could study. Leslie completed about nine months of his three-year 'pre-medical' course – the prelude to four years of 'full medical' – before leaving for New York to 'roam about a bit' and discover what he wanted to do. Leon broke the bad news by letter to George, who promptly stopped Leslie's allowance. He was deeply hurt that Leslie had dropped out, and had no other way of expressing his anger and disappointment. He never forgave Leslie, and Leslie never forgave him for cutting him off and leaving him to starve and freeze in Harlem during the vicious winter of 1917. Nor did Leslie forgive Leon for informing George of his defection.

Leslie had never intended to qualify as a doctor. As far as he was concerned, the medical-school plan was simply a way of getting off the island and away from his family. Far from committing himself to seven years of study with an older brother monitoring his progress, he wanted to experiment with life in a new world without any responsibilities. However, he could absorb academic and other information almost as easily as he could remember music; and later, when his capacity for reinventing his past had become almost boundless, he still retained sufficient grasp of anatomy and surgery to convince people that he had qualified as a doctor. When on tour in the thirties, he even went so far as to show a lad in his dressing room a case of golden surgical instruments, provenance unknown, which, he said, were a graduation present. On press releases that went out with his records, Hutch claimed to be a trained lawyer, possibly feeling that the law carried more social and intellectual cachet than medicine.

After dropping out from Meharry, Leslie visited Grenadian friends in Washington and Boston. By 1920, he was living in Harlem at 2394 Seventh Avenue, where his landlady was Corene Grant, Grant being a Gouyave family name. At that time, immigration was much easier than later, and numerous West Indians were well settled in New York. As inter-island travel in the Caribbean was difficult, those from different islands often met there for the first time. A variety of benevolent associations, such as the Grenada Mutual Association, not only laid on sponsors for those coming to America but also provided contact and support, largely through meetings every Sunday. West Indian immigrants needed all the help they could get. Whatever their qualifications, they usually had to take menial low-paid jobs, and blacks were always last hired and first fired. Housing was just as discriminatory: blacks had to pay two or three times as much as whites, and were forced to live in bad areas. Furthermore, in most parts of New York, there were few places where they could eat, drink, wash or relieve themselves; they could not even sit on park benches.

These restrictions did not apply to Harlem. It had been built in the nineteenth century in the north of Manhattan as an opulent suburb for wealthy whites. Then, around 1900, a surge of real-estate speculation led to a series of bankruptcies. To get cash, the speculators split up the lavish apartments and rented them to blacks. By 1920, with its wide avenues, mass of trees and not yet dilapidated apartment buildings, it had become the finest black enclave ever in the USA at that time. However, it was over-crowded and noisy and rife with poverty, prostitution, gambling, drugs, disease and gang warfare. What it didn't have was white people; as Paul Robeson's wife Eslanda wrote, 'Only negroes *belong* in Harlem . . . it is a place they can call home.'[2] It attracted ambitious immigrants from many parts of the world throughout the 1920s, and Louis Armstrong found it to be full of 'brilliant and talented musicians and actors and poets of our race' and declared it to be 'the city where most of our coloured genius today is to be found'.[3]

Even within Harlem and away from white bigotry, Leslie faced marked prejudice against West Indians among American blacks. They were seen as tireless hustlers after everyone else's jobs; as would-be entrepreneurs up to every sort of trick. Moreover, because they had no direct experience of slavery, which had been abolished in America only fifty years earlier, they often riled the American blacks by adopting superior attitudes; by playing cricket, waving the Union Jack and displaying fervent loyalty to the British. In Harlem, they were particularly associated with insurrection and crime. It was often said that a revolutionary always turned out to be an over-educated West Indian out of work. A Jamaican, Caspar Holstein, became 'king' of the lottery racket until ousted by Dutch Schultz, a big downtown bootlegger; and another Jamaican, Marcus Garvey, founded the Universal Negro Improvement Association promising 'new freedom for Negroes in a land of their own sans Jews', until he was sent to prison for his part in a massive steamboat scam designed to transport blacks back to Africa.

Leslie had to adapt fast to survive and fit into Harlem. Coming from Grenada, a claustrophobically close community where every-one knew him, to a city where he was unknown, unemployed and practically penniless was frightening. By his own account, even 'the walls, the skyscrapers all round me scared me stiff. It was like being in a cage. I had to get a job so I became an elevator boy in a palatial New York hotel. But by the winter of 1917 I was out of a job again and absolutely broke. Imagine winter in New York when you are down on your luck – the blizzards, the biting cold and the mercury still falling, the grey damp pavements and oh! that smell of food from restaurants.'[4] Despite that, Leslie somehow had the application and resources to rechannel his partly self-taught classical piano technique into the jazz idiom. To this end, he played every day for hours and hours on the pianola, a self-playing pianoforte that was activated by a perforated roll of paper. This early form of piano recording flourished in the 1920s: 'player pianos' accounted for 53 per cent of the piano industry's sales in 1923. Many pioneers of ragtime and jazz piano, including Scott Joplin, Luckey Roberts, Eubie Blake and Jelly Roll Morton, made piano rolls; James P. Johnson made over fifty piano rolls in 1917 alone. From these, Leslie learned his style in minute detail by pressing down the keys while the rolls played; he also learned the styles of leading players from listening to them live.

Basically stride piano is a percussive, romping, two-fisted affair and most of its exponents, such as Willie the Lion Smith, tended to use the right hand to embellish the melody; by contrast, Johnson used his right hand to improvise new themes on the chords of the melody. Indeed, he was altogether a far more subtle pianist than his epithet 'the father of stride piano' implies: educated in the European classical idiom, he was influenced by a wide range of genres including church music, dances, ragtime, reels and blues. He wrote extended classical works, scores for Broadway shows and such popular songs as 'Runnin' Wild', 'Old-fashioned Love' and the number that launched the famous knock-kneed dance craze, the charleston. In her autobiography, *His Eye Is on the Sparrow*, the singer Ethel Waters paid him this tribute:

All the licks you hear, now as then, originated with musicians like James P. Johnson. And I mean *all* of the hot licks that ever came out of Fats Waller and the rest of the hot piano boys. They are just faithful followers and protégés of that great man, Jimmy Johnson. Men like him, Willie the Lion Smith and Charlie Johnson[5] could make you sing till your tonsils fell out . . . They stirred you into wild joy and ecstasy. They could make you cry.

Through imitation, practice and hard work, Leslie became a sound stride pianist and entertainer; and, like all black musicians, he resented the many whites – including, later on, several English critics – who assumed that he played from a natural talent. From James P. Johnson, he picked up ragtime clichés such as the double-handed break, the displaced accent and the bell effects in the treble; he also absorbed 'the walking bass figures and chordal arabesques in the treble' that the jazz historian Frank Driggs admired so much in Johnson's playing.[6] Of particular significance to Leslie were the ways in which New York pianists assimilated some of the harmonies, chords and techniques of the European concert pianists. As the jazz critic George Hoefer has noted, 'Unlike jazz and ragtime pianists from other parts of the country, New York striders were steadily in the aura of big-city sophistication and closer to the rhythms of Broadway.'[7] Years afterwards, European musicians would marvel at Leslie's dexterity. His hands were large enough to stretch tenths or, some said, twelfths. He could explore a single theme almost endlessly, and he delighted in finding new chords or variations and making his hands play separate rhythms and melodies. Musicians also noted how much he disliked anyone taking notes during his performances.

On 10 September 1923, Leslie made his debut in a recording studio. He accompanied a minor vaudeville singer, Ruth Coleman, on 'Original Charleston' and 'She Walked Right Up', and is given a credit on the record. Three weeks later, he accompanied a slightly more blues-oriented singer, Hazel Meyers, on 'Graveyard Dream' and 'Low Down Papa'.

Electrical recording was not introduced until 1925. For these and other early recordings made in the acoustic era, Leslie had to sit in a small and far from soundproof studio and play into two crude round microphones, or 'horns', hung halfway up the wall. Balancing the sounds made by different performers was difficult and, on the Hazel Meyers tracks, Leslie is too close to the horns and, at times, threatens to swamp the singer. He plays in a way which, if lacking in originality, is sprightly and confident with neat runs and trills. In style, he is far closer to Clarence Williams, the pianist, composer and all-round musical fixer, than he is to James P. Johnson: in fact, Williams's playing on Bessie Smith's debut record, 'Downhearted Blues', is virtually indistinguishable from Leslie's backing on the Hazel Meyers titles.

Leslie was always an outstanding accompanist, acutely sensitive to the styles of different singers, as well equipped to point up their good features as he was to compensate for their deficiencies. These performers were not, of course, classic blues singers such as Ma Rainey, Bessie Smith and Sippie Wallace: for the classic singers, the blues was an emotional release, a way of facing up to life by singing about loneliness or bad times, about the jinx that brings bad luck, the lover who betrays, the good times and the evil days. Ruth Coleman, Hazel Meyers, Lizzie Miles and the other performers that Leslie backed were in the vaudeville idiom, roughly the equivalent of English music hall, which, while borrowing some of the themes and shape of the classic blues, set out to divert rather than make an emotional impact. Inevitably, there was extensive overlapping: Bessie Smith, for instance, often sang vaudeville numbers, while revue artistes such as Ethel Waters sometimes dipped into the blues repertoire; classic blues singers also often joined vaudeville performers on stage but, when they did so, they adapted their singing to match the parodic, innuendo-packed blues of the vaudevillians.

The market for vaudeville blues was created by 'Crazy Blues' by Mamie Smith. This, the first jazz vocal performance to be recorded, launched in 1920 the issue of so-called 'race records' aimed specifically at Afro-Americans. At a time when a record was an expensive novelty, 'Crazy Blues' was a best seller. For the first time ever, American working-class blacks could hear 'their' music; and, if black performers could not cross white thresholds, their music could: race records soon became a fashionable cult among wealthy whites nationwide, although they were advertised and distributed only in black areas in the North and available only by mail order in the South.

'Crazy Blues' made Mamie Smith a sensation everywhere. From being a struggling blues-shouter of twenty-seven, she soon had long queues outside the theatres where she played in 1920 and 1921. She bought three palatial homes in New York – each with an electric player-piano in many of the rooms – and wore richly bedizened and feathered gowns. While she knew how to play the lady, she was also a hard drinker, a tough broad who drew most of her lovers from her own band, and had rows with them with them on and off stage. Willie the Lion Smith, the stride pianist who played on the 'Crazy Blues' session, described Mamie Smith as 'a pretty bossy girl – one of the best looking women in the business'. On 'Crazy Blues', she delivers the vocal in an assertive, almost hectoring contralto voice with little blues intonation or shading. The accompaniment is typical of the bump-and-grind pit bands of the period.

'Crazy Blues' paved the way for over two hundred women singers on race records. Some, like Bessie Smith, recorded over a hundred titles each; several made a few dozen; while others made only one or two. Throughout the 1920s, Mamie continued to tour the black theatres which had recently been organised into the TOBA, the Theatre Owners' Booking Association, or, unofficially, Tough on Black Asses. If the act went well, there were often two more performances around midnight exclusively for white audiences. Prohibition had been the first reason white people went to Harlem, in search of clandestine drinking rooms; soon black stage stars became popular with a wider public.

In September 1924, Leslie may briefly have been a member of Mamie's band. He certainly recorded two songs with her, 'Remorseful Blues' and 'Just Like You Took My Man Away From Me', in that month; but the band, the Choo-Choo Jazzers, was a pick-up group, assembled only for the recording. At various times, the fluctuating personnel of Mamie's band, usually called the Jazz Hounds, had included jazz stars such as Coleman Hawkins, Bubber Miley and Joe Smith, but at the time Leslie recorded with Mamie, the only name of note in the six-piece group was Elmer Snowden, a banjo player. According to the mass of longhand notes at the Institute of Jazz Studies at Rutgers, New Jersey, most of them unsigned and undated, Leslie first met Snowden around 1922, and their fortunes were to be sporadically linked for some years.

Snowden was born in Baltimore in 1900, and became a virtuoso banjo and guitar player as well as, in time, bandleader, agent, impresario and song plugger. When he was only fifteen, he played in the band of the pianist Eubie Blake, also from Baltimore; and in 1919 he was in a trio with Duke Ellington in Washington, DC. In 1920, he left to work with Gertie Wells, a pianist whom he later married; and by 1922 he was leading his own band in Atlantic City, at the Music Box, where he first met Leslie. The band went to New York and found that its promised pianist, Fats Waller, had already been hired for a show. Snowden recruited Ellington as a substitute. When the band members suspected that Snowden was short-changing them, they ousted him and the group became Duke Ellington's Washingtonians, a sextet that was to grow into the greatest and longest-lived big band in jazz history. During the changeover, Leslie sometimes sat in as relief pianist.

The venue was Barron's on the corner of Seventh Avenue and

134th Street. After the Big Three – Connie's Inn, the Cotton Club and Small's Paradise – Barron's was the best-known Harlem night spot. It opened in 1915 and both James P. Johnson and Mamie Smith appeared there before 1920, but when it hit its peak in the early to mid-twenties when practically every major stride pianist played there. So, too, did Leslie, filling in for Fats Waller, who later said of him, 'I knew him well when he didn't have a pair of pants to his ass.'[8]

Its star attraction was a light-skinned black singer and dancer, Ada Beatrice Queen Victoria Louisa Smith, known as Bricktop because of her startlingly red hair. She was to become one of the great nightclub hostesses in Paris, Rome and Mexico City, but here in Harlem in 1923, she was just another struggling performer in need of a good accompanist. So she befriended Leslie.

In her words, Barron's was 'THE Harlem spot. Only light-skinned negroes could get in . . . Every night the limousines pulled up . . . and rich whites got out, all dolled up in their furs and jewels. [They] were the Who's Who of New York's Roaring Twenties; gangsters rubbed shoulders with high society, and people in show business came uptown after the Broadway theatres closed.'[9]

Leslie also played at four other clubs: the Exclusive Club, the Hollywood, the Bamville and the Nest. Descriptions of them evoke the glamorous side of Harlem of the time – the Harlem of Ellington's 'Black and Tan Fantasy' and the pictures of Edward Burra with their cocktail bars, broad-shouldered pimps and cloche-hatted tarts. It was said of the Exclusive that 'the place never gets started before one o'clock at night. It is frequented by white men.'[10] Near the Exclusive Barron Wilkins, its owner and a leading black politician and man about town, was knifed to death by Yellow Charleston, a celebrated dope fiend, because Wilkins, who controlled much of uptown life, had refused to pay for some booze. His brother Leroy, who ran a nightclub of the same name, was one of the few who never admitted whites.

The Hollywood Club at 203 West 49th Street opened in 1923 but, after Snowden and Leslie had finished there, it became the Kentucky and James P. Johnson moved in with a band that included two future saxophone stars: Sidney Bechet and Benny Carter. The Bamville Club at 65 West 129th Street had been opened by a popular black tenor, Henry Broadway Jones, in 1920 as Broadway Jones's Supper Club. When the management changed from Jones to Johnny Carey, it became the Bamville, and the Palm Beach Orchestra made way for Snowden's unit with Leslie. The club was still flourishing in the late 1920s when *Variety* reported it to be one of 'eleven class white-trade night clubs' frequently visited by the British heiress Edwina Mountbatten, who 'really knew these dumps'. By then, 'to see the High Hats mingle with the native stepper [was] nothing unusual'.[11] After three weeks at the Bamville, Snowden's band moved to the Nest Club at 169 West 133rd Street, a luxuriously louche establishment noted for its superior music and Chicago gangland atmosphere.

During his seven years in and around New York, Leslie made numerous friends and contacts, many of whom he saw frequently in later life. Broadway Jones was a vaudeville entertainer well known in Harlem high society, who featured at the Thursday-afternoon entertainments of the black millionairess A'lelia Walker. Many of the performers and guests at these functions were 'dictys', or blacks who tried to be as white as possible and looked down on other blacks. Leslie felt completely at home in their company.

It was probably through Jones that Leslie got to know and work with Alberta Hunter, a jazz singer from Memphis, Tennessee. Having made her name in Chicago, she came to New York in 1922 to star on Broadway with Sidney Bechet in *How Come?* She also wrote 'Downhearted Blues', with which Bessie Smith made her phenomenally successful recording debut in 1923. Alberta was well known to both Bricktop and Leslie for many years, and continued to sing well into her eighties. Among her papers was found a photo of Leslie, resplendent in a dinner jacket, signed to 'Brick, my pal'; it is a duplicate of his passport photograph taken in 1924.

Another Harlem friend was Florence Mills, a diminutive singer and dancer who sprang to fame in the musical *Shuffle Along* on Broadway in 1921. Opal Cooper, another singer, got to know Leslie at this time. They would meet again in Paris, and later perform together at the Palladium and elsewhere. Turner Layton and Tandy Johnstone sang duets to Leslie's rippling piano and, with the support of the Mountbattens, they were to precede him to London. And Florence and Palmer Jones were Harlem friends long before Leslie frequented their nightclub, Chez Florence, in Paris. Leslie also struck up with the cornet player Cricket Smith, when Smith was playing with Jim Europe's orchestra on the roof of the

New Amsterdam Theatre where they featured Ziegfeld's *Midnight Frolics*. After Europe's death, the band was led by Noble Sissle, a singer-songwriter with whom Leslie recorded in the late 1920s in London. Cricket Smith later played in Leslie's band in Paris.

By far the most important musician Leslie encountered was Duke Ellington. Shortly after assuming command of Elmer Snowden's band, Ellington reigned supreme in Harlem until 1930. Then, owing to touring and film commitments, he made way at the Cotton Club for a relief band led by Cab Calloway, the scat-singing 'Hi-de-Hi' man, who had been forcibly transferred from the Savoy by the Mafia. Ellington believed that musicians originated the 'new music' not in New York but, from 1910 on, in New Orleans, Chicago and the West Indies. He recruited accordingly, his best-known West Indian bandsman being the trombonist Juan Tizol, from Puerto Rico, whose skin was so pale he had to black up to match the rest of the band. In Ellington's view, it was only when these influences came together in New York that jazz emerged as an art form. Even more cosmopolitan than Ellington were the actor and singer Paul Robeson and his wife Eslanda: they knew Leslie well in Harlem, and were to meet him again in Paris, Venice and London.

Another international figure was the rich socialite Carl Van Vechten. Osbert Sitwell described Van Vechten as 'the white master of coloured revels' and invoked a Harlem joke of the day to illustrate the enterprising mix of his parties: 'Good morning, Mrs Astor,' says a porter at Grand Central Station. 'How do you know my name, young man?' 'Why, ma'am, I met you last week at Carl Van Vechten's.'[12] At these functions, close encounters between black and white sometimes precipitated bizarre incidents: when Van Vechten's wife, the ballet dancer Fania Marinoff, gave Bessie Smith a standard valedictory kiss, the great blues singer belted her across the face and shouted, 'That's enough of that shit!' Although married, Van Vechten was a homosexual with a penchant for black lovers. It is probable that he found Leslie, who was twenty years his junior, physically attractive; and 'Carlo' may even have been Leslie's first famous homosexual partner. Dorothy Parker once commented that he wrote 'with his tongue in someone else's cheek', and Van Vechten promptly accused her of envy. More seriously, Van Vechten was a latterday Maecenas who encouraged many aspiring writers in Harlem, including Langston Hughes,

Countee Cullen and Wallace Thurman, and vigorously promoted them in the white literary world. Leslie would have met them at parties.

Leslie also got to know a Senegalese boxer called Louis Phal, better known as 'Battling Siki'. He had a lion as a mascot, served French wine and, in the disapproving words of the *Chicago Defender*, 'paid little attention . . . to women of his own colour'. He probably kindled Leslie's interest in boxing; from now on, Leslie was to follow the sport closely, and later, in England, he was often asked as a guest celebrity to watch key bouts from a ringside seat.

After six years in Harlem, Leslie was very well equipped for the life that lay ahead in Paris and London. The smart parties polished his social skills to produce confident, attractively relaxed manners, an impressive conversational range and the ability literally to charm the pants off almost anyone. He also became an accomplished dancer at Harlem parties where everyone was expected to master the intricacies of the black bottom, the shimmy, the camel and, of course, the charleston. For years, the rich whites on Park Avenue had engaged blacks to teach them to sing 'darkie songs' and 'talk nigger'; now they were learning to dance with elegantly controlled frenzy. Later, in Paris, both Bricktop and Leslie were employed to induct the Prince of Wales and other members of the international *beau monde* into the mysteries of the dance which had, within two years of being featured in the 1923 James P. Johnson musical *Runnin' Wild*, swept the world.

Leslie also developed great stamina as a performer. Along with recording jobs and work in nightclubs and on the vaudeville circuit, he played at rent parties. These were private dances that charged admission, often in order to help pay for accommodation. The entrance fee for these functions – also called 'jumps', 'shouts' or 'struts' – was as little as a quarter. For that, people could eat ham hocks, pig's feet, black-eyed peas and fresh corn bread; and, for a modest further outlay, wash them down with beer and bathtub gin. The parties started any time after midnight, and howled and stomped on until dawn or beyond in a miasma of smoke, bootleg booze, collard greens and hot music. At the more ambitious struts, around three in the morning, James P., Willie the Lion, Claude Hopkins, Fats Waller and Duke Ellington would arrive to play and vie with each other to see who could 'beautify' a melody the best. In these cutting and carving contests, one pianist would often leave his successor a particularly challenging key such as A major or F sharp. Musicians tended to boost their energy by drinking; and, after the highs generated by nerves, concentration, successful performance and applause, would often engage in epic drinking bouts, egged on by an admiring audience. As a result, many jazz musicians became alcoholics: prominent among them was Fats Waller, who died of all-round overindulgence, virtually exploding in a train, aged only thirty-nine, in 1943. Leslie witnessed numerous variations on the theme of excessive drinking, and always claimed to despise its manifestations such as foul language and loss of control. For all that, he learned to use drink as a tool to see him through a lifetime of double and triple performances on a single night.

Leslie also became an adept showman, a maestro of presentation. Most performers, whether racing drivers, chess players or tennis champions, go through idiosyncratic routines to generate an atmosphere of concentration. Pianists, in particular, tend to address the piano with a host of individual flourishes. James P. Johnson, who was himself noted for the series of grandiose gestures with which he sat down at the keyboard, much admired the routine of Jelly Roll Morton, who slowly and carefully used to fold his overcoat inside out and put it along the top of the piano so that everyone could see its spectacular lining. Next, he shook out a large white silk handkerchief and dusted his stool. Then he sat down, hit his trademark chord and let rip. Fats Waller used to disarm his audiences with a megawatt smile, paying nominal obeisance before performing on his own terms and blatantly flirting with specific women in the audience. When he performed his great hit 'Ain't Misbehavin', he used to leer at them, rolling his eyes and singing, 'Savin' all my love for you . . . and you . . . and you.' This flagrant formula nearly always worked, as Leslie was to find when he used the same bantering line to pull women in his audiences. By watching his competitors closely, Leslie developed a stage-setting technique of his own: settling his coat-tails with great deliberation, putting his handkerchief on top of the piano and shooting his cuffs. Many Europeans found these mannerisms affected, but they were minimal compared to the elaborate routines he had seen in Harlem.

He also copied the pronounced sartorial style of the great pianists. James P. Johnson wore jackets with elaborate pleats at the back; Duke Ellington used to ring the changes in the course of an evening, often changing from a pale-blue suit to a glittering dinner jacket of wild silk; Willie the Lion Smith always appeared in a derby puffing an outsize stogie. As a local Harlem journalist, Floyd Snelson, wrote, 'Everyone dressed in the height of fashion . . . gay Lotharios were bedecked in full dress suit, tails, English walking suit, and silk hat and cane, and sometimes a modest sack tuxedo. Everyone wore their "black cloth" to a "swell function" every night, everyone lived like a millionaire, everyone went for higher-priced cars.'[13] Leslie followed suit, and ever after dressed himself immaculately. A photograph taken in 1917 shows him when his self-presentation skills were still in embryo. He sits at the piano with a smug smile and very short hair, done up in starched shirt and a natty bow tie, very much the all-American college kid. Leslie commissioned the picture, as part of a promotional handout, from the famous New York photographer Strand; it was the first of many such portraits taken by society photographers such as Tanqueray and Baron.

While he was in America, Leslie also acquired a wife. Although he always claimed that the wedding took place in Brooklyn, no record of it survives. Nor is there any record of his wife's birth. Leslie told the French authorities that his wife's name was Ella, née Byrd, and that she was born in Beach in 1894; if so, assuming they were married in 1923 or 1924, she would have been thirty, six years older than Leslie. A member of the Hutchinson family is sure that Ella came from Beach, Georgia (there is another Beach in North Dakota), where some scant records reveal that a child registered as white, and called E. B. Bird, was born in 1894. Beach had been named in 1870 after a prosperous local landowner called William Washington Beach. By 1900, it had a population of 200, and was no more than a scattering of 'shotgun' houses, temporary structures put up to house itinerant black workers during brief periods when a sawmill and a turpentine factory created jobs.[14] Beach does not appear on modern maps, and it is now impossible to place it exactly. In the surrounding area, Ware County, there was a large white family called Byrd, many of whose black slaves, following the convention of the time, took on the name Byrd; there were also some Chinese families. Leslie later described his wife as Anglo-Chinese. It is not surprising that there are no surviving records of

Ella's family and upbringing. Despite Leslie's description of her and the record of E. B. Bird being white, she was predominantly black and therefore, especially given the character of this rural area, unlikely to be documented in any way.

Considering his ambitions, it is odd that Leslie married so early in life. Photographs taken later in Paris show a pretty, smiling woman, so he may simply have fallen in love. Or he may have contracted a 'visa marriage' to confirm his right of residence with the authorities. Or Ella may have helped Leslie to overcome some financial crisis. These three motives, which can only be speculative, are by no means mutually exclusive.

It is easier to see why Leslie left America in October 1924, while apparently on the brink of a breakthrough. After he died, a friend recalled Leslie saying that, together with Broadway Jones and a band, he had gone to Palm Beach, Miami. They lodged in the black quarter across a narrow bridge from the white millionaires' playground. One hot evening, on a hill overlooking the city, there appeared a flame that fanned out into the fiery cross of the Ku Klux Klan. Nationally established since 1867, this organisation proclaimed that the enemies of America were alcohol, loose women, Jews, blacks, Roman Catholics and anyone else who was not a native WASP. By the early 1920s, there were 4 million members across America, frequently dressing in sheets and masks like huge dunce's caps with slit eyes, and thirsting for racial violence. 'I knew the real ague of terror that night,' Leslie later confided. 'My legs trembled as the Klansmen passed in parade. Without legal rights of search, they kicked open doors, flashing torches on our faces, demanding to know if we were harbouring their intended victim. When we gave our innocent answers, furniture was smashed and our possessions thrown around.' The unknown friend added that he never forgot that experience and 'left America as soon as it could be arranged and went to work in Paris'.[15]

Despite all the fun of Harlem, Leslie was also generally getting tired of the cruel refinements of American racism. 'Nigger Heaven!' a black character remarks in Carl Van Vechten's 1926 book of the same name.

That's what Harlem is. We sit in our places in the gallery of this New York Theatre and watch the white world sitting down below in the good seats in the orchestra. Occasionally, they turn their faces towards us, their cruel hard faces, to laugh and sneer, but they never beckon. It never seems to occur to them that nigger heaven is crowded, that there isn't another seat, that something has to be done.

Life was demeaning for well-bred and educated blacks like Leslie because their social ceiling was low despite the current vogue for lionising them in Manhattan. Furthermore, American blacks were very shade-conscious. Leslie had long ago discovered that, while it was desirable to be light-skinned in Grenada, in the USA he was apt to be denigrated as a 'high yaller' by darker-skinned men. Indeed, in 'Young Woman's Blues', Bessie Smith proudly proclaims, 'I ain't no high yaller, I'm a deep mahogany brown,' an expression of contempt for miscegenation. On the other hand, there was a widespread demand for hair straighteners and bleaching creams, and Wallace Thurman's novel *The Blacker the Berry* (the title comes from the folk saying, 'The blacker the berry, the sweeter the juice') is about a dark-skinned girl whose rejection by lighter-skinned blacks makes her feel far more isolated than the blatant racism of white men. And Nancy Cunard, the rebellious daughter of Emerald Cunard, the famous society hostess, wrote in her book *Negro*, 'There are near-white cliques, mulatto groups, dark-skinned sets who will not invite each other to their houses . . . The snobbery around skin colour is terrifying.' Thurman wrote more specifically that:

> mulattoes of light brown skin have succeeded in absorbing all the social mannerisms of the white American middle class . . . They are both stupid and snobbish as is their class in any race. Their most compelling if sometimes unconscious ambition is to be as near white as possible, and their greatest expenditure of energy is concentrated on eradicating any trait or characteristic commonly known as negroid.[16]

Some fifty years later, a journalist upbraided Leslie for considering himself an honorary white man. Leslie almost certainly agreed; after all, he had been trying to slough off his blackness ever since he came to America.

Apart from his friendship with Van Vechten, it is impossible to know how much exposure in America Leslie had to 'ofays' as

blacks called whites (probably from *au fait*). He later claimed that
one evening, when his fortunes were at their nadir, after nights of
sleeping illicitly on a bench in Central Park, he met in the street a
patron of the hotel where he had worked. The man was looking
for a pianist to play at a smart party that night. Leslie proposed
himself, borrowed a dress suit and took the job. The hosts of the
party were much impressed, and turned out to be the Vanderbilts,
at that time America's closest equivalent to a royal family. This
astonishingly lucky break led to their becoming Leslie's friends and
patrons in Paris and London. They were very influential, with
social connections at the highest level: for instance, one of the
Vanderbilts married a woman, Gloria, whose sister, Thelma Fur-
ness, was the mistress of the Prince of Wales; and it was Thelma
who introduced the Prince to her friend Wallis Simpson.

At the Vanderbilts' and other downtown parties, Leslie would
have met the white hosts on a business footing when making
arrangements for payment. And he probably attracted a following
of socialites who came to hear him in Harlem, thus generating a state
of affairs, in both senses, that persisted almost to the end of his life. As
a black, Leslie had numerous scores to settle with whites; and it was
probably while he was in New York that he set about wreaking his
revenge by seducing white women. At any rate, he would have
generated enough experience to be reasonably confident that he
could hold his own in white society socially and professionally.

Leslie had made a modest name for himself in Harlem in the
eighteen months before he sailed for France; but he must have
realised that, as a jazz musician, he would never be more than a
good as opposed to a great player – and there were too many great
players around. When Duke Ellington made a list of the 'great
piano players' he included such famous name as Fats Waller, James
P. Johnson, Count Basie and Art Tatum, but there is no mention of
his friend Leslie. Though a competent exponent of Harlem stride
and an excellent accompanist, he had little of the originality and
talent of the great jazzmen, all of whom, unlike Leslie, composed
much of their own music. In the event, his departure for Europe
was to prove a sound commercial move. While many stars were
unable to earn a living by playing jazz in the 1930s – even Sidney
Bechet had to open a tailor's shop for a time – Leslie was to earn a
fortune playing in the café-society genre.

He also knew that he had still a lot to learn. He later claimed that he went to Paris to be a concert pianist; and he may at the time have liked the idea of undergoing formal classical training. It would have offset his failure to complete his medical studies; and, should he go on playing jazz, the likes of James P. Johnson, Fats Waller and Jelly Roll Morton believed that the study of classical music did much to enhance its performance. In truth, Paris beckoned simply because it was a smaller stage where he would shine more brightly. His French, learned from his mother, was perfect. Black musicians spoke of good living conditions, less colour prejudice and excellent scope for work; for them, Paris was the alternative to Harlem – everything happened in one or the other location. And many of the exalted white patrons whom Leslie had seen in Manhattan would take more notice of him in Paris. In addition to the Vanderbilts, they included the Prince of Wales, Lady Mountbatten, the theatrical producer Charles Cochran and the revue singer Beatrice Lillie.

So Leslie set sail for Le Havre on 18 October 1924. Ella probably went with him, though she may have followed later. According to his passport, he had grown four inches in the eight years he had been in America. He had grown in many other ways, too. He had survived; in a small way, he had succeeded; now it was his turn to be famous.

Chapter Three

I Love Paris
1924–1927

In Montmartre, in Montmartre
Everybody is playing a part.

Douglas Byng

After a three-week crossing by ship from New York, Leslie reached Le Havre on 5 November 1924. Within two weeks of arriving in France, he went on to Madrid, probably leaving his wife to settle into a flat at 26 rue Constantinople, Paris 8e, near the Gare St Lazare. His destination was the royal court, where Queen Ena, wife of King Alfonso XIII of Spain, wanted him to teach her children the piano and give twice-weekly recitals to court audiences.[1] As the Queen liked her family to be abreast of fashion, he probably also provided accompaniment for charleston lessons. Queen Ena – her full name was Queen Victoria Eugenie of Battenburg – was a granddaughter of Queen Victoria and a cousin of Lord Louis Mountbatten. She was attractive, elegant and amusing and, in 1923, the romantic novelist Elinor Glyn described her as looking 'like a fairy queen, so young and fresh and lovely. In her silver turquoise and aquamarine lamé dress . . . a dream of beauty all the time.'[2]

It is possible that she employed Leslie on the recommendation of Edwina Mountbatten, as Edwina could well have seen Leslie perform in Harlem and at Palm Beach.

Leslie afterwards claimed that he lived and taught in the palace for a year, but Queen Ena's daughter, the Infanta Beatriz, said that the lessons were infrequent and that his stay was only brief, probably about six months. Leslie later told a friend that Queen Ena was devoted to him, but it is now impossible to know whether this was bragging or hinted at his first royal romance. Just before the Spanish Revolution, Lord Dudley was introducing them at a London party when Queen Ena smiled and said, 'We are old friends'; she and Leslie then spoke intimately for the rest of the evening.[3] She and the deposed King Alfonso lived in London from 1931 to 1939; they then divorced, and she settled in exile in Switzerland.

While in Spain, Leslie may have met some old friends from Harlem: Cricket Smith, the trumpeter; the pianist Palmer Jones and the drummer Creighton Thompson. They had played 'under the command of the King of Spain' in the Pyrenees in 1922,[4] and Cricket Smith took a band to Spain in 1925. Soon after, Leslie was playing in a band with both Thompson and Smith in Paris at the invitation of Rollen Smith. Rollen Smith was an alto saxophone player whom Leslie knew from Elmer Snowden's band in Harlem in 1923. The band was respected, experienced and soon made a name for itself. Cricket Smith was the star. Langston Hughes cites him as among 'the cream of negro musicians then in France'; and Noble Sissle said that even 'if Cricket Smith didn't know the name of a chord, he certainly didn't miss any of the notes . . . when he improvised, it was right on the nose'.

In the 1950s, as a guest on the British radio show *Desert Island Discs*, Hutch requested 'Navarra' by Isaac Albéniz 'because I have spent three years of my life in Spain'. This was certainly an exaggeration of the extent of his visit, but Leslie was there long enough to pick up the language. On his recording of 'Besame Mucho', his accent is perfect; and in the 1960s he ordered a journalist drinks in fluent Spanish, and told him that he had learned the language in Madrid as a protégé of the Spanish royal family. Hutch's friend Bill Pilkington confirmed that he spoke Spanish well, adding that he also spoke German. During the years Leslie was based in Paris, he spent as much time elsewhere in Europe as he did in France, and Berlin may well have been one of his ports of call; he would certainly have been well suited to the decadent ambience of Weimar Germany.

When Leslie travelled, he always left Ella behind. Although she did not initially speak French, she coped well but lived quietly. She soon got used to Leslie's being away so much; and, when he was at home, to his sleeping through the morning and staying out all night. She was neither white enough nor black enough to fit easily into any group. She had no performing skills or social presence. So Leslie did not take her anywhere; thinking, possibly with some justification, that she would let him down in front of the international set through whom he sought to advance his career. Ella lived in partial ignorance of his relationships with white people, punctuated by some nasty surprises; but she must have been deeply upset by the ways in which Leslie slowly abandoned her without actually leaving her. When the wives of other black musicians were similarly isolated, they either left or made themselves harder to dispose of. Ella adopted the latter course: she became pregnant, and the only child of the marriage, a girl christened Leslie Bagley Yvonne, was born on 9 April 1926. To announce her arrival, her proud parents sent out pink and gold engraved cards.

Shortly after Leslie arrived in Paris, Battling Siki, the Senegalese boxer and compulsive party giver, turned up to fight a series of bouts. He paraded his pet lion along the Seine, and cut just as bizarre a figure in the ring at the Velodrome: in his match against the French heavyweight champion, Morelle, he grinned throughout, and turned round so that his opponent could pound his back and sides. The referee judged this burlesque to be a foul, and declared Morelle to be the winner. Siki returned to America, and was murdered a few weeks later.

On leaving Rollen Smith's band in 1925, Leslie played as a soloist at the Romance, a nightclub in rue Pigalle, and at a club called the Boite. Soon he was off on his travels again, with a band, on a tour that started in Constantinople and took in Vienna, Budapest and most of the capitals of central Europe. This came about because Mustafa Kemal, later known as Atatürk, had heard the band on a visit to Paris and (according to Leslie) been most impressed by it. As he was a 'hot jazz' fan and keen to update his country on the latest Western trends, he ordered his Paris agent to summon it to perform in Turkey. Being bisexual, he may also have been motivated by a weakness for Leslie. When the band arrived, he met them in person and also received them at his private residence in Çankaya, near Ankara. The band played at several informal and formal functions. The latter included a great ball, presided over by Atatürk. In the course of this drunken revel, eleven of Atatürk's political rivals were hanged in the main square in Ankara. It was ironic that Leslie had only recently left America, in part to escape violence at the hands of the Ku Klux Klan, to find himself playing for a man who had ordered his henchmen to commit multiple murder only four miles away.

France, especially Paris, was very appealing to black musicians in the 1920s, largely because black music appealed so much to the French. A number of black American soldiers had fought in the First World War, and the Parisians welcomed them as heroes. The Parisians also liked jazz for its brazen strutting sound, and associated it largely with blacks. Furthermore, unlike most white American tourists at the time, many black visitors took the trouble to learn French. On arrival in Paris, US musicians were amazed to see black men and white women on the stage together. 'White Americans appear positively silly over here,' Alberta Hunter observed. 'They do their utmost to cause trouble – to try to start the colour question – but to no avail . . . I am only praying no coloured person will ever cause the French people to dislike us, as Paris, in fact, all of France, is heaven on earth, for the black man or woman.'[5]

The French were not in fact actively hospitable; although they did not feel threatened by the black newcomers, they kept them at arm's length. Prejudice was not wholly absent. And Langston Hughes commented, 'Less you can play jazz or tap dance, you'd just as well go home,' which he did.[6]

The biggest star of the black invasion was Josephine Baker. She was to be a friend of Hutch's for many years. Late in 1925, she led a troupe of two dozen musicians, singers and dancers in *La Revue Nègre*. Fifty years after the opening night, Josephine Baker was still 'fresh . . . sensual, exciting' in the memory of Janet Flanner, for many years the Paris correspondent of the *New Yorker*.

She made her entry entirely nude except for a pink flamingo feather between her limbs; she was being carried upside down and doing the splits on the shoulder of a black giant . . . She was an unforgettable ebony statue . . . [a] magnificent dark body, a

new model that to the French proved for the first time that black
was beautiful . . . She was the established new American star for
Europe.[7]

The impact of the show worried some commentators. A distinguished ballet critic, André Levinson, feared *La Revue Nègre* would
result in black culture permeating the mainstream of American and
European culture. Other reviews warned that miscegenation
would result in the lower black gene contaminating and eroding
the quality of the higher white gene. Phyllis Rose, in her biography
of Josephine Baker, makes some useful definitions:

> An enthusiasm for African statues is one thing, for black flesh
> another. I would call one primitivism; and the other, exoticism.
> Compared with racism, exoticism is merely decorative and
> superficial. It doesn't build death camps. It doesn't exterminate.
> Exoticism cares mostly about its own amusement and tends to
> find differences of colour amusing where racism finds them
> threatening. Exoticism is frivolous, it hangs out at nightclubs,
> will pay anything to have the black singer or pianist sit at its table.
> Exoticism grew up rich and a little bored. The racist is hedged
> around by danger, the exoticist by used-up toys. If one is to be
> treated as a thing, one would rather be treated as a rare and pretty
> thing, than as a disgusting or dangerous one. But that is still to be
> treated as a thing. As Josephine Baker said wryly, 'The white
> imagination sure is something, when it comes to blacks.'

Leslie's old Harlem friends Alberta Hunter and Bricktop were both
in Paris, but they had fallen out. 'Bert' felt superior and ill-disposed
to 'Brick' because Bricktop was loud-mouthed and raunchy. This
dislike had intensified when she learned later that while they were
still in Harlem, Bricktop had picked up a telegram from Paris
addressed to Alberta. It was the offer of a good job at a nightclub in
Montmartre called Le Grand Duc as a replacement for Florence
Embry, a beautiful singer from Harlem who had quarrelled with
Bullard and left to open Chez Florence. Bricktop immediately left
for France and grabbed the job. The fact that someone as good-
natured as she was would act so ruthlessly shows just how desperate
black performers were to escape from America. Langston Hughes
recalled that Le Grand Duc had been 'empty of black musicians for

a while', but 'Brick liked everyone, and made everyone like her' and soon made a great success of the club.[8] The part-owner and manager of Le Grand Duc, Gene Bullard, was a former prize fighter and much decorated war veteran who had been the only black to serve in the Lafayette Flying Corps. He was to become very friendly with Leslie.

At Le Grand Duc, Bricktop met two Americans who defined the Jazz Age: the novelist F. Scott Fitzgerald and the songwriter Cole Porter. In fact, Bricktop became everyone's confidante. She was a wise, sympathetic woman whose views were often sought by the mostly neurotic and immature artistes around her. She said of Josephine Baker that 'she wouldn't go round the corner without asking my advice'; and when, a few years later in London, the sex lives of both Paul Robeson and Leslie were embarrassing their white friends, Bricktop was brought over from Paris to restrain them.

Late in 1925, soon after Cole Porter met Bricktop, he started giving charleston parties with her as a teacher. Because Bricktop thought Leslie by far the best accompanist in Paris, she asked him to play for her dancing lessons, and they became a team, 'Hutch and Brick'. Bricktop always called Leslie 'Hutch', and by late 1926, so did everyone else, apart from close friends. From now on, this book will do the same.

Among their dancing pupils were the Aga Khan, Elsa Maxwell and the Prince of Wales, whom Bricktop first met at a party given by a Boston millionaire called Amos Lawrence. At the party, while Bricktop was performing a song with Hutch's band, the Marquise de Polignac invited her to teach the Prince the black bottom, which was fast superseding the charleston as the new dance craze. 'It didn't take long for him to catch on,' Bricktop remembered. 'He was a very good dancer.' Later that evening, the Prince decided to give a party, and Hutch volunteered Bricktop's new nightclub, the Music Box, as the venue. In Bricktop's words, 'That was all we needed to put the Music Box over. I had him and I had Cole Porter, and that was enough to pack the place every night. Spencer Williams who wrote, "Everybody Loves My Baby", and Hutch took turns at the piano . . . The club was a fantastic success.' Leading jazz musicians met there to jam. In his autobiography *As Wonderful as All That?*, Henry Crowder, a jazz pianist and, more significantly, lover of Nancy Cunard, noted that it was briefly fashionable, and that 'Nancy was a regular client of the place and always took her friends there . . . she also went downstairs to have earnest conversations [Crowder's euphemism for sex] with the cook, Fred.'

The Music Box soon folded, because of complaints from rival nightclub owners. For a while Bricktop returned to Le Grand Duc to recoup her finances. Her next club, the soon to be legendary Bricktop's, opened in October 1926, on the rue Fontaine. In her memoirs, the American writer Kay Boyle describes Bricktop in evocative, if overblown, terms.

> I liked her . . . clear-eyed poise in the dancing, drinking, worldly turmoil of the place. Her ability to be at the heart of, and yet remain detached from, the activity around her, gave them − the others − the look of ants in panic, and she, doe-eyed, was the warm, sweet mammal, with daisies in her ears and a cud as sweet as honey in her mouth . . . The decisions she took in the hour we spent with her that night were made as quietly as turning the pages of a book, taken, there could be no doubt, out of some unshakeable recognition of right and wrong, some individual and untroubled concept of natural law.[9]

At Bricktop's, the white torch singer Helen Morgan often got up and sang. She had been partly blinded as a child when someone threw a can of paint in her face. Born in 1900 in Danville, Illinois, she began singing in Chicago speakeasies and progressed to Broadway, where she starred in a Ziegfeld show. Later, in *Showboat*, she sang 'Can't Help Lovin' Dat Man' in her uniquely shaky little voice. Alcoholism, illness and broken marriages inflated her celebrity, and numerous saloons and speakeasies were named after her. After visiting Paris, Helen Morgan would move on to London, where Hutch recorded with her in 1927.

The knockabout comics Mutt and Jeff were cavorting across the stages of Berlin, London and Paris at this time, and Hutch shared a bill with them in 1926 when they appeared at the Théâtre des Champs Elysées at a charity event. Hutch was billed as 'Les Hutchinson', and he appeared with his Royalty Six and his Quartette Royal; both groups featured his old colleague Rollen Smith on alto saxophone.

One of the most outrageous people with whom Hutch was on

intimate terms was the American actress Tallulah Bankhead. He met her in April 1926, when he was working at the Boite. The club owner, a black American called Gerald Hall, asked Bricktop to help him attract clients, and one of the people she introduced to the club was Gene Bankhead, Tallulah's sister. Tallulah was currently the talk of London, where the realism of her performance in Noël Coward's *Fallen Angels*, as a hectic, drunken wife, had aroused a furore of discussion and condemnation in the press. The society photographer Cecil Beaton thought she looked like 'Medusa, very exotic, with a glorious skull, high pumice-stone cheekbones and a broad brow'. Her deep, husky voice was like 'the sound of a man pulling his foot out of a pail of yoghourt'.[10] Her mother had died giving birth to her in 1902, and her father, Will, was the love of her life, but he was a racist. Tallulah opposed his views and publicly condemned the Ku Klux Klan and the treatment of blacks in the South. In the idiom of the time, she was 'highly strung', and, in 1925, shortly before she met Hutch, she had made a half-hearted suicide attempt. It was said that she had abortions as other women had permanent waves. Much later, the US comedian Milton Berle remembered her as 'a Southern Belle, a foul-mouthed free soul with little respect for morals and rules of behaviour . . . a flower child in a Coco Chanel suit, uninhibited, basic and bent on self-destruction'.[11] Bricktop described her more kindly as 'really some-one special. She had everything – beauty, grace, wit, personality and intelligence. When Tallulah walked into the room, she was the centre of attention, and she expected to be.'[12] If she failed to attract that attention, she would 'sniff some snow' (cocaine) and do her famous cartwheels; and, if that did not work, she removed her knickers. Once, in New York, when he refused to play for her, she tried this tactic on Arthur Rubinstein, but to no avail. Truman Capote recalled that 'Tallulah turned up for a swimming party, wearing nothing but a string of pearls, because she wanted to prove that she was a natural ash blonde.'[13]

Pearls also play a central role in a gesture she made just after the birth of Hutch and Ella's baby. Bricktop wrote, 'Tallulah loved Hutch . . . and was there [at the Boite, Gerald Hall's club] the night that Hutch's wife gave birth to their child. As the champagne went to work, Tallulah got all emotional about "that beautiful child and her mother being in some lonely hospital room away from those who loved her".' Tallulah insisted on going to the hospital, cleaving her way through protesting doctors and nurses and bursting into the room where Ella and the baby were asleep. 'After "oohing" and "aahing", Tallulah dramatically took off her pearls, and held them out to the baby. "They are for you, darling. Keep them, and remember me always." Then she placed them on the pillow.' Early next morning, Tallulah woke up with a hang-over and, regretting her generous impulse, sent her sister Gene to ask Bricktop to recover the pearls. Bricktop refused and, despite continued pressure from Gene over several days, went on refusing. Then, one night, when Tallulah came to the club, she said to her, 'nice and loud, "Gene wants me to get back the pearls." Tallulah looked daggers at Gene, who stuttered, "I was telling Brick we must get back the pearls you gave to Hutch's baby." Tallulah got ready for one of her balcony projections. "Darling, I definitely don't want them back. No, no, no. I gave the pearls to that precious little baby. I want her to have them." ' Having made her point loud and clear, Tallulah whispered to Bricktop on the way to a table, 'Brick, I do wish you'd get the pearls back. I'd like to have them.' But, to Bricktop's knowledge, she never recovered them.[14]

Tallulah described Hutch as 'simply divine'. They were lovers for a while, but she proved too erratic for Hutch, who dropped her. However, they remained good friends, and admirers of each other's performances, into the 1950s.

While there is no instance of Hutch's ever being used by others, he was always ready, if it helped him in any way, to make use of his sexuality. One of the most important affairs of his career began in 1925 when he met Cole Porter. It is just possible that they met at the Schola Cantorum. Hutch later claimed that he had trained to be a concert pianist at the Conservatoire or the Schola Cantorum at 269 rue St Jacques. Neither institution has kept its old registers, but it seems unlikely to be true. He was too busy making money and a name for himself to have had much time for formal study. Cole Porter certainly attended the Schola but, despite his proud and frequent references to his studies and his work with the composer Vincent d'Indy, there is little evidence of either: Porter's recordings show him to be an indifferent pianist, and there is minimal evidence of co-composition with d'Indy. It is conceivable that Hutch may have accompanied Cole to the Schola, but that is probably the closest he came to rigorous musical studies in Paris.

The nearest both men got to classical music of real stature was in the person of Arthur Rubinstein. Hutch met the legendary pianist through Cole, and was enchanted by him, 'one of the greatest pianists I have ever heard'. Rubinstein was also the leading exponent of Chopin, Hutch's favourite composer. One evening, in the company of the Prince of Wales and the eccentric Princess Violette Murat,[15] they listened to the poet and artist Jean Cocteau playing the drums. Afterwards they sat side by side at the piano and, in Hutch's words, 'showed each other our favourite piano tricks . . . he was fascinated by some rather unorthodox chords I showed him.' Hutch and Rubinstein had much in common. Away from the piano, both men shared an insatiable, often destructive need for love. They were deeply suspicious, short-tempered and bore grudges; were extravagant, self-indulgent and dressed expensively. But they were also genuinely charming, sometimes very generous with money and excellent company. Both men lived beyond rules and without roots; and were incapable of developing close relationships.

It is much more likely that Cole and Hutch first met through Bricktop. In any case it was appropriate – indeed, almost inevitable – that they should meet in Paris. American artists and writers since the days of James McNeill Whistler and Henry James had looked on the city as the great intellectual centre and the source of the finest food and drink. The rich came to enjoy the leisurely, stylish pace of the world's most fashionable capital while the less rich were attracted by the promise of the good life in cheap surroundings. In some ways, Paris was closer to New York than it is now. During the 1920s it became a playground annexe to New York, a reminder to a puritan society that work is not all there is to life, and that there are options other than the American pattern of hard work and violent relaxation. The young composer Virgil Thompson summarised the motives behind the invasion when he wrote that Americans flocked to Paris 'to get screwed, sharpen their wits and eat like kings for nothing'.[16]

Cole Porter lived in Paris throughout the twenties. He came from a rich family and had started composing at the age of six. Although he had studied law at Yale and Harvard, he never practised, but pursued his vocation for words and music. Photographs of him aged thirty-three, when Hutch met him, show a licentious, clever dandy with a secretive smile and suggestive pop-eyes. By this time he had already had some success as a songwriter. He spoke excellent French, fair Italian and a little Spanish. His favourite composers were Stravinsky, Bach, Mozart, Gershwin and Rodgers; and his favourite lyric writer was P. G. Wodehouse. Like Hutch, he loved Spain; he told the Duchess of Alba, 'Spain and its flamenco gave me . . . the abiding influence with . . . regard to basic beats, changing tempos and pure melody and scale at their purest and most primitive.'[17] He owned sixteen dressing gowns and nine cigarette cases. His house in Paris, at 13 rue Monsieur, in the fashionable quartier des Invalides, had an interior in the Art Deco style. Inside, zebra rugs lay on gleaming marble floors; white kidskin cushions on red lacquered chairs; suede covered sofas; one room had platinum-coloured wallpaper; and the huge, mirror-lined basement was solely devoted to parties. This adventurous approach to interior design stemmed from Cole's rich, elegant wife, Linda. At least ten years older than Cole, she acted as a very sophisticated finishing school for numerous men, but principally her husband. 'Because she was so worldly, she taught him a lot,' the socialite Brooke Astor said. 'He could never have written the type of songs he wrote without her. She launched him into that world. It was not the fast lane, it was the chic, intercontinental European set. That is how and when it all began.' She had so many admirers that the librettist Moss Hart said, 'To fall in love with Linda Porter was as much a part of a young man's first trip to Paris as eating snails at Fouquet's or climbing the Eiffel Tower.' At this stage of their marriage, Linda was happily resigned to her husband's being, in the words of the lyricist Alan Lerner, 'a homosexual who had never seen the closet.' In particular, he had a well-known *faiblesse* for black men.

Eight years older than Hutch, Cole Porter had an immense amount to teach his protégé – socially and intellectually, as well as about music, sex and clothes – and Hutch was keen to learn. Cole was a kind and graceful mentor; later in life, Hutch emulated him by passing on helpful advice to young people without patronising them. Cole had about him a subversive irony which he used to oust pomposity in favour of style. This swiftly became a key component of Hutch's way of presenting himself. Like Hutch, Cole was perpetually reinventing his past: for instance, he mendaciously claimed that he had joined the French Foreign Legion. While it is understandable that Hutch, who came from a humble background and had restlessly moved from one continent and social world to another, should have felt so insecure that he had to mythologise himself, it is very strange that Cole, who was born to so much privilege, should have done the same.

While Hutch was Cole's lover, their partnership was mostly professional and mutually admiring. The actor Monty Woolley said that Cole often told male friends that Hutch's talents went far beyond the keyboard; he believed that their affair went on well into the 1930s.[18] They shared expensive tastes, and Cole delighted in Hutch both as a companion and as a performer. While Cole was very generous to Hutch, there was never any question of Hutch living off him or anyone else, which is why he was relaxed and amused about singing Cole's song specially written for him, 'I'm a Gigolo'. Hutch may well have been bisexual before he came to Paris; once there, where bisexuality was fashionable, he became confirmed in this part-time habit. Under the influence of Cole, Hutch also became ever more particular about his appearance. Cole dressed with a precious, dearly bought camp verve, and his lithe, glowing appearance was the end result of afternoon naps, swallowing a variety of pills every day, and having his skin well oiled. Hutch, very impressionable at twenty-five, copied Cole in many ways, even down to wearing a carnation in his buttonhole. Cole may have been the first rich man he knew intimately, and many of his ways of spending money, enjoying himself and organising his day were, in time, to become Hutch's own. The popular writer Michael Arlen claimed that, having dressed in riding clothes and 'written a song or two', Cole would appear at half past twelve at the Ritz, where he would order champagne cocktails and claim to have had a marvellous ride.[19] His guests at the Ritz often included the playwright Philip Barry (author of *The Philadelphia Story*), the poet Archibald MacLeish, Prince Michael Romanoff, Groucho Marx and Scott Fitzgerald.

Cole, in turn, appreciated the rare combination of attributes – musical ability, good looks, quick wits, great skills in acting and timing – with which Hutch brought a song to life. The two men sat for hours at Cole's house, trying out new numbers face to face on a white double piano. Hutch quickly became one of Cole's favourite exponents of his songs, and Cole showed him exactly how he wanted them played and sung. Hutch later acknowledged that he was 'lucky in being in Paris at the time when Cole Porter was starting to write his really big hits. Cole took me under his wing, taught me how to sing his songs, introduced me to the right people and I was later introduced to London society through him.' Hutch also said that Cole was 'the greatest man in music ever known. He's an education.'[20] Cole's songs are rife with society names and in-jokes – 'Anything Goes' is an outstanding example – and aimed at diverting an exclusive social set. However, because of their beautifully turned lyrics which only Noël Coward could rival, and their brilliantly catchy tunes, his songs transcend their topical references; many of them are classics of the genre, almost as enjoyable now as they were sixty or seventy years ago.

Although Cole Porter had been writing prolifically ever since his Yale days, only a few of his musicals had been staged, and many of his songs had only been performed informally: he called them his 'secret songs', and handed them to Hutch, Bricktop, the society hostess Elsa Maxwell and others to sing at private parties. His breakthrough came in 1927 when a producer, Ray Goetz, urgently needed extra material for a musical called *Paris* starring Irene Bordoni. Cole came up with a clutch of numbers, and soon became one of the top songwriters of the day along with Irving Berlin, Jerome Kern, George Gershwin and the team of Richard Rodgers and Lorenz Hart. His songs have lasted because they have a depth, a regret, an intensity, sometimes even a bitterness which elevate them into haunting dramas. These qualities stem from an uneasy private life in which Cole could never quite find the love, or even the friendship, about which he wrote so heartbreakingly.

Cole wrote three of the songs most often associated with Hutch: 'Let's Do It', which dates from this period, and, in the 1930s, 'Night and Day' and 'Begin the Beguine'. The composition of the second was to give him more problems than the other two. At one point, Monty Woolley advised him to abandon the struggle, and Cole retreated for the weekend to Vincent Astor's cottage in Newport. There, as they dined, a downpour caused a broken drain to drip persistently. 'I must have that eave mended,' Mrs Astor said. 'That drip, drip, drip is driving me mad!' This remark sent Cole straight to the piano, where he triumphantly completed 'Night and Day'. Destined in 1932 to become Cole's biggest hit, 'Night and Day' was unique in that, instead of the thirty-two bars traditional in songs up to that time, it had forty-eight. 'Begin the Beguine' had, according to some accounts, even more exotic beginnings. While on the *Franconia* on a world cruise in 1935, Cole, Linda, Moss Hart and Monty Woolley stopped at a village on Alor, one of the Sunda Islands in what was then the Dutch East Indies. There the party witnessed a traditional dance, the rhythms of which inspired Cole to write 'Begin the Beguine' back on board ship.

The Coleporteurs, as they were called by *le tout Paris*, hired Hutch and his band to play at their parties in Paris and later in Venice. The guests often included Tallulah Bankhead, Noël Coward, Elsa Maxwell, Lady Diana Duff Cooper and the American actress and singer Fanny Brice, all members of the international set who were to make Hutch famous. They found him irresistible; gossiped about his love life; hired him to play at their parties, and followed him around to nightclubs. 'Cole Porter, Leslie Hutchinson, Noël Coward and Elsa Maxwell were all singing in Nicky Ginsberg's flat one evening to entertain us,' recalled Princess Sita of Kapurthala, who went to Paris every year at this time.

> Cole Porter always arrived in Paris by about May and, whichever house you went to, he was always there. His wife was so charming and beautiful, too. They clearly got on so well together. I remember Leslie Hutchinson at Daisy Fellowes's parties, too, in Neuilly and at Les Ambassadeurs. He was very well educated and good-looking and he was invited to these parties as a guest and not just as a pianist.

To be socially accepted by a hostess as grand as Daisy Fellowes – she was the Honourable Mrs Reginald Fellowes, granddaughter of the sewing-machine magnate Isaac Merritt Singer and a compulsive entertainer in both London and Paris between the wars – was a great step up for Hutch. He fervently wanted to be treated on a par with other guests; and, through Cole, he was now moving beyond the servant caste. As he saw it, not having to sing for his supper meant that he was being accepted for himself. This was illusory: the expatriate Americans were being daring in crossing the colour line, but they were far from home, in a city where blacks happened to be fashionable. They were only toying with the exotic. But for Hutch, this was the start of 'five of the greatest years of my life'.[21]

'During the next two or three years all the young men were twenty-six years old,' Gertrude Stein observed. 'It was the right age apparently for that time and place.'[22] She knew of Hutch, as did Ernest Hemingway and the Scott Fitzgeralds. Hutch also got to know leading French entertainers like Maurice Chevalier and Mistinguett.

In exchange, Hutch pimped for Cole and his friends. He took them to the lowlife nightclubs of Montmartre, and organised sleazy parties for them. Hutch also frequently played at their parties. The most notorious of these was given by the Porters in Venice in August 1926, when the fashionable world had moved to the Lido. From being a pleasantly chic Adriatic resort, the Lido had become the best-known beach in the world, a magnet for the fashionable of Europe and America. This was partly due to the energy of Elsa Maxwell, one of the century's most tireless and enterprising hostesses. Her projects on the Lido included a golf course and boat races; and the mayor of Venice, Count Brandolin, frequently sought her advice on other initiatives. That summer, Cole and Linda Porter had rented the two-hundred-room Palazzo Rezzonico, where Byron had stayed and Browning had died. The ballroom could accommodate a thousand guests, but they wanted something different, so they decided to give a grand party on a dance boat, known locally as a *galleggiante*; Sibyl Colefax, one of the guests, described it as three barges roped together with a floor to cover them to make a floating nightclub. The local press reported that 'a negro jazz orchestra is being brought from Paris to play and there will be dancing'. This was Hutch's band. All the socialites in Venice vied with each other for invitations.

In the event, the party was a disaster. There was a storm, all the guests were seasick, and there were no lavatories. After that, the barge was firmly moored close to shore, and an angry letter appeared in the local press.

> The whole of Venice is up in arms against Cole Porter because of his jazz and his negroes. He has started an idiotic night club of a boat . . . and now the Grand Canal is swarming with the very same negroes who have made us all run away from London and Paris. They are teaching the Charleston on the Lido Beach. It's dreadful. The Porter's renting of the Palazzo Rezzonico is characteristic of the nouveaux riches.[23]

According to Monty Woolley, the choreographer Sergei Diaghilev was prominent among 'the whole of Venice': on hearing that the Porters had hired an all-black band, he went into a racist tirade.[24]

Hutch revelled in the publicity. Alongside Bricktop, he and his band also performed at various other functions in Venice, from 5 August to the start of September; most notably, in a 'Charleston Cabaret' on the Lido at the massive 700-bedroom Excelsior Hotel, which was always packed at this time of year. Hutch, Bricktop and the band were all grateful to Cole Porter for exposure to so many potential employers, and for the opportunity to consolidate their finances while enjoying the luxuries of the Lido.

A programme among Hutch's papers states that on 23 August at 10 p.m. 'A Moonlit Night' was staged on behalf of two charities. 'Hutchinson's Royal Six' played two sets; and Miss Bricktop, Miss Maxwell and various socialites appeared once. The charleston was performed by an international cast including Lady Northesk, Duca della Verdura, Mrs Scott Fitzgerald, Count Andrea di Robilant and his wife, and Baron de Gunzberg. Manning the bar were Lady Abdy, Lady Diana Duff Cooper and Mrs Cole Porter. To get the socialites to rehearse, Bricktop had enlisted the help of the influential Princess Jane di San Faustino. A tall, white-haired woman, grandmother of the Fiat chairman Gianni Agnelli, she was born Jane Campbell in New Jersey. In Venice in the 1920s, she dictated who was 'in' and 'out', and was responsible for launching the Porters. That night was Bricktop's birthday, and Count Andrea di Robilant carried in a cake for her, a richly deserved tribute.

An even more exclusive performance took place by royal command after a visit to the Fenice Theatre to hear Puccini's *Turandot*. Hutch and the guests had seats near the royal box. Over thirty years later on *Desert Island Discs* he told the story of the evening:

About halfway through the performance, an equerry came round and said that the royal personage was getting bored, and could we please keep an eye on him. When he dropped a handkerchief, that would be a signal for us to leave our boxes quietly, and go downstairs to the side entrance, where gondolas would be waiting to take us to the palazzo for the party. We all watched out of the corners of our eyes; we saw the handkerchief drop, and down we went. We got into our gondola, HRH got into his, both craft swung round into midstream, and collided.

We were nearly sunk. We all got very wet. However, once the party got going, we all forgot about that. It was a fabulous party.

Then, citing Puccini as his favourite operatic composer, he opted for 'Nessun Dorma' ('None Shall Sleep') from *Turandot*.

Back in Paris, Hutch returned to work at Zelli's, a club across the road from Le Grand Duc in rue Fontaine, run by Joe Zelli. An Italo-American, Joe had previously run a speakeasy in New York, but was now 'king of the nightclub district' in Paris.[25] Some contemporary promotional copy reads:

> Joe is a great, grinning, good-time guy, and he will give you a gladsome hour. And there are 740 girls, more or less, to dance with, and every one is affectionate, hungry, thirsty or broke . . . Joe is worth a million dollars now. All made in seven years and with personality. Nothing else. Go into Zelli's next year, open three bottles of wine. Stay away three years, come back, Joe will rush to meet you and call you by your first name and you will love it.

One window at Zelli's was full of pictures of entertainers and topless bar girls and a vast electric sign, visible from half a block away, beckoned to customers. When Americans came in, Zelli greeted them with his catchphrase, 'I give you the royal box.' He and Hutch respected each other's success and got on well together. According to Bricktop, it was Zelli's that inspired Cole Porter to write 'Love for Sale': when Cole asked one of the taxi-dancing girls what she did, she answered 'I've got love for sale', and given the title, Cole got to work on the song. It was later a great hit for Hutch and many others, especially Elizabeth Welch (who had sung 'Charleston' in *Runnin' Wild*).[26]

One of the patrons at Zelli's in 1926 was Edwina Mountbatten. In New York she had often visited Harlem 'to hear Jazz at the Tent and Plantation' as 'she never tired of jerky syncopated dance music, sentimental love songs and the sound of the wailing saxophone'. She may even have seen Hutch perform there or in Palm Beach. She enjoyed 'unconventional places to dance and dine', and was sometimes introduced to them by her sister-in-law, Nada Milford-Haven, who was mostly lesbian by inclination, and 'had a nose for peculiar nightclubs'.[27] Paris also met those needs, and, from 1922 on, when Edwina went there, she liked to go to Zelli's for cocktails and dancing before moving on to Montmartre. By the time Edwina met him at Zelli's, Hutch had dropped Tallulah Bankhead, having had enough of her antics. And Edwina, once she had formed a relationship with Hutch, decided to devise a way to get him to London, and have him closer to her for more of the time. Their affair was to last intermittently for nearly thirty years.

As a spoilt heiress, she was used to having her way. Her grandfather, Sir Ernest Cassel, a banker, had been a close friend and financial adviser to Edward VII; and, at the turn of the century, he was said to be 'the richest man in the world'. Edwina was heir to Brook House in Park Lane and its priceless contents; she also had an annual income of £30,000, and a number of estates. In 1922, at the age of twenty-one, she married Lieutenant Louis Mountbatten in an elaborately mounted wedding. He was a great-grandson of Queen Victoria, born in the year before her death.

Their differences soon emerged. Mountbatten was a naturally domestic and monogamous man; he was sentimental rather than passionate, and a loving father. He was also handsome, vain, insecure, mentally limited and ambitious to emulate his father and be admiral of the fleet. Edwina was complex and clever and Mountbatten had neither the confidence nor experience to satisfy her; indeed, as Mountbatten's biographer Philip Ziegler wrote, it was doubtful whether 'any one man could have given her what she wanted'. The harsher, more specific verdict of the historian Andrew Roberts is that she was 'a spoilt playgirl, a nymphomaniac and bisexual'.[28] In any case, Edwina liked constant attention, and, finding that she had a 'terrible rival' in the Royal Navy with her husband away at sea, she became bored, lonely and restless. As a result, she diverted herself with, in her own words, 'a life of complete hecticness'. Nothing was spared to enhance her considerable beauty, and her Chanel suits and fox wraps, and diamond bracelets, caused her to be named one of the six best-dressed women in the world in 1925. The Mountbattens had agreed to lead separate lives and she took several other lovers in the same year as she started her affair with Hutch.

Edwina had much in common with Hutch. They were both extreme characters with ebullience and charm. They were both beautiful, elegant and sophisticated. They were swift-witted, funny and shared a love of practical jokes and banana-skin humour. They were perfectionists, and each gave the other an entrée to worlds that intrigued them but that they could not enter alone. Hutch had far more to gain socially from Edwina's company and contacts; but, through him, she could relax in a milieu which amused her, away from the responsibilities and restrictions of her marriage. Above all, they both had immense energy, loved experimental sex – and did not mind at all if they shocked other people.

Getting Hutch to London did not present Edwina with any problems. She invited him to play at 'one of those brilliant receptions for which she is famous' at Carlton House Terrace which she was giving with a socialite friend, Lady Gibbons,[29] in the autumn of 1926. Hutch came over, and the party was a great success. Many of his audience often went to Paris, and even if they had not experienced Hutch at first hand at the Music Box, La Boite or elsewhere, they would have known of him as the rage of the boulevards and the talk of intimate soirees. Newcomers to Hutch were delighted to welcome an accomplished and original performer. At the party, Hutch sang 'Two Little Babes in the Wood', Cole Porter's ingenious satire on the Dolly Sisters, a vaudeville duo. Hutch later recalled, 'It was the first song I sang when I came to dear old London, and I'll never forget the warm-hearted way they welcomed me to town. Maybe, I'd been feeling something like a babe in the wood myself.'[30]

Edwina's next move was to ask Charles Cochran, the great impresario, to employ Hutch in the pit orchestra for his next revue at the London Pavilion. Through Bricktop and Cole Porter, Cochran was already aware of Hutch's existence, and he had heard Hutch being warmly applauded at Edwina's party, which had been conceived largely as a showcase for his talents. Anyway, he would never have agreed to sign up Hutch if he had not been impressed by what he heard. Some record sleeves wrongly claim that Cochran discovered Hutch at 'Joselli's', but the fact of the matter is that Edwina wanted Hutch close to hand, and, rich and manipulative as she was, she arranged matters to suit herself. As it happened, her arrangement also suited Cochran and Hutch.

In February 1927, Cochran announced that he was planning to 'present an intimate revue. It will be short, late and expensive.' Cochran was then in his fifties and had been staging successful revues and shows with music in London since the end of the First

World War. He had a gift for spotting new talent and for using established performers in fresh combinations. A risk-taker with a great enthusiasm for the theatre, he created shows that were among the defining events of the period.

Before he committed himself to a permanent move by buying a house and moving his family, Hutch stayed with a West Indian doctor in north London. He needed more than success at Carlton House Terrace to be sure that he could support himself, Ella and little Leslie in London. That aside, it must have been very hard for him to leave Paris. He had always felt at home there, French was his second language, and his identification with Paris is apparent in the fervour with which he later sang Cole Porter's 'I Love Paris'; and in the wistfulness and pride in his rendering of other songs about France, among them, 'Paris Is Not the Same', 'Bon Voyage, Cherie', 'Somewhere in France with You', 'A Small Café in Notre Dame' and, most memorably, 'La Mer'. As in Harlem, he had been in the right place at the right time.

Hutch had changed completely, and, from now on, was often to boast of the culture and sophistication he had acquired in Paris. Apart from enhancing his musical and social skills, he had also become a gourmet. Eating and drinking at Le Boeuf sur le Toit probably launched him as a *bon viveur*. As well as being a meeting point for intellectuals with a penchant for jazz, this restaurant, in the words of a 1925 guidebook:

> symbolised very well the work of Jean Cocteau, its godfather: the wildest fantasy within established traditions. At the Boeuf, one encounters the artistic trend of the moment . . . [and] if one hears the most astounding declarations that are being made in Paris, one is at the same time certain to eat exceedingly well.

From being a hungry, impoverished musician, whose only entrée to a grand restaurant would have been as an employee, Hutch now walked in and commanded service with all the authority he had gleaned from being entertained in expensive venues. In time, there was little Hutch enjoyed more than to be identified and fawned on by the maitre d', and to show off to waiters and sommeliers the expertise of a gourmet and an oenophile.

Apart from a love of French cuisine, Hutch had picked up another skill which was to serve him well in England. He attracted the attention of Natalie Clifford Barney, a wealthy American lesbian who had lived in Paris since 1900. She galloped her horse daily through the Bois de Boulogne, dressed in bowler and black bow tie, and invited Hutch to ride with her.

Like anyone who has ever lived and loved there, Hutch felt possessive about Paris. It influenced much of his thinking and became for him the ultimate yardstick of civilised living. He was often to return there; to court various women, eat at fine restaurants, stay at elegant hotels and look up his wide circle of friends. As Ernest Hemingway wrote, 'If you are lucky enough to live in Paris as a young man, then wherever you go for the rest of your life, it stays with you, for Paris is a moveable feast.'[31]

Chapter Four

London at Last
1927–1930

To men like you we pay no living wage
And all their work is swept away like snow
Yet you have left your footsteps on the stage
The world is richer for the Cochran show.

A. P. Herbert

H utch had always stressed that he was British by birth and not, as most people supposed, American; and, like many colonial entertainers, he was keen to make his mark in his mother country. He would have liked to show his father that musicians were not just vagabonds and wastrels, but his father was now dead of tuberculosis. Hutch longed for the acclamation of British audiences: if only he could get them to accept him as one of their own, he would feel secure and satisfied.

C. B. Cochran had said that *Blackbirds* of 1926 would be his last revue; but when it proved to be sensationally successful, he changed his mind. In part, this was due to the Prince of Wales, who, in the words of the singer and dancer Edith Wilson, 'used to come all the time . . . I used to do a number on stage, and he'd do it right along with me. He'd be in the box – they had curtains you could draw so you couldn't see from the side – and he'd be dancing right along with the show.'[1] The show was also a personal triumph for Hutch's old friend from Harlem, Florence Mills. As the star, she became a popular cult figure. But only briefly: on her return to New York in 1927, she died suddenly, after an appendix operation, aged only thirty-two. Prominent in her 150,000-strong funeral procession, as it wound slowly through the streets of Harlem, was a tower of red roses perched on a car. Signed 'From a Friend', they had been ordered by an unsigned cablegram from London; many believed them to be from the Prince of Wales. As the ceremony came to a close, two aeroplanes flew low over the crowd. The first released a flight of blackbirds, while the second scattered a cloud of roses.

The revue is a swift series of short items – songs, dances and sketches – often with a gently satirical slant. Up to the early 1920s, under the aegis of impresarios such as André Charlot in Britain and Florence Ziegfeld and George White in New York, revues were mostly spectacular entertainments. But between the wars this type of revue made way for the 'intimate revue' largely pioneered by C. B. Cochran. He launched the genre with *Odds and Ends* in 1914, and continually redefined it with a series of increasingly elaborate shows that stopped only in the late 1940s, when he concentrated more on musicals. Douglas Byng, a brilliant female impersonator who appeared in many of his shows, wrote that Cochran:

> had a magnificent disregard for expense. If someone suggested a backcloth from the greatest artist in Spain, or an iceberg from the polar regions, it was immediately sent for . . . What one admired most, was his courage and his perfect taste; once you had seen a Cochran revue, all others seemed tawdry by comparison. He was so sure of himself, and so sure of exactly how far to go.[2]

His shows featured many of the major interwar stars, including Jack Buchanan, Beatrice Lillie, Jessie Matthews and Gertrude Lawrence. He also used writers and songwriters such as Noël Coward, Cole Porter and Herbert Farjeon; choreographers like Mikhail Fokine and Léonide Massine; and leading designers including Rex Whistler and Oliver Messel.

For his 1927 revue, Cochran tried to sign up Noble Sissle and Eubie Blake, who, as well as writing *Shuffle Along*, Florence Mills's debut musical of 1921, had also made a large contribution to *Blackbirds*. But they reluctantly declined, as Blake was keen to return to America. So Cochran commissioned Richard Rodgers and Lorenz Hart instead. The show was called *One Dam' Thing After Another* – a sound definition of any revue. 'Even without the "n" in *Dam*' in the title, this struck Larry and me as a racy title for an English revue.' Richard Rodgers commented in his book *Musical Stages*. 'Others apparently thought so, too, since the show was usually referred to as "the London Pavilion Revue".' Cochran himself gave the show two further names, 'The Kindergarten Revue' and 'The Ol' Man's Pleasant Evening', because the company was so young.

Rodgers wrote that Cochran:

> lined up an impressive cast, including, in her first major part, a very young bright-eyed and toothy doll of a girl named Jessie Matthews. Also in the cast was Edythe Baker, a brilliant American pianist, whose trademark was a large white piano. A second pianist, for the pit, was Leslie Hutchinson, an extremely personable black man known as 'Hutch'. He used to appear at all the society parties, and was so popular that it was a real coup to have him play in the theatre orchestra.

Douglas Byng remembered Hutch as 'an expansive personality, who loved life, especially riotous parties'. The show previewed in Manchester, where, after a very late dress rehearsal, Hutch 'threw a splendid affair at the Midland Hotel which continued until the very late hours of the morning. One of the Young Ladies – the chorus girls – went to give Cochran a goodnight kiss, and returned with a note from him which read, "Ladies and gentlemen, please remember we open this evening."' During this and later Manchester openings, Hutch made some extra money by performing after hours in the Trafford Room of the Midland Hotel.

The Young Ladies included Marjorie Robertson, later, as Anna Neagle, to star in many English films, often directed by her husband Herbert Wilcox; Mimi Crawford, who, in the true Gaiety Girl tradition of marrying into the peerage, was soon to wed the Earl of Suffolk; and Mimi's understudy, Sheilah Graham, who, after breaking off her engagement to Lord Donegall, went to Hollywood and became Scott Fitzgerald's partner in his declining years. Also in the cast were Sonny Hale, a comic song-and-dance man who later married Jessie Matthews; and Max Wall, then a chorus boy but later to become one of the most original stand-up comedians of the century. He also became a close friend of Hutch.

Over the weeks before the premiere, Cochran's press office released details of the cast, costumes and decor as a form of advance publicity for the show. Edythe Baker's cape was to coruscate with 600 ostrich plumes, and Coco Chanel had designed the dresses for the fifty chorus girls. On the eve of the opening on 20 May, women queued on camp stools outside the London Pavilion, and had to be moved on by the police because they caused traffic congestion. They were allowed to return at five in the morning. As well as being devotees of Cochran revues, many of them were avid to see the Prince of Wales arrive for the first night.

With the Prince came Lord Lonsdale, who, at the sight of Edythe Baker, dropped the large cigar that had become his trademark. Richard Rodgers wrote that he was delighted by the Prince's presence because he assumed it would ensure the success of the show. But Cochran, wise to the ways of London audiences, was doubtful: given the choice, they were more inclined to watch royalty, and emulate reactions from the royal box, than watch what happened on stage.

The Mountbattens took a box for the opening night and from it showered sweets on Hutch at his Steinway in the orchestra pit. In the interval, he played alone under a single spotlight, and most people remained in their seats to listen. As the only black man on the audience's side of the footlights, he was conspicuous, and was admired as a talented, handsome exotic in exemplary evening dress. After the show, Lady Portarlington gave a party for Edythe Baker, where Hutch played again. This was attended by numerous socialites, many of them coming straight from the premiere; the guests also included Fred Astaire and his sister Adele.

The first-night curtain had fallen to only perfunctory applause, but ecstatic notices appeared five or six days later; Cochran always rigorously excluded critics from the theatre until the show had had time to settle down.

Cochran's latest revue will have a long run [predicts a cutting among Hutch's papers]. It seems to have all the components of revue success, such as bright humour, lively tunes, pretty

costumes and daring dances. But, comically enough, the uproarious hit of the show is just a lady pianist, Miss Baker . . . the
amazing legend is that this real artist knows not one note of
music and plays entirely by ear.

The *Evening Standard* agreed: 'She can dance, she can sing, she can
play ragtimes on the piano . . . doing all of them remarkably well
with the aim of enjoying herself and being amused at herself . . . I
need not add that she is young and wickedly pretty.' The *Sunday
Pictorial* was more to the point: 'She moves in an aura of admiration, seeming to be receiving bouquets with her eyes, and gets so
much sex appeal into playing the piano that one suspects that she
would be entrancing even with a double bass.'

In those days, black entertainers could not normally expect an
accolade in the white trade press. The *Amsterdam News*, a black
newspaper in New York, deplored the fact that the London
edition of *Variety*, a New York magazine, applauded unsuccessful
white performers but never even mentioned Hutch. The press felt
that flattering reviews of blacks gave them too much power and
could easily propel them over the colour line. The *Amsterdam News*
tried to compensate for this by referring to:

> the clever pianist and baritone playing with the big London
> Pavilion orchestra in *ODTAA* . . . I daresay there hasn't ever
> been a pianist and singer who has come to London and achieved
> such wonderful success as Mr Hutchinson, also entertaining at
> two very exclusive night clubs in the West End, and at least two
> private parties every night. It is Lord and Lady Mountbatten,
> who are related to HRH the Prince of Wales, that have made it
> possible for him to get in with this class of people.

One reason Hutch played in the orchestra was that racial prejudice
disbarred him from appearing on stage with white women. As a
result, Jessie Matthews, for instance, hardly knew him. Then, one
evening after rehearsals at the Pavilion, she was crossing the stage
when she heard 'this simply amazing piano playing' rising from the
orchestra pit. So she peered down, and:

> There was this handsome black man playing the piano without
> music, and with only a solitary rehearsal light . . . it was the best

sound I ever heard in my life. I had never heard an English
pianist play that way, the nearest thing to it was the negro pianists
I had heard in the little jazz clubs in Harlem on my first visit to
New York.[3]

Many confirm Jessie's claim that it was she who first encouraged
Hutch to start singing as well as playing. She also chose him for her
accompanist when she went to record 'My Heart Stood Still', a
Rodgers and Hart song from *ODTAA*, and 'Just a Memory' in
October 1927. Hutch is billed as Leslie A. Hutchinson.[4] Hutch
always gratefully remembered Jessie's kindness, and they remained
lifelong friends. Forty years later, he said, 'But for this girl, my
career would never have happened.'

'My Heart Stood Still' became one of the runaway hits of 1927.
Some three weeks after the show's opening, the Prince of Wales
went to a dance at the Royal Western Yacht Club in Plymouth,
and asked the bandleader, Teddy Brown (on leave from the Café
de Paris), to play the song. Brown did not know it, so the Prince
sang it until the band copied the melody, at which point the Prince
joined in on the drums. Next day, a headline in the *Evening News*,
'The Prince dictates a foxtrot', had long queues of people at the
Pavilion and at music shops, wanting to buy sheet music and
records of the song. 'My Heart Stood Still' was soon the biggest-
selling song since Vincent Youmans's 'Tea for Two' in 1922.

Years later, Cochran gave Hutch a photo of himself that read, 'To
my old friend of the Pav days – Hutch – Whose brilliant virtuosity
helped to make My Heart Stood Still – In gratitude, Charles B.
Cochran.' It is possible that Cochran inspired Hutch to emblazon
photos of himself for friends and fans with similarly grandiloquent
flourishes and mildly patronising messages. One, written to the
songwriter David Heneker, reads, 'To David – Thrilled with your
progress. Soon you will be another Kern. Ever, Hutch.'

The musical director at the Pavilion, Ernest Irving,[5] was irritated
when he found that Hutch was extemporising while the rest of the
orchestra faithfully followed the arrangements written for the
show. But he recognised Hutch's exceptional musical talent,
and did not do anything about it. One night Irving noticed Alfred
Cortot, a French pianist, in the stalls, so he sent a note to Hutch,
asking him to play a chorus in the style of Chopin as a gesture to the
great soloist who was renowned for his Chopin interpretations.

Hutch immediately produced a masterly Chopin pastiche, followed by a chorus in the style of Schumann. After the show,
Cortot, who may well have met him before in Paris, came
backstage to congratulate Hutch. Irving ruefully conceded that
he would have been proud to spend two hours transcribing the
improvisations which Hutch had just played. Indeed, he was so
impressed by Hutch's ability to ad lib that, having previously
opposed jazz in all its forms, he now declared himself a convert.

Just as, every Sunday evening at Gouyave, Hutch used to wait
for the chance to deputise for his father at the organ and receive
plaudits after the service, so, now, did he wait for something to
happen to Edythe Baker so that he could step in and triumph. Luck
was on his side. A few weeks into the run, Edythe Baker fell ill.
Hutch was allowed to replace her on stage at her white piano. He
too became an overnight sensation; presumably he must have
appeared without any white women on the stage.

On recovering, Edythe returned only briefly before retiring
from the stage to marry Gerard d'Erlanger, brother of Princess Jean
de Faucigny-Lucinge, a fan of Hutch from Venice days. Hutch was
thrilled to attend the wedding, a gathering of international society.
And he was delighted to take over Edythe's piano for the rest of the
run at the Pavilion.

While in *ODTAA*, Hutch also performed for six weeks at the
Café de Paris, then a large and luxurious nightclub on the north
side of Leicester Square. Harry Gold, the veteran bandleader and
bass saxophone player, was impressed by the way that Hutch lulled
his audience into a state of 'complete restfulness'. As in Paris,
women treated him as an exotic pet and followed him from club to
club. This is hardly surprising. Hutch was clever, handsome, hugely
talented and a great lady-killer. And, in the words of one of his
audience of the time, Barbara Cartland, he was also 'the first nigger
many of us had ever talked to'. After his spell at the Café de Paris,
he played for more than a year at a far smaller and more exclusive
venue, Chez Victor; its regulars included the Prince of Wales, the
King of Spain, Alfonso XIII, and, inevitably, the Mountbattens. 'I
followed Hutch around everywhere,' said Joan Vyvyan, who was
then a young socialite.   ?

He played and sang so effortlessly, everyone fell under his spell,
and the room used to burst into thunderous applause when he

finished. The waiters stopped dead as if petrified when he sang.
He had a liquid magic voice. He could inject more sex into one
bar of music than most people knew in a lifetime. At Chez
Victor, he used to sing directly to Edwina Mountbatten, who,
on one occasion, took off her chiffon scarf and put it round his
neck and kissed him while he was playing. He sang 'The Man I
Love' to her.[6] He was madly attractive and intelligent. How we
envied her! But everyone was in love with him, wherever he was
playing was completely booked out, it was impossible to get a
table.

The relief pianist at Chez Victor, Norman Hackforth, thought
'Hutch was the grandest man I had ever met. He had a joke Oxford
accent and enormous presence as a performer. I just tried my best
to copy him.'[7] By now, Hutch was so well known that he was
often referred to by other performers. Around the same time,
Hackforth also accompanied Douglas Byng, who sang a song about
Cole Porter's party in Venice which included the couplet:

Where we met all the well-known madonnas and such,
As they loll on the Lido with Lifar[8] and Hutch.[9]

After his scheduled appearances, Hutch was usually driven in a
large car, with his white piano strapped to the roof, to entertain at
the homes of social celebrities; he was engaged that season for more
private functions than any other artiste. Hutch's skill, grooming
and personality ensured his position as England's leading cabaret
performer from the late 1920s to the late 1940s. He had all the key
qualities: he was handsome, a superb musician and an excellent
singer. He also had an irresistibly magnetic presence, and could
make each member of his audience feel that he was performing
only for him or her; he later found that he could also cast this spell
over huge variety audiences. His nearest rivals were Turner Layton,
a black American pianist who had known Hutch in America, and
his vocalist partner Tandy Johnstone. They sang beautifully and
were deservedly successful, but they did not have Hutch's ability to
feel and act the lyric. 'When Hutch sang, he made love to you,'
one of his fans recollected; 'he held your hand, he danced with
you, you knew that he could and would and did . . . no other
performer made you feel that way.' And, the favourite accompanist

of so many others, Hutch also accompanied himself, an underrated skill. He gradually developed a dark rich baritone voice, variously compared to peat, velvet and chocolate, and he dominated his audience without ever seeming to raise his voice. When Coleman Hawkins taught Thelma Carpenter how to put over a song, he could have been describing Hutch's performance:

> You've got to regard it as if you're making love. You greet the song, then slowly get closer to it, caressing it, kissing it, and finally making love to it, and, when you bring your performance to a climax, you don't just end it there and then, you have to be just as tender as you were when you began, so that the audience feels the flow of your expression, and they end up peaceful and satisfied.[10]

In Hutch's style of intimate cabaret the performer has no hiding place. There are no rhythm sections, prompters, amplifiers or speakers. Instead, alone and spotlit under the narrow eye of a sophisticated and highly critical audience, he must hit all the right notes and say and sing all the right words. He must have an inexhaustible arsenal of funny stories and a stream of patter to match every sort of mood. He must also be alert to regular patrons, and make an apt response. He also has to rise above the collective challenge of drink, smoke, food, chatter and the clink and clatter of glass, china and cutlery. Night after night, Hutch transcended these obstacles to become a great master of a notoriously difficult art. His particular skill was to conjure up a mood of intimate reverie among the people clustered round his piano.

On the piano lid or up his sleeve, there was always a large lawn handkerchief; at emotional moments during his act, he would use this to mop his brow with an operatically flamboyant movement. Over the years, this became a trademark gesture, especially with variety audiences, but it was not just a gimmick: partly under the heat of the lighting but more from nerves, Hutch used to sweat profusely. As a fellow pianist, Patrick Baring, said, 'Hutch had an animal energy which could light up a building. It's not surprising that he used to sweat like crazy.'

The aftermath of the First World War had left a moral and philosophical emptiness and, more obviously, a social vacuum. Certainly the new life which came to fill it was happy to dissociate itself from any prewar behaviour. It was youthful, playful, escapist, wild and, for the most part, well-born. Its exploits provided the press with columns of free and easy coverage. In 1924 the *Daily Mail* stamped its exponents with the collective label of the 'Bright Young People', which soon more often became the Bright Young Things or BYTs. They affected a callous disillusionment with everything and their daring cynicism and ruthlessness became their trademark. Bisexuality was the goal of their fashions. Men were languid, bloodless and foppish. Women wore their hair, which had been bobbed after the war, shingled, edging towards the Eton crop. Chests were flattened, boyish slenderness sought after, with an extravagant amount of silk stocking on display. The craze for the charleston and the black bottom and the shimmy and other dances made their elders wax indignant over the sexual overtones of their uninhibited indulgence in jazz rhythm at the endless round of parties and nightclubs.

In the twenties, there were numerous nightclubs in London. One of the first, the Cave of the Golden Calf, was opened in 1913 by August Strindberg's second wife Frida Uhl, an ex-actress with a Viennese background. Its walls and columns were decorated by Jacob Epstein and Wyndham Lewis, and it became the haunt of artists, army officers and the demi-monde who went there, so they said, to listen to Galician Gypsies play accordions and to feathered sirens singing 'Popsie-Wopsie'. The war saw a spread of tackily discreet 'clubs' – many of them virtually brothels for officers – but by 1923, most of those who crowded the stifling back rooms and cellars called nightclubs were Bright Young Things escaping from chaperones and all out for a good time.

Prominent among the club owners was Mrs Kate Meyrick, who had started with a dubious tea-dance club in Leicester Square in 1918. By the mid-1920s, she was the owner of a chain of clubs all over the West End, including the famous '43', once the Cecil Club, in the Charing Cross Road. When she was tried for breaking licensing laws, 'Ma' Meyrick claimed that her clubs were purely for the convenience of those who required an early breakfast. When Mr Justice Avory asked what time breakfast began, Ma famously answered, 'Ten p.m.'[11] The sale of alcohol had been severely restricted by legislation passed during the First World War. Altogether, between 1924 and 1928, police raids resulted in sixty-five prosecutions for illegally extending hours and serving alcohol without licence. Nowhere was safe: even the Kit-Cat Club, virtually a second home for the Prince of Wales, was raided; and, as a result, security measures became ever more elaborate. For instance, the Quadrant had three bolted doors, the third of which had a wicket. At the entrance, there was a foot-operated button that could sound the alarm in both the bar and the lounge. This element of risk made the nightclubs more alluring than ever to the BYTs.

Pops in Soho Square was yet another haunt of the Prince of Wales and the Mountbattens, and there was Chez Henri, on a first floor in Long Acre, where Charlie Kunz was resident pianist. At one time or another, Hutch played at all those clubs. He also provided cabaret at the Lido Club in Newman Street; at Uncle's Club at 13 Albemarle Street; and at breakfast, probably rather later than 10 p.m., at the Dutch Room. To fulfil all these commitments, Hutch often had to cram three or four engagements into a night that lasted from 10 p.m. to around 8 a.m. or later.

Hutch also frequented many clubs as a visitor rather than a performer. These included the Gargoyle Club in Meard Street, in Soho, owned by the Honourable David Tennant, then married to the actress and singer Hermione Baddeley, with a membership rigorously limited to celebrities of society, stage and screen. A rich self-styled clairvoyant, N. St John Montagu, had elaborate dinner parties there, and Hutch was frequently a guest. Hutch took girlfriends to the Florida in Bruton Mews, later a showcase for Ken Snakehips Johnson. This club featured a revolving glass door and telephones on the tables so that patrons could ring round the room for partners.

Hutch was less popular in the clubs owned and largely frequented by blacks. According to Don Johnson, who played in Snakehips Johnson's band, he 'acted like the uncrowned black king of Mayfair'; and although he could have done much to further the careers of numerous black musicians, he rarely mixed freely with them, let alone offered any help. As well as finding his airs and graces insufferable, they also thought his music was bland and over-refined, and suitable only for white audiences. Hutch never played at black clubs now. In fairness, as a solo artist, Hutch did not work closely with other musicians, and that may have made him seem much more aloof than he had been as a band member in Harlem and Paris.

Together with a song plugger named Ted Morgan, Hutch often went to the Nest, a tiny club that vibrated to legendary jam sessions starring hot players from British dance bands together with visiting stars such as Benny Carter, Coleman Hawkins and Fats Waller. Run by a woman called Millie, the club played host to the Prince of Wales who, often drunk, took over the drums in the small hours. On these occasions, the staff contrived to clear the street so that, when the Prince had finished, he could be unobtrusively slipped into a taxi and driven back to York House in St James's, sometimes accompanied by Hutch.

Hutch was probably more at ease at Frisco's, a piano and drinking club in Shepherd Market which he often visited on his own to see the eponymous proprietor, another old friend from Harlem. Just below Frisco's was 33 Shepherd Market, a drinking club for toffs and blacks, and another favourite retreat of Hutch's.

'Before the war, clubs were posh and elite,' Don Johnson recalled; 'soon afterwards they were just dumps. Then, there were marvellous women of the night, later they were just tarts. There was very little colour bar before the war. London was exciting, so clean and safe.' Johnson also remembered Jigs on the corner of Wardour Street and St Anne's Court in Soho, where the doors firmly closed and gambling started every night at eleven. Also in Wardour Street, on a top floor, was Hatch's. Ike Hatch, another old friend of Hutch's, was both proprietor and performer. Flamboyant in tails and gleaming topper, he sometimes stood outside on the pavement, a chucker-out in reverse, shouting at likely customers, 'Yowzer [you, sir], come on in!'

Hutch's position in society was equivocal. 'You have no idea how much colour prejudice there was in London in those days. Many times I was asked to go and sing at big parties at grand houses, I had to go in by the servants' entrance. At the time, I just accepted it as the way things were, but it makes me mad as hell now,' he said in the 1960s. Even when he was invited to a party as a guest, he would be expected to use the servants' entrance. Although by no means all fashionable society shared the craze for black musicians, during the 1920s society people increasingly 'took up' theatrical and musical stars, and sometimes treated them at least superficially as social equals. For instance, Don Johnson recalled Lady Iris Mountbatten[12] whisking off the band at the Café de Paris for two nights at her country house; there, the members were served meals by staff in the dining room. Other society patrons would have told them to help themselves in the kitchen, along with the servants.

Racism could be rationalised as class snobbery. Dame Barbara Cartland remembered that, when she used to have Hutch to lunch, 'just like an ordinary friend', he, 'like Ambrose, that bandleader, always knew his place, and did not presume on the fact that we were friends. There was a barrier, not because he was black, but because he was a paid performer.' Writing of her grandmother, Lady Diana Cooper, Artemis Cooper stated:

> People of Diana's class and generation divided the world into servants and the served. You could talk and laugh with servants, be interested in them – they did such funny things – and you could get very fond of them. But, ultimately, they were another race, who existed to perform certain menial tasks on the fringe of your own life. Any 'lady', who had an affair with a servant, was obviously a nymphomaniac. (It was different for gentlemen, of course.) I think Duff and Diana thought about blacks in that way, too. Most of the blacks they met, were servants or entertainers, and those who were not – i.e. the inhabitants of Africa – were charming primitives who were very lucky to have the British Empire to run their lives for them.

For all that, Hutch's charm and talent for being what people wanted him to be caused many prejudices to be set aside, and many social barriers to melt. Photographs bear witness to his skills as a social chameleon. The clean-cut all-American kid vanished in Paris, to make way for the aggressively sensual jazzman, who was, in turn, subsumed by the suave cabaret performer who became the darling of London society. By the late 1920s, Hutch's singing voice bore no trace of his lives in Grenada, New York or Paris. Instead, he sounds like an extraordinarily polished Oxbridge man, entertaining his peers after dinner; once again, demonstrating the way he reflected and echoed the characteristics of those around him, showing himself to be less an original than an original conglomerate.

Hutch commanded the voice and vocabulary to match four different idioms, all in the English language: West Indian, black Harlem, white American and upper-class English. He would sometimes switch from one to the other in mid-sentence: if he was talking to West Indians and white people suddenly appeared, he would promptly start speaking from his throat to dilute his accent. When he was young, he had a light speaking voice strangely inconsistent with the booming baritone of his singing voice: from late middle age on, he spoke in a lower key, and the contrast disappeared. The way in which he sedulously cultivated the accent, attitudes and character of the patrician class had much in common, possibly more than either would readily have acknowledged, with Noël Coward's reinvention of himself. Both men came from relatively humble backgrounds and were anxious to identify, and be identified, with a smarter social level.[13] Up to the mid-1950s, as films of the period show, many entertainers and film stars aped the mannerisms of the 400.[14]

There was another reason why Hutch adopted a British upper-class accent. Before the Second World War very few English people knew much about blacks, let alone the Caribbean islands, and if a man was black, he was assumed to be an American. As a sensitive West Indian who considered himself to be profoundly un-American, Hutch found this very offensive. Some Americans too, such as Tandy Johnstone, Turner Layton's partner, detested having to follow show-business convention and assume a Deep South 'you-all' drawl. Ever since he first met the Hudsons and McIntyres in Gouyave, Hutch had copied the accents and manners of the English; now he had the perfect arbiter elegantiarum on which to model himself – the Prince of Wales.

Described by a friend as 'a clobber merchant, who spent a bomb on stuff from Savile Row and Jermyn Street', Hutch always dressed in correct, extremely well-cut clothes. In 1927 he opened accounts in several posh outlets and one of them, Anderson and Sheppard, still has his measurements and several addresses for delivery. In the late 1930s, Hutch had at least twenty-four suits of evening tails. When in London, he always bought a red carnation in the Dorchester Hotel; and, in the provinces, there were often frantic searches for buttonholes. One lover remembered that Hutch soused himself in Chanel No. 5. In those days, anything more than a dab of eau de cologne on a man was looked on as vain, foreign and effeminate. A variety entertainer observed a star going into the number-one dressing room at a theatre, sniffing the air and affecting to reel backwards from the heady blast of scent. 'Hutch must have been here this week,' he cracked, and the company laughed in recognition of an old joke. But years later the actress Beryl Reid said he smelled like a privet hedge being cut.

Given his strong connections with the Prince of Wales and Edwina Mountbatten, Hutch had easy entry into the thick of London café society, now a melting pot of aristocrats, nouveaux riches, the famous, the foreign and the weird. Sir Steven Runciman remembered him at a party in Wilton Crescent, Belgravia, in 1927. When Runciman was talking to his sister-in-law, the novelist Rosamund Lehmann, he noticed a flurry in another part of the room, and was afterwards told that it was Hutch putting himself up for auction and being won by Brenda Dean Paul, a leading society femme fatale and drug addict. Apparently, they rushed upstairs and burst into a bedroom where they found their host's parents, trying vainly to go to sleep.

Rosamund Lehmann, like so many other women at the time, loved Hutch because he seemed to sing especially for her. Allanah Harper, a BYT, remembered Hutch as being 'very attractive to both men and women [and] the only pianist worth having in the twenties . . . we treated him as an equal'. The biographer Elizabeth Longford first met her husband at a commem ball at Oxford, and afterwards noted, 'It was Hutch's band – I evidently took this as a good omen!' The writer and aesthete Harold Acton found Hutch 'elegant, charming and intelligent', but most men were less impressed. The novelist Anthony Powell found him 'impossibly arrogant', and the historian Peter Quennell complained that 'this big black chap was everywhere we went'.

If Hutch was ubiquitous at society parties, he was the only black man who was, and this was no kind of disadvantage, rather the reverse. The BYTs were a decade younger than Hutch, and many of the girls found his exoticism and air of international sophistication preferable to the callow gaucheness of their white partners. He had lived a much wider, more exciting life than most of them, and could often beat them at their own games. He looked spectacular and rode well in Rotten Row, and, to the delight of spectators, would often scoop up his bowler from the ground at full gallop. He rode out with the aristocracy at Melton Mowbray, a centre of fox hunting and horse breeding in Leicestershire, and loved racing: from a vantage point in the paddock where he was on first-name terms with all the trainers and jockeys, he quickly became a knowledgeable judge of horses. He played good tennis, danced beautifully and had courtly manners. He never drove, but always had a car – a Rolls-Royce or a Daimler, hired or owned outright, depending on his finances – and a chauffeur. 'He was fastidious, and liked the best of everything,' said Gwenol Heneker, the wife of his old friend. 'Insecurity made him that way. Coloured people always felt like that with Englishmen.' Although there was much to make him insecure, pressures did not weigh heavily on Hutch at this early point in his English career. Possessing charm, wit and talent, he was also gentle, graceful and tender, and that gave him an edge on most men in London society. To find your way into the heart of English café society has never been easy: it has always been a treacherous environment, intolerant of nonentities and phoneys; an arena in which adventurers are prepared to kill to avoid expulsion. Hutch came slowly to realise that; but for the time being he revelled in his success.

While most of the parties that Hutch attended were fairly decorous, some were scenes of open debauch. In an age when sex outside marriage was regarded as serious immorality, Allanah Harper thought they were like scenes of hell painted by Hieronymous Bosch. In particular, she remembers Hutch at the soirées of Peter Spencer Churchill, 'a bad lot [with] a lot of pederast friends'. In sexual matters, the 1920s were comparatively naive, though they have acquired a reputation for naughtiness and general licentiousness. In fact, outside Mayfair there was a strongly puritan element in the country, particularly in the press. Beverly Nichols remembered how much trouble there was when he wrote 'syphilis' in an article in a national newspaper where everyone else had previously written 'a certain disease', rape was 'a certain suggestion' and pregnancy was 'a certain condition'. When King George V discovered that a peer was rumoured to be a homosexual, he said, 'I thought men like that shot themselves.' Homosexuality was seen as a failing not to be discussed in society. Viva King, a clever and beautiful Chelsea hostess, who claimed also to have been one of Hutch's lovers, writes in her autobiography that she usually left parties before they degenerated into orgies, as she wished to avoid contamination by such a 'maelstrom of iniquity and self-destruction'.[15] More specifically, the wife of Sir Nicholas Hildersley, Audrey, known as 'Mauve', used to entertain her decadent friends at their home in Swan Walk, Chelsea. While her husband, often with his fellow philatelist George V,

worked on his stamp collection in the basement, the guests, stimu-
lated by drink and cocaine at his expense, used to chant, 'Hey, hey, let
Nicky pay!' Hutch and Mauve, armed with a musical saw, used to
sing and vigorously enact 'Let's Do It'. Mauve was a vain woman, in a
cloud of Turkish cigarettes and Chanel No. 5, who avoided having
children for fear of losing her beautiful figure. Although Hutch
probably tried various drugs – Billy Milton, a rival pianist, claimed he
took cocaine – he did not become dependent on the stimuli of the
very fast set, limiting himself to being a lifelong heavy smoker and
drinker.

Typical of Hutch's clients and/or lovers was Elvira Mullens,
daughter of Lord and Lady Mullens. Three pianists – Hutch, Billy
Milton and Carroll Gibbons – all played at one of her parties,
which always featured modish theatricals. Appearing the same
night was a close-harmony turn, the Three New Yorkers. Elvira
was briefly married to one of them, a Mr Barney. The marriage
ended, and scandal erupted, when Elvira took a lover and shot him
dead. Elvira was arrested and confined to the infirmary of Holloway Prison, where, to keep up her spirits, she displayed a photograph of Tallulah Bankhead. At the same time, Mr Barney tried to
blackmail her father by threatening to expose details of her private
life, including her cocaine habit. In the event, Elvira was acquitted.
To celebrate, she threw a huge party at the Berkeley. People were
horrified and soon afterwards she committed suicide in Paris.

Many of Hutch's female lovers were rich and had nothing to do,
and had little or no self-esteem. Desperate for affection and
attention, they lived in gilded misery, drifting from party to party
and, inevitably, attracting men who despised, exploited and dis-
carded them. Noël Coward's song in *This Year of Grace* is a pointed
elegy to them:

> Dance dance dance, little lady
> Youth is fleeting to the rhythm beating in your mind
> Dance dance dance, little lady
> So obsessed with second best no rest you'll ever find
> Time and Tide and Trouble
> Never never wait
> Let the cauldron bubble
> Justify your fate.

Hutch represented all that was 'naughty but nice' to society women, many of whom cultivated him solely to add a black notch to their bedposts. As a prominent BYT, David Herbert, said, 'All the married women of the twenties were crazy about Hutch.'[16]

Prominent among Hutch's unmarried girlfriends was Zena Naylor. Their affair started within two months of Hutch's arrival in London. She was the daughter of Langton Douglas, 'an art dealer and historian of ambiguous reputation'[17], whose other child was Lord Douglas of Kirtleside. Viva King writes that Douglas 'started his career as a clergyman, but was, not surprisingly, unfrocked for his amorous activities, and was married more than once . . .' Douglas discovered Tuscan Renaissance painting 'long before Bernard Berenson'. He often went into old village churches where, in exchange for a dusty Sassetta or Giotto, he would offer the priests bright new paintings of negligible worth. In this way, he became both knowledgeable and rich. His daughter was conceived in Siena and was named Zena after the town. David Herbert remembered her as 'not really pretty, but loud, fun, short and daring, rather stocky with bad legs, and a great one for bed'. Viva King describes her as:

> pretty in a Pekinese-type way, witty and amusing. But she had that quality which destroys . . . she was extremely romantic and always in love, without her many affairs leading to a happy conclusion. The real love of her life was Eugene Goossens [an orchestral conductor] . . . later, when Gene married in America, it was a cutting blow to her. Her loose conduct . . . did no good to her father's business . . . on one occasion, when he entered the drawing room to show some rich clients his Botticelli, Zena and one of the 'Blackbirds' were discovered on the sofa, doing what comes naturally, with the Botticelli looking on. It was the end of Zena in Hill Street.

It is possible that Viva King mistook Hutch for a Blackbird.

Carl Van Vechten identified her as a character called Gala Jersey in an obscure novel, *Going Somewhere* by Max Ewing, published in 1934: 'A young English girl with dimpled, rosy cheeks who did not drink or smoke, but who atoned for the lack of these semi-precious vices by describing in an endless monotone the various forms of her amorous transports, and the characteristics of the persons with whom she enjoyed them.' She also inspired a feckless character called Noma Ridge in Van Vechten's own novel *Parties*.

Zena also features in the diaries of Evelyn Waugh. Early in 1927 Waugh was infatuated with Olivia Plunkett-Greene, a BYT, who was, in turn, intrigued by 'negroes'.[18] On 28 February Waugh notes a backstage sortie to see the cast of *Blackbirds* – 'niggers and negresses in their dressing rooms' – and later a visit to 'a night club called Victor's to see another nigger, Leslie Hutchinson'. Two days later, he goes 'to tea at Hill Street with the Douglases. The situation of a distinguished old man's illegitimate daughter receiving in his house her black lover and her black lover's wife and baby might seem improbable in a book. However, there it was.' This was, of course, before the Botticelli debacle. On 10 March Waugh went to a party given by 'Layton the black man' at the studio of a painter called Stuart Hill. 'All very refined – hot lobster, champagne cup and music. Florence Mills, Delysia, John Huggins, Layton and Johnstone and others sang songs.' On the next day, Waugh lunched with Olivia, among others, before calling on 'black Hutchinson who is having a row with Zena. To dinner at Hill Street with Zena.' Five months later, Waugh dined and drank 'a great deal' at Kettner's before going on to the Gargoyle, 'drank a great deal', and then to Victor's, 'drank a great deal more . . . Lady Kinross, Patrick Balfour and an absurd French nobleman and masses of other people. I talked endlessly to Hutchinson who was wearing a terribly smart French waistcoat.' On 9 December Waugh reported on a serpentine tangle of sexual entanglements: 'Zena returned and I sent her flowers I could ill afford. She is in love with David and declares Hutchinson slept with Babe. Honor Henderson[19] also in love with David.' David was the brother of Olivia Plunkett-Greene. Nearly seven foot tall, he was an accomplished pianist who drowned himself at the stately home of Longleat, Wiltshire. Babe was Babe McGustie, heiress to the Ladbroke bookmaking fortune. Waugh noted in his diaries that she lived in 'an opulent house in Grosvenor Square with a common stepfather called Bendir and an animal called a lemur'. David Herbert recalled that when Babe married David Plunkett-Greene, who was his cousin, their aunt, Lady Maud Parry, yelled into the ear trumpet of his father, 'The girl must be mad. We all know that giants can't.'

It is likely that the character of Chokey, Margot Beste-Chetwynde's pompous black lover in Evelyn Waugh's first novel,
Decline and Fall, published in 1928, was mainly based on Hutch;
Chokey being a bad pun on the word 'Choccy'.[20] The presentation of Chokey, a malicious yet hilarious caricature of Hutch and
the less educated Blackbirds, shows the kind of racist clichés then
current in that society.

> After him, like the first breath of spring in the Champs-Elysées,
> came Mrs Beste-Chetwynde – two lizard-skin feet, silk legs,
> chinchilla body, a tight little black hat, pinned with platinum and
> diamonds, and the high invariable voice that may be heard in any
> Ritz Hotel from New York to Budapest.
>   'I hope you don't mind my bringing Chokey, Dr Fagan?' she
> said. 'He's just crazy about sport.'
>   'I sure am that,' said Chokey.
>   'Dear Mrs Beste-Chetwynde!' said Dr Fagan; 'dear, dear Mrs
> Beste-Chetwynde!' He pressed her glove, and for the moment
> was at a loss for words of welcome, for Chokey, though graceful
> of bearing and irreproachably dressed, was a Negro.

Mrs Beste-Chetwynde goes on to say, 'You can't move Chokey
once he's seen an old church. He's just crazy about culture, aren't
you, darling? . . . He plays just too divinely.' She then insists that
Fagan listens to Chokey's new records, and comforts her protégé,
'Now, darling, don't get discouraged. I'll take you over and
introduce you to Lady Circumference. It's his inferiority-complex,
the angel. He's just crazy to meet the aristocracy, aren't you, my
sweet?' Some onlookers say that their friends in Savannah know 'a
thing or two about niggers. Of course, it's hardly the thing to talk
about before the ladies, but, to put it bluntly, *they have uncontrollable
passions* . . . You can't blame 'em, mind; it's just their nature.
Animal, you know. Still, what I do say is, since they're like that, the
less we see of them the better.' Then a further caricature appears.
' "'Pon my soul," Colonel Sidebotham was saying to the Vicar, "I
don't like the look of that nigger. I saw enough of Fuzzy-Wuzzy in
the Soudan – devilish good enemy and devilish bad friend." '
    Properly introduced by his real name, Sebastian Cholmondely,
Chokey launches into an impassioned harangue about his race,
education, appreciation of Shakespeare, religion, architecture and

how 'the poor coloured man has a soul the same as you have'. Soon Mrs Beste-Chetwynde says to Lady Circumference, 'I sometimes think I'm getting rather bored with coloured people . . . I daresay you'd be good with them. They take a lot of living up to . . . He gets gay at times, you know. It's only when he's on his best behaviour that he's so class-conscious.' In the next chapter, after Chokey has had a row with someone over the late development of the rood screen and its connection with colour prejudice, the ingenuous hero, Paul Pennyfeather, asks his scapegrace friend Captain Grimes what he makes of the relationship between Mrs Beste-Chetwynde and 'that nigger'.

'Well, I don't suppose she trots with him just for the uplift of his conversation; do you?'
   'No, I suppose not.'
   'In fact, I don't mind diagnosing a simple case of good old sex.'

With Hutch's name synonymous with sex and scandal from the start of his arrival in London, Ella must have led a humiliating existence. Hutch was ashamed of her; whenever possible, he rigorously excluded her from his social life, and limited his conjugal responsibility to paying bills. Hutch saw her and his daughter sporadically, only when it suited him. However, he was sometimes very proud of his daughter, and Evelyn Waugh told one of Hutch's later lovers that he had seen a doting Hutch encouraging Leslie, then about three, to do the hulahula on table tops at parties. By 1930, there are no more press mentions of Ella accompanying her husband anywhere; indeed, few of Hutch's later friends or lovers knew that he was married, and even the rare visitors to his house were unaware of her existence, or else Hutch introduced her as his housekeeper.
   Ella's life was confined to the house in Hampstead which Hutch had bought in 1928 and lived in for most of the rest of his life. She kept chickens in the garden, played bridge with women friends, laundered Hutch's shirts and sent them to wherever he was performing. Always a retiring person, she lived very quietly, and devoted herself to her daughter. She and Hutch probably enjoyed each other's company and shared their delight in little Leslie. Ella may have accepted the odd terms of her marriage to

Hutch in exchange for financial security. A guest who stayed at their house for two weeks was surprised that Hutch used to telephone Ella daily for long chats. He also saw that she was never short of money. It would have been daunting for her to leave Hutch and strike out as a lone parent in a huge city she hardly knew.

At the house Ella had the company of Hutch's brother Ivan, who had come over in late 1926 and become a permanent member of the household. And for Hutch, she provided a buffer between him and women who might otherwise have been far more demanding: while she lived, there was no indication that Hutch asked any of his girlfriends to marry him.

The house, at 31 Steeles Road, NW3, was designed by J. M. Brydon, also the architect of Chelsea Town Hall, and built in 1874. It was called Spring Bank and described as 'a small house in the suburbs in the Queen Anne style'. When the Hutchinsons lived there, visitors found it full of massive oak furniture and depressingly dark; in the drawing room, the penumbra was relieved by a display, on top of the piano, of glinting silver knick-knacks, all inscribed to Hutch.

The Steeles Road area is now more Chalk Farm than Hampstead, but the house has retained its association with the world of entertainment: the distinguished actor Derek Jacobi now lives there, and his neighbour is the film star Bob Hoskins.

Chapter Five

London After Dark
1927–1930

High hat
You've got to treat them
High hat
Don't let them
Know that you care
Act like a frigidaire
You'll win them like that

George Gershwin

W hile being black and talented in Britain ensured success
within a small and elitist social circle, racism was never far
away. English society was wary, sharply stratified and deeply
xenophobic. Even well-educated and sophisticated people had
little or no experience of meeting black people and did not think
that normal rules for behaviour applied to their dealings with them.

Colonial history and literature had done much to shape and
reinforce the prejudices of educated Britons. To them, blackness
meant the threatening, mysterious primitive rather than the noble
savage: Africa, the Dark Continent, represented the reverse of
Western civilisation and was thought to be – or, rather, felt to
be – a black hole seething with every sort of chaos and sexual excess.

Scare stories from America about blacks getting their own back by the rape of white women also crossed the Atlantic and were believed, even though they were only put out to justify the lynchings committed by white Southerners. In London, a painting by John Souter called *The Breakdown* caused a furore when it was hung in the Royal Academy Summer Exhibition in the early 1920s. It showed a black musician sitting on top of a prone statue of the goddess Minerva, staring at a naked white girl dancing the charleston. The fears it aroused were such that the picture was removed from the show.

In the 1920s as later, black people in Britain frequently ran the risk of humiliation. In 1929, some friends of Hutch's, Robert S. Abbott, the black founder and publisher of the *Chicago Defender*, and his wife arrived in London. They were asked to leave their hotel because white American guests had complained to the management for letting them in. A more reverberant scandal erupted when, again following protests from American whites, Paul and Essie Robeson were turned away from the Savoy Grill. They said that they had often gone there before, but the management told Robeson that the hotel 'did not permit Negroes to enter the rooms any longer'. When fielding a question about the incident in the House of Commons, the Prime Minister, Ramsay Macdonald, said, 'It is not in accordance with our British hotel practice, but I cannot think of a way in which the Government can intervene.' Hotels sometimes refused to admit Hutch because of his colour – the Adelphi, a prestigious hotel in Liverpool, was one of them – and this may partly explain why he often stayed in boarding houses. Henry Crowder, the pianist, relates in his memoir that he had the same experience with his lover Nancy Cunard on a visit to London in 1929. 'We were refused at place after place . . . London and England are infinitely worse for coloured people than New York and other cities in the US. It is the shock from the terrible humiliation from being refused so unexpectedly that cuts. And all because of one's colour.'

In *As Wonderful as All That?* Crowder frankly describes his experience of white women in Europe in the 1920s. He states that black men were convinced that white women imagined white men were inferior as lovers to black men who, in exchange for sex, expected financial favours. 'Nancy has often told me that she had never met a coloured man who did not want money. I tried to explain to her that when a white woman became intimate with a black man he usually expected to get money from her.' Crowder also remembered a white Londoner who said that, while he had no prejudice against blacks, he 'somehow had a queer feeling' when he saw one dancing with a white woman. Asked how he felt when the position was reversed, he said he did not 'have the same sort of feeling'.

Responding to insults, some took a sexual revenge. This was even true of men as rich, confident and attractive as Aly Khan, an Indian aristocrat. Once, when riding a horse to the finish in a race, he asked the front runner to move over and let him through. 'Shut your mouth, you goddamned nigger!' the jockey shouted back. Expanding on the incident, Khan said, 'They called me a bloody nigger, and I paid them out by winning all their women.'[1] A common white male racist fear is that generously endowed black men will win 'their' women, and Hutch played up to this stereotype. He boasted to fellow musicians that his penis was 'the biggest in the world' and while obviously unable to confirm this, several of his lovers have volunteered that it was massive. Promiscuity was wholly natural to Hutch; and, for many, much of his attraction lay in his uninhibited, totally relaxed approach to sex. While most people keep this hidden and separate, Hutch made no bones about it; both he and his brother Ivan were given to boastful genital exposure. Hutch could never understand why many people found this behaviour so crass and crude; and he frequently overestimated the extent of his attractions, especially when he was drunk. In this he was not alone.

'When a white woman takes a Negro man as a lover, she usually lowers him and herself too,' wrote Essie Robeson to her errant husband Paul. 'White people and Negroes feel that she has a bull or stallion or mule in her stable . . . and view the affair very much as if she had run away with the butler or the chauffeur; she is rarely – almost never – a first-class woman, and neither the black nor the white people think the Negro has won a prize.' She scathingly compared him to Hutch who 'took pride in displaying presents from white women'.[2] Edwina Mountbatten, Tallulah Bankhead and Peggy Ashcroft (who had a passionate affair with Robeson when playing Desdemona to his Othello) were hardly second-rate, but they were secure enough to ignore censure. This released them to experiment – or even to fall in love. Henry Crowder took a similarly astringent line with his lover:

Nancy seems to have forgotten that, instead of raising the lowest of the black race to her level by associating with them, she lowers herself to their level. And because of that, many black men make the most complete fools of themselves over what is practically the dregs of humanity and proudly disport themselves with nothing more than whores – as long as they are white.[3]

Hutch was always quick to take offence at any racial slight. Normally, he expressed this by becoming cool and stiffly correct, but, when he was drunk, he got very aggressive. Then he could become incoherent with rage like a thwarted child, and, if someone turned down an invitation of his, Hutch would embarrass onlookers by saying that it was because of his colour. For instance, Peggy Cochrane, wife of the bandleader Jack Payne, wrote in her autobiography *We Said It with Music* that Hutch:

the brilliant coloured pianist, asked if I would lunch with him. I truthfully replied that I had a friend with me, and we had already made arrangements to dine at a restaurant. At this, some angry mutterings issued from Hutch, who was under the impression that I had turned him down because of his colour, as in those days it was not done to be seen in the company of a coloured fellow . . . One night, about a year later, I returned to my hotel in Blackpool. I put my nose into the bar, and there spotted a good friend of mine, Reg Connelly, the publisher of so many books of the 40s and 50s. Reg was talking to Hutch, who immediately recognised me and yelled at Reg in a very drunken and abusive way, 'There's that bitch of a woman who refused to have lunch with me . . .' Reg tried to calm Hutch down as he was very drunk, and at the same time whispered to me to get out of the bar. This I thankfully did.

In the same way, Hutch was never aggressively lecherous unless he was drunk. Several women firmly state that they never knew him make an unwelcome advance: if they rated fidelity, he respected them; but if they did not, he was always game. However, Gwenol Heneker remembered with affectionate exasperation that 'Hutchie was incorrigible. My husband was his great friend, but David only had to go out of the room for him to try and kiss me. He could be tactlessly intrusive, too. He sat for hours between us on our bed on our honeymoon night, singing, "It was just one of those things". For him, it certainly was.'

Hutch sought the company of whites – in particular, of white women – rather than blacks for various reasons. As white people were his clients, he needed to cultivate them constantly to stay in their good books. He was also far more at ease with them than with American blacks, who were unable to share his West Indian culture; not that he got on much better with West Indians, as they rarely came up to his level of sophistication. Above all, he showed off his white conquests because he thought they conferred kudos on him and were symbols of his having 'arrived'. And, until he began to feel its effects, he also revelled in notoriety.

Hutch can fairly be charged with having what is now scornfully called 'the crossover mentality'. White audiences accepted him because he played 'white music' and did not look very black. A few modern black performers – Michael Jackson is an obvious example – have lightened their skins through cosmetic surgery; both Nat King Cole and Ray Charles bleached their performing styles in ways that proved detrimental to the quality of their music. Neither was true of Hutch. Grenadian shade consciousness had always stressed how much whiter – and, therefore, more enviable and privileged – he was than most of his fellow countrymen. And he improved out of all recognition when he switched to café-society music from trying to play jazz. For a time he sustained a comforting illusion of progress by the tireless social climbing which took him from lower to upper class and from ethnic minority to quasi-WASP. But, by aiming to be anything but himself, he became exiled not only from his background but from his own emotions. Yet his white audiences and associates saw him as simply black. So while Hutch knew that he was British because he held a British passport, white people knew he was a black foreigner who happened to have a British passport. This made him fundamentally rootless and disoriented.

Regardless of the singer's sophistication and his distance from the cotton fields, black singers were expected to sing stereotyped spirituals. In 1903, the vaudeville team of Bert Williams and George Walker sang 'Evah Darkie is a King' to the future George V who, as so often, failed to see the joke. And black performers as diverse as Louis Armstrong, Leontyne Price and Harry Belafonte all recorded spirituals. Bernard Shaw was both cruel and right when he advised Paul Robeson on how to address a public meeting, 'Don't talk politics, but sing "Ol' Man River".' However, once Hutch had generated a successful repertoire of more sophisticated songs, he dropped numbers like 'All God's Chillun'.

The white response to various shows about or involving blacks during the 1920s and 1930s gives an indication of popular attitudes. On 31 December 1927, right-wingers in Vienna, then as now a notoriously illiberal city, demonstrated against the opening of Ernst Krenek's jazz-inspired opera *Jonny Spielt Auf* at the Operntheater. Jonny is a black musician – Alfred Jerger played the part in blackface – who cuts an erotic swathe through the women that surround him. In Josephine Baker's first talkie, *ZouZou* (1934), Baker and her co-star, Jean Gabin, hardly touch, but she and a blonde girl kiss and caress each other. Oddly, while any sort of romantic or physical interplay between white men and black women – or vice versa – was as inadmissible in drama as male homosexuality, a faint hint of lesbianism was acceptable. As Billie Holiday wrote, 'They still make it hot for a negro girl who walks to the corner with a white man. But a black chick and a white chick can be married and carry on and everything's cool as far as the what-will-people-think people are concerned.'[4]

While some critics took Paul Robeson to task for playing Uncle Tom roles in white entertainments, most leading blacks felt that any exposure of the race, even if it was demeaning, was better than none. Robeson's most notorious excursion in this sphere was playing the good black chieftain in *Sanders of the River*, Korda's 1935 film about a British colonial servant trying to keep the peace among belligerent west African tribes; the US title was *Bosambo*. In Hollywood, blacks could only play servants or low comics: Eddie Rochester Anderson specialised in such parts; Louis Armstrong played a series of deeply degrading roles – notably, the King of Jazzmania's tiger-skinned trumpeter in *A Rhapsody in Black and Blue* – and, as late as 1947, Billie Holiday made her only screen appearance as a bouncy parlour maid in *New Orleans*.

But of all entertainers, black or white, the duettists Layton and Johnstone had a career that most closely mirrors that of Hutch, and provides the most telling insight into his rise and fall. Both came from very well-educated families. Turner Layton was the son of a leading black musician in Washington, and Clarence – nicknamed Tandy – Johnstone was a qualified orthopaedic surgeon. They performed at society parties for the Astors and the Vanderbilts; and, as we have seen, the Mountbattens encouraged them to come to England – where, on their arrival in 1924, they were vigorously promoted by the Prince of Wales. When they performed at the Café de Paris in Leicester Square, Ray Langley of Columbia Records immediately signed them up on the back of a menu. Soon they were rich: each owned a Rolls-Royce, and both hunted with the Quorn. They returned to the Café de Paris at £400 a week. There, one quiet Sunday evening, Johnstone looked over the balcony at the sparse audience and stalked back to his dressing room, shouting, 'They're Jews! I'm not going to sing to such a small crowd of terrible people.' The Café de Paris fired them, and it was soon rumoured that the duo were getting on so badly that, to avoid off-stage contact, they came on stage from different sides. They quarrelled and finally split up in 1935. Johnstone overspent, ran up huge debts and eventually was declared bankrupt to the sum of £40,000. He divorced his wife and married a white woman. After that, no one hired him; and, after divorcing again, he died, broke, in New York, in 1953, aged sixty-eight.[5]

The year in which Layton and Johnstone – and virtually every other black celebrity in London – reached their apogee of social desirability was 1928. Early in the year, the Thames flooded and, to raise money for the victims, Noble Sissle staged 'the greatest all-star coloured show' at the London Pavilion in the afternoon of 29 January. Taking part were Layton and Johnstone; three other well-established duos, Williams and Taylor, Russel and Vivian, Jackson and Blake; James B. Lowe, the Uncle Tom of the film *Uncle Tom's Cabin*; and, giving one of the first of numerous charity performances, Hutch. He was joined by two old friends: Alberta Hunter, who hurried over from Monte Carlo, and, arriving at the eleventh hour from Paris, Josephine Baker. Due to immigration difficulties – the authorities did not readily issue work permits for foreign musicians – Alberta had to invoke the name of the Lord Mayor of London before she was nodded through. Accompanied by Hutch, she sang 'Just Another Day Wasted Away'; sadly, this duo never made a record. On the strength of her performance, Jerome Kern and Oscar Hammerstein cast her as Queenie in the London run of *Show Boat* which opened on 3 May. Her male lead was Paul Robeson, who consented to play the part only when he had persuaded Hammerstein to change the word 'niggers' to 'darkies' in the lyrics of 'Ol' Man River'. Alberta, who had known Robeson in New York, was thrilled to be performing with him: 'I'd look up at old Paul and sing, "Can't help lovin' dat man". Oh Lord, that was a knock-out.'[6]

Later in the year, Paul and Essie Robeson gave a large party in St John's Wood, which became front-page news in the black newspaper the *Chicago Defender*. In a letter to Gertrude Stein, Carl Van Vechten wrote, 'there was a great deal of food and champagne. All the distinguished Negroes were there: Layton and Johnstone and Leslie Hutchinson accompanied by some. . . .'[7] Other distinguished guests included Mrs Patrick Campbell, Lady Ravensdale, Lord Beaverbrook, Lady Laski, Hugh Walpole and most of the English stage.' The latter included Athene Seyler, Ivor Novello and Constance Collier; also present were Johnny Payne, Fred and Adele Astaire, Alberta Hunter and Harold Browning of the Harmony Kings. Many of Robeson's guests reconvened later at another 'our-folks' party in Maida Vale: together with Layton and Johnstone and, on a rare outing with Ella, Hutch, were the comedians Johnny and Mildred Hudgins, the pianist Larry Brown and the singer Marian Anderson, who had just given a triumphant concert at the Wigmore Hall, accompanied by Sir Roger Quilter. Every time black people performed successfully in public, it was not just an individual success; it helped to reduce prejudice, or so it was hoped.

In 1928, Hutch appeared in two shows. In the first, Cochran's *This Year of Grace*, 'the most popular jazz pianist of the smart nightclubs' was used 'in the orchestra only'.[8] Noël Coward wrote the book, music and lyrics; Oliver Messel designed the scenery; and, once again, Cochran assembled a fine cast. It included Joan Clarkson, Dougie Byng, Jessie Matthews, Sheilah Graham and Marjorie Robertson (Anna Neagle). The biggest hit was Tilly Losch from Vienna; a light-headed singer and dancer known to café society as 'Silly Tosh'; she was later briefly married to the aesthete Edward James. In his autobiography *I Had Almost Forgotten*, Cochran recalled that his favourite number 'was "Dance, Little Lady" . . . sung by Sonnie Hale, and Lauri Devine, pale of face and ascetic, dancing with strange precision, was followed by queer masked figures, and created a sensation. Jessie Matthews sang "A Room with a View" delightfully.' The Manchester preview attracted favourable notices, and the show opened at the London

Pavilion in the usual blaze of publicity. Always anxious to keep distractions in the auditorium to a minimum, Cochran asked King Amanullah and Queen Souriya of Afghanistan not to come on the first night. Even so, the audience glittered with celebrities. They included Edythe Baker, now d'Erlanger; Lord Northesk and Lord Portarlington, both lasting friends of Hutch; the novelist Arnold Bennett, the department-store proprietor Gordon Selfridge, Evelyn Laye, George Gershwin and Syrie Maugham. The ex-wife of Somerset Maugham, she was a pioneer interior designer, with a penchant for white.

The show ran for 316 performances, and earned Noël Coward the astonishing sum of £1,000 a week in royalties. As ever, Hutch was also appearing in nightclubs and, a solid earner throughout his London career, performing at debutante dances. These included a dinner dance given by Lord and Lady Beauchamp for Lady Mary Lygon. The Crown Prince and Princess of Sweden were among the guests who listened to Hutch singing highlights from *Showboat* and *This Year of Grace*.

HMV also commissioned Hutch to record, accompanying himself at the piano, in March, April and June of 1928. He recorded songs from *This Year of Grace* but, possibly because the original cast recording had already been issued, along with versions by Layton and Johnstone and by Coward himself, the records were never issued. At the March session, Hutch sang 'Two Little Babes in the Wood' with Carroll Gibbons, then head of music at HMV, but that was not released either. There are no comments in the files. Hutch left *This Year of Grace* before the end of its run, in order to appear in his second show in 1928. This was *Good News*, an American 'co-ed musical' that opened at the Carlton Theatre, Haymarket, on 15 August. It ran for 132 performances. Hutch was the first to sing its hit song, 'The Best Things in Life Are Free', but he did not record it until February 1941.

In April 1928, Hutch met a woman who would be loyal to him for life. Joan, then nineteen, was beautiful, well-born, intelligent and independently wealthy although, like most women of her class, she was uneducated. As a comparison between appointment diaries for 1927 and 1928 shows, her sudden infatuation with Hutch marked a complete change in her life. In 1927, she had lunch with the Gwens, Irenes, Margots and Nancys; went to 'Mummie's At

Homes' and the 'Flickers'; motored to Henley for tea with her aunt; attended dress fittings, dances and a garden party at Buckingham Palace. The 1928 diary starts in the same vein; then Joan goes to *This Year of Grace* and, through Dougie Byng, meets Hutch. The entries for 27 and 28 April both state, 'Lunch with Hutch', and after that Joan was too busy either to record meetings with relations and girlfriends or to arrange them in the first place. For the rest of the year, activities with Hutch – occasionally 'Hutchie' – fill the pages: they often lunch at the Café Royal; they have tea at the Alhambra; they drink cocktails at the Lamp Post Club and the Devonshire; they dine at the Berkeley and 'go on to' the Bat, the Lido, the Gargoyle, the Silver Slipper, Uncle's (or 'Nunky's'), the Kit-Cat, the Florida. They go to Lords, Wimbledon and greyhound racing. They attend the Hendon Air Display, racing at Hurst Park and first nights, including a Beatrice Lillie show at the Palladium. They go to the Chelsea Arts Ball; to parties in London and the country; and they go to the hairdresser – on Hutch's account, not Joan's.

Hutch certainly knew how to give a girl a good time; and Joan's breathless catalogue of events is proof of his astonishing energy. He contrived to fit Joan into parts of most days or nights, but enjoyed many other people and events without her. Some diary entries suggest that, although she only went by herself to see Hutch perform in public, she was pretending she was with him. She loved fame and glamour. Her court presentation photograph shows a provocative, wilful, spoiled young woman with limpid, tantalising eyes under the mandatory spread of ostrich plumes. She also looks rich. After fame, she loved money and was greedy. Her mother was a widow who adored her only son, Maurice, and they excluded Joan from their relationship. In return, Joan fought both of them out of their inheritances, and wrangled ferociously over every piece of jewellery and stick of furniture. And, to offset her isolation and show she was indifferent to it, she went all out to shock. She made friends with theatrical homosexuals and, once attached to Hutch, she clung on to him. At first, he gave her much time and excitement, but his attention soon wandered. But Joan remained a constant support and lover for the rest of Hutch's life, with the minimum of encouragement. She was in love with love, and her longing to bask in the reflected glory of someone famous was a desperate, obsessive need.

Joan was unaware of the birth of Hutch's first son, Gordon, in Liverpool in August 1928. He was born in his grandmother's theatrical boarding house, near the Hippodrome. Gordon's step-father was a ventriloquist who, like Hutch, was often away from home, touring on the variety circuit. He generously accepted his wife's misdemeanour as a casual encounter on a lonely night, and treated Gordon with great kindness. Even so, the situation must have been very difficult for all concerned. At this time, it was a frightening and alienating experience for a woman to have an illegitimate child. It was also an easy mistake to make: sex educa-tion was negligible, contraception rudimentary, and abortion both illegal and risky. Society ostracised both mothers and children, and they were often threatened lifelong with blackmail or exposure. As well as these miseries, Frances and Gordon had to bear the stigma of the mixed-race child, whose very existence was a permanent reminder of the indiscretion. Women had to be brave to survive these circumstances, and many of them understandably abandoned their children or offered them for adoption.

The next year, 1929, saw a breakthrough in Hutch's recording career. Parlophone signed him up, and Hutch made a batch of outstanding titles that demonstrate his technique, diction and personality. Among them were 'He Loves and She Loves', 'I'm a Gigolo', 'You're the Cream in My Coffee', 'Huggable Kissable You', 'Thou Swell', 'Button Up Your Overcoat', 'I Wanna Be Bad' and 'Ain't Misbehavin''. Possibly the most brilliant and characteristic was 'High Hat' with its wit, frothy style and superb piano playing. He sang almost against the beat of the accompani-ment to produce a unique rhythmic effect; the fill on the piano dovetails perfectly with the vocal passages; and the performance has a polished integrity that very few could equal.

This was an *annus mirabilis* for Hutch. He stretched his wings and became more adventurous in many ways. As well as continuing with his usual activities, he signed on with one of the top show-business agents, Charlie Tucker, and set about turning sporadic appearances into a steady and very remunerative career in variety. In January, he took a professional partner for the only time in his career, performing at the Café de Paris with his old friend from Harlem and Paris, Opal Cooper. On one night, there were four members of royalty in his audience, all at different tables, and, at yet another, Tallulah Bankhead. They sang 'Moonlight on the Ganges' and 'Because I Love You', two songs they had recorded for Vocalion in 1927. They also briefly appeared at the Holborn Empire; thereafter, Hutch had the limelight to himself.

The Cochran revue *Wake Up and Dream*, with words and music by Cole Porter, opened on 27 March. It had a typically dazzling Cochran cast with Elsie Carlisle joining the line-up that had helped to make *This Year of Grace* such a success: Tilly Losch, Lauri Devine, Sonnie Hale, Dougie Byng, Jessie Matthews and George Metaxa. Oliver Messel and Rex Whistler produced twenty-four settings and 500 costumes, and the two big hits were 'What Is This Thing Called Love?' and 'Let's Do It', a number that Hutch was to make the most of for the rest of his working life.

Rather than discourage celebrities for the first night, Cochran doubled the charge for the stalls seats, announcing that 42 shillings was the price for seeing the unique spectacle of a Cochran Pavilion Revue First Night Audience; from the second performance on, prices retreated to the normal level. The first-nighters got their money's worth. Cole Porter's friends – many of them Hutch's patrons – came from Paris and included Sir Charles Mendl, Lady Abdy, Mrs Reginald Fellowes and Gordon Selfridge. Also present were the biographer Lytton Strachey, Lord Berners, Lady Juliet Duff, Lady Colefax and Lord Curzon. The *Morning Post* described the interval as like the royal enclosure at Ascot plus the Ritz Bar. As the première was, in fact, the first uninterrupted dress rehearsal, Cochran came up to the footlights before the show and told the audience, 'Circumstances have been against us. I am afraid you will be disappointed in our performance tonight. Later, we shall have a fine show.' That summer Cochran and Mistinguett, the queen of French music hall, wrote the *Dictionary of Theatrical Terms*, feted in camp circles in Britain. One entry struck a particularly telling note of schadenfreude: 'First Night Audience: a body of optimists wanting to have fun whilst hoping all will turn out bad in the end.'[9]

Although scrappy, the revue provided an excellent showcase for Hutch, who attracted far more attention than any mere pianist could expect. On 31 March the *Sunday Express* reported, 'There were present two scores of these strange young people who now think they represent the last word in highbrowism and the last word in smartness. They sniggered at each other. "Hutch ought to

Leslie in New York, 1916/17.

Hutch's early passport.

Gouyave, 1900.

Mamie Smith's Jazz Hounds, 1920.

Palm Beach, Florida, 1923.

Hutch (left), Florida, 1923.

Hutchinson's Royal
Six visiting the Lido,
Venice, 1926.

Cole Porter in
Venice, 1923.

Joe Zelli's, Paris, 1925.

Tallulah Bankhead, London.

Edwina Mountbatten, 1925.

Edwina Mountbatten at
Wimbledon, 1924.

Edwina Mountbatten on
the beach at Deauville, 1925.

Joan, 1927.

Jessie Matthews and
C. B. Cochran, *circa* 1927.

Jessie Matthews in a
Cochran revue.

Hutch in London, 1928.

be on stage," said one when that clever negro pianist accompanied one of the dances from the orchestra. They are all Hutch fans.' Two weeks after the opening, Hutch started a residency at the stately Carlton Restaurant, where he sang 'Let's Do It', and word went round that he had known the words before Cole Porter wrote them down; which, in a way, was true.

In the same month, April, the *Daily Express* announced that Leslie Hutchinson, 'the genial West Indian pianist of Cochran's "29 Revue" ' was to open a cocktail bar called Hutch's Hutch in Mayfair. 'A kind of select club,' said Hutch, 'where I shall serve esoteric cocktails and entertain my friends with music.' This idea may have been a flight of fancy which was abandoned because it threatened to commit Hutch for too long in one place. It is also possible that Hutch did briefly realise the concept in the Rag-Bag Club. In his autobiography *A Bundle from Britain*, the historian Alistair Horne wrote that his socialite mother, Auriol Horne, wrote a song called 'Ladies Prefer Negroes', a variant on the title of Anita Loos's best-seller *Gentlemen Prefer Blondes*. Hutch accepted this 'with delight, performing it with great gusto at his fashionable "Rag-Bag Club" and across the West End in 1927 [sic]'. Loelia Ponsonby, soon to become the Duke of Westminster's second wife, thought that the 'American entertainment with Hutch was marvellous' at the Rag-Bag Club.[10] For all that, the enterprise foundered quickly. So, among much else in 1929, Hutch was finding out what did not suit him.

Also in April 1929, Hutch at Chez Henri was the first male cabaret singer to perform Cole Porter's daring song 'Love for Sale'. Curiously, Hutch never recorded it. A rich young man called John Gardiner, who saw Hutch perform, gives a revealing account of his life at that time. 'A girlfriend called Claire Luce was having a brief affair with Hutch and I went to meet him with her on the balcony of the Chateau de Madrid, a smart club overlooking the Thames, opposite Dolphin Square.' Gardiner then did the rounds of nightclubs and restaurants with Hutch over the next three weeks. They went to the Blue Train in Stratton Street and to Romano's in the Strand where, 'thanks to Hutch', supper was 'on the house'. He saw Hutch in action at the Kind Dragon in Ham Yard, Soho.[11] 'And from the club next door we used to collect Frieda Roberts, a beautiful hostess who married Al Bowly, the renowned singer, who was bisexual, of course. Years later, she became notorious as a drug addict.'

Hutch's chauffeur Fred drove Hutch and Gardiner everywhere at all hours. They went to the Chateau de Madrid, later named the Ballroom Club because of its massive dance floor, and listened to piano duets by John French and Norman Hackforth. Fred would then drive them back to Hutch's house in Steeles Road, together with Hackforth and two hostesses. There, Hutch played the piano and drank brandy provided by Gardiner before taking one of the women upstairs. Hackforth then played the piano until Hutch reappeared, and Gardiner got taxis to take Hutch's guests home. 'I never saw anyone else in the house . . . though I got the impression his wife lived there.' Gardiner adds that Hutch could be both humble and vain. 'Once when I expressed my admiration of his sapphire cufflinks and waistcoat buttons – he always wore tails for his act – he boasted that not only his jewellery, but all his clothes, were paid for by women.'[12]

Late 1929 was the time of the Wall Street crash, setting off the Great Depression across the world. Churchill described it as an economic blizzard that was turning Britain into one vast soup kitchen – soon there were 2 million workers on the dole. But the Depression had yet to affect the world in which Hutch moved.

The actress Claire Luce often came to watch Hutch in cabaret at Taglioni's, in Gerrard Street, Soho, where the social press commented on her backless black velvet gowns.[13] Here Hutch launched his first band of British musicians, which he conducted. The *Melody Maker* commented on the 'very novel and striking . . . costumes of the boys . . . white serge suits with blue velvet collars, blue silken lapels [with] the letter 'H' embroidered on the breast'. The band of 'well-known London musicians' included Eric Coleridge on saxophone and violin, and Julian Vedey on drums.[14] They played at Tag's from late 1929 to February 1930.

With and without Hutch, the band continued for another year or so. In September 1930, a US newspaper reported:

Two Negroes have found firm fame in London as Jazz Band Leaders, both have become institutions in the music world. They are Jack London, 'The Ebony Flash', who represented Britain in the Olympic Games in Amsterdam and Hutch Hutchinson, pianist and guiding spirit of the orchestra at C. B. Cochran's revue at the London Pavilion. As for Hutch, he is an institution in London's theatrical world. Numerous negro bands and bandmasters have come and gone, but the lanky pianist in Cochran's orchestra has outlived them all. He introduced London to its first steady diet of real rhythm and subtle syncopation. Now Hutch has a band of his own which is available for those denizens of Mayfair and other places of great social altitude who have developed a craving for the best of dance music.[15]

Hutch cannot have been essential to his band's performance – significantly, he played only second piano – because he frequently left London to appear in variety. Posters and programmes presented him as the 'celebrated society entertainer and Parlophone recording artiste'; and, after serving his apprenticeship with a few false starts in unrewarding cul-de-sacs of the entertainment world, he found that, although they were very different, he could entertain variety audiences as well as society audiences. Variety suited him because it set him challenges that he could handle brilliantly; so much so that, after only a few shows, he was sometimes topping the bill.[16] He was also very well paid. Certainly, there were sticky moments and teething problems. Many people had never seen a black man, and were far from sure they wanted to: when he came on stage at Chatham in 1930, the audience booed him off, but an intrepid manager persuaded the audience to give Hutch a hearing, and his performance soon won them over. Members of his public were impressed by his 'immaculate evening dress and his excellent posh voice'. One noted that Hutch was 'the first person of African origin I had seen until I went into the RAF'. Another referred to a:

> magic night . . . when a handsome black man sat at a piano with a white hanky reposing on the piano on the right-hand side . . . He was the first Black Man we had ever seen. I was completely charmed by the beautiful music he played . . . the audience must have been struck dumb as they did not join in the singing as they usually did.

There were a few brave souls who befriended Hutch when he was touring in the provinces in the twenties. Dorothy Thackeray Spencer was a tall, glamorous redhead who attended art college

in Manchester and modelled on the catwalk and for advertisements
too. She drove an Austin 7. Embarrassed by the way her contemporaries nervously ignored Hutch, she invited him home for
supper.

'I've never been to anyone's home in this area,' said Hutch
immediately. 'I would be glad to accept.' So Dorothy's stepmother
was briefly informed that a famous pianist was due for dinner that
night.

Dorothy had a marmoset who used to examine visitors from
upstairs and if it did not like them it would fly through the air and
land on their shoulders or head; if it did like the look of them, it
would walk quietly down the stairs.

At eight o'clock came the ring at the door. Dorothy was not
ready so her stepmother went to answer it. She took one look, gave
a piercing scream and fainted. Hutch carried her in.

The marmoset decided it liked him. It strutted downstairs on its
best behaviour, wearing a red outfit and fez, and tried to take his
hand.

Hutch plonked his hostess down in a hall chair. She moaned and
came round and, seeing Hutch, fainted again.

'She later said she thought she was in hell,' Dorothy explained.
'She was very uneducated and had been my mother's maid. She
had never seen a black man in her life.'

Throughout 1929, Hutch saw Joan but, after the initial frenzy,
rarely more than once a week, and then often with his brother Ivan
or her brother Maurice in tow. He invariably took her to the same
places, not out of sentiment but as a way of pigeonholing her and
avoiding other girlfriends; the common round was Nunky's,
Kettners, the Kit-Cat, the Winter Garden and the Blue Lantern.
The incidence of more mundane activities increased with visits to
Hutch's tailor, dentist, doctor, Chappell the music publisher; and
often Hutch did not take Joan out at all: instead she picked him up
from the stage door and drove back him to her flat. By the end of
1929, the lunching ladies – the Gwens, Irenes, Margots and Nancys
– are filling up her diary again.

Joan's main rival was Peg, a woman who, soon after her
husband's death in 1929, had a torrid affair with Hutch for at
least a year. She was about thirty and a natural blonde, chic, clever
and with a come-hither look. Long after the affair, she would
describe what a wonderful lover Hutch was, and how sweet he had

been to her. The family legend says that Hutch took her to Paris and gave her a marvellous time. 'It was all very hush-hush, but she also went into a private clinic and had an abortion.' When he left Peg for another women, she was so angry that she hurled all her Hutch records down the stairs after his retreating figure. Several of them smashed on his head. Significantly, Peg's sister said of her, 'If there wasn't trouble when Peg got there, there would be by the time she left.'

In 1930, Hutch continued to appear in cabaret in London: in early January, he performed at Pops Club, and in late March at the Not, a nightclub under the Café Anglais in Leicester Square which brought Parisian informality to the West End. Patrons did not have to wear evening dress or order champagne. Many did, but others wore day clothes or, fair-isled and plus-foured, came straight off the golf course, and they often drank beer. As people poured in, more and more tables crowded onto the floor, confining the dance area to little more than a square yard, as in the best *boîtes* in Paris; and when there were not enough chairs, people lay on the floor round the piano.

Hutch also featured in cabaret at the Midland, Manchester, in what was virtually a dry run for a famous radio feature, *Henry Hall's Guest Night*. The outstanding cast included 'Monsewer' Eddie Gray, a juggler who later starred with the Crazy Gang; Florence Desmond, a comedienne; the Delfont Brothers, dancers who later became the impresarios Bernard Delfont and Lew and Leslie Grade; and the juvenile lead star and pianist Billy Milton. The experiment was short-lived since the lyric of 'Two Little Babes in the Wood' proved too suggestive for Arthur Towle, the hotel manager.

In February Hutch left, in the words of the *Melody Maker*, to take 'a trip to Buenos Ayres for the combined purposes of health, business and pleasure', relinquishing his band-leading role at Taglioni's to the first pianist, Bob Probst. Hutch's passport confirms that he went to Spain, and he probably travelled onwards from there to Buenos Aires. With its large, rich expatriate community, it was a favourite place for European entertainers such as Mistinguett and Josephine Baker.

It is impossible to know whether or not Joan went with him. Her diary for the second week in February is uncharacteristically blank and when it resumes, there is no mention of Hutch for a

month. Hutch may have taken Joan; but, if so, it is odd that she did
not note the trip among a gleeful welter of preparatory arrangements. The blank may indicate only that she was pained that he
preferred to go with a rival or, in the words of one of his songs, to
travel alone. It is possible that she did go, and never committed a
word about it to paper, because it was such a daring thing to have
done. In April, Joan's diary mentions meetings with the wife of a
South American millionaire, a Madame de Pena who may have
helped to arrange Hutch's trip to Argentina. Through Madame de
Pena, Hutch and Joan met Prince Bismarck und Wallenburg, but
after a fortnight that new friend disappears from the diary.

The last Cochran show in which Hutch appeared was the unim-
aginatively named *Cochran's 1930 Revue*. Its cast was rich in
national and international performers. With Dougie Byng – the
sole survivor from the line-up of the two previous revues – were
Maisie Gay, Ada May, Roy Royston, Joan Clarkson and a very
young Richard Murdoch; there were two celebrated Parisians,
Sacha Guitry and Yvonne Printemps; and strong representation
from the Ballets Russes with Serge Lifar, Alice Nikitina and
choreography by Georges Balanchine. There were sixteen of
Mr Cochran's Young Ladies, and the sets and costumes were
by Oliver Messel, Rex Whistler, Doris Zinkeisen and the veteran
Paris couturier Worth. Having had brilliant scores from Coward
and Porter respectively for his, last two revues, Cochran had
difficulties, largely of his own making, with lesser talents over
the *1930 Revue*. At first he gave the job to the composer Vivian
Ellis, but he then broke his promise and commissioned Ivor
Novello. Mysteriously, Novello never did anything, and Cochran
then handed most of the assignment back to Ellis, with the writer
and socialite Beverly Nichols as librettist, and Lord Berners contributing the music for two balletic turns. In the event, Ellis and
Nichols made a good team, and became lifelong friends. Peter
Spencer, now Lord Churchill, also contributed to the book. And
Rodgers and Hart, although responsible for just one number,
delivered the show's biggest hit, 'With a Song in My Heart', also
a great hit for Hutch.

There was an eleventh-hour crisis over Hutch. On the day
before the opening night, 27 March, it was reported:

★   ★   ★

All seats for tomorrow night's '1930 Revue' are sold . . . For three years, Hutch has played in the theatre orchestra [for] £25 a week, which was a perquisite of his wife's, since regularly he earns large sums as a cabaret turn and at private parties. Until Monday, Hutch and Mr Cochran had agreed that Hutch should have a rest. But he will be in his usual place tomorrow night.

This confusion may have arisen through Hutch being in Argentina and beyond contact.

The other successful song from the show was 'Wind in the Willows' by Vivian Ellis, sung by a chorus of Botticelli angels and staged by Balanchine. Ellis loved Hutch's version of this song, and frequently played it until the end of his life. Richard Murdoch remembered that Hutch liked the song and played it, together with 'Body and Soul', at many of that year's cabarets. That said, two good songs do not make a show, and the fortune spent on mounting the revue – between £15,000 and £20,000 – initially failed to conceal its mixed parentage and scrappy development. The reviews for the Manchester try-out were bad: the show was under-rehearsed, overran by forty minutes and 'lacked good tunes'. However, these shortcomings must have been dealt with by the time the *1930 Revue* reached the London Pavilion, because it attracted unqualified praise from the critics, with Hutch specially singled out.

The first night dazzled as usual. The audience included the playwright George Bernard Shaw, the photographer Cecil Beaton, the film director Anthony Asquith and the millionaire hostess Emerald Cunard. Backstage, Ivor Novello took 'an undue interest' in Hutch; and when two Grenadians came to see their local boy made good, they found Lady Mountbatten 'demeaning herself' with him. The show ran for 245 performances.

Every night after the show, Hutch performed at both the Ambassadors Club and Chez Henri in Long Acre, 'not far from the Covent Garden brussels sprouts . . . a romantic haunt that has built up a steady reputation during the past few years . . . the floor is glassy and the atmosphere very peppy'.[17] He now asked a high price for extra engagements. When the American embassy in Brussels asked him to fly over and give a brief cabaret, Hutch asked for £100 and overrode attempts to cut the price. After three years in London, Hutch was more popular than ever. He played to

smart crowds at the Café Anglais and the latest West End restaurant, the Trafalgar. He was also hugely in demand for debutante
dances, and when Princess Ottoboni was launching her daughter,
she was firmly advised to settle for no one but Hutch for the
cabaret.

Ted Morgan, a song plugger for the music publisher Lawrence
Wright, who became a friend of Hutch during the *Cochran 1930
Revue*, provided some interesting glimpses of him at this time. The
two men used to dine twice a week at the Piccadilly Hotel, and
Morgan remembered Hutch giving money to a woman called
Mary, who always used to beg at the entrance. 'He always said,
"How's your little girl?" . . . and talked to me often of his
daughter, Leslie. But he never went home till 3 or 4 a.m.' They
also lunched at Frascati's in Regent Street, where Hutch used to
order mixed grill with the new Escoffier sauce. ' "Must have the
sauce," he would boom.' Ted also went with Hutch to the Old
Bailey and the House of Commons in the 1950s, and was amazed
when he found out that Hutch's claim to have trained in the law
turned out to be untrue.

Hutch was occasionally employed by the legendary Rosa Lewis
at the Cavendish Hotel.[18] In 1930, Daphne Weymouth went to a
party there in the Elinor Glyn Room, given by Aly Khan and
Michael Beary. She recalled Hutch playing the piano, and Rosa
reminiscing about everyone's grandparents over champagne. The
actor John Mills, who first met Hutch at a weekend party given by
the actor Henry Mollison at West Drayton, also had some revealing insights:

> He used to play splendid tennis and was great fun. He was
> lionised by everyone, but was a surprisingly nice man. I re-
> member we men all showered together in Henry's bathroom.
> What a man! He was a fine pianist and a tremendous showman. I
> met him also at Noël Coward's house in Gerrard Row. They
> used to play the piano together and entertain us and each other.

In the course of their weekly meetings, Hutch and Joan went to
numerous films and plays, including the first night of Coward's
Private Lives at the Phoenix Theatre, newly refurbished in the Art
Deco style, in Charing Cross Road. On her free evenings, Joan's
other friends, mostly gay theatricals such as Dougie Byng and Billy

Milton, acted as walkers. Sometimes they went to see Hutch in cabaret but just as often they went elsewhere. So, although she was still in love with Hutch, Joan had recovered her dignity and, with it, a more balanced social life. Even so, she was never happier than with Hutch.

Although 1930 was less adventurous than 1929 for Hutch, he was still broadening his range in various ways. He made his first film appearance in a small part in *Big Business* in which he sang 'Always Your Humble Slave', written by Oscar M. Sheridan, who directed the film, and Hubert W. David. He also appeared before a static camera operated by Paul Tanqueray. Tanqueray attracted fashionable subjects to his studio at 8 Dover Street in the West End. He produced memorable portraits of, among many others, the film star Anna May Wong, the dancers Anton Dolin[19] and Tallulah Bankhead, and blazed the trail for such portrait photographers as Cecil Beaton, Yevonde and Baron. Hutch's picture filled a full page in the *Tatler*.

In August, Carl Van Vechten was back in London. When reporters asked him whether he was going to see Paul Robeson at the Royal Albert Hall, he said, 'The Albert Hall is not on my street. I expect to go to Betty Chester's to hear Hutch play.'[20] Betty Chester was one of the Co-Optimists, a troupe of sophisticated West End pierrots led by Melville Gideon and including the young Stanley Holloway and Phyllis Monkman, a girlfriend of the Duke of York, later George VI. They were all well known to Hutch.

Hutch soon appeared again at the Café de Paris. It was the peak of cabaret success, just as starring at the Palladium was the ultimate in variety. The Café de Paris was an underground restaurant in Leicester Square which was an exact replica of the Palm Court in the ill-fated *Lusitania* (a passenger liner torpedoed in the First World War). Jack Poulsen, the manager, skilfully generated an atmosphere that was formal and, at the same time, clublike and relaxed. Tails were mandatory for his exclusive clientele, although, largely thanks to the influence of the Prince of Wales, dinner jackets and soft shirts were to follow later. On the balcony, distinguished people could dine in ordinary clothes, but were not permitted on the dance floor. Many habitués had their tables kept for them until 11.30 p.m. or later. Poulsen also had intimate knowledge and instant recall of his clients. This enabled him to 'dress' the room; and occasionally he would deliberately place a divorcing wife and husband, who were in separate parties, at adjoining tables so that everyone had some sort of floor show until the cabaret started.

Although the Café de Paris always used top artistes, its customers sometimes reacted in a surprisingly contrary fashion to even the most expensive stars. Someone might be at the top in their particular niche, but he never knew, until he had negotiated the curved staircase to the dance floor, whether he would return to the dressing room on the wings of applause or slink away in leaden silence. Hutch, unsurprisingly, triumphed. Stéphane Grappelli, later the virtuoso violinist and pianist with the Quintette du Hot Club de France, reflected the general view in congratulating Hutch on being a wonderful artist. The whole ambience might have been made for him; and it certainly provided a suitably glamorous setting for the start of an affair with one of his most spectacular girlfriends.

At the Café de Paris were five young hostesses supervised by a duenna, Barbara Crosby. She had just returned from the Spanish court, where she had been teaching the children of Hutch's old employer Queen Ena to dance. Like Cochran's Young Ladies, the hostesses were noted for their charm and style, but Barbara was required to keep them on a tight rein: they ate at their own table on the balcony, and provided company and light conversation for clients, but there was no question of sex. They also had to wear evening clothes bought out of their salaries. Among her charges was Nora Turner, later Lady Docker; she became a lifelong friend of Hutch's, and in the 1950s he often gently parodied the excesses with which she relieved the drabness of postwar Britain. Another of the five was a nineteen-year-old girl from Calcutta called Queenie Thompson. Encouraged by Barbara's sister Catherine Courtenay 'to register as an Oriental maid or something', Queenie was to be the first Anglo-Indian film star. Experimenting with names, she at one point called herself Mary O'Brien until one of her lovers, Charles Sweeny, suggested she adapt this cheerfully mundane Irish handle to the more exotic Merle Oberon.

Merle's biographers Roy Moseley and Charles Higham write, with approximate accuracy, 'While she was at the Café de Paris, Merle took a major stride up the social ladder. She set her cap at none other than "Hutch", Leslie A. Hutchinson, the rage of London society.' They then expand on Hutch's professional triumphs, his irresistible appeal to society women, unseen wife and 'humdrum domestic household' before stating, 'By sleeping with Hutch, Merle gigantically elevated her career . . . undoubtedly, this is how she met the many aristocrats who later became her friends, as well as some predominant figures of the movie world.' One of Hutch's less appealing features was his unwillingness to promote anyone other than himself, so he must have liked spending time with Merle, and admired her for her beauty, nerve and ambition; at that time, she was also unspoiled and lacking in confidence. Other writers mention their affair. In his biography of Norma Shearer, Gavin Lambert touches on Merle's involvement with 'a popular Jamaican nightclub singer known as Hutch'. Sheridan Morley mentions in his biography of David Niven (*The Other Side of the Moon*) that 'David first met Merle in London in the early 30s when she was a hostess at the Café de Paris, living with Hutch, the great cabaret pianist, and David was on his nightclub rounds'. Niven was to have his fling with Merle in Hollywood in 1935. As for Morley's view that Hutch was 'living with' Merle, Hutch hardly had time to live anywhere, nor did he or Merle wish to devote themselves exclusively to anyone.

Indeed, at the time of her affair with Hutch, Merle was also the girlfriend of Charles Sweeny, a handsome American playboy. Sweeny often went to hear Hutch at the Café de Paris, and when he heard years later that Merle had been two-timing him with Hutch, he said, 'If I'd known that Merle was going out with that nigger boy, I would never have allowed her to.'[21] In his autobiography, Sweeny wrote that he was ashamed to be seen entertaining Merle at the 400 (because she was part Indian), but did so because she badly wanted to go, and people envied him for escorting such a beauty. Sweeny married Margaret Whigham, later the Duchess of Argyll, in 1933. Alexander Korda, the Romanian film producer and director, also fell for Merle's charms. In 1985 his nephew Michael Korda wrote a fictional biography of Merle called *Queenie*. Hutch appears in it, strangely disguised as a French photographer called Lucien.

Hutch returned to Paris for the Columbus Day Ball at the American embassy in October 1930. In entertainment terms, *le tout*

Paris performed: most of the casts from Le Moulin Rouge and the Folies Bergères; Josephine Baker; the band of the Hot Club de France; Mistinguett, whose legs were insured for a million francs, and her lover Maurice Chevalier, then enjoying a great hit with 'Louise'. All these stars were old friends, and they must have had a ball within the ball, catching up on events since they were last together. The occasion is described in a novel called *The Weeping and the Laughter* by Noel Barber, who was Paris correspondent for the *Daily Mail* for some years.

> The most prestigious social event of the Paris season – in fact the first ball of the winter of 1930 – was undoubtedly the Columbus Day Ball at the American Embassy on 13th October . . . the 1920s had not only been symbolised by the Charleston and the new short dresses and new hair styles for women, but by 'le jazz' . . . it was rumoured that the singer Hutch would entertain . . . 'I wonder if he'll insist on bringing his girlfriend along with him,' Father wondered . . . 'Edwina Mountbatten. Married to Lord Louis Mountbatten, Queen Victoria's grandson. Fine way to carry on, but they say she's fond of dark-skinned men . . . They're particularly well-endowed, you know.'

Then his guests go the ball, where the principal guest was Raymond Poincaré, who had recently rescued the franc from devaluation.

'Anything Goes' might have been the anthem of the BYTs, but most English people in the 1920s were deeply conservative and very censorious. Hutch's philandering was becoming a threat to his career. He seemed incapable of accepting the difference between mores in Grenada and Britain. On the surface, sartorially and socially, he fitted in; but his solipsism blinded him to the need to conform at a deeper level. From what he said later, he seems to have thought that the mothers of his first two outside children had made unfortunate mistakes which caused him inconvenience. He had known and needed their mothers only fleetingly. His attitude was that they knew the risks. In 1930, the birth of another child caused greater misery.

For about a year, a woman called Elisabeth had been besotted by Hutch. She came from a quintessential establishment family: her grandfather had been a naval commander; her father, a product of Eton and New College, Oxford, joined the Foreign Office, was knighted and later became High Sheriff. Elisabeth was clever, musical, pretty and the leader of a smart social set. In March 1930, her grand wedding in Chelsea to a captain in the Guards made the papers. On 29 September she gave birth to a daughter at a private nursing home in Earls Court, London. Elisabeth's husband either knew or suspected beforehand that he was not the father. On the day of the birth, he wrote to confirm that a Miss Markes, a midwife with links to adoption agencies, would be well paid for removing the baby and looking after her until she was adopted. On the same day, he wrote another letter to Miss Markes, asking her to allow one of his fellow officers to examine the baby. The wife of that officer remembered the circumstances:

> Elisabeth had an infatuation for Hutch, used to do his letters, she became a sort of stooge. She married when she was pregnant. I don't know if she knew at the time or not, but we felt she probably cheated him. I was pregnant, too, and we lived in the same block, both fatties together. While she was in labour and before my baby was born, Elisabeth's husband came to see us both, and said, 'If it's black, I can't bear it and I don't want to see it. Please go and see for me.' He wept on what was left of my lap, 'What shall I do?'

The fellow officer admired the newborn, undeniably coffee-coloured baby. When the baby was two months old, Elisabeth's husband referred all communications concerning her to his solicitor, W. Rollo of Withers & Co, an ex-Guards officer who specialised in acrimonious society divorces.[22]

Elisabeth's father was so incensed that he went all out to wreck Hutch's career. To prevent him leaving the country, he got the Foreign Office to remove his passport, but Hutch seems to have had it renewed without any difficulty. Rollo forced Hutch to pay a large sum into court, probably £1,000, conceivably £10,000: on one of her annual visits to Withers & Co, the little girl, now called Gabrielle, craned to see the figure among the papers on Rollo's desk, but never succeeded in seeing the amount clearly.

A brief reconciliation between Elisabeth and her husband

produced another daughter eleven months later, but Elisabeth left him soon after, and they got divorced. Elisabeth remarried, and became a magistrate noted for handing down severe sentences to prostitutes.

Chapter Six

From Revue to Variety
1931–1938

Love and scandal are the best sweeteners of tea.

Henry Fielding

Having been in the last three Cochran revues, Hutch must have felt strange to be sitting in the audience of the *1931 Revue* on 31 March, a week after the London opening. Because he had so much other work and no longer wanted to be tied up in a long engagement, he had abandoned Cochran. In the event, his timing was good because the show failed, running for only thirty-seven performances, despite having some excellent songs. Hutch recorded some of these, including Noël Coward's 'Half-Caste Woman', a haunting, tender salute to one born of 'some queer magic'.

That February, Hutch had opened at the Not. Joan and her friends used to see him perform there every night. The racing journalist Richard Baerlein had a girlfriend who worked at the club, and he also used to take out a glamorous singer, Marion Rodgers, who performed Marlene Dietrich numbers at the Not; Baerlein remembered her as 'rampantly oversexed'. He knew

Hutch as a regular visitor to the races at Kempton: 'He was well known to trainers and pretty knowledgeable. We all used to go and see him at the Not, which we called "the singing brothel" . . . It was a tiny little club, but we all fitted in somehow.'

The Not was one of three nightclubs owned by Jack Poulsen and his partner Stocco. The others were the Café Anglais, to which it formed a sort of annexe, and the Café de Paris. The Not acted as a proving ground for new talent: if performers succeeded there, they graduated to a larger audience, more money and fame at the Café de Paris. The club gave many cabaret stars – including Florence Desmond, Hildegarde and Dougie Byng – their first significant breaks. But the club also featured established acts like Hutch. By 1931, the BYTs crammed the Not every night, and it was described as 'one of the smallest, most amusing, most ridiculous, most exclusive, little dance haunts in the world'[1] so it was no step down from the Café de Paris for Hutch to perform there.

The *Daily Sketch* compared the Not to a speakeasy, 'even though drink does stop at midnight'. There follows a breathless litany of 'in' people including Lady Davina Lytton, her brother Lord Knebworth, Lady Castlerosse, wife of the *Daily Mail* gossip columnist, and 'two pillars of the German Embassy, Count Bernstorff and Prince Bismarck, sat at a table which looked far too small for them'. And looming behind Hutch was 'the cheerful, rosy visage of Evelyn Waugh . . . full of the conviviality of the returned traveller . . . He staggered the waiters by producing a purse of gold sovereigns, which he poured on to the table when paying the bill. "You have to have gold in most parts of Africa. They won't take notes", he explained. Then, open-handed, he began distributing the coins to his friends.'[2] Dame Barbara Cartland also saw Hutch at the Not.

Hutch went on to the Bobbin, a new nightclub where evening dress was also optional; and in April he returned to Chez Henri. However, for much of 1931, he continued to appear at the Not at midnight, and became the main reason for its success. He was probably the only cabaret singer in London with the personality and repertoire to attract the same people again and again. Among his highlights was Cole Porter's notorious 'Love for Sale'. Because it was still almost impossible to hear the words anywhere else, people went to the Not just to hear that single song:

> Love for sale
> Who will buy?
> Who would like to sample my supply?
> Who's prepared to pay the price
> For a trip to Paradise?
> Love for sale
> If you want to buy my wares
> Follow me and climb the stairs,
> Love for sale.

That was the kind of sophisticated material that Hutch's public expected of him. When that summer he released a record of 'River, Stay Way from My Door' and 'O Lord, Send Us the Sunshine', two numbers of the sort that black artistes were expected to sing, the *Melody Maker*, calling Hutch 'the Michael Arlen of cabaret artists',[3] remarked that 'in spite of his colour, the mockspiritual does not become him. West Indians are too cultured a people to get excited about a river or a sun. Cannot we have a record of the Hutch we know, just playing the piano?' Hutch may have hoped to gain a wider audience outside the West End by the use of such ethnic material. His versions of these songs are, of course, quite adequate, but hardly sincere. Other black solo singers refused to sing spirituals on the grounds that doing so encouraged whites in their belief that blacks should be confined to the 'darkie' repertoire. Regrettably, this was not Hutch's last venture in this genre.

In September, Poulsen decided to close the Not for two reasons. Its mainstay, Hutch, was going to leave and start another dance band; and, as the Café Anglais was now admitting people in ordinary clothes, the Not had lost much of its point. However, many mourned its passing. It had been innovatively informal, and had had an intimate friendly atmosphere all too rare in London restaurants and nightclubs, the most popular meal there being kippers and lager beer.

Hutch launched his new band on 14 September 1931 at the Empress Rooms in the Royal Palace Hotel, on the site now occupied by the Royal Garden Hotel, Kensington. The Royal Palace was one of the more ornate links in a chain of restaurants and hotels all over London and the provinces, owned by Messrs J. Lyons. It included the Trocadero Restaurant in Piccadilly and a number of Corner Houses. Those on key sites in Leicester Square and Oxford Street had an orchestra on each of their four floors.

Although there were a number of very accomplished West Indian musicians in London at the time – including two fine trumpeters, Hutch's namesake Leslie Jiver Hutchinson and Dave Wilkins – Hutch employed only whites. He had made an enterprising choice, taking on several future stars of British jazz and light music. The six-piece band comprised Bram Crossman, trumpet, brother of the more famous Joe who later played with Bert Ambrose's band; Micky Amstel, tenor saxophone; Jack Shields, alto saxophone; Stanley Black, piano; Harry Sharman, guitar; and Ginger Conn, drums. They played every afternoon and, except on Sundays, every evening for customers well versed in the intricacies of the foxtrot, quickstep and waltz.

Sydney Lipton, whose band also played at the Empress Rooms and was for many years resident at the Grosvenor House Hotel in Park Lane, admired and envied Hutch for his cultivated English, excellent French and 'languid baritone', but felt that his 'strong personality' was wasted sitting at the piano in a dance band, and that band-leading was, anyway, not his forte. Stanley Black agreed. He was only sixteen at the time he was hired as pianist and enjoyed being taken by his mentor to Wheeler's in Old Compton Street and sitting up at the bar. He felt that Hutch 'was a beautiful rhythmic pianist . . . naturally an individual performer . . . but never a conventional bandleader'. No sort of team player, Hutch was an erratic leader, intolerant of his colleagues' calls on his time and attention; and, when he himself took time off, remarkably cavalier about rehearsal times.

A photograph of Hutch in his dressing room at the Palladium hints at the difficulties musicians must have had with him. Wearing only a sleeveless vest, Hutch challenges the camera with a camp, defiantly provocative stare. The picture is timeless, and could well be of one of today's rock icons.

Predictably, the personnel of his band changed frequently. Within weeks of its launch, the rhythm section, apart from Black, had changed to Bob Thomas, guitar, Dick Ball, double bass, and Percy Hampton, drums; while Micky Amstel, on tenor saxophone, had given way to Buddy Featherstonhaugh, who was to become one the best British jazzmen of the 1930s and 1940s.

As ever, Hutch found that his residency at the Empress Rooms

left time for other London dates. He occasionally used a microphone and a loudspeaker at this time but without much success. 'It
results in unpleasant distortion,' complained the *Melody Maker* in
December 1931, 'which negatives the novelty element.'

In November 1931, Hutch and his band appeared at the
Palladium in 'Buy British Week'. Although he shared the bill
with a scatter of variety acts and dance bands, it was largely Hutch's
show. He appeared 'most effectively at a cream-coloured piano',[4]
and the *Melody Maker* reported that his 'vocalisms went down well,
whilst his piano work must have tickled anyone with a knowledge
of that instrument'. The magazine also paid a tribute to Hutch's
band: 'Considering that it was its first appearance in variety, the
band rallied round Hutch quite nobly, dealing very convincingly
with part of "Tiger Rag", and providing some rumba rhythm with
all the appropriate instruments, including a tambourine! There is
plenty of co-operation between the different sections of the band,
which seems brimful of promise.' Altogether, the London press
deemed Hutch's first big break in variety a great success.

Meanwhile, in Grenada, Marianne Hutchinson was walking in
the hills when a thorn scratched her eye. The resulting infection
spread, and she was soon blind and wholly dependent on her
sisters-in-law. Feeling alone and afraid, she sent frequent letters to
her favourite son asking for help. Hutch occasionally replied, and
even invited her over to stay. He told friends he was very worried
about his mother and showed them photographs of her. But
Marianne was far too feeble to make the trip, and Hutch was
not going to make the arrangements himself, let alone go and fetch
her. He did not really want his smart friends to meet Marianne.

So his mother died without seeing him again, and there is no
trace of her grave among the greening stones of the churchyard at
Gouyave.

Hutch's fame was still growing, and on his birthday, 7 March 1932,
he returned to the Palladium to star in a variety show directed by
George Black, the impresario who ran the Palladium from 1928 to
his death in 1945. Released by 'kind permission of the management of the Empress Rooms', Hutch appeared once, in the last slot
before the interval. He almost certainly featured many of the hits
named in an advertisement in the programme, promoting his
recordings for Parlophone. They included 'If I Didn't Have

You', 'Life Is Just a Bowl of Cherries', 'When Your Lover Has Gone', 'Memories of You' and a piano solo, 'Gone'.

At that time, the Palladium was billed as 'London's High-Speed Variety Theatre which sets the Vaudeville Pace for the World'. The premier theatre of the Moss Empires chain, it priced its seats as follows: boxes from 18 shillings; 'A Few Special Imperial Fauteuils', seven and ten pence; Imperial Fauteuils, four and tenpence to six shillings; Imperial Circle, three and eightpence; Stalls and Grand Circle, two and fivepence; Upper Circle, one and thruppence and Balcony, 11 pence; 'Tea and Coffee served in the auditorium by request'.

At the end of March, Hutch appeared for the first time with great success at the Victoria Palace, for many years home to the Crazy Gang comedians and later to be affectionately referred to by the royal family as 'our local'. The bill also starred Doris Hare and Ted Ray, 'who fiddles and fools for a living'. The *Era* found Hutch 'in fine voice and splendid in his pianoforte playing', and the *Performer* filled its front cover with his photograph captioned, 'The incomparable Hutch'. It even rates 'Lawd, You Made the Night Too Long' as 'the greatest semi-spiritual of our time', in vindication of Hutch's return to the overtly black repertoire.

For much of the 1930s, Hutch appeared at both the London Trocadero Restaurant Cabaret and the Grill Room Suppertime Show known as 'Trocabaret'. Although both venues were in the same Lyons-owned building, they were quite separate. The restaurant engaged only star artistes, while Lyons contracted C. B. Cochran to organise the cabaret in the Grill Room. The latter always featured the Young Ladies, often with minor mime artistes, 'dumb shows', from the continent, and only occasionally with big stars such as Hutch. One of the Young Ladies spoke of rules set by Lyons that were even more draconian than the code for hostesses at the Café de Paris. Visiting and 'exploring outside one's own work domain' was forbidden; so, too, was use of the main entrance; instead, the chorus girls had to go through the kitchen quarters and run a nightly gauntlet 'through a barrage of soap suds thrown by cheeky washers-up and risk breaking an ankle on the slippery floor'.

In April 1932, after finishing for the evening at the Empress Rooms, Hutch moved east from Kensington to the West End to appear with Eddie Fox's band at the Monseigneur, a nightclub near Piccadilly Circus, now a cinema. By May, Norman Impey had taken over from Buddy Featherstonhaugh in Hutch's band; Bert Jackson had replaced Percy Hampton on drums; and Alec Blackford was now leading the relief band from the piano. As always, this restlessness in the personnel reflected the volatility of the leader, who was clearly ready to move on.

Over the past four years, Hutch's variety dates had taken up less than a third of his working life; by 1932, they accounted for at least half of it. He left behind disordered heaps of press notices of his shows, sent by Durrant's Press Cuttings, and some, dated May, report a great triumph at the Glasgow Empire, a venue notorious for the hostility of its audience towards Sassenachs. Comedians fared particularly badly: Bob Monkhouse once had to fake a heart attack in order to leave the stage without attracting a shower of pennies from the gallery; Mike and Bernie Winters were greeted with a shout of 'Oh God, there's two of them!'; and Les Dawson wrote in his autobiography, 'I didn't die there, but an undertaker in the audience threw me a tape measure and some embalming fluid.' Along with Scots, Irish, Jewish and Geordie acts, black performers were traditionally far better received. Hutch was no exception. He sang what the programme described as 'the syncopated spirituals of America's sunny south', including that lachrymose stand-by 'Lawd, You Made the Night Too Long'. And the *Glasgow Evening Times* acclaimed 'the cabaret idol of the exclusive set who has blossomed out as a variety star' and stated that he had made 'a fine impression' despite being 'only known to Glasgow on the gramophone'.

Back in London, Hutch again starred in June at the Victoria Palace, where he struggled with a heavy cold and earned praise for appearing. August found him at the Holborn Empire, his favourite theatre, where he always made what his friend Ted Morgan called his 'abdication speech, telling the audience how much he loved them, and had missed being there'. Featured numbers included the inevitable and embarrassing 'Lawd, You Made the Night Too Long' and 'Happy Go Lucky You'. He returned to the Palladium in a splendid bill with the singing comedy duo of Flanagan and Allen 'with a tumultuous spate of Flanagisms with ad lib accompaniment of "Ois"; Teddy Brown, "may his shadow never grow less!" gets the audience singing with gusto as we welcomed his brilliant xylophone music'; G. S. Melvin 'proves his unique versatility by his uproarious "Song of the Policewoman" and lots more'.[5]

One of Hutch's more glamorous cabaret venues at this time was the Blue Train Grill in Stratton Street, Mayfair, a replica of the Côte d'Azur luxury express on which he sometimes travelled with Edwina Mountbatten. An illuminated station sign showed the way to the grill room; there were luggage racks on the walls; and there was a mural of hurrying porters. Regular passengers included Gloria Vanderbilt and Freda Dudley Ward, former mistress of the Prince of Wales. By August, Hutch was back at the Trocabaret, which celebrated its thirty-sixth anniversary in October by reprising the successes of the Naughty Nineties stars who had appeared in the music hall which had previously occupied the site of the restaurant. The audience went home in some style in the last surviving fleet of hansom cabs.

Throughout the decade, Hutch gave an increasing number of charity performances. In February 1934, he went to Brighton to join a spectacular bill – it included Alice Delysia, Max Miller, Flanagan and Allen, Naughton and Gold, Billy Caryll and Hilda Mundy, Frances Day and Vivian Ellis – to raise funds for the Brighton and Hove Jewish Board of Guardians. The *Brighton Standard* noted that 'Hutch raised quite a storm of applause'. In June that year, he accompanied a troupe of debs at Claridge's in aid of Alexandra Rose Day. One of them recalled, 'We had to sing a ghastly song called "Only a Rose", supporting an aged opera singer called Maggie Teyte . . . I also have a feeling that Hutch must have been joining in.'

Geoff Tansley, a saxophone-playing veteran of dance bands and pit orchestras between the wars, remembers a row between Hutch and the conductor Sir Thomas Beecham in the newly built Lewisham Town Hall. Beecham complained that the hall was stuffy, because the staff had neglected to open the windows. When he found they were stuck, he violently tried to prise them open with his baton. Hutch explained that the building was air-conditioned, then a rare luxury, and the windows were not designed to open. He added it was absurd that someone from humble origins like himself knew more about such refinements than the exalted conductor; and ended by saying that, if Beecham did not apologise for castigating people for something that was not their fault, he would not perform in the concert with him. Beecham apologised, and the concert went ahead. Conditioned at school in Grenada to stand up to bullies and fight for fair play, Hutch was shocked by Beecham's famous irascibility and the conductor's abuse of his authority. Although Hutch flared up in response, he was firm, reasonable and well in control. Tansley recalled other instances of Hutch championing the underdog, but on the whole he tended not to score points off powerful whites, however wrong they were. But he still seethed inside.

An American girlfriend sent Hutch a cutting from Walter Winchell's On Broadway gossip column of June 1931 that read, 'Lady Ashley, England's celebrated blue blood, is making Leslie Hutchinson, the negro, the rage of London by attending nightly the Café Anglais, where he warbles, in sports clothes. Lady Mountbatten is often there, too.'[6] As Winchell's column suggests, Edwina's affair with Hutch continued. Now that the initial possessive passion had worn off, she was less demanding, and the relationship was following the relaxed, no-strings pattern that would persist well into the mid-1950s. Because the long, intimate connection was so central to Hutch's life, it prevented and distorted much biographical information about him. The affair reverberated through the memories of many people, each with their own angle on its character and details; and the result is a rich – and, inevitably, often inconsistent – amalgam of hearsay, written information and oral testimony.[7]

On 29 May 1932, the downmarket Sunday newspaper the *People* shattered the settled peace of this stage in their relationship by publishing an unusually frank article. It pulled together strands of recent gossip, and ran a story loud with finger-pointing in-nuendo. Under the headline 'Society shaken by terrible scandal', its column 'Behind the Scenes' read:

I am asked to reveal today the sequel to a scandal which has shaken society to the very depths. It concerns one of the leading hostesses in the country – a woman highly connected and immensely rich. Her association with a coloured man became so marked that they were the talk of the West End. Then one day the couple were caught in compromising circumstances. The sequel is that the society woman has been given hints to clear out of England for a couple of years to let the affair blow

over, and the hint comes from a quarter which cannot be
ignored.

By modern standards, it may seem extraordinary that the news had
not burst earlier. But until the mid-1960s the media were generally
far more reticent; and the two great press lords, Rothermere and
Beaverbrook, were particularly discreet concerning royal matters.
For example, while fully aware of the friendship between the
Prince of Wales and Mrs Simpson from mid-1934 on, they did not
reveal the news until December 1936.[8]

The 'society woman' was easily identified as Edwina Mountbatten, and 'the quarter that cannot be ignored', with equal
certainty, as Buckingham Palace. Salacious rumours went round
concerning the exact nature of the 'compromising circumstances';
the most popular referred to Hutch and Edwina being inextricably
united through vaginismus, a rare and temporary medical phenomenon; and having to be taken in flagrante delicto by ambu-
lance from the Mountbattens' home at Brook House to hospital.[9]

A copy of the piece went to Malta, Lord Louis's current station,
where the Mountbattens were entertaining, among others, the
King of Spain. The Palace said that steps must be taken to 'deny the
imputation on two counts: that Edwina was having an affair with a
coloured man, and that the Palace had suggested that she should
live abroad'.[10] Before returning to London in July 1932, the
Mountbattens took legal measures to sue for libel Odhams Newspapers, the publishers of the *People*.

The Lord Chief Justice's court sat at the unusually early hour of
9.30 a.m. and the whole matter was heard and finished before
anyone, particularly the press, knew about it. Richard Hough gives
this account of it in his biography of Edwina:

> One of the greatest advocates of the day, Norman Birkett, acting
> for the Mountbattens, opened the case: 'It is not too much to say
> that it the most monstrous and most atrocious libel of which I
> have ever heard.' He also prevailed upon the judge, Lord
> Hewart, to make an exception and allow the Mountbattens
> to go into the witness box. This display of co-operation allowed
> Edwina herself to stand up and state strongly that she had never
> in her life even met the man referred to, who had been identified
> by her friends; and for Dickie to explain that the reason Edwina

had come out to Malta was that he was serving there as an officer in the Royal Navy, and that she had certainly not flown from scandal in London. For the defendants, Sir Patrick Hastings, could only make an unqualified apology – 'genuine and deep regrets'. A denial and apology would be given prominence in the newspaper. Edwina refused all damages . . . the case led to damages of another kind all round with long-lasting effects.

The *People* duly published an apology soon after, and Edwina returned to Dickie (her husband's nickname) in Malta.

In the event, it was not Hutch but Paul Robeson who took the blame for the affair. This was largely because he was the most famous black man in the world at that time. Essie Robeson said, 'It is incredible that people should be linking Paul's name with that of a famous titled Englishwoman, since she is just about the one person in England we don't know!' But she was probably trying to conceal the fact that she had not been seeing much of her husband, and had lost touch with his movements; the 'we' was loyal, wishful thinking. The untruth was echoed in Edwina's diary: 'A coloured man I've never even met!!!!' The character of her diary suggests that she was writing for posterity, and it contains a number of other attempts to rewrite history.[11]

Two years before, after his brief affair with Peggy Ashcroft Robeson was involved with another white actress, Yolande Jackson. A *Daily Herald* reporter asked Essie whether she had filed for divorce, and whether Lady Louis Mountbatten had been named as co-respondent. From America, Robeson confirmed that he was separated from his wife and had been seeing an Englishwoman. He added that she was neither Peggy Ashcroft nor Nancy Cunard, and that, if he decided to marry her, he was 'prepared to leave the US if there was any stir about it'.

While there is no direct evidence of an affair between Robeson and Edwina, the writer Mary Seton, who knew both parties, says that Robeson himself told her that he and Edwina 'went to bed once', and that she had taken the initiative in the matter. Robeson had been to some of Edwina's parties at Brook House when he had often been the only black man in the room other than Hutch. He later recalled that he had been 'made a fuss of by Mayfair'; and, at the time of the libel suit he was distressed that Edwina, friend and briefly lover, should deny that she had ever met him when

hundreds of their friends had seen them together. He believed that
the court case hinged on the colour of his skin, and was convinced
that racism in England was as pernicious and profound as in
America.

This did not deter him from returning to England in the
following year and throughout the 1930s. Early in 1933, John
Krimsky, co-producer of the film of Eugene O'Neill's play *The
Emperor Jones*, which featured Robeson, met both Mountbattens
with Robeson at the Dorchester;[12] and, soon after, Robeson was
seen in Kingston, Jamaica, with Edwina, who was on holiday with
her friend Doris Delavigne. Jamaicans recalled the scandal of their
bathing naked by moonlight after Robeson had given a concert on
board ship.

Edwina's sister Mary[13] later told Richard Hough that Edwina
admitted that she had lied in court. Long after, Edwina made the
same admission while having dinner with Catherine Courtenay
and her husband in Kandy, Ceylon. Mountbatten talked openly of
'the whitewash in the court case with Robeson. Edwina just stayed
silent, until she said, "It's over now. What else could I have done?"
At the time, Dickie had a very pretty girlfriend called Lindsay, and
they led separate lives.' Hough states that Edwina was furious at
being forced to have lunch at Buckingham Palace the day after the
court case.

> It was intended to show that there was nothing to forgive and
> that solidarity prevailed, rather than that all was forgiven. The
> Palace was not pleased that it had had to take the extreme step of
> obliging the Mountbattens to appear in court to teach Edwina a
> lesson. As for Edwina, she was outraged at the whole business, its
> covetousness, hypocrisy and censoriousness and the way she
> cravenly submitted to the royal command.

Clearly, the traditional royals were determined to reprimand
international upstarts for their unseemly behaviour. No wonder
Lord Louis quaked at the way in which his wife's amours were
threatening his chances of promotion and, worse still, putting at
risk his efforts to be accepted as royal by right, despite his
undesirable German connections. And no wonder Edwina, so
used to getting her way without let or hindrance, reacted furiously
to the royal reproof. She never forgave the King and Queen, was

increasingly critical of the monarchy, and became more and more left-wing. She also became tougher, more cynical and, if anything, more amoral.

Much later, Lord Louis was to say, 'Edwina and I spent all our lives getting in and out of other people's beds.'[14] For many highly placed people, marriage in those days was a social, financial, dynastic and sometimes political arrangement; and in the 1980s and 1990s there have been constant reminders of how deeply adultery is ingrained in the British ruling classes. Still, the case put a great strain on the Mountbattens' marriage.

Soon after, Edwina set off with her sister-in-law Nada Milford Haven to travel from the Black Sea across the deserts of Persia to the Persian Gulf. Gloria Vanderbilt, who went to say goodbye to them at Lyden Manor, heard Nada tell reporters that they were only taking the clothes 'we stand up in and one change, as well as a light tent and two sleeping bags'. Edwina and Nada went to 'Constantinople and Palestine, purchased an ancient motor car and, within three months, they covered approximately 10,000 miles, 6,000 by airplane and 4,000 by automobile, crossing both the Great Salt Desert and the Great Sand Desert.'[15]

Over half the people who knew Hutch also mentioned Edwina. This is hardly surprising as they were an inconstant constant, acting for each other as tokens of successful rebellion; intermittently for over thirty years they appeared together at parties, nightclubs and at Hutch's variety dates, with Edwina being both proprietary and demonstrably affectionate towards him. As news of the court case was largely confined to London, some of Hutch's girlfriends never heard the story; and to those who did, he shamelessly implicated Robeson. 'It wasn't me,' he said to Virginia and others, 'it was him.' He later told a friend, Bill Pilkington, that Robeson and Edwina had indeed had a affair, brief but long enough to infuriate Hutch at Edwina's needing Robeson as well as himself. When confirming the facts behind the court case, David Herbert said that Edwina gave the damages awarded her in court to charity; and that 'Hutch was very much more sophisticated than poor Paul Robeson, it was absurd to think that Edwina and Paul would have spent much time together . . . but Hutch suited her tastes very well.' Many people in London knew that Robeson had been unjustly blamed. As one aristocratic Indian remarked, 'We knew all about it at the time. It was giggle chitchat. I remember my mother, who was a great friend of Hutch in Paris and later in London, used to talk about it, but only when the servants had left the room.'

It was tacitly decided in high places that Hutch should be penalised. Because nothing much happened for a time, he probably thought he had got away scot-free, but he was eventually damaged in the area that hurt him most, his career. He was never asked to appear at a royal command performance and Val Parnell, the manager, understood that the Palace did not want him at the show. Lord Beaverbrook put Hutch on his 'white list' of people who were not to be mentioned by name in his newspapers. A junior reporter on the *Daily Express* in Glasgow recalled that after the scandal broke, any reports of variety shows in which Hutch featured omitted his name. After mention of other stars, there would be an anodyne phrase like 'the rest of the programme was made up of musical interludes'. Other transgressors were treated in a similar way. Internal memos at the BBC show that Hutch's radio broadcasts were curtailed.

All this embittered Hutch, who seems never to have accepted that his failure to toe the social line would result in censure. To think that he could publicly enjoy an adulterous relationship with a semi-royal white woman and be immune from obloquy, was deeply unrealistic. When Hutch found restrictions closing in on his career, he was humiliated and uncomprehending, and, like Robeson, felt victimised for his colour. Another area of his life had run out of control.

A perceptive friend who first met Hutch in 1937 said, 'Hutch had a fixation about prisoners. Perhaps that is why he often volunteered to entertain them. He himself behaved as though he was always unfairly under constraint. He never felt himself a free man, but he believed passionately in freedom.' In fact, Hutch's real belief was in licence to do whatever he liked without taking the consequences. Alongside that, he wanted the British aristocracy to accept him as one of Edwina's lovers, and give him the same immunity from comment and censure that the others enjoyed. Even so, a small instance shows that the court case did dent Hutch's self-confidence. Late in 1932, a singer's accompanist failed to show up at a party. Hutch proved a brilliant substitute, and the singer invited him to a party of her own in Dolphin Square. Hutch sent her a bottle of champagne, and regrets that he could not attend. Later, he explained to her that he did not want his presence to compromise her. Behind his seeming humility, this incident betrays a note of ostentatious pride in his increasing notoriety.

Although her daughters categorically deny it, the unauthorised biographers of socialites of this period consistently accept Hutch's relationship with Edwina.[16] Hutch himself occasionally boasted of the affair in the 1930s, and much more frequently in later years. When he was appearing at the Trocadero, he told a fellow musician about his 'promiscuous relationship with a well-known female member of the aristocracy'.[17] And he later described her to a friend as 'a wonderful woman and a great lay'. A BBC producer, Bobby Jay, recalled their brazen behaviour:

> I was at a grand party. Edwina interrupted Hutch playing the piano. She kissed his neck, and led him by the hand behind the closed doors of the dining room. There was a shriek and, a few minutes later, she returned, straightening her clothes. Hutch seemed elated, and, before he returned to the piano, told me that, with one thrust, he had flashed her the length of the dining-room table.

Elsa Lanchester is said to have referred to Hutch behaving in the same way at parties, 'in a constant state of deshabille'. In the 1950s, Hutch frequently spoke about Edwina in New York and India, and in the 1960s, in Hong Kong, he often recalled the affair.

On his variety tours, Edwina went with Hutch whenever she could. Sometimes, like itinerant royalty – which, in a way, she was – she hired the dressing room next to his for more privacy in more space; several artistes were amazed to recognise her backstage.[18] Fellow musicians also saw them together. A singer at the Palm Beach nightclub remembered, 'Hutch used to come into Palm Beach with Lady Mountbatten in 1939. He just *slid* in, he was so high! Lady Mountbatten used to come in late with Hutch's brother.'[19] Jack Bentley, who played at the 400 Club and with top bands led by Jack Hylton, Ambrose and Sydney Lipton, saw the couple on numerous occasions. 'Of course, Hutch had an affair with Lady Mountbatten. She wasn't at all reticent about it, and made no attempt to disguise that she went where he went. It went on all through the war, too.'

A sustaining characteristic of the affair, one common to most long-running relationships, was a shared sense of humour. Hutch and Edwina constantly played jokes on each other. One fan who often saw Hutch in the 1930s related that when they were catching the famous Blue Train from Paris to the Côte d'Azur, Edwina was frantic because Hutch had not turned up as arranged. Then, when the train left, he emerged from some hiding place on the train, and strolled past Edwina's compartment, saying, 'Anyone for coffee?' In the late 1940s, Hutch appeared on Terry-Thomas's television programme, and amazed his host by saying, without any warning, 'This one's for you, Boo Boo.' Afterwards he told Thomas that he had been addressing Edwina, who he knew was watching him.

Gifts flowed from Edwina to Hutch. In the late 1950s, Hutch showed some variety artistes in a recording studio an astonishing jewelled penis sheath made for him on Edwina's orders by Cartier.[20] She also gave him a bejewelled gold cigarette case with an 'affectionate inscription'. Hutch displayed this pointedly and often: it glinted on his mantelpiece at home, and was once handed for safekeeping to a member of the audience before a show in Calcutta. She gave him a large gold swivelling ring with her coat of arms hidden on the inside and a gold and diamond watch. Hutch also received valuables from other sources. These would not always have been love gifts. After parties, it was customary for performers to be given expensive presents instead of fees. For instance, the Prince of Wales gave Max Miller a diamond-studded Rolex watch after Miller had entertained the servants at a Windsor Christmas party in the 1930s. Friends gave each other valuable presents, too. The bandleader Harry Roy gave Hutch a gold watch in 1937 in recognition of their friendship and partnership at the Mayfair Hotel.[21]

In May 1932, the same month as the court case, the *New Yorker* commented on two of Hutch's recent record releases: 'Note to collectors of Leslie Hutchinson. He does Everything with "You Try Somebody Else" . . . The spare is "Was It the Moon or Love?", and it doesn't matter terribly.' The former song provided a timely, if ironic, comment on Hutch's affair with Edwina:

> You try somebody else
> And I'll try somebody else
> And when we do, we'll both be blue
> And be back together again.

Although they had no claim to the implied romantic idealism of the lyric, the song provides a telling leitmotif for their relationship over the years. Moreover, opposition to their liaison presumably sharpened and sustained its attraction for both of them.

Even when he and Edwina had been leading separate lives for some years, Lord Louis could become very distressed about her relationship with Hutch. Van Straten, a fashionable bandleader at both the Not and Quaglino's, noted in his diary a night in the early 1930s when Lord Louis came in to Quaglino's very drunk and sat with him. ' "I am lonely and drunk and sad", he complained. "That nigger Hutch has a prick like a tree trunk, and he's fucking my wife right now." '[22] In the hearing of one socialite, Joan Vyvyan, Mountbatten exploded, 'If I ever catch that man Hutch, I'll kill him.' In both cases, the violence of his language has the ring of truth and speaks of pent-up pain and jealousy.

It is hard to tell when Hutch's intermittent affair with Edwina finished. An autograph hunter, outside the Dorchester in 1949, recalled, 'Hutch was going out as Lord and Lady Mountbatten were coming in. She looked delighted and kissed Hutch warmly. "You remember, Hutch, don't you, darling?" Lord Mountbatten said, "Good God, I thought he was dead!" in a voice like thunder and swept into the hotel. Lady Mountbatten turned round, and went off with Hutch.' About a year later, a theatrical agent heard Edwina inviting herself into Hutch's dressing room. 'Hutch treated her very contemptuously, and was annoyed that she had come to see him.' When the cricket commentator Brian Johnson dined with him in the 1950s, Hutch frequently said he was off to see Edwina afterwards.

Moss Empires owned about eight out of ten of the variety theatres nationwide. Apart from the Palladium, the circuit included five more large and prestigious theatres in London: the Victoria Palace, the Holborn Empire, the Finsbury Park Empire and the Prince of Wales. It also owned major theatres in Birmingham, Newcastle, Glasgow, Edinburgh, Liverpool, Nottingham, Sheffield, Swansea, Sunderland, Chatham and many other cities. Stoll Theatres was a smaller circuit, but just as prestigious as Moss Empires, and sometimes more rarefied in its offerings: its leading theatre, the Coliseum in St Martin's Lane, featured excerpts from ballets and operas, and such stars as the French playwright and actor Sacha Guitry, the

actor-manager Seymour Hicks, the dancers Anton Dolin and Alicia
Markova and the Lunts, the celebrated acting couple. Stoll also ran
the Alhambra, and the Empires at Wood Green, Chiswick,
Shepherds Bush and Derby. Until the Second World War there
were more than eighty theatres within twenty miles of London,
and a 'barring clause' in contracts prevented performers from
working for more than one management within a five-mile zone.
In his heyday in the 1930s and 1940s, Hutch appeared at all the
main theatres many times, often topping the bill; variety repaid him
by making him a national star.

Variety shows were a hangover from the music hall, which, in
turn, developed from tavern entertainments. In the 1830s, these
were staged in theatres attached to pubs, thereby getting round the
laws that protected the theatrical monopoly of stage entertainments. With changes in theatrical licensing laws, the pub connection gradually diminished, although most music halls had bars
around the auditorium so that people could drink while they were
being entertained. What with further laws in 1902 banishing drink
from the auditorium, and films, recordings and radio presenting
ever-growing competition, music hall started fading and, by the
mid-1920s, it was virtually dead. By the early 1930s, though, the
competition was rekindling an interest in variety as the public
wanted to see the flesh-and-blood people behind the broadcasting
and recording successes. The promoter George Black was largely
responsible for exploiting this interest and staging 'spectaculars',
sometimes in combination with new film releases, which featured
such stars as Gracie Fields, George Formby and Hutch. Many
people first saw Hutch when he played between double features in
the cinema; some turned up specifically to see him, and left after his
performance. Variety in theatres lasted into the early 1960s, and
Hutch was a star throughout its history.

As the League is to footballers, so were the variety circuits to
show business. Beginners started in third-division theatres in
smallish towns, for instance, the Penge Empire, Dulwich, and
then graduated to larger, plusher theatres in better locations, for
example, the New Theatre, Oxford; and the chosen few, schooled
up through the grades, appeared on the number-one circuit in
cities like Birmingham, Liverpool and Glasgow, and, when they
were established as top performers, in London at the Palladium.
Thanks to his appearances in Cochran's shows and his celebrity as a

nightclub performer, Hutch started out in the second division and, within four years of arriving in England, was at the Palladium. In autumn 1932, he was featuring for the first time in week-long shows at large provincial theatres such as the Empires at Birmingham, Finsbury Park and Glasgow; the Palace, Hull; and the Shakespeare Theatre, Liverpool.

In major theatres such as the Palladium and the Coliseum ticket prices were higher, but in the provinces the most expensive seats, usually in the dress circle, were four shillings; stalls were half a crown; and space in the gallery, where people sat or stood, often leaning over the rails, cost sixpence. The audience – looking respectable, but not dressed up – watched shows lasting about two hours. They were staged twice nightly, usually at half past six and a quarter to nine, but people could go in at any time and stay as long as they liked. Usually there were five acts in the first half; an interval of fifteen minutes; then a further five acts. When there were twelve acts, they were strictly limited to ten minutes each. Lit-up numbers on either side of the proscenium arch enabled the audience to keep track of the programme, and the top performer was always the penultimate act. Bad language on stage was forbidden: a licence from the Lord Chamberlain was required for a performer to say 'bloody'.

The veteran entertainer Max Bygraves, in his book *I Wanna Tell You a Funny Story*, claimed that while some acts 'like Wilson, Keppel and Betty, Max Miller, Gracie Fields and George Formby would have 'Standing Room Only' boards outside . . . class acts . . . like Ronald Frankau, Flotsam and Jetsam, Oliver Wakefield and Hutch, didn't seem to have the same appeal.' But Hutch's chameleon-like skills were to serve him well: he adapted his material and performing style to match different regional demands. At the start of his career in variety, he relied on the expected black repertoire, and only slowly varied it with current hits, mostly sentimental numbers. Hutch abandoned many of the extravagances that made up his cabaret persona. There were no songs by Coward or Porter, whose subtle sophistication would have had little appeal. And although brow-mopping stayed in the act – partly from necessity, partly as a gambit – he never flourished his handkerchief in the old languid, playful West End style.

If his repertoire was more restrained, Hutch's piano playing was increasingly impressive. The comedian and pianist Reg Varney remembered him as:

> a great solo performer, with enormous hands . . . a great man for chords, he struck handfuls of them with obvious pleasure. Hutch mostly did an eighteen-minute turn as the star. He sang all the old evergreens, once he was well-known. He gave every word value, and could sell the story of a song. Your material must suit your age. He knew that. He was a big, handsome guy who admired the women, and did they chase him!

Working-class women were just as direct as upper-class women in their approach to sex – and to Hutch. They could not leave him alone, even when he was having an after-show drink in an all-male group; and he was invariably charming to them. While some recall that Hutch 'absolutely oozed charm, and mixed a lot with members of the band, to whom he was always considerate', other fellow performers found him less appealing. The more successful he became, the more he avoided them and stayed in his dressing room. (In the 1940s, Beryl Reid noticed that the door of his dressing room bore the sign 'Nesting'.) Ben Warriss, of the Jewel's and Warriss comic duo, recalled, 'We were often on the same bill but had only a slight association. He was toffee-nosed and objectionable, which apparently attracted the women. Leslie was always very busy with the white girls. He was good-looking and a very, very fine performer. I admired him professionally. But he was not a friend.' In fairness, part of this aloofness derived from the conventions relating to a top-of-the-bill star. George van Dusen, a variety performer who appeared at the Hackney Empire with both Hutch and Max Miller, explained:

> Hutch didn't come into the bar like the small acts, of which I was one. Top-liners had visitors in their dressing rooms every night, and had their drinks there. He went down terrific and was a big draw with the audience. Coloured ladies and white ladies used to queue up to see him after the show. As a top-of-the-bill star, I wasn't surprised he kept himself to himself.

Another performer, Len Lowe, found Hutch 'rather aloof and frightfully West End cabaret. He used to place a lady in the wings, often as not, and work her as well as the audience. If I met him, he'd say, "Hello, dear boy, how are you?" Which meant, "Make way, Hutch is here", but I thought he was elegant, not arrogant, and that was just his way.'

If anyone with talent impressed Hutch, he always had time for them and often learned from them. Just as he had admired Jimmy Durante in New York as a comic, he now appreciated the professionalism of Bud Flanagan, Stanley Holloway, Max Wall, Harold Berens, Teddy Brown, Terry-Thomas, Cyril Fletcher and others; they came from diverse backgrounds, but they shared intelligence, exuberance, originality and great timing. Hutch was helpful to his talented friends in the business, and some of them reciprocated his kindness. Some paid him the compliment of impersonating him. These included Terry-Thomas:

> Hutch was extremely helpful to me at the Hippodrome in 1938. He was a big star, and my name appeared in the minutest letters on the posters. I had a sweat before I got my laughs, because I used to go on when the audience was still cold. Hutch, one of the nicest fellows in show business, understood my nerves. From then on, I made it a point to bring his singing voice into my act.

Terry-Thomas (his stage name was a reversal of his two first names, Thomas Terry) played up his aristocratic and military background, toted a bamboo cigarette holder, and dressed with caddish lavishness, designing the fancy waistcoats in his 'vestry' himself. A charming and cultured comedian with a splendid singing voice of great range, he appeared in more than one hundred films. Despite the trademark gap between his front teeth, for a generation of Americans, he was the quintessential upper-class Englishman in films such as *Carleton-Browne of the FO* and *It's a Mad, Mad, Mad, Mad World*. He and Hutch had hunting and many other interests in common, and when Terry-Thomas was on *Desert Island Discs* in 1970, he told the host, Roy Plomley, 'If it were possible, I would have all Hutch records because I got such a kick out of his work and Hutch as a person.'

Hutch was also a close friend of Max Wall. He met the comedian in 1927 when they were in Hutch's first Cochran revue, and thereafter they often worked together. Wall was not a pianist but, with his deep resonant voice, he could imitate Hutch's singing quite well. They had an act which started with Wall going to the piano and bringing the house down with his impression of a Hutch performance. He then said:

> That, ladies and gentlemen, is *my* act! Hutch knocked it off from me after seeing me one night at the Fire Station in Birmingham! I was getting 15 shillings a night, and use of hose, when he came in looking for one of his old flames. He saw me doing the song, and pinched it. When he comes on in a minute, I want you to know that it's me playing in the wings, and he's bashing away at a rubber keyboard!

Hutch loved this send-up, and the audience roared when he walked on the stage behind Wall as he was doing the routine. The idea inspired Wall's comic character Professor Walloffski, a concert pianist who endlessly circles his instrument, falling onto and into it, and never coming to terms with the keyboard.[23]

Another Hutch impersonator was Leslie Sarony of the Two Leslies, a diminutive Cockney comic whose most famous song was 'Wheezy Anna'. His Hutch act comprised a version of 'I'm Dreaming of a White Christmas' which so affronted one Hutch fan that she wrote a letter of complaint to Sarony. Sarony replied that Hutch was a good friend who endorsed his efforts.

Teddy Brown was also a friend of Hutch, and they both had the same agent, Charles Tucker. Born Abraham Himmebrand in America in 1900, he was an exact contemporary. He learned to play timpani, and for four years was a member of the New York Philharmonic Symphony Orchestra. In 1919 he switched from classical to dance music, and played the drums in Joseph C. Smith's band, also learning the xylophone. On the strength of being discovered by the Prince of Wales, whose passion was drumming, Brown came to London in 1926, the same year as Hutch. He formed his own band and played at the Café de Paris, and also performed at the Kit-Cat Club and the Silver Slipper. After 1930, his career still running parallel with Hutch's, he appeared in variety as a solo act using xylophone and drums. A vast man of over 20 stone, he used to divert audiences by running backwards and forwards along his xylophone. He had a special door made for his Rolls-Royce so he could get into it, and was a popular performer

on stage, screen and radio. He appeared in the royal variety
performance at the Palladium in 1931; and – a great honour for
a foreigner – was crowned King Rat in 1946. (Like Variety, the
Grand Order of the Water Rats is a charitable organisation
comprising leading show-business performers. Each year, they
elect a 'King'). He died in the same year in Birmingham, while
on tour.

Brown used to meet Hutch and other performers at Olivelli's in
Store Street, or Jones's Corner House on the corner of Leicester
Square (now a Whitbread pub), after the variety shows, between
eleven and two in the morning. They sometimes moved on to
Brown's flat in Ridgmount Gardens, just east of Tottenham Court
Road, where Brown's cook often cooked doughnuts, great fa-
vourites of Hutch, until six in the morning.

Hutch also formed a friendship with Cyril Fletcher when they
were in a road show, *Boys of the BBC*, with two other comics,
Billy Bennett and Oliver Wakefield. This went on tour for some
ten weeks playing to capacity at Moss Empires' number-one
halls. Hutch and Fletcher always opted to stay at the top hotels,
and usually met for a midday drink in the bar. Fletcher found
him:

> a highly educated man and a great musician. His act was polished
> and sophisticated, and was as right for the grandest cabaret as it
> was for the halls . . . To see him take a call was an education in
> itself. At our morning sessions . . . I learned a lot of the world,
> and how to cope with show business from him. He was in every
> way a gentleman. His manners were impeccable. He was great
> company. Some time after . . . in Cardiff, when Hutch was
> topping the bill at the New Theatre . . . passing the stage door, I
> popped in and . . . was shown in to his dressing-room at once.
> Hutch had just finished his act . . . and stood, stark naked, being
> wiped down by a blonde lady. At once, he introduced us, 'Do
> you know the Hon Sheila . . . ?' But he was fond of his missus.
> He told me so.

Another young protégé to whom Hutch was kind – although
possibly with ulterior motives – was Judy Shirley who sang with
the bandleader Maurice Winnick at the Piccadilly Hotel, London,
dispensing what their publicity material described as 'the sweetest

music this side of heaven'. Some time in the 1930s, when Judy was just starting with Winnick, Hutch finished his act and said,

'You're not nervous, are you?'
'Not a bit. Can't you hear my knees knocking?'
'You're too beautiful. Get on there.'
It was very nice of him to encourage me. Some of the other musicians were so jealous, they were ready to tear him apart. He had a chauffeur and sometimes gave me a lift. The band boys would look down their noses and make nasty remarks. His best advice to me was, 'Keep it quiet. Gently make them listen. Make them feel that they might miss something.' I never forgot it. Whenever he heard me in the future, he would send me notes saying, 'Just shake your knees.'

Hutch's exhortations about stage fright came from the heart: he often suffered it himself, and said it accounted for his heavy sweating. George Elrick – a drummer, crooner and, later, presenter of *Housewives' Choice*, a long-running record-request radio programme – remembered being taken on as a drummer at the Malmaison in Piccadilly, and finding the pianist was none other than Hutch.

He had asked for me specifically, so we had a few rehearsals and worked out some duets where I sang the harmonies and added some vibraphone touches. It was a great experience, not least because up to then I hadn't bothered much with girls, being too busy working, but Hutch was a master at pulling them – a different one almost every night. I think he could afford them, but I was afraid I couldn't . . .[24]

Hutch was also capable of placing a fellow female star on a pedestal. When sharing a bill with Evelyn 'Boo' Laye at the Chelsea Palace, he sent her a daily present of scent or flowers. This gallantly reverential treatment may have come about because Hutch first met her as an established actress and variety star at Cochran's house. She continued to sing his praises for the rest of her long life.
The singer Doris Hare was also an enthusiast. 'Everyone was mad about him, a marvellous bloke. We often shared variety bills. My sister Winnie played the piano and accompanied me – she

wasn't very good, in fact, she was bloody awful. Hutch used to watch her from the wings, and she used to tremble.'

Hutch befriended another female star, José Collins, when they were both on the same bill at the London Coliseum. José, who made her name in *The Maid of the Mountains* in 1917, was so shocked when she found she was billed second to Hutch that she refused to go on stage and sing. The theatre manager, Phil Hyams, explained to the audience why Miss Collins had left the theatre, and declared, 'The money thrown away over this engagement would be enough to feed a dozen families for a week.' José stayed in her Park Lane flat, sturdily unrepentant: 'I consider my attitude completely justified. In the seventeen years I have been a star, I have always been top of the bill.' Hutch said he was 'amazed'; two court actions followed; and the business never forgave José for infringing the unwritten law that an artist, regardless of any disagreement with the management, never lets down the public.

Despite this upset, Hutch took to her. This was hardly surprising as she was established, well connected – her husband was Lord Robert Innes-Ker – and no threat to him. They were friends for some years, and Hutch did what he could to help her to regain her former success. His efforts were doomed, as, by the mid-1930s, José was, according to one observer, 'well and truly passé: short, rather plump, a rather heavy drinker and really not at all attractive . . . she was finished.'

Hutch always dressed to the nines, and looked most conspicuous on tour in the provinces where his Mayfair trappings were very rare. Off stage he wore a vicuña overcoat, brown suit, a fawn shirt and burnished brogues or, sometimes, half-boots of reversed calf from Tuczon of Clifford Street. He wore a massive gold ring, a black or grey homburg, and always carried a cane. The daughter of a landlady described him as looking like 'a Threadneedle Street banker'. When in Liverpool or Birkenhead, he wore a tweed suit of singing bottle-green to Aintree racecourse, and also rode, immaculate again, at Sefton Park. His expensive suits of mohair, a material rarely worn by men at that time, glowed resplendently on stage; and to avoid creasing them, he used to stand in the wings before going on.

When on tour, Hutch used to stay in bed all morning, then have drinks and lunch with friends. He always practised the piano some time during the day, and often went to private drinking clubs in the afternoon. He sometimes spent the day in his room with a girlfriend or went racing or played golf. Whenever he could, he went riding. Hutch also accepted invitations from select members of his audience to visit them in their homes and while away the time before his next performance.[25] The comedian Jimmy James said that he always arrived at the venue just in time to do his first turn, then went to his hotel for dinner, and returned for the second spot. Once when he was late, James went on instead, and Hutch was very contrite and grateful.

Despite all his diversions, Hutch got bored on tour sometimes, and if there was nothing else to do, he drank too much and behaved badly. One woman, whose parents owned a large hotel near the Hull Palace, had bad memories:

> Hutch came to Hull two or three times a year in the early 1930s. He always needed sobering up. He used to chat up my mum. He was an arrogant pig, a snide devil and a rude man. He used to strut about . . . and his wallet was always left in his dressing room, and he ran up big bills all week. After his last performance, my dad and other creditors used to wait at the stage door to get their money. Nine times out of ten, he'd get away through another exit. Then everyone would hurtle to the midnight train at Paragon station, Hull, to catch him . . . A loveable rogue he may have seemed to some, but he had a woman in every port. He hurt people.

Later, in the mid-1930s, Hutch and a girlfriend arrived in a chauffeur-driven Daimler to play a round at Northenden Golf Club in Cheshire. Before he left, he bought drinks all round at the clubhouse. He then put a book on a van parked close by. The driver told him to remove it; Hutch said he would not be a moment, and would not harm the van, but the driver protested vehemently. Hutch, who was tipsy and throwing his weight about to impress the girl and other spectators, said, 'See that Daimler over there. Go and scratch your name across it; it doesn't matter to me.' As so often, Hutch was assuming racism on the part of the driver, and hitting back in as condescending a way as possible.

Leslie Berens, brother of the comic Harold Berens, ran a cinema in Boscombe and, whenever Hutch visited Bournemouth on tour, used to ride with him in the New Forest, 'resplendent in his kit'.

He observed that Hutch could be choosy: 'There was a cow owned the swanky hotel. She was very hoity-toity, but Hutch wouldn't go to bed with her. He could be an aloof sod when he wanted. And musicians who played there then, recall with amusement that Hutch moved out to the Imperial Hotel, Lansdowne, to escape her clutches.' Hutch used to make 'an entrance at parties, and then stand by himself at the back of the room. I used to tell him, "You're spoilt, you're a conceited bastard", but he just laughed and loved it.'

Another of Hutch's riding companions, Arthur Prothero, who was Harry Roy's lawyer, first met him when Hutch was performing in a nightclub in Regent Street, the Versailles. One day, when riding at Windsor, they were joined by an American singing star, a pretty young woman – possibly Nina Mae McKinney, a veteran of *Blackbirds* – who was very upset that Hutch had not met her as promised; and Hutch was displeased at her pursuing him.[26]

> She had a white maid with her, and left in a black Rolls for London. Hutch galloped on ahead, and I was thrown and my horse bolted. Hutch just abandoned me, leaving me floundering in a ditch . . . a sort of equine bloodwagon was dispatched to send me home. I was angry with him.
>
> Another time, we were staying at the Metropole in Brighton and galloping on the Downs. Someone was acting the fool and whacked Hutch's horse, which bolted. Hutch was obsessed by the possibility of damage to his hands.
>
> I was envious of the way women fell for him. He was a novelty, the only black man I had ever met. I shared a bathroom with him once and noticed immediately that he was massively endowed. He used to boast that he was a marvellous lover.

Once at Bourne End, then a fashionable weekend retreat in Buckinghamshire, a young man called Tony Wheeler arrived with his girlfriend Lorna. Hutch was also one of the guests. After he had sung 'My Secret Love', he disappeared with Lorna. Wheeler found them in bed, got out a gun and threatened to shoot Hutch. 'Hutch jumped out of bed, half-dressed, and ran down the stairs shouting, "Good God, have you gone mad?" We laughed about it later. I suppose I was about twenty-three and he was ten years older. He was so marvellous, women were bound to behave that way with him.'

Elizabeth Welch, the American singer, knew Hutch well throughout his career, but not 'as a visiting friend'. She paid tribute to his good looks and smart clothes; confirmed the Edwina Mountbatten rumour was true; and had qualifications about some of his mannerisms: 'that hanky thing irritated me'. She continued:

> His wife Ella was very seclusive. His brother Ivan wasn't very friendly with Hutch, who didn't like having him around. Ivan was not a socialite and not a smartie, he just ran around with ordinary musicians. Hutch was still a lot of fun later on in life, never depressed. His music seems corny and old-fashioned now, because he added sex to it. He was never a favourite of mine, though I respected him as a performer. He looked at the ladies while he was singing, it was not my kind of wooing. I remember him singing, 'I'm a Gigolo'. He was.

While no one doubted Hutch's professionalism and perfectionism, people were wholly divided about his character. Terry-Thomas, Cyril Fletcher and many others spoke of his kindness, generosity, modesty and fine manners; others referred to his cruelty, meanness, arrogance and rudeness. On attaining national celebrity, Hutch became increasingly complex and contradictory. He could be ebullient, sociable and extrovert and, minutes later, reclusive, moody and selfish. But he was consistent in that he tended to mistreat anyone who failed to flatter or serve him; and, when crossed, he showed his overweening self-absorption.

Chapter Seven

Touring and Climbing
1931–1938

Love not to talk, love not to boast
Grief comes to him who brags the most

Traditional Grenadian children's rhyme

B y the mid–1930s, Hutch was a superstar. He continued to be driven in a Rolls–Royce or Daimler by a chauffeur, and was earning some £500 a week in variety.[1] He was mobbed by crowds, especially in the North. Police horses kept back the throng, and chanting women used to bombard hotels and theatres with thousands of gifts, especially lawn handkerchiefs. During his act, men used to leave for the bar, because they were bored or jealous of seeing their women going crazy for him. Some threw their knickers on the stage; many screamed and wept, or fainted and had to be carried out.

Once, Hutch was on tour in Ireland with his agent Charles Tucker, an amiable American hustler who had started out in variety as 'Strolling Vagabond and Violin' before marrying a minor English singing star, Violet Essex, and becoming both an agent and a producer of premier-league tours largely featuring his own stable of stars. Hutch and Tucker were chatting and drinking in their suite when a crowd gathered outside their hotel and began shouting for Hutch, who pretended not to hear them. When Tucker at last persuaded him to acknowledge his fans, Hutch stepped out from his suite onto a first-floor balcony and looked down on the tumultuous surge of women. He gave a regal wave, plucked the carnation from his buttonhole and skimmed it down into the crowd. The impetus of this gesture threw him off balance, and he fell down into the street below and broke his arm. The crowd howled with horror, and Hutch drawled to Tucker, 'The show *won't* go on. And I *shan't* take your advice again, dear boy.'

Racist behaviour was rare among musicians in Britain, but variety performers, like their audiences, were quite unused to blacks, especially on stage, there being only Hutch, Layton and Johnstone, and G. H. Carlyle who sang Jamaican songs. Many white performers thought it humorous to call the blacks 'spades' or 'schwartzers'; and when Scott Sanders, a Scots comic, was due on stage after Hutch's act, his son would bawl out, 'Hurry up, Dad, the golliwog's on!' There is a story about a comic coming off stage to desultory applause from a tiny audience on a wet Monday night, and meeting Hutch in the wings. 'How are they?' asks Hutch, elegant in white tie and tails. 'Not worth blacking up for, 'Utch lad,' comes the answer. Billy Bennett is said to have coined this phrase, which is still used in the business to describe a poor audience, but it has also been attributed to Jimmy James, Frank Preston and others. It may well be apocryphal, as it is unlikely Hutch would have been confronted by a near-empty house at this time.

Jim Casey remembered visiting his father, the comedian Jimmy James, who had burst an ulcer and was coming round from an anaesthetic. 'I'm fine,' said James. 'He's doing a good job, whoever this fellow is,' glancing at the drip-and-blood canister. 'I hope to God it's not Hutch.'

Hutch joined in the jokes about being black, and certainly appreciated the 'blacking up' story, but he often misjudged people's sensitivities, usually when he was the only black person present. To amuse friends in Scotland, he once wore a Black Watch tartan until a girlfriend told him to stop embarrassing his host.

In 1933, Hutch was making some of his finest records. In October, the music critic Robert Tredinnick wrote, 'That much waited-for song from Cole Porter's *The Gay Divorce* which opened in Birmingham on Monday night, is sung very well indeed by

Leslie Hutchinson. It is the sort of song he puts over with genuine artistry . . . Hutch at his best.'[2] Tredinnick was right. 'Night and Day' is arguably Hutch's best recording. Its fervour and yearning are still moving, and he somehow reconciles the urgent rhythm with an easy, unforced style in a way unique to himself, making 'Night and Day' an intimate love song, intense and uncontrived. Another critic wrote, 'The first few bars of 'Night and Day' would be impossible to transcribe. By breaking up the 'accepted' metronome rhythm he creates a tension which, when resolved into 'Night and Day, you are the one . . .' produces a quite magical effect.'[3] One of Hutch's lovers said the record was Hutch's own favourite of all his output. At the same time, Hutch recorded 'Body and Soul', a lovely song by Johnny Green with a haunting minor-key verse and chorus with beautiful modulation in the middle eight. Hutch sings it superbly as a personal statement, while exploring all its poetry. Other successes of 1933 include 'Dusty Shoes', a sequel to Bing Crosby's Depression classic 'Brother, Can You Spare a Dime?', also an addition to Hutch's growing portfolio of Depression songs; the previous year, he had recorded two ironically escapist numbers by Brown and Henderson, 'The Best Things in Life Are Free' and 'Life Is Just a Bowl of Cherries'. In a March 1935 *Radio Times* feature, 'Famous artists reveal their preferences', Hutch said pompously:

> I always try to 'live' a song, to interpret it according to my own individual reading of the composer's intentions – with the result that composers have sometimes told me that 'You have made my song sound a better song than I thought it was'. As you know, I also have the inestimable advantage of being my own accompanist. I have always maintained that it is impossible to get the best out of a song unless due attention is paid to the piano accompaniment, an integral part of the song, and by accompanying myself I am able still further to singularise my interpretation of a song. Thus the songs I most enjoy singing are those that give the fullest play to my own interpretative sense . . . [for example] 'Smoke gets in your eyes', and 'Mrs Lowsborough-Goodby', with Cole Porter's excellent lyrics.

With notable exceptions such as 'These Foolish Things', most of Hutch's hits in the 1930s were American. Oddly, although London had 'a heaven full of stars', it had no songwriters of its own apart from Noël Coward and, to a lesser extent, Vivian Ellis and Harry Parr-Davies, who both wrote a number of West End musicals. If British composers had produced scores for specific stars in the way that American composers wrote for the likes of Ethel Merman and Clifton Webb, musical theatre would have been better able to compete with such rival modern attractions as the talkies and the motorcar. This was demonstrated in 1935 when Ivor Novello identified the gap in the market and started writing songs again. Novello, a Welshman whose real name was David Ivor Davies, had scored a spectacular success in 1915 with his song 'Keep the Home Fires Burning', but during the 1920s and early 1930s he devoted himself to acting on stage and screen and writing straight plays. Between 1935 and 1939, he wrote and composed four romantic musicals of great middle-brow appeal: *Glamorous Night*, *Careless Rapture*, *Crest of the Wave* and *The Dancing Years*, all staged at Drury Lane. The first of these had an ending that made Queen Mary cry and when George V complained of this to Novello, it was changed; the last of the four, revived in 1942, became a permanent feature of the wartime theatre scene. Novello appeared in nearly all his own shows, and by the time of his death in 1951, when he was appearing in *King's Rhapsody*, he was known as 'the last of the great profiles'. Hutch greatly admired him, and was briefly his lover. In 1959, he chose 'Glamorous Night' on *Desert Island Discs* 'for its sheer beauty of melody and because of the admiration I had for the composer'.

Hutch's unique success came from his ability, first recognised by Cole Porter, to sing a popular song with emphasis on the words, as though he meant every one of them. He never makes poor rhymes rhyme; nor does he force equal syllabic stresses onto words to iron out an ill-written line, any more than he upsets the lyric by letting the tempo swamp the sense. Instead, he sings lightly and confidently and tells an extremely tuneful story. After listening to a number of his records, it is easy to hear which songs Hutch enjoys and which he finds hard work. Those he loved, such as 'Night and Day', live on. Hutch was always bound to succeed in a sector of natural inferiors, because he was so intelligent, sophisticated and accomplished. It is tragic that, arrogant though he was, he never recognised this. Bill Pilkington felt that if he had had an agent with more vision and enterprise,

Hutch might have stretched his talents to the full, giving solo concerts on the international circuit.

As well as solo recordings, Hutch also recorded five songs with Harry Roy's band, of which two, 'I've Got to Sing a Torch Song' and another Johnny Green number, 'I Cover the Waterfront', were pensive, charming and successful. *Wireless Magazine* for October 1933 found it:

> hardly feasible that Hutch, a quiet, one might say, confidential, singer, and Harry Roy's Band, a breezy affair, would make an ideal recording combination. Strange things do happen, and here we have an ideal light vocal record. Both tunes are quite popular hits. Those of you who run gramophone dances in the winter, should make a note of the number – the record is admirably suited for sitting-out periods.

At the time of the recordings, Harry Roy and Hutch were appearing together at the Mayfair Hotel, and this collaboration led to a close friendship; Roy claimed they were also occasional lovers. Nat Temple, a clarinettist and later a bandleader himself, thought that the records stemmed from the on- and off-stage relationships between the two men; and also from encouragement by Oscar Preuss, recently appointed manager of Parlophone. Temple remembered that Hutch, unlike other 'coloured artistes', was often invited to sit with guests after performances. Davy Kaye – who, with Ivor Moreton, formed a frenetic two-piano turn billed as the Tiger-Ragamuffins[4] – said that Hutch was 'full of humour and very hail-fellow-well-met. He used to enjoy himself on the piano, and was a fine player and an excellent musician.' In March 1934, his recording company put excerpts of Hutch titles on one of their 'Parlophone Presents' discs; these were showcase samplers for their best-selling artists. Two piano solos, 'It's Only a Paper Moon' and 'Everything I Have Is Yours', came out in the same month, together with 'This Little Piggie Went to Market', a hymn to the pleasures of parenthood, and 'I'll Follow My Secret Heart', Noël Coward's covert announcement of his homosexuality.

Hutch's musical accomplishments did not include the gift of composition, yet he always wanted to be seen as a songwriter. So much so that, in March 1933, he declared that he was inspired by the warmth of his reception in Coventry to write a song, 'Blue

River Roll On'. It caught on, and he used it in his Trocabaret act and made a record of it. In its review the *Gramophone* accused him of partial plagiarism: 'At least, one third of it is his, the other two-thirds being the brain-child of the Cole Brothers' fellow performers.' As Hutch had attended the funeral of one of the brothers, Tommy, in March, it seems graceless of him to take sole credit for the song. However, despite the review, he repeated his false claim in an interview a month later.[5] When his fictions burnished his image and made wishes seem reality, Hutch often lied. As Leslie Berens put it, 'He could spin it.'

Hutch's inability to write songs himself was further rubbed in when, in 1937, Ralph Boosey approached Norman Hackforth and asked him to write a signature tune for Hutch. Hackforth turned out a lilting, cheerful song, 'Singing for You'; and on Norman's copy of the record, Hutch wrote a few words to confirm that it was now his official signature tune. However, 'Singing for You' never caught on because variety theatres continued to herald Hutch's entry by playing 'Begin the Beguine', the Cole Porter tune which combines a flamenco effect with the beguine rhythm. As audiences assumed this was Hutch's signature tune, it became just that. To acknowledge his association with the song, Hutch rerecorded 'Begin the Beguine' in the 1950s.

Hutch's choice of material hinged on his relations with music publishers and record companies. If they were caught bribing recording artistes to sing their songs, publishers were banned for two years; but then as now, 'bribe' was an imprecise word, and many vocalists, including Hutch, formed cheerfully expedient links with Teddy Holmes and Jimmy Henny at Chappell; with Ralph Boosey of Boosey and Hawkes; with Lawrence Wright, a composer as well as a publisher; and with Ted Morgan and other song pluggers. He had less benign relations with record companies, because he was always trying to renegotiate contracts by brandishing offers from their rivals. Once a Parlophone employee, A. Kraut, left to join Decca as recording manager, and tempted Hutch to come with him. Hutch encouraged him long enough to extract a draft contract from Decca, which he promptly sent to Oscar Preuss at Parlophone. Oscar Preuss was displeased, but paid out the extra £250 necessary to retain Hutch. Hutch was to perpetrate other similar manipulations in the future, leaving Preuss increasingly disaffected.

At this time, the press described Hutch as a 'hotcha' or 'hotcha-machacha' pianist, meaning he was something of a character who played 'hot' piano. Harry Roy was often billed as 'Your little Hotchamachacha' or 'His mother's little Hotchamachacha'. Not content with pigeonholing him simply as a singer and pianist, other reports describe Hutch as an 'actor-vocalist', 'an entertainer at the piano' and 'a musical raconteur'. Despite Hutch now being a pillar of British variety, writers in the press continued to describe Hutch as 'a darkie singer', 'a pleasing coloured singer', 'a gentleman of colour' or 'a negro singer'; and although their comments were usually lauda-tory, there was an underlying hint that musical prowess came easier to blacks. A typical review reads, 'He is a pianist of the first water, and his voice has a deep rich quality peculiar to his race.'[6] 'The soul of music and romanticism seems inherent in every North-American negro,' another reviewer states,

> but in none does it shine more effulgently than in that greatest of living basses, Paul Robeson, and in that greatest of swing singers, the incomparable Hutch. Nor is Hutch one of the many crooning coons; he is a superb singer and a truly great artist in song. He has a pure tenor of a range and richness that almost any opera singer in the world might envy. It is not his physical appeal, but his amazing spiritual gift of making romantically real and dramatically poetic even the most commonplace of lyrics that elevates Hutch above all would-be rivals.[7]

For both stars, the 'spirituality' was a way of distancing themselves from humiliation and, possibly unconsciously, of ingratiating themselves with white audiences. To avoid implicitly mocking their material, they had to be convincingly sincere; and as part of this charade, Hutch assumed a modest, disarmingly hesitant air. And, contrary to the writer's assertion, the popularity of both men depended much on their physical appeal.

In the early 1930s, Hutch featured only rarely on radio. He topped a *Vaudeville Saturday Night Show* in October 1931, and advance publicity promoted him as 'the brilliant Negro pianist, who, for several seasons, has delighted night-club audiences at the Café de Paris'. In technical terms, radio – in those days called the wireless – was still very primitive, all programmes were live rather than recorded, and when Hutch appeared on a music-hall broadcast in 1932, the press excoriated its presentation. 'Almost every artist had his or her performance marred by some defect, either personal or mechanical . . . Leslie Hutchinson was almost inaudible since the microphone picked up the piano, and quite neglected Hutch's not very powerful voice. An unnecessary fault this . . . [only] Miss Gracie Fields had proper control of her exquisitely-trained voice.'[8] There were rumours that Hutch also used a microphone on stage, secreted in his carnation; this seems imaginative, considering the size of microphones at this time. In fact his voice carried well in theatres, and audiences were anyway spellbound in silence when he started to sing. Professionals initially dismissed microphones as 'gobsticks' or 'crooner's crutches', but later in the decade, microphones were widely accepted, and Hutch used one quite often.

Hutch could also be seen on the silver screen. In September 1932, a Pathétone news film showed him at the Malmaison. Unlike cabaret today, the performance furnished a backdrop to chat, laughter, clinking glasses and bustling waiters. Hutch sings 'What Makes You So Adorable?', a charming number with an elaborate piano interval. He has no sheet music, and never looks down at his hands. He often smiles round his audience, and a few couples exchange glances and reach lovingly towards each other. As the song goes on, the noise dies down, and, at the end, the applause is terrific.

Two months later, Hutch cropped up as a guest artist in *Say It With Music*, the first talkie to feature Jack Payne, leader of the BBC Dance Orchestra. The film, named after Payne's signature tune, was 'a vehicle for Mr Payne's talent. Mr Payne sings, plays, conducts and stars. His film is a song of the air made visible.' Along with Hutch, it features Anona Winn, Billy Bennett, Albert Whelan and Flotsam and Jetsam. Hutch sings 'Love Is the Sweetest Thing', but the film's main attraction was its setting, the inside of a BBC studio.

Also in November 1932, the Prince of Wales made a brief speech to mark the tenth anniversary of the BBC, and attended in the studio an all-star variety concert. In effect, it was a minor-key royal command performance featuring Jeanne de Casalis, Jack and Claude Hulbert, Cicely Courtneidge, Florence Desmond, Clapham and Dwyer – and Hutch, because the Prince of Wales evidently overrode the Palace ban.

On 11 July 1935, a British feature film, *Cock o' the North*, opened at the Prince Edward Theatre in London. Its all-star cast included Naughton and Gold, a duo from the Crazy Gang; Mrs Simone Rogers, the original 'Mademoiselle from Armentières'; and, appearing in his first full-length talkie, Hutch. The London Midland and Scottish Railway Company granted special facilities to the producers so that the film could chart the involvement of the engine driver, his workmates and their families. Hutch sang 'To Tired Eyes' and 'Wake' in sequences that reappeared in the 1943 film *Down Memory Lane*.

Hutch often attended cricket matches at Lord's and the Oval with Gordon Crier, a BBC producer; Roy Plomley, an actor and writer, who originated *Desert Island Discs*; and two BBC commentators, Brian Johnson and John Snagge. The five men became great friends, and the other four went on to become founder members of the Lord's Taverners in 1950 a drinking club for cricketers and their supporters. Sometimes Crier would come home and say, referring to Hutch, 'I had an hour at the cricket with Ginge today', 'ginge' being short for 'ginger beer' and Cockney rhyming slang for 'queer' or, possibly, a substitute for 'dinge', a slang word for 'black'. Crier used to entertain Hutch at home, and both Hutch and Edmundo Ros, a drummer from Trinidad who had a successful Latin-American-style band after the war, would help cook for Crier's parties. Gordon and his wife, who had performed in pantomimes, saw Hutch perform at the Not and the Café de Paris, where they met Joan, whom they thought gorgeous.

Like many show-business people, Hutch was a devotee of boxing and was very knowledgeable about the sport, not least because many of his fellow stars had started out as prize fighters. Before he came to England the singer, Al Bowly had been a prominent amateur boxer in South Africa; Bud Flanagan had tried his hand at 'mitt-slinging'; Jimmy Durante, who came to England in the 1930s to star in his first British talkie with Richard Tauber, was originally a boxer; and Errol Flynn, the Australian star of the sensational pirate film *Captain Blood*, had represented Britain in the 1928 Olympic boxing team.

Hutch also continued to spend much time and money on racing; as off-course betting was then illegal, he used bookie's runners but was never caught at it. In 1937 he told the press that he owned several racehorses, but research suggests that part-ownership of a steeplechaser was the closest he ever got to having a string racing under his colours. He continued to hunt and ride; and he greatly upset his new girlfriend, Virginia, a young dancer, when he abruptly left her to accept an invitation from Lady Ursula Filmer-Sankey, the daughter of the Duke of Westminster, to hunt and ride with her. Lady Ursula was a generous friend to many people in the business; and she was described by Douglas Byng in his autobiography as 'the kindest and most unselfish friend I have ever had . . . she has that ethereal beauty which reminds me of a painting by Botticelli'.

The Prince of Wales often commanded Hutch to perform for him. As well as delighting in his company and artistry, he derived added pleasure from irritating his elders – the choice of Hutch as companion was nothing less than outright rebellion, and both men must have been amused when, after long evenings of roistering, they met under the constraints of a formal occasion. On 12 March 1935, Hutch was one of many who performed at the Portuguese embassy for the Prince and seventeen ambassadors. Hutch played on a grand piano on a dais, just in front of the seats of honour, which were occupied by the Prince and a slim dark lady called, the performers were told, Mrs Simpson. Significantly, none of the extensive press reports mention Wallis Simpson's presence. Instead they focus on the jewellery and frocks of other guests and the 'three white ostrich feathers which decorated the dinner table . . . It was the best, grandest and most amusing party we have had in diplomatic circles for some time.'[9] Mrs Simpson shared the Prince's admiration of Hutch, and subsequently the couple would spend many happy hours listening to him.

That year Hutch was at the apogee of his career. When George V gave one of his broadcasts to the Empire, the BBC planned to fly Hutch from Bournemouth, where he was on tour, to London so that he could represent the West Indies on the programme. However, as the *Bournemouth Daily Echo* (10 May 1935) reported, 'At the last moment, it was found that the plane could not land in the dark. So he actually came by road'; adding the wry comment that 'it would not have been quite the same in 1910: then there would have been no BBC, so Hutch would not have needed to dash to London'. The King addressed his huge audience as 'my children' and, just by being royalty, elicited great love and gratitude throughout the British Empire. Typical of numerous encomiums in the press was this comment: 'What a marvellous thing is this broadcasting! Just think of it – for the second time within four days you will hear the voice of the King in your homes.'[10]

When the *Sunday Express* stated that the ideal variety programme would include 'Will Hay and his scholars, Elsie and Doris Waters, Jack Hylton, Leslie Hutchinson, Beatrice Lillie, John Tilley and Douglas Byng',[11] this too showed that Hutch had well and truly arrived as a variety artist.

Hutch was also flattered by being selected as the subject for an experiment in live recording. In March 1935, some apparatus on stage at a Leicester theatre recorded Hutch in action, and the audience heard the recording played back immediately afterwards. The impression was then used to make records for the open market. The novelty was deemed a success: 'Believe it or not,' said the *Leicester Mercury*, 'it is amusing and clever.'

'Two-Ton' Tessie O'Shea, an immense Irish comedienne who for many years embodied the spirit of the Golden Mile at Blackpool, remembered a bizarre sequence of late evenings she spent with Hutch in 1935.

> A friend of Hutch's owned a supper club just off Regent Street which finished by about 1.30 a.m. From wherever we'd been working or spending the evening, Hutch, Anton Dolin and I met, on Wednesdays mostly, at that time, at least twice a month for a whole year. Hutch would play classical piano, like Tchaikovsky, and I would dance with Anton Dolin for a couple of hours . . . I had always wanted to be a ballet dancer.

Two-Ton Tess, whose sobriquet was well merited, seems an unlikely ballerina, but her poignant wish was fulfilled in an empty club. Dolin, who knew Hutch from Marc Anthony's gay salons and similar places, toured England with Alicia Markova in the late 1930s. Accompanied by their own symphony orchestra, they presented highlights from famous ballets. They also starred successfully in variety.

In this splendid year, Hutch recorded 'Hands Across the Table', which, wrote a critic, 'is guaranteed to make sentimental young people feel more sentimental than ever'.[12] That said, there is nothing glutinous or obvious about Hutch's performance; for all the effusiveness of the genre, he sings and plays purely and directly. The same is true of two more 1935 hits, 'Blue Moon' and 'I Only Have Eyes for You', the live performances of which prompted the *Manchester Guardian* critic to write, 'Hutch sang his songs so skilfully that we believed that everyone in the theatre must have a heart.' Later in the year, he recorded two mellow successes, 'East of the Sun' and 'My Heart Is Haunted'. Unrecorded, possibly because it was too risqué, was 'I'd Love to Be a Girl, But I Really Can't Decide', a number which hugely diverted his cabaret and variety audiences.

Hutch may have learned a lot from the most famous of his music-publisher friends, Lawrence Wright. The music-hall artiste George Robey described Wright as 'Britain's Irving Berlin' with some justification: under a variety of pseudonyms, Wright had written numerous hits, including 'Shepherd of the Hills' and 'Red Sails in the Sunset'. He was known as 'the Daddy of the Alley', the 'alley' being 'Tin Pan Alley'; in fact, Denmark Street, which was rife with the offices of music publishers, off the Charing Cross Road in London. In March, Hutch was one of the many 'leading lights of the profession in the throng'[13] present at a pageant and ball held at the Royal Opera House, Covent Garden, to mark the launch of Wright's song 'An Invitation to Dance' and his twenty-fifth year as a music publisher. Wright was a sharp, manipulative tyrant. If a star refused admission to his dressing room, Wright would rap on the door and throw in his chequebook. The ruse always worked. Fat and drink-sodden, he often got his employees to spy on each other, and no woman was safe from his advances. In the 1930s, he gave Hutch a cigarette case inscribed 'To Hutch, Love is like a cigarette, From Laurie'.[14]

On 20 January 1936, King George V died at Sandringham. There was a BBC radio silence, save for the ticking of the clock in the background, and every quarter of an hour the announcer told the nation in hushed, sepulchral tones, 'The King's life is moving peacefully to a close.' In some ways, Hutch's heyday was also coming to an end. The King's death confronted Hutch's royal patron, the Prince of Wales, with an appalling dilemma: whether to become king and sacrifice the love of his life or go into exile with her. Further, it was increasingly clear that war was inevitable; a war that was bound to do away with the socio-economic conditions within which Hutch had prospered so mightily.

Night after night, the Prince of Wales and Wallis Simpson sat over dinner in the downstairs room at Quaglino's, with Hutch's soft songs providing a mellow bourdon to their tense discussions. They danced and nearly always stayed late, and the world speculated on what would happen next. These were the couple's last few months of relative happiness, before they linked their fortunes and committed themselves to lifelong exile. In the 1950s they sometimes returned to Quaglino's to hear Hutch again; these visits must have evoked feelings of bittersweet nostalgia.

Once Edward VIII had abdicated, Hutch no longer had a friend at court. So when the BBC Television Booking Department suggested to Cecil Madden, head of light entertainment, that Hutch might be invited to appear 'during a Marconi EMI week, his previous appearances being on the Baird system', Madden sent a brisk note in pencil: 'Please hold off for a bit. Reasons explained personally.' Clearly, Hutch was still in disgrace.[15]

In January 1936, Parlophone issued Hutch's recording of 'Love Is Like a Cigarette' with, on the reverse, 'The Morning After', two Sam Coslow numbers from the film *Hands Across the Table*, a romantic comedy. Hutch does both songs full justice, and deftly improvises the piano interludes; but, in his idiosyncratic pronunciation of the word 'morning', with the rolled 'r' and hint of a 'g' at the end, his self-burlesque begins. Although barely discernible to the lay ear, other artistes identified it immediately, and the first Hutch impressions were soon under way. Having introduced 'Lights Out' to variety audiences, Hutch recorded this Lawrence Wright hit; its flip side was a song that soon became a standard, 'These Foolish Things'.

It was written by Eric Maschwitz, later to follow Cecil Madden as the BBC's head of light entertainment. He was then in his flat in Adam Street, not long down from Cambridge, unshaven, still in his pyjamas, and wondering how to tackle the problems of writing a song. 'By some accident, I hit upon "These Foolish Things" and, then and there, between sips of vodka and coffee, I drafted the verse and three choruses of the song:

'Gardenia perfume ling'ring on my pillow
Wild strawb'ries only seven francs a kilo
And still my heart has wings,
These foolish things remind me of you.'

Maschwitz and the composer, Jack Strachey, tried unsuccessfully to get the song published; and Keith Prowse, who had Maschwitz under contract, signed a release so they could sell it elsewhere.

One day, a manuscript copy – by that time, rather dog-eared – attracted the attention of Hutch, who found it lying on top of my piano. With characteristic enthusiasm, he sang and played it through, took an immediate fancy to it, and agreed to record it. From the day his record appeared, the song was made. Artists all over the world clamoured to be allowed to sing it.[16]

Over the next twenty years, the song yielded Maschwitz £1,000 a year. He followed it up with 'A Nightingale Sang in Berkeley Square' and 'Room 504' in 1940 and 1941. Both were triumphs for Hutch. For many people, Hutch singing 'These Foolish Things' epitomises the 1930s. The lyrics drive this sad *chanson noire* – 'The winds of March that made my heart a dancer / A telephone that rings but who's to answer?' – and slowly unfold a doomed cosmopolitan love affair. The song, especially Hutch's version of it, is as poignant now as the day he recorded it. A present-day critic, Robert Cushman, observed that he:

sings a verse . . . with the blunt enquiry, 'Oh, will you never let me be?' It goes on to set up the song with a reference to 'those little things . . . which bring me happiness and pain'. Most singers have tipped that balance in one direction or another. Hutch keeps it exquisitely poised; he suggests that he has the heart for grief but would never dream of wallowing in it. His voice, famously, throbs; but it throbs with dignity. He is suffering greatly, but he knows how to live with it. His cut-glass diction, with its outlandishly elegant vowels, actually contributes to his haunted sound: the upper crust of the soul. He must have sensed that in this still obscure song he had found the perfect showcase. He sings it as if it were already a standard.[17]

Like most performers, Hutch found the high fees offered by advertising agencies hard to resist, and he made several promotional records. In the late 1930s and early 1940s, Hutch was chosen to make a series of programmes to promote Persil, because Lintas, Unilever's in-house advertising agency, reckoned that he was the soap-powder users' favourite star. Radio Eireann broadcast the series, and Hutch was accompanied by a band led by Peter Yorke, a pianist and arranger who had worked with Jack Hylton among others. Joyce Brazell, a continuity girl in the radio and films department of Lintas, remembered:

> Hutch was a delight to work with. His professionalism was immaculate, his technique, his phrasing, his diction, impeccable. We recorded at the Decca studios, then in Frognal. Hutch would arrive on time, his only request being that a bottle of champagne should await him on his grand piano. This at 9 a.m! I remember sharing his glass on one occasion and feeling wildly sophisticated at such an early hour! He would tell the most amusing, risqué, not to say ribald stories, not recorded, and then slide into one of his lushly romantic numbers without a break.

She also recalled a respectable yet mysterious mouse of a woman in a blue suit, who always sat quietly in the corner of the recording box. Hutch said that he had no idea who she was, but that she always turned up wherever he was. They never spoke, and one day she disappeared for ever.

The recordings of the broadcasts, on Vynalite, are excellent, and fully capture Hutch's unique timbre and limpid piano playing. There were few retakes, which was important in those days of wax masters before the introduction of easily handled magnetic tape. The banter between Hutch and Yorke is embarrassingly contrived; worse still, Hutch's tone barely conceals his impatience and feelings of superiority to any mere accompanying bandleader.

Hutch recorded several extended jingles. The best of these was a nonsense song. Hutch recorded it early in 1938 as part of an 'Eat more fruit' campaign, and clearly enjoyed singing along with an unknown female singer:

You can always tell it's summertime when we put back the
    clocks,
You can always tell a golfer by the colour of his socks
You can always tell a burglar by the way he picks the locks
And you can always tell a Jaffa by its juice!

The *Sunday Referee*, in a piece that reads suspiciously like a
doctored press release, commented, 'It is so wittily contrived by
all concerned that there is no trace of sordid advertisement about it,
and the title might easily pass into currency as the catchword of the
day.'[18] Five hundred records were pressed, and Lawrence Wright
waived the copyright fee with a fanfare of self-congratulation.

Wright was one of the main figures behind a record business that
encouraged the British public to remain blindly loyal to its
favourites – Hutch, the Lancastrian singer and comedienne Gracie
Fields, the Australian singer Peter Dawson, the Austrian operetta
singer Richard Tauber and the dance bands of Jack Hylton and
Bert Ambrose – at the expense of encouraging new talent. Still
worse, the public was conditioned to regard with scepticism any
change of style or direction on the part of their favourites. The
result was a turgidity in the record industry – and, come to that, in
variety. In a long, thoughtful article in the *Daily Herald*, Spike
Hughes deplored this chronic lack of enterprise and blamed it, in
part, on 'the high prices one has to pay for these shellac slices of
musical history'. He regrets that record libraries are impractical:
'The literary value of a book is not diminished by a dirty thumb
mark . . . but each playing of a record by even the most meticulous
needle-changer affects the quality of reproduction.'[19]

Hutch's complicated love life continued to flourish. He formed a
relationship with a woman he met in the Caledonian Hotel,
Edinburgh, while on tour in 1936.

I used to be invited to sit in the wings and watch his show.
Hutch was very conscious of his colour, where he could go and
where he couldn't. I was married, and whenever I talked about
leaving my husband, Hutch always dissuaded me, saying, 'You'll
be full of regrets.' He told me of his affair with Edwina
Mountbatten . . . He doused himself in Chypre perfume, and
loved dark red carnations. We had great fun together – in

Scotland, in London and on the Wirral, when he was playing at the Argyle.

In 1938, a woman who owned four shops in West Kirby, on the Wirral, instructed her solicitor to make them over to Hutch on condition that he set up house with her. Later that year, Hutch borrowed a happily married woman from her husband without anyone raising objections. On tour in Cardiff, staying at the Angel Hotel, Hutch asked to be introduced to 'that clean girl' at the bar. The Titian-haired woman, Wendy Tonkinson, went with Hutch up to his suite and watched him practise for almost two hours. She then took him home to meet her small daughter, who enquired resonantly, 'Why's that man all black?'

Wendy and her husband took Hutch to the docks, where they ate Spanish omelettes and drank red wine – from coffee cups, because Cardiff was dry. 'Hutch had a gold cigarette case which my husband admired. It had "Edwina" written inside it. He was tall and elegant. I had three children by then, and was having a serious affair.' These latter factors notwithstanding, they became friends.

Wendy Tonkinson was a flaming redhead with beautiful legs, described by her son as 'a queen in her flapper generation. The great played around and the provincial beauties imitated them with knobs on. She suggested that I should make a family tree of her lovers.' Wendy seduced the music master at school and her best friend's father. She trained at Great Ormond Street Children's Hospital, where she was a rebel against authority and a mocker of convention. She was left-wing, but a tremendous snob who pulled rank and discomfited the insecure. She loved the theatre and especially musicals; Fred Astaire was an idol. She was knowledgeable about classical music too. She was a perfectionist in all domestic matters – the food in her elegant house was excellent and she was always immaculate. When Wendy ordered champagne in the Café Royal in London, Hutch said, 'You're costing me a pretty bit to take about'; eliciting the arch response from Wendy, 'But I am a pretty bit to take about.'

'At that time, he was very much involved with Edwina,' Wendy thought. 'A chauffeur arrived and whispered to him. A large limo was outside, and she was waiting for him.' Wendy had a stormy affair with Hutch in which she threw his records on the fire with a great smash as a melodramatic gesture of pique.

When a compulsive hostess, Countess Betty Dumas, wrote about her giddy social and domestic life in the *Evening News* (28 April 1936), she incidentally showed how Hutch mingled with his clients in his free time. Like many others, she had the time, resources and driving need to lionise celebrities. So, every weekend, her Roehampton villa in southwest London seethed with guests, ranging from the Duke of Manchester to the boxer Larry Gains; from Lord Victor Paget and Lord Selby to Hutch. While staying in London, Hollywood film stars such as Norma Shearer and Joan Crawford paid fleeting visits. From Friday to Monday, it was open house, with hordes of social and theatrical luminaries sweeping in for food and cocktails as the mood took them. Her husband, Peter, was a friend of Princess Jane San Faustino, who still dominated society in Rome and Venice. The Princess urgently needed a pianist for a charity concert at the Excelsior Hotel on the Lido; all was set for a repeat performance of Hutch's great triumph at the same venue in 1926.

> Peter and I knew Hutch very well, and Peter promptly tele-phoned to the Café Anglais in Leicester Square where Hutch was appearing, asked him to come to the Lido by airplane from Croydon on the Saturday to appear on the Sunday, and told him that the fee would be £300 which he, Peter, would pay. Only the fact that Mr Poulsen stopped Hutch from going, because he could not at short notice get a substitute for the cabaret, saved my husband that £300.

Countess Dumas sounds vulgarly entranced by a fee that must have sorely tempted Hutch to break his contract; Jack Poulsen must have been a strong character.

Hutch's film career continued with two further minor appear-ances. In June, a Pathé Pictorial, a bland 'magazine' that formed part of the supporting programme in British cinemas for many years, featured Hutch in a release typically entitled 'Airs – Open and Musical'. And, early in 1936, *Beloved Impostor*, based on a novel by Ethel Mannin, went into production. Hutch's role was to sing 'Nothing but Dreams'. On set, he suggested that an actress 'keep her peepers open under the arcs', and she was grateful for his advice. Hutch often observed other acts closely, and often made tactful, constructive suggestions which were usually well re-ceived.[20]

Always a man of extremes, Hutch was meticulous about his appearance, small courtesies, piano practice and performance schedules; but he was wholly undisciplined about sex, smoking, money, food and alcohol. By the late 1930s he was prosperous, and he was getting fat. In January 1937 he went to Paris for three days with Leslie Holmes (of the Two Leslies comic partnership) and Stanelli, a brilliant violinist. Then, according to *Radio Pictorial*, 'The Christmas party brought Stan and Les back home, but Hutch, complete with sun glasses and mountain boots, went for three weeks' holiday in the Swiss Alps at Valmont.'[21]

Blandly misrepresenting his trip as a holiday, Hutch went for the first of many stays in a sanatorium to combat the stress symptoms of being overweight and of drinking. A postcard to Joan read: 'Darling, Is this hotel hidden enough? I am surrounded by snow and mountains. Wonderful air, but how lonely. Love, Leslie.'

The cure did not prove effective: Hutch's drunkenness persisted throughout 1938 and 1939, and his friend Bill Pilkington recalled having to douse him with cold water and manoeuvre him on stage several times in those years.

> Hutch was foul-mouthed when drunk, and it started happening too often by the late 1930s and got worse during the war. Once, when he was at the Shakespeare, Liverpool, he was very drunk half an hour before he was due on as the last act. The whole company rallied round to strip him and give him a cold shower, and try to pull him round fast before he had to go on. Astonished by his nakedness, one young artiste shivered and exclaimed, 'Someone's married to *that*.' This comment put Hutch into an even blacker mood, and he sat drinking black coffee and shaking. We got him into his trousers and white tie, combed his hair, and put talcum powder on his face so that it didn't shine. I did up his cufflinks.

Hutch went on stage 'without a backward glance or stagger . . . to roars of applause . . . and performed brilliantly as though nothing had ever been wrong'. After bidding the audience goodnight and blowing kisses, he came backstage and collapsed. 'Women waited outside for him until midnight, but we didn't wake him. It is no wonder people didn't realise he had a problem.'

The weekend country-house parties continued. Hutch accepted

invitations only if he was asked in his own right, and was not asked to perform. In mid-1930s, he often stayed at Wadhurst Park in Sussex with Grant MacLean, a solicitor who invested heavily in show business. He had made his fortune by winning a case over a disputed diamond land claim in South Africa. MacLean built a nine-hole golf course by the lake, and the estate was reckoned to be the best duck and pheasant shoot in southern England. A tremendous *bon viveur*, he died after the war from cirrhosis of the liver. Hutch also went to stay several times with the actor Gerald du Maurier at his house built like a ship on the river at Fowey in Cornwall. Also there one weekend were Jack Buchanan and his on-stage partner Elsie Randolph; the actor-manager Lewis Casson and his wife Sybil Thorndike; the Prince of Wales and Edwina Mountbatten. Hutch also used to visit Broadlands, the Mount-battens' home outside Romsey, Hampshire.

For recordings, 1937 was another vintage year for Hutch. He sang many of the lachrymose ditties so popular at the time, but he also recorded versions of standards that stand up well today. Given a good tune and intelligent lyrics, Hutch came up time and again with two or three minutes of beautifully turned music characterised by off-beat timing, superb piano interludes and the easy, nonchalant style that come only from great technique and long practice. His skills are perfectly illustrated in two January releases, 'The Way You Look Tonight', a Jerome Kern song from the 1936 Astaire–Rogers film *Swingtime*, and 'When I'm With You' by Mack Gordon from the Shirley Temple film *Poor Little Rich Girl*. The next month, 'Easy to Love' backed by 'I've Got You Under My Skin' showed Hutch's rapport with Cole Porter's songs to be as robust as ever. And later in the year, Hutch's 'monthly soul-pouring'[22] included 'I Need You'; 'Where Are You?' from *Top of the Town*, a musical variety film; and 'They Can't Take That Away from Me' from Gershwin's score for the Astaire–Rogers film *Shall We Dance?* Hutch was fortunate to flourish at the same time as a group of lyricists who did not write down to the public and composers who wrote ambitious, sometimes complex music. Hutch himself declared his favourites to be 'Cole Porter for sophistication and the marriage of music and lyrics; Jerome Kern for irresistible melodies, and Richard Rodgers and Irving Berlin'.[23]

In the spring of 1937 Hutch went to New York to play at a 'Barnyard Frolic' party. This was given by Elsa Maxwell at the Waldorf Astoria in the Starlight Room, so called because its electrically retractable roof can expose it to the stars. At the top of the hotel, permanent tenants had, and still have, apartments collectively known as the Waldorf Towers. Elsa and the Cole Porters were among the first to move in (later tenants included the Duke and Duchess of Windsor, President Hoover and, more recently, Henry Kissinger, Richard Nixon and Marilyn Monroe). The party was attended by the Porters and Merle Oberon, among many others, all rustically clad as animals or farm workers. One of Hutch's girlfriends, then attached to the Pentagon, travelled up from Washington, much enjoyed his performance and dined with him afterwards.

From Waldorf Towers, Cole and Monty Woolley often went to Harlem to trawl for black male prostitutes, and it is probable that Hutch occasionally accompanied them. During the 1930s, in New York as in London, the gay scene was necessarily secretive; reviled by outsiders, yet perceived as an exclusive club because it included talented, sought-after men such as Cole, Noël Coward and Lorenz Hart.

Later in 1937, Cole sustained a serious riding accident: he fell off his horse, which collapsed onto him, crippling him so severely that he spent the remaining twenty-seven years of his life in a wheelchair in considerable pain. Shortly after the fall, Cole said, 'It just goes to show that fifty million Frenchmen can't be wrong. They eat horses instead of ride them.'[24]

It was after the Barnyard Frolic that Hutch cruised to Trinidad and then made his clandestine detour to Grenada. Returning to London, he must have come to the realisation that he couldn't go home again. At any rate, he left it at that.

The coronation of King George VI took place in May 1937. As part of the celebrations, the BBC lavished a record budget on some all-star variety bills which, regal embargo temporarily forgotten, included Hutch. Practically every hotel had famous visitors; Prince Chichibu of Japan was at the Hyde Park, for example, and the Aga Khan was at the Ritz. Numerous people went to the hotels, made a half-crown cocktail last an hour or so, and watched the celebrities come and go. Special licences allowed dance halls and nightclubs to postpone closing time for hours; and 'gala dinners' for coronation night featured special menus, souvenirs and cabarets. That night Hutch and Alberta Hunter broadcast live on NBC to the USA.

In late 1937, Hutch featured at the Paradise Club at 189 Regent Street. Its distinguished members paid seven and sixpence for entrance, and had to order bottles in advance from an agent in Bruton Mews. It was popular with both royalty and stage stars: the Mountbattens and the Kents were often there; so were Tommy Trinder, Douglas Byng, Eddie Cooper and Jack and Daphne Barker. Along with Hutch's cabaret, there were two bands. People danced all night and, before leaving, had an early breakfast of bacon and eggs. The club was closed early in 1938, when Josephine Baker precipitated a police raid by ordering a bottle of wine.

In the same year, Hutch became friends with Harold Berens; they first met when Berens was still a shirtmaker in premises over Ecu de France in Jermyn Street.[25] 'He was the first coloured man I ever measured,' Berens recalled. 'He smelled better than most of my clients. My dad used to sell him Havana cigars. It was rare to be friends with a coloured man.' Berens left shirtmaking to become a comic, and his capacity to create zany accents and burlesque languages later prompted Peter Sellers to pick him as a guru. Like his brother Leslie, the Bournemouth cinema manager, Harold used to go riding with Hutch.

> We used to ride near Brighton, galloping over the Downs, and in Richmond Park. Leslie's horse – I always called him Leslie – shied there once, and put its hoof through the back window of someone's car. It was all his fault for showing off, he used to make it rear by urging it on and holding it back at the same time. Bloody fool! Leslie used to ring and say, 'What about getting pissed tonight?' Once, when he was visiting, my mum was sick over the weekend, and we moved the piano upstairs to her room, and he played to her for hours.

Hutch enjoyed Berens's company, and often asked for him to be put on the same bill. They always stayed at the best hotels, and Berens remembered him looking 'very obvious in dark glasses', drinking champagne and being 'in every way a lover of good living'; and being made much of in Glasgow, Brighton, Bourne-mouth and, especially, Edinburgh. 'There were always numerous

Hutch on horseback, 1920s.

Hutch with the usual
accessories, 1920s.

Ivor Novello, 1920s.

Noel Coward, 1920s.

Hutch in his dressing room at
the Palladium, 1929.

Peg, 1929.

Mauve

Gabrielle, born 1930.

Elisabeth, mother of Gabrielle.

Merle Oberon

Hutch in the 1930s.

ladies at the stage door. He was a bristols man[26] but he always told me he wasn't fussy, as long as women wanted him badly and told him so.'

A dancer, Hy Curtis, reversed the usual pattern: although much fancied by Hutch, she never became his lover. She came over in the cast of *Blackbirds*, and was married to a show producer, Clarence Robinson, who staged most of the extravaganzas at the Cotton Club for more than a decade. They returned to London in 1937, because Robinson brought the *Cotton Club Review*, in which Hy featured, to tour France and England. They appeared at the Palladium with the Teddy Hill Orchestra, which then included a twenty-year-old Dizzy Gillespie as a section man; the featured trumpeter was Shad Collins.

> The first person who was crazy about Clarence and I was Hutch. He was so fond of me. He said if I wasn't Clarence's girl, he would give me the works! He was very elegant, and lived in a beautiful house. We went there often for dinner and cocktails. Hutch was very successful and full of airs – the West Indians are like that, anyway, when they're successful. He had a big house and servants but there was no woman there. We were over a couple of times a week. He'd play the piano, have me sit by him. He had a real crush on me but Clarence didn't mind. He was really elegant, too, and sophisticated about these things. Hutch was charming, tall – full of crap, as they say now![27]

But the Jazz Age was over, and Hutch's tastes now seemed out of place. After he appeared as a singing waiter in a radio play called *The Melody Man* written specially for him by Norman Hackforth, the BBC distributed a series of 'Internal Circulating' memos, starting in September 1937. Headed 'Alexandra Palace – Alcohol Refreshments – Confidential', and with a palimpsest of pencilled addenda, these provide ironic comedy and bleak insight into the start of what was to prove a tragedy for Hutch.

> From the report of the Commissionaire at Alexandra Palace on September 16th, I note that at 8.30 p.m. the chauffeur and valet of Mr Hutchinson, who was appearing in the television programme, arrived at the Reception Desk with a bottle of champagne. The situation was explained on the telephone to Mr Bax, who gave

permission for this to be taken up to Mr Hutchinson's dressing room, stating that it was being used on medical grounds.

The pencilled marginalia from various hands are reminiscent of Mr Hewitt's comments in Hutch's primary school in Gouyave: 'I don't think this sounds at all convincing and I don't consider Bax has authority to make such decisions'; 'Agreed, though this artist is now apparently unable to perform without alcoholic stimulant. Mr Bax was the senior executive official on duty and acted on his own responsibility in the belief that otherwise the artist would not have appeared . . .'

> September 17th . . . Members of the Productions Staff here will corroborate that Hutch never goes on stage or on the set for filming without drinking half a bottle of champagne, and I think the time has now come for me to make clear to you that a great many 'star' artists – perhaps unfortunately – could not give a performance at all unless they followed this practice . . . Mr Noël Coward, who would have walked out on us had he not been allowed to gargle, unfortunately on one occasion rather loudly in front of the microphone, with port. I could go on quoting numerous other cases . . . Had Hutch brought in the bottle of champagne in his dressing-case no-one would have been any the wiser provided he took the 'empty' and the cork away with him!

> 19th November. I am just putting on paper what we agreed verbally yesterday regarding alcoholic refreshments at Alexandra Palace.
>   1. That as far as possible alcohol should be barred from our premises.
>   2. That artists should not be in any way encouraged to go out and get drinks at the local Bar before performances, and
>   3. In what you consider are exceptional circumstances artists may be permitted to bring in and drink stimulants or send out for them, the authority being vested in . . . In all cases, where this latter privilege is exercised, you are to be informed . . .

This memo is copied to eight employees, and an educated hand replies in pencil, 'Back to the fourth form again!' It is likely that the

BBC executives recalled the famous incident when Commander Tommy Woodroffe was commentating on the review of the fleet at Spithead in 1935, part of George V's jubilee celebrations. Having been plied with drink by former shipmates in the ward-room, he came out into the cold air and could do no more than repeat delightedly, 'The fleet's lit up'; the words became a national catch phrase and, soon after, the title of a show at the Palladium.

If Hutch spent much of his time with either Edwina or Virginia in 1938, the last season before the war, he spent even more with Princess Marina of Greece. She had arrived from exile in Paris to marry Prince George, the Duke of Kent, in November 1933. Margaret, Duchess of Argyll, wrote in her autobiography that Marina's natural elegance outshone that of every other woman in the room, with the exception of Queen Mary. As it provided the first royal pageantry since the wedding of the Duke and Duchess of York in 1923, their marriage generated great fervour and enthusiasm. It was also the first royal occasion to be broadcast by wireless worldwide, though the BBC commentator, Howard Marshall, was not permitted in Westminster Abbey. He resorted to giving the commentary from the remote roof of Westminster Hospital; the control room was set up in the crypt, under the Tomb of the Unknown Warrior.[28] The couple took their honeymoon on a West Indian cruise. One of her biographers says that Princess Marina is 'now mostly remembered as a tragic beauty, who gave a certain chic to the dowdy Windsors . . . an elegant princess walking with a slight limp onto the Centre Court at Wimbledon to give winners their prizes'.[29] Hutch fell for the limp.

Marina had been married for four years to the incorrigibly immature, bisexual and unfaithful Prince George. He was also the most cultured, talented and intelligent of the princes. He had charm, taste, a good knowledge of art, and a flair for interior decoration. A good sportsman, he also loved ballet and most types of music including jazz, and spent long hours in nightclubs playing the banjolele. His brother, the Prince of Wales, had given him rooms at York House, St James's Palace, where he often met Hutch. Prince George had been addicted to drugs and, in what some have described as the Prince of Wales's sole unselfish act, dried out by the Prince. He was a wild young man, even by late-twentieth-century standards, and had been engaged several times.

As Sir Steven Runciman said, 'No one of either sex was safe with him in a taxi.'[30] Prince George saw no reason to change his ways on marriage, and was fortunate that newspapers were then so discreet. However, public ignorance of his numerous affairs did little to palliate the hurt for his wife, who loved him. Luckily, Marina had been brought up to survive trials independently, and had the love and support of her family. She determined not to be destroyed by her husband's neglect. She also decided to choose a lover and amuse herself in private during his many absences.

Marina was Greek, Russian, Danish and German by blood, and had been born in a palace in Athens and brought up there by her parents, Prince and Princess Nicholas of Greece. In the early 1920s, the family went into exile in Paris, where the Prince rented a studio in Auteuil, and the Princess and her three daughters went to live in a small flat in Trocadero. Young Marina grew up to enjoy the art galleries with her father, and to work hard on behalf of Russian refugees with her mother, who had been the Grand Duchess Helen of Russia; together with her two sisters, she sold their jewellery to help them. They were an exceptionally close and happy family. Early in 1934, when she was staying with her sister Olga, she went to a dance given by Emerald Cunard, and met Prince George. He had been employed at both the Foreign and the Home Offices, and impressed her with his liking for humanity, intelligence and fun. 'We laugh at the same things,' he said on their engagement; 'she can beat me at most games, and she doesn't mind how fast I drive when I take her out in a car.'

Marina and Hutch also had much in common. Edwina knew them both, and must have known of the affair. Lady Iris Mount-batten had been one of Marina's bridesmaids, and also knew Hutch well. In 1923, Marina had spent time on Brownsea Island in Poole Harbour, Dorset, with Hutch's pupils of two years later, the Infanta Beatriz and Infante Alphonso.[31] Marina knew the West Indies from her honeymoon; and her life of exile, humiliation and poverty in Paris was easily understood by Hutch. Like him, she had connections with England that went back to her childhood; she was brought up with nursery rhymes in English, which was her first language. She loved to ride and paint, and enjoyed acting and the theatre. She was uninhibited, independent, unselfconscious, generous, warm and witty; and, like Hutch, something of a chameleon, able to take on a different personality to suit her company. Although dutiful, she was easy-going by nature; and, without being very clever, she was swift and observant. She was also beautifully dressed, a feature that greatly appealed to Hutch. In Paris, although she made her own clothes and set her hair, she had acquired a Parisian's dress sense. Because she showed them off to such advantage, enterprising dress designers offered her their creations at temptingly low prices. This paid off, for Marina proved to be a great setter of fashions. She launched tiny, veiled pillbox hats, and made 'Marina blue' famous. She also boosted British industry by insisting on using only British fabrics: cotton, Nottingham lace, Scottish tweeds. She set other trends. She got rid of the Art Deco furnishings in her house, the chrome furniture and razzle-dazzle cushions, saying that she did not want to live in a bar. She thought it bad manners to make up in public – 'running repairs' had been an acceptable practice since the mid-1920s – and did not invite women who did. She promoted lighter dinners, more enterprising mixes of guests and better conversation.[32] She also pushed her own pram, and prompted other fashionable women to take their children about with them. Her brief fling with Hutch in 1938 got her through a bad stage of her marriage. It also led to a loving, mutually respectful friendship with Hutch that lasted for the rest of their lives: they still dined together in the 1960s.[33]

Prince George was killed in 1942 when his plane crashed at Eagle's Rock, Scotland, on the way to Iceland. Typically, Marina did not go into mourning; after a brief initial collapse, she assumed all the Duke's duties while continuing with her role as commandant of the Women's Royal Naval Service (the Wrens). She was also patron for the POIPH (Promotion of Industries for the Physically Handicapped); took on Alexandra Rose Day, a charity for the blind; and, having trained as a nurse at University College Hospital, London, under the name Nurse Kay, she helped out at the local cottage hospital at Iver, west of London. Marina died the year before Hutch, in 1968.

Chapter Eight

Reserved Occupation
1939–1945

And when they ask us
We never will tell them
How we fought in some café
With wild women night and day
Twas the wonderfullest war you ever knew

Cole Porter parody of
'They'll Never Believe Me'
by Jerome Kern and Otto Harbach

Although the first night in October 1938 was ruined by 'a bad gale which topped trees aplenty in the district', Charles Tucker's show *Tops Everything* was a diverting entertainment with a cast that almost lived up to its title. Jewel and Warriss, the Colleano Brothers, Olive White and Max Wall joined Hutch on a bill that toured the Empires. The *Performer* judged the most amusing sketch to be that in which Hutch and Olive White bore the brunt of Max Wall's guitar playing.[1] Wall's wicked burlesque of Hutch's impassioned pianistics was launched in *Tops Everything*. Although Hutch's fans were not sure at first whether to laugh or be indignant, Hutch's appearance, joining in the joke, banished uncertainty. This double act was to give great pleasure to performers and audiences alike for some twenty years. In his autobiography, Wall wrote, 'It was a very funny and original act, because Hutch had never before spoken on stage, apart from his own announcements of songs, and had never at that time performed as an actor of sorts with another artist.'

Hutch was initially more critical of the way in which Harold Berens sent him up in *December Follies*, a new cabaret at the Café Anglais. Berens injected the strain of malice, the edge vital to any effective imitation, and Hutch violently objected. However, Berens must have placated him, because Hutch later said to Terry-Thomas, 'Only Berens has my permission to do impressions of me.'

Tops Everything transplanted successfully from the Kilburn Empire to the Holborn Empire in January 1939, and Max Wall extended his solo act with its mischievous imitation of Hutch. Later in the programme, Hutch joined forces with Wall, and there was doubt as to who was accompanying whom. Wall's bizarre antics dazzled Hutch, who usually enjoyed being guyed by his comedian friends; but he preferred to be there to join in the fun, playing the decently puzzled man to the zany. The double act ended with Wall expressing a surrealistic ambition to go to Hutch's funeral in brown boots, on a bike without a bell.

The theatre critic of the *Sunday Times*, James Agate, reviewed the show. Although his piece reads strangely now, Agate, who rarely covered popular shows, spotted that Hutch felt ambivalent about some of his material: on one level, he disdains its banality but, instead of sending it up as Fats Waller did, he puts it across with seeming sincerity and passion because, on another level, Hutch needed to believe that the romantic fantasy of the songs had some substance.

There are two 'Hutches'. The 'Hutch' who bows his acknowl-edgements is the child of sophistication, glossier and starchier than anybody since Vesta Tilley. He is playboy and exquisite – in a word, civilisation's coloured top. Or with his suave smile and dimpling knee, you might take him for a coloured boxer who just doesn't trouble to box. That is the first 'Hutch'. The second is the figure seated at the piano, and it is a very creditable imitation of primitive man. This 'Hutch' sings love songs, such songs as might have fallen from the lips of Umslopagaas, the executioner in 'Salome', Masrur in 'Hassan' or the personal attendant of Ozymandias . . . I don't know the make of piano Mr Hutchinson is using, but I do know that Messrs Steinway, Bluthner, Erard, Broadway and the entire family of Collard

never made strings as vibrant as those of this singer's heart . . . Mr
Hutchinson's delivery of these Sapphic trifles is a masterpiece of
veiled insincerity. He plays with passionate monotony on the
one note which to women is the whole of music – the assurance
that Man is better off kissing her hand than in setting his own to
the work of a Shakespeare, a Wren or Beethoven. I do not think
there is a Lieder-singer in the world who is Mr Hutchinson's
equal in this tongue-in-cheek virtuosity.[2]

By now, Hutch was offering mimics an increasingly soft target.
Like many performers at the height of their careers, he sometimes
verged on self-caricature: his mannerisms became more exaggerated, and his playing and singing more and more affected. Song
pluggers remembered that he used to play their offerings perfectly
when he first saw them, but later abandoned his crisp and careful
delivery in favour of a maudlin tremolo and other oppressively
theatrical touches. Hutch was fully aware of what he was doing.
His variety audience applauded these effusions; and Hutch was
simply giving them what they wanted. However, by demeaning
his talents in this way, he coarsened himself as an artist and,
eventually, undermined his belief in himself. In the end, Hutch's
variety audience was the death of him as an artist who could blend
words and music in a subtle, understated way. The purity of his
music was irretrievably lost, and he gradually became a parody of
himself, which was, in turn, all too easy for others to parody; in
time, Hutch became a ripe target, not just for friends such as Max
Wall, Terry-Thomas and Harold Berens, but for virtually every
impressionist from Peter Casson to Leslie Sarony, who, to Hutch's
dismay, used to perform a long, brazen song, punctuated by blue
jokes, called 'The Night That Hutch Forgot His Handkerchief'.
    A Merseyside critic wrote, 'As a single music-making unit,
Hutch is not less mighty than the Orpheans. His voice reverberates
in a series of sentimental songs which might be described more
aptly as musical orations.' He was now aiming not to please but to
impress. This self-vulgarisation exposed him to erosions of privacy:
by reducing his female audiences to a highly emotional state,
Hutch, like the sorcerer's apprentice, generated a following over
which he had no control. One couple, who stayed in a hotel at the
same time as Hutch, described the experience as 'hellish'. Women
clamoured for entry at all hours; heaps of presents blocked the

stairs; flowers choked the lobby; the establishment revolved around Hutch, and there was little service for anyone else. They moved out after one night. Small wonder Hutch became more and more of a recluse.

At the same time, his manners were getting more outrageous than ever. Leslie Perowne, a BBC producer, met Hutch for lunch at La Coquille, a fashionable restaurant in London, in July 1940. 'He flirted with the female he had brought with him with his hand in her knickers, and then blow me down if he didn't flirt with the waiter, too.' He later sent Perowne a picture of himself – all bare, rippling torso and lazy, lascivious smile, taken outside a Cotswold country house. It is easy to misconstrue such exhibitionist behaviour as insensitive; in fact, it betrays a great lack of confidence.

Bill Pilkington, who was Hutch's compere at the Argyle, the broadcasting theatre in Birkenhead, provided revealing glimpses of Hutch at the end of the 1930s. 'He had a most annoying habit of cracking his knuckles, and used to pick up a toothpick at the very ends of the back of his fingers and snap it to demonstrate their strength.' Hutch also told Pilkington in 1938 that he had sired some eight children, and that the women and children concerned should consider themselves lucky to have been so favoured. 'Marriage was a disaster,' he added, 'just not for me. Perhaps it's my own fault, perhaps I was too young.'

With heterosexual friends, Hutch was always explosively homophobic. When drinking with Pilkington at the Adelphi Hotel in Liverpool, they saw a noted homosexual, 'Sadie', dressed as a woman, at the other end of the bar. 'I just hope he doesn't get any closer,' said Hutch, 'or I'll flatten him.' Until many years later, Pilkington had no idea that Hutch was himself bisexual; nor that he was still married; instead, he seemed entirely independent, 'as though disowned by his family'.

While Hutch envied his friend's zest for exercise – Pilkington was both a jujitsu black belt and an exponent of kendo, Japanese swordsmanship using bamboo staves – he never took any himself, although he was concerned about his health and particularly prone to indigestion and colds. Once, on stage at the Shakespeare Theatre in Liverpool, he told the audience in a hoarse but audible whisper that he was unable to sing to them. A low moan of disappointment tempered by sympathetic 'aahs' filled the theatre. After the show, the stage door was invaded by women bearing cough mixture; and, later, while walking in Sefton Park, Hutch was approached by a woman intent on rubbing his chest.

Pilkington greatly admired Hutch's presence and authority on stage. 'He could make people listen: as he sat down at the piano and gazed around, there was complete silence . . . he was more than a singer, he was an actor who sang.' When he finished, he made it seem like a great effort to part company with the stool; once standing, he held onto the piano and bowed. Glinting on one wrist could be seen a gold identity bracelet which Pilkington knew was incised with the name Edwina. Pilkington noted that Hutch was obsessed with social advancement at various levels. In Liverpool he often courted the company of Lord Derby, saying 'I'm sure that man could do something for me'; and, a prized speaker at ladies' groups and masonic lodges, Hutch was also keen to become a mason, but the invitation never came; 'I'm always on the doorstep, never in the parlour,' he said to Pilkington. However, when approached by a religious group to join their number, Hutch refused; afterwards he said that he was not religious, and that 'You should stick to what you believe in, and believe in what you stick to'.

Pilkington found Hutch, when sober, 'a lovely companion, humorous and kind'; but he was also chronically restless, never content, and incapable of being on his own; he was 'an exhibitionist who had to have an audience'. Hutch was also very unpunctual. After being let down twice, Pilkington stopped making arrangements to meet him.

Early one morning he saw Hutch outside a rundown house in Bedford Street in Toxteth, one of the poorest parts of Liverpool. 'He was obviously sorry to be caught there. "Oh, fuck, not you, dear boy" was all he said.'

Pilkington wrote a statement that read, 'I will give of my art and talent to all men to entertain, to educate, amuse and please, irrespective of their skins, their race, their rank or their creed.' This grandiloquent manifesto greatly appealed to Hutch, who mounted it on a card and afterwards carried it everywhere. It elevated his role to that of universal entertainer, of someone whose on-stage function was so heavy that he could be excused all other responsibilities.

Throughout Hutch's life, commercial radio was prohibited in the UK. To get around this, advertisers used stations on the continent, such as Radio Luxembourg and Radio Normandy, whose signals were strong enough to reach many parts of Britain. In February 1939 Hutch appeared on a Radio Luxembourg programme sponsored by the makers of De Reszke Minors, cigarettes that were promoted by the slogan 'Ten minutes to wait – and mine's a Minor!' On it, a fulsome linkman exclaims, 'Sophisticated Hutch! You think of him in sumptuous settings, in beautifully tailored evening clothes. That's the stage Hutch. The Hutch you meet on Sundays is a different man. An out-of-doors man, happiest of all when he's galloping over the Downs. After a hard day's riding, we meet him in his flat.' This may have been a flat in the Dorchester Hotel in Park Lane, rented to save time commuting from his home in Hampstead; and also, possibly, to simplify the presentation of his private life. Olive White, a versatile American who played violin, saxophone and guitar, and was Hutch's partner in the Max Wall sketch in *Tops Everything*, appeared on the programme to test Hutch's famed ability to read music on sight. Hutch feigns reluctance and shouts 'Taxi!', but excels when he sings and plays 'I'm a Different Me' to Olive's violin obbligato. As he had been performing the number for many weeks in *Tops Everything*, the test was palpably phoney, and the high quality of his performance is hardly surprising. On the same show he sang 'They Say', a sweet simple tune, one of the last to be performed in his old unselfconscious style.

Given his pride, Hutch must have been humiliated by the constraints on his career which stemmed from the regal decree: quietly yet firmly, the BBC, the Beaverbrook press and Val Parnell, among others, were consistent in stressing that, in some ways, he was persona non grata. To avoid brooding on the results of his indiscretions, Hutch plunged into a work schedule more frenetic than ever. On top of his twice-nightly appearances in variety and performing in two or more nightclubs well into the small hours, he had a daunting schedule of recording sessions and broadcasts on commercial radio which delighted in flouting an establishment embargo.

At its zenith at this time was Hutch's five-year affair with Virginia, the young dancer who objected so fervently to Hutch's frequent hunting sorties with Lady Ursula Filmer-Sankey. That was at the start of the affair in 1937, and as she was then only eighteen, and Hutch was her first lover, Virginia may be forgiven for being rather proprietary. With her, he had embarked on a new kind of relationship which reflected his age, if not maturity. Previously, all the key women in his life had been contemporaries, but he was twice Virginia's age; and, at 37, starting to need the comfort of young flesh to assure himself of his own agelessness. Given his penchant for giving constructive advice to younger performers, he may have enjoyed playing a paternal role and being less of a lover and more a guide to life. Virginia, while clever and beautiful, was too independent and wilful to be moulded satisfactorily; but, that notwithstanding, the relationship was typical of many others that followed.

She had been trained by Victor Silvester as a ballroom dancer, and it was one of her exhibition dancing partners, Bobby Hooker, who introduced her to Hutch. It was some time before her father, a rich Virginian living in Jersey, heard about the affair. He may not have been very outraged, since Virginia was used to shocking her family and friends, and resilient enough to take care of herself; indeed, her enterprise soon secured her a good part in a revue, *Black Velvet*, with Teddy Brown and Vic Oliver, a violin-playing Viennese comic who had recently eloped with Winston Churchill's elder daughter, Sarah. A bookmaker, Chummy Govanter, remembered her as being very beautiful and a bit naive, and added, 'I always noticed Hutch at the races because she was with him,' which confirms that Virginia met two of Hutch's desiderata – by paying court to him and being demonstrably attractive.

Hutch insisted on Virginia adopting his own attention to sartorial detail, and was very stern if her petticoat showed or her gloves failed to complement the rest of her clothes. He was angry if she swore. He was also extremely jealous, and if she was not at home waiting for him to ring her, she was 'deluged by irritable telegrams'. Unless he had specifically given her permission, he never let her come backstage. The one time she broke this rule, he was otherwise engaged, and had her turned away. But the strictures did not go just one way: Virginia warned Hutch that, if he did not cut down on whisky, he would get cirrhosis of the liver. More positively, he enjoyed her 'very infectious laugh' and the way in which she imitated his walk, 'tripping forward on his toes when on stage'. She believed he was largely faithful to her.

He always took me to the best places . . . we used to go to a pub
in Maidenhead and hire a punt for the day . . . the publican said,
'I see you've settled down now, Hutch.' 'Yes, I'm very happy,'
he replied. We were good companions. Sex wasn't a predominant thing, though he made love to me whenever he could. I
was so inexperienced, I was probably a terrible lover. He was
very much in love with me, I think.

And very probably, she with him: as Virginia recalled the affair and
watched Hutch on video, tears ran down her cheeks. He told
people he was ready to settle down with her, but she sensibly did
not believe him. She never met Ella, though she knew of
her existence and often spent nights with Hutch at 31 Steeles
Road, too.

She also recalled Hutch's chauffeur Ernie, who sometimes fell
asleep at the wheel, possibly as a result of driving his employer
round into the small hours of the morning. 'We were always
waking him up. When Ernie applied for a new job, he was
congratulated by his employer for speaking English so correctly.
"I should do," Ernie replied proudly, "I was Mr Hutch's chauffeur." '

In 1941, Virginia was a dancer at the Café de Paris. On 4 March,
just after her act, she rushed to meet Hutch off a late train. Ten
minutes after she left, at half past nine, the Luftwaffe dropped two
50-kilo high explosives. One bomb exploded in the gallery just
above Ken Snakehips Johnson's band, who with one exception
were killed outright; the second broke on impact with the floor,
then crowded with dancers.[3] Society people of the time still recall
where they were that night, much as people can summon up the
same details regarding when they heard of President Kennedy's
assassination or Princess Diana's car crash. When Hutch sauntered
up the station platform to Virginia, she saw that his face and neck
were smudged with lipstick kisses. These he shamelessly – and
strangely – attributed to fooling around with some waiters. But her
date with him had saved her life.

The affair ended in 1944 when a bomb blew up Virginia's flat at
49 Hallam Street, between the BBC and a synogogue. Hutch
never called to commiserate. 'I might as well have been dead for all
he cared. That finished it. I hardly saw him again.'

She never married, but claimed that her later lovers included

Clark Gable and Duke Ellington. She made films in Hollywood and Britain, notably appearing in *Fanny by Gaslight* with James Mason in 1944.

Hutch gave Virginia a photograph of himself inscribed 'A toi. I wonder how many people really know me.' Ironically, the person, who knew him least was he himself. He was perpetually reinventing his past, trying to ignore racial barriers, and presenting himself in different ways. His aim was to gain security and acceptance; these he denied himself by setting himself impossible targets, and then he felt cheated by the world. Because he was cocooned in admiration – and drink – Hutch came to see himself as a world citizen of unique sophistication and unparalleled skills, who transcended conventional restraints. And while so many people worshipped him, no one could have the effrontery to plumb the depths of so complex a person.

Most people consolidated Hutch's illusions by ministering to his vanity and self-importance. These included Lawrence Wright who, in 1939, briefed Jacob Epstein, the great Polish sculptor, to do a bronze bust of Hutch, and thereby create an idol for the idolatrous. Earlier in the year, Wright had commissioned Epstein to produce massive figures of Adam and Eve 'to live in Blackpool always'; the cost was £7,000 for Adam and, oddly, £15,000 for Eve. Wright, ever the shrewd businessman, charged holiday crowds a shilling each to see each of them. On the first half-day, some 12,000 people saw Adam, and Wright soon made a handsome profit on his seemingly altruistic investment.

In late August 1939, a photograph of Hutch, looking smug and provocative at the piano, appeared in the *Radio Times* to advertise a programme to be broadcast on a Sunday. This marked the triumphant conclusion of a campaign waged by the *Daily Mail* for brighter Sundays; at that time and for many years afterwards, retail outlets and places of entertainment were almost all closed on Sundays; and radio broadcasts were sombre and devotional in character. It persuaded many thousands of listeners to write letters complaining of drab Sabbath fare, and the BBC, without prior announcement, had completely capitulated. The *Daily Mail* crowed:

A short while ago, if Leslie Hutchinson were engaged to sing at a piano on a Sunday, most of the BBC higher command would have thrown a million fits. Someone would have been hauled over red-hot coals . . . Hutch, though a first-rate artist, would never in the Reith days have been allowed near Broadcasting House on a Sunday . . . for he sings popular songs in the popular way. And that would never have done.

Once, when reading with Hutch in bed while on tour in the West Country, Virginia had bravely challenged him about Edwina. Hutch issued his standard response, 'It was never me, it was him,' referring to Paul Robeson. She did not ask again. But in fact, while necessarily intermittent, the affair still carried on. Fellow artistes often saw Edwina on tour with Hutch, frequently with Hutch's brother Ivan acting as a sort of minder. A week after the historic Sunday broadcast, on 31 August, a small crowd formed outside Dartmoor Prison, where Hutch had been performing for the inmates at the end of a tour round Torbay. The onlookers were admiring a huge gleaming black car attended by a chauffeur when Hutch swept through the gates, arm in arm with Edwina, 'looking beautiful, smiling, elegant and wearing a bandeau. A murmur ran through the wondering assembly, "It's Lady Louis".'

Three days later, war was declared, and several of them never forgot the juxtaposition of events.

Hutch and Terry-Thomas shared a bill at Northampton on 2 September. In his autobiography, Terry-Thomas later wrote, 'For some reason (I can't remember her name) Hutch had not been able to reach the theatre from London in time. I went on and impersonated him, singing, "Life is Just a Bowl of Cherries". And I suppose it had been, until then.' Next day, they heard Chamberlain's announcement on the radio, and drove into London in Hutch's car, each nursing a bottle of champagne.

We were just in time to hear that ghastly siren sound for the first time . . . After the panic of the air-raid warning, Hutch suggested we should get out of town as quickly as possible, so we arranged to meet at his local, 'The Load of Hay', in Haverstock Hill, Hampstead. When I arrived, he was standing outside with a large glass of brandy in his hand. He looked into the sky, and said in that fabulous voice of his, 'Terry, you know I'm beginning to get used to this war already.'

In the first fortnight of war, the authorities closed all places of entertainment. A leaflet headed 'War Emergency' among Hutch's papers reads:

> All cinemas, theatres, dance halls and places of public entertainment will be closed until further notice. When it is seen how the air attacks develop, it may be possible to allow reopening of such places in some areas. They are being closed because if they were hit by a bomb, large numbers would be killed or injured . . . Never crowd together unnecessarily . . . Do not take too much notice of noise in an air raid. Much of it will be the noise of our own guns dealing with the raiders. Keep a good heart: we are going to win through.

More than anything else, it was the blackout that convinced the civilian population that there was a war on. Every evening, darkness fell unrelieved like a pall. No street lamps went on; torches and car headlamps were dimmed down to a faint glow. People thought twice before turning on lights, and, even when they did, the bulbs often shone an odd, muted blue. When a theatre is closed, it is called 'dark', an apt word for the world of entertainment in the first few weeks of the war.

The first theatre to reopen was the Windmill, with the slogan 'We Never Closed', on 16 September. Others soon followed. In her autobiography *Vocal Refrain*, Vera Lynn recalled:

> When it was realised that all cities would not be instantly destroyed, the industry pulled itself together, the theatres gradually reopened, the hotels reinstated their dances, and there was a boom in the whole cheer-up business . . . And maybe the public had grown fatalistic; if Hitler was going to drop a bomb on you, he might as well catch you having a laugh in the stalls as hiding under the stairs. You'd do your shows in the late afternoons and evenings, and go to service camps, munitions factories, works canteens and hospitals earlier in the day. There were informal singsongs when the raids were on.

To revive spirits and regain lost business, managements fielded unusually strong bills. In the third week of the war, the Birmingham Hippodrome featured Hutch, Max Miller, Teddy Brown and G. S. Melvin. The local papers reported that the theatre seemed determined to 'do a very big bit in brightening the blackout', and commented on how effective the show had been in 'taking thoughts away from serious matters for an hour or two'.[4] Escapism had always been the prime function of variety, but never more so than during the war.

Two months later, Hutch was again sharing the bill with Max Miller, at the Brighton Hippodrome. By now, the Lord Chamberlain allowed every kind of joke to belittle the Axis leaders. Miller was famous for coming on stage with two sticks and raising each in turn. 'Hitler's right leg', 'Hitler's left leg'. He then went into the wings, and returned with two immense potatoes held over his crutch. Once a slow collective laugh had spread through the audience, he would shake his head and say, 'You're wrong, ladies and gentlemen, you're wrong. They're King Edwards.' As for Hutch he left topical references alone, and concentrated on romance.

That autumn Hutch was fined £2 for 'failing to obscure the lights' in the Queen's Hotel, Southsea; the magistrates decided that if the management had efficiently blacked out a hotel, it could hardly be held responsible if a careless guest allowed a light to be seen.[5] By the time the case came up in Portsmouth, Hutch was in Liverpool, attracting excellent reviews ('The idol of millions of radio fans, his husky voice crooning lilting melodies is unforgettable'[6]). He made a broadcast from the Palace Theatre, Blackpool; the programme was sandwiched between 'A Public School in Wartime' and 'The RAF in Command'.

Another of Lawrence Wright's grandiose enterprises in Blackpool, the Castle Club, had opened the same month the war broke out. Luscious paintings and a vast parquet dance floor helped to create an ambience of opulence. The members of this residential club included Evelyn Laye, Frank Lawton, Max Miller, Turner Layton, Henry Hall – and Hutch, who delighted in this flamboyant retreat. Even at smart hotels, such as the Palatine on the Promenade, he was all too exposed to his importunate following. That was why he generally preferred discreetly anonymous boarding houses. Among these, his favourite in Blackpool was owned and run by the Wiebencer family. When Hutch stayed there, he insisted on being the only guest apart from the 'secretary' he brought with him. 'There was always a different Mrs Something,' said George Wiebencer, 'who was usually blonde and well-spoken. They never emerged before noon.' Hutch made the house a home from home, and the family was happy to indulge his whims. He appreciated good home cooking, especially his landlady's apple pies. He also liked having the run of the kitchen and doing his own, very enterprising cooking, to much applause. He loved gamey dishes, and spent days marinating partridges in red wine, brandy, spices and herbs until they were pungent. When the son of the house took a portion of this dish to work in his lunch box, his mates begged him to throw it away and stop polluting the atmosphere.

Hutch made a lasting impact on his fans, providing the foundation for endless emotional fantasies. Jessie of Manchester cannot forget him:

> Hutch became part of my life in my teens at the start of the war. I was unable to go to anyone for love and comfort. I lived alone with a tyrannical father who abused me, so in no way could I hang around a stage door in the hope of an autograph. Wherever I went, so did Father. I was captivated by the contrast Hutch represented. It was a combination of talent, charm, elegance and his lovely smile, the way he seemed to glide on stage, which added to the charisma. Why, after fifty years, am I still besotted and can't let him go? Had I been one of his circle of friends or just a girl in the street and he had beckoned, I would have gone and not counted the cost.

As many did. A year or so earlier, Jessie might have been less impressed, but Hutch was now looking much better than before his stay in Switzerland. He was still drinking too much, but he looked good and had immense energy. Like all singers, he dreaded throat infections; and when he caught one, he made a great fuss. On tour in Swansea that autumn, he went every day to a clinic to have his throat sprayed. The nurse vividly remembered that she had

> treated a very handsome coloured gentleman, apparently a VIP, though I had never heard of Hutch before. He insisted on

coming in every morning and every evening before going on stage to have his throat sprayed by me. He was very charming. After two days, he gave me a ticket to see him at the Empire and his card and invited me backstage to see him after the show. I went and enjoyed it, but I did not go backstage.

In contrast to her, a blonde teenage girl caused a ripple of comment from the audience when, after Hutch had paid particular attention to her as she sat in the front row of the stalls, she obeyed his gesture to join him backstage. The incident happened early in 1940, when Hutch was appearing in a Sunday-night variety concert at the Longford Cinema in Stretford, near Manchester. One member of the audience, a girl two rows behind her, said, 'As we were teenagers ourselves, just like her, at the time, we thought it rather daring, especially as we considered him to be "an older man".' His colleagues were much impressed with Hutch's capacity to attract girls at long range, not only for himself but for others. Max Wall was one of many who put in requests for him to procure 'the dark one with the long hair in the third row'.

Hutch's wartime performances gave him a chance to show fortitude and elicited a new form of devotion, pure gratitude. A Manchester fan wrote: 'The bombing started during his performance, but Hutch just carried on playing the piano and singing, also mopping his brow as usual. He helped us to forget the Blitz for a while. When we came out of the theatre, the Coliseum Picture Palace opposite had had a direct hit and was in ruins. Hutch was a real trouper.' A man from Liverpool wrote as follows:

I never missed a show when the band played his music the audience applauded before he walked on the Stage he was a very popular Man always well dressed I would say a Ladies Man he would walk bowing to the audience toward his Piano, Sit Down place his handkerchief on it, he was always a Real Class Entertainer, he always had the audience under is Spell the full 45 minutes he was on. I was once told by the MD at Band Call on a Monday morning when he sang Lords of the Air they would stop working while he was singing. In the War I loved him like a Brother.

When required, Hutch was brave and unflappable. Once, at Wolverhampton:

> Suddenly the air-raid warning boomed out. Everything stopped. Hutch rose from his seat at the piano, held up his hand and spoke to us, 'Ladies and gentlemen, there is an air-raid warning. Anyone wishing to leave, please do so (the firefighters and other officials then went) but, if you wish to stay, I will carry on playing.' Most of the audience sat down again, and he played 'Land of Hope and Glory'. We all joined in with him. It was terrific and he received a standing ovation.

A similar tribute came from Glasgow:

> In the midst of his performance, the air-raid siren went off. He just shrugged and went on singing. Shortly after, the All Clear went, he said in a defiant way, 'Let's sing our answer to that.' He then played 'There'll Always Be an England', and the audience sang loudly too, and then he had a tumultuous reception from all of us. We wouldn't let him leave the stage. I was about 22 at the time, and I adored him.

A letter from Bolton mentions a rare tour *en famille*:

> I remember a charming man immaculately dressed, with a beautiful soft voice and flourishing the whitest handkerchief ever. He was with his lovely wife and daughter. Hutch brought the house down that night. He was the first black singer I had ever seen, and I was mesmerised by him. He transported the audience with the sheer magical quality of his velvet voice. I remember many people were reduced to tears and sobbing. I felt embraced by him, and needed the comfort at that time of war when everything was so frightening. Something of Leslie Hutchinson has stayed with me over the years. So much so, that when my daughter was born, I naturally called her Lesley.

Although he didn't show it in his performances, Hutch felt very frightened during air raids. Marjorie Lipscomb, then a BBC producer in Bristol, recalled travelling with Hutch by train from Temple Meads station to Bath during an air raid. 'He went quite white, speechless and shaky.' Like many people, Hutch could keep firm charge of himself when responsible for his audience, but when he was off stage and threatened by immediate danger, he went to pieces. Usually, though, he was very busy since first-class acts were, like practically everything else, in very short supply; at the start of the war, the government had repatriated most foreign performers and banned the entry of new overseas talent; many British performers had joined the services, and others had departed hurriedly for safer, less restricted zones.

During the Battle of Britain, Hutch was particularly in demand. After the Luftwaffe had dropped 10,000 firebombs on London, and destroyed the Guildhall and eight Wren churches in September 1940, night life entered a frenetic mood of living-on-the-edge and tomorrow-we-die. Behind the blackout, many restaurants and nightclubs overcame rationing and shortages of various foodstuffs, and the wartime regulation limiting the cost of a meal to five shillings; somehow, they continued to produce elaborate dinners and keep the liquor flowing. Bands played on, and Hutch went on performing cabaret. And, like George Formby and other variety stars, he went down into the London Underground stations, which many people used as air-raid shelters, and entertained for hours on end. 'He was brave to do it without his piano, but his voice was soothing, and he led singsongs, and we all felt cheered by his courage and kindness.'

An anonymous woman rang to tell me that she bought Hutch's records as they came out all through the war. 'I preferred to listen rather than watch him. He was electric on stage, which I found disturbing, very sensual with a dramatic way of moving his body, and his mouth was a bit coarse.' She sounded too inhibited to concede Hutch's appeal and thereby enjoy her obsession. Significantly, she only called me on Sundays when her husband was out.

Another keen collector of Hutch records was more direct in her response to Hutch. Having just left school, one girl went to a skating party on the frozen lake of Cirencester Park in the Cotswolds. Because of the raids, there were no bonfires, but the stars shone, and the gramophone boomed out Hutch singing Eric Maschwitz's three top hits: 'These Foolish Things', 'A Nightingale Sang in Berkeley Square' and 'Room 504'. On hearing his 'very manly . . . deep, rich, velvet voice', she recalled that her 'pony found itself a widower. I must marry such a man. I suddenly guessed one might do more than just lie side by side fully dressed in bed, once married. It was a most romantic and thrilling evening.'

Although wartime communications were very difficult, telegrams continued to flow from Hutch, a significant number of them to his loyal Joan. In a typical month, 1940, she received about twenty from all over England, expressing a diversity of needs. They ask for hotel reservations and appointments to be made or cancelled; beg her to remember her lover; and thank her for letters and presents. They ask her to order special dishes, to collect his shoes and get his watch repaired. They enquire why she was silent or absent, and what she was doing or thinking. They instruct her to rent a small furnished house in Amersham, Buckinghamshire, and, finally, from St Ives, Oxfordshire, they make her panic with, 'Narrowest escape ever. Extra luck saved my life. See today's papers. Badly shaken. Leslie.' This was probably a bomb, but such incidents were not reported in wartime. These telegrams show how much Joan contributed to the smooth running of Hutch's life, and also how he relied on her for security and affection. Because of her multiple roles, Joan knew, even during his long absences, that she was essential to Hutch. This was his intention; but, despite using her as a constant support, he did not return the same level of loyalty and devotion. In *Howards End*, E. M. Forster wrote that he mistrusted relationships based on 'telegrams and anger'; in other words, to leave everything to the last moment and take partners for granted is a recipe for bitterness and disillusion. Hutch aimed to be everything to everyone all the time: he was like a juggler with too many balls in the air, whose only hope is to keep juggling and disregard, for as long as possible, the resulting nervous strain.

Early in the war, Ella and Leslie, now seventeen, were evacuated from London 'for the duration' to Bangor, where, from 1943 on, the BBC had its recording studios for light entertainment; up till then, after moving from London, the studios had been in Bristol. Phyllis Rounce, the BBC employee in charge of Hutch's performances, recalls a time when broadcasting with him live from a bombed-out church in Bristol:

The end of the church caught fire. We provided the only contact the troops had with England, so it was vital to get the shows out

. . . the boys would think the worst had happened if they did not hear us. And it was *all* done live. There was no recording. It wasn't easy because you never knew if a performer would be alive by the time they were next scheduled. None of us might have been. The Germans were always aiming at the suspension bridge in Clifton where we were. Sir Adrian Boult and his orchestra[7] would pedal bikes up Whiteladies Road on their rims – there were no tyres. He was always very upright with a butcher's basket on the front of his bike which carried his batons and musical scores.

Like most producers, Phyllis admired Hutch's professionalism and deplored his female fans: 'They were a menace. They fell for him like ninepins and put him on a pedestal. I used to try to head them off so that we would not be disturbed when we were working. I did not permit audiences.' Phyllis found Hutch 'rather moody and touchy'; this may have been because he disliked being answerable to a woman or because she denied him access to others.

With the war, the ban on Hutch's radio appearances was tacitly withdrawn, and Hutch was soon busily engaged on a round of outside broadcasts. Typical of these was a *Workers' Playtime* programme from Blackpool, where a team on the assembly line making Wellington bombers sought his autograph and kisses. 'I doted on him at the time,' said one of them. 'It was so very nice of him to stop and chat and make us feel happier.' Stephen Williams, the producer of *Workers' Playtime*, remembered that Hutch 'had a terrific eye for the girls, and they fell for him lock, stock and barrel. He enjoyed himself no end.' Williams had devised *Break for Music*, a series of lunchtime concerts for workers that toured factories nationwide, before the war. When war broke out, he gained the support of Ernest Bevin, then minister of labour, to launch a variant, *Workers' Playtime*, which featured variety acts rather than music. 'I remember doing a *Workers' Playtime* with Hutch once near Chester as the bombs were falling. Later, we were turfed off the train at Crewe during an air raid on a Sunday. We got separated but met again later and fell on each other's necks. Then we did *Variety Bandbox*, a music-hall programme, together. On another *Workers' Playtime*, a Manchester fan heard Hutch introduce 'his daughter, Evelyn, and she sang "The Man I Love" '. He did make such an introduction, but it is not known who she was.

Like other radio stars (including Ben Lyon, Bebe Daniels and Vic Oliver), Hutch had to fulfil an annual six-week quota of broadcast and other performances for ENSA, which stood for Entertainment National Service Association or, more familiarly, Every Night Something Awful. For broadcast performances, artistes were paid two-thirds of the standard fee; for other shows, a flat £10 a week.

This makes a stark contrast with the weekly £500 Hutch commanded at venues such as the Ritz Cinema, Birkenhead, an Art Deco showplace strident with red plush and chrome. He usually performed between two full-length feature films. The actress Jean Boht, widow of Southan Morris who managed the Ritz, recalled that 'the Ritz put on massive stage shows. A new film would be released in Leicester Square, and the entire cast would travel next day to Birkenhead to promote it.' This scheme once put Hutch on the same bill as the Hollywood star Gregory Peck, who took great exception to sharing the stage with a black man. Southan Morris's son Stewart remembered Hutch at a white piano performing on his father's *Replica Royal Variety Show*, probably the nearest Hutch ever got to appearing under the regal banner. Hutch, who could choose his own compere, opted for Bill Pilkington, who often presented him at the Ritz and the Argyle, the broadcasting theatre, in Birkenhead, and at several of the five theatres in nearby Wallasey, then a larger holiday resort than Blackpool and, allegedly, with more millionaires than Paris.

Pilkington had vivid memories of Hutch's kindness to the disabled and the elderly. At a charity coffee morning at a house in Wallasey, Hutch entertained people, some of them with:

> hideous deformities. Hutch shook hands where possible. He told the blind ones that they were his most avid listeners, and made them feel ten feet tall. He was one of nature's gentlemen. Hutch had a need to belong, so he was always happy to contribute to charitable entertainment.
>
> Every woman fell for his charisma. He used to play for tea dances at the Adelphi, Liverpool, in the afternoons. As he looked at the women, they were hypnotised. I once saw him with a 64-year-old fan, who came to his dressing room. He just sat and looked at her, and then gently touched her cheek. She just melted into tears.

Always a man of extremes, Hutch was renowned throughout his career for being an erratic tipper. Grandiose by instinct, he rarely did good by stealth. Instead, he preferred to spend money ostentatiously to secure good service and praise for his generosity.[8] Early in the war, after performing for Mrs Churchill's Aid to the Russian Red Cross Fund, Hutch tipped the orchestra leader £5 to buy the musicians a drink, saying, 'I never forget I was once just a working musician and I know well how little you get paid.' He tipped a Liverpool taxi driver £1, double the fare: 'There's never been anyone like Hutch. He was a real gentleman.' In Yorkshire, Hutch went to a country inn full of aircrews and pilots of the Whitley bombers from Dishforth. He joined them for home-cured ham, eggs and game birds, and insisted that everything was 'served on silver, from teaspoons to plates. After the meal, he not only left a tip, but . . . congratulated the cook . . . and gave her, the two waiters and the two waitresses one pound apiece, a lovely gesture. My wife was the cook, I was on leave. One disappointment, he never gave us a turn, his contract forbade it.' Or so he said. One woman recalls Hutch staying at the Seaburn Hotel in Sunderland, and giving an impromptu concert on the piano in his rooms, playing in the dark, because of the blackout, with uncurtained windows framing the moonlight on the sea.

Reviews now gratefully referred to him as a long-established entertainer, implying that he was providing a sense of stability and continuity particularly valuable in wartime. Commenting on an appearance in variety at the Palace, Manchester, in late 1940, a critic wrote:

> The warmest applause of a full house was given to Hutch as to an old friend. He was as charming as ever, as much at home in his musical rhythmical element, with the same brilliance and delicacy in his fingers, and the rather full and unrestrained expressiveness of voice that transforms at moments, the most banal love songs into poetry.[9]

At this time, Hutch's main cabaret engagement was at Quaglino's, usually called Quag's. While imprisoned by the Japanese in Kuchin, John Gardiner wrote a nostalgic round-up of London nightclubs and described Quag's as:

one of the nicest restaurants in London . . . in Bury Street, just off Jermyn Street and cars may be parked outside. A taxi to Piccadilly Circus costs 9d. Before the war, it was presided over by the brothers Quaglino, John and Ernest, but since Italy's entry into the war, they are no longer there. The restaurant itself is a very pleasant room, with comfortable sofa seats around the walls. The food is very good, perhaps excellent . . . it is fashionable for both lunch and dinner. Dress is compulsory in the evening, where there is dancing to a good band and a cabaret at midnight.

Bill Cotton, son of the bandleader Billy Cotton, remembered Hutch as being 'the darling of quite a wide set at Quaglino's. He bedded a lot of white women. He looked terribly important and had gravitas, an aura of being very well connected.' Cotton also recalled his father's band being on the same bill at Watford in a fund-raising enterprise typical of time, 'Wings Week', with audiences contributing to the purchase of a Spitfire fighter plane.

Hutch would have been only sporadically available for cabaret in London, as he also appeared, from mid-November 1940 until mid-1941, in *Mayfair Follies*, a touring 'Song and Laughter Show', with, among others, Nat Jackley, 'the India-Rubber Man'. A local Northampton paper shows Hutch – cross-legged, arms folded and grinning broadly – flanked by girls in the show with their arms round him. Hutch's lighting plot for the show survives. He gives detailed instructions for different illumination to highlight the variations in mood of each number. Several artistes recalled Hutch's scrupulous insistence on every detail of this facet of his performance. He was equally stringent about the make and position on stage of his piano; the orchestra's timing; the fall and shade of the backing curtains; indeed, every facet of the presentation which made his act so impressive. Small wonder theatre managements respected his professionalism.

During rehearsals for *Mayfair Follies* at Nottingham, the chef arrived from the best local hotel to discuss Hutch's evening menu. For half an hour, while the other cast members stood around, Hutch gave the chef exact instructions on how to prepare his pheasant and woodcock, and on which wines to uncork and when. Hutch did well for himself throughout the war, despite the official rationing from 1940 of butter, sugar, bacon, meat, tea, margarine and cooking fats, together with, from 1941, a points system that extended even to vegetables and canned foods. When others were turned away, hotels and restaurants would serve him delectable meals; and in the teeth of regulations, farmers used to send him a steady stream of parcels containing butter, eggs, pork and chicken. While colleagues not invited to share Hutch's lavish menus were resentful of his unpatriotic gourmandising, many of his friends admired his capacity to forage so successfully.

When *Mayfair Follies* reached Rochdale, a stagehand was briefed to keep Hutch supplied with ice for his face because of his sweating: the handkerchiefs were also liberally flourished. One night a couple were imitating Hutch's mopping and laughing between themselves so loudly that Hutch looked up, saw why and, for the rest of his performance, did not use his handkerchief. At the Hippodrome, Wolverhampton, a fan noted a pile of snowy white handkerchiefs on the piano, and, on Hutch's little finger, 'a beautiful diamond ring . . . which flashed in the lights . . . real or not, it was a whopper'. An idiosyncrasy that affected his fellow performers rather more was Hutch's 'complete non-adherence to the conventional beat and the way he hung on to ad lib cadences'; this often led to an 'awful tangle'.

In 1940, an incendiary bomb landed in the garden at 31 Steeles Road, and several nearby houses were bombed. Hutch's brother Ivan decided to move to Wolverhampton, where he met a tall, attractive blonde whom he soon afterwards married. Over the ten years he had been in London, he had run numerous errands and acted as secretary to Hutch and minder to Edwina. In the 1990s, people in Wolverhampton still recalled Ivan and his wife Molly. At first he attracted attention from the local press, simply because he was Hutch's brother – Ivan's only real distinction. 'Hutch Gives First Show in Wolverhampton' ran a headline, with the bathetic follow-up, 'But he is brother of stage-star.' The rather laboured story runs:

> Like Leslie in appearance, Ivan does not play the piano, although he confessed to having all the opportunities to learn when young. His voice, however, is deeper than Leslie's, and admirably suited to the song he sung, 'Mighty lak' a Rose' . . . Ivan hopes to go on the stage before long, but would not say definitely whether he would appear with his brother or as a

single turn . . . Modest and retiring, Ivan admitted that people
had often remarked on the excellence of his singing . . .

In fact, Ivan was nothing like good enough to turn professional.

Early in 1941, Ivan joined a Defiant Assembly Section at the
Boulton-Paul Aircraft Factory in Wolverhampton. A fellow work-
er – Ivan's partner on much of the two-handed riveting vital to
aircraft assembly – said that, while Ivan was extrovert and lost no
time in saying who his brother was, he was also likeable, well
educated and well spoken. Ivan's mate stood in awe of him
because, except in films, he was the first black man he had seen;
moreover, at Ivan's insistence, he had accompanied him to the
lavatory so that he could see for himself how well endowed Ivan
was. When Ivan asked, 'What d'you think of it?', the mate replied,
'It's all right', a noncommittal response which Ivan found deeply
unsatisfactory. When other workers heard about this incident, they
'rolled in the aisles'.

When Hutch played the Hippodrome in Birmingham, Ivan and
several of his mates went to hear him; in the interval Ivan went
backstage to ask Hutch whether he would come and entertain
them at the factory. When he came back, 'we pestered him,
"What'd he say? What'd he say?" Slowly, a bit sad, Ivan told us,
'He said, "Fuck off." ' In the event, Hutch did go to the factory,
and performed to a huge lunchtime audience. The factory revelled
in the Hutchinson connection.

Early in 1942, Ivan joined the RAF. When on leave, he used to
sing duets with Molly in the local clubs; their most notable
performance was for the Dutch armed forces at the Civic Hall.
Although there was space for them in Molly's family home, they
lived in their own house. Her niece explained, "Molly Rawlings
was my aunt, a half-sister to my father, a lovely young woman,
very tall and very fair. My mother was somewhat strait-laced about
colour and much else, and refused to have her name mentioned. It
was a taboo subject in our family.' A Grenadian who knew Ivan as
the warden at a hostel for West Indian students after the war,
remembered Molly as 'Jewish, I think, and loud and flamboyant.
She used to chase all us students. Ivan seemed resigned to this
behaviour.'

Unsurprisingly, Ivan and Molly eventually divorced. Molly
married a Dutchman and went to live in the Netherlands. 'She

never got on with her brother-in-law, Hutch,' her niece said. In the late 1940s, Ivan became a postman in Kilburn, sometimes visiting pubs also frequented by his brother, and always 'quiet, taciturn and resentful of Hutch', the musician Don Johnson observed.

Far from supporting him in any way, Hutch seems to have exploited Ivan and put him down, both explicitly and implicitly. He bullied and despised him for being less bright, less talented, darker-skinned and infinitely more ordinary. Ivan is a shadowy, depressed figure: cuckolded by his wife, who finally left him; bereft of a career or a separate identity; and dependent on a brother who was dismissive of him and would not even let him enjoy his own reflected glory. He was insignificant, and Hutch did not let him forget it.

In 1942 Lawrence Wright told a reporter that once, when having supper with Mistinguett in Paris, he had heard a middle-aged violinist in the restaurant play an arresting melody. The tune, 'Jealousy', turned out to be written by the violinist, Joseph Gade, who came from Copenhagen. Wright paid Gade a large advance on prospective royalties, but the tune, published as a conventional tango, flopped. Then it was set to words by Winifred May (later better known as Patience Strong, the writer of uplifting doggerel in popular newspapers), and Wright approached Hutch to perform and promote the song. Like Wright, Hutch immediately spotted its potential, declared 'It is a great song', and sang it in the show *Happidrome*. He matched its dramatic swoops and flounces with his own ornate touch, and 'Jealousy', backed by Wright's promotional resources, was soon, in the words of his sales force, 'selling something terrific'. Sadly, Joseph Gade, a Jew, died in a concentration camp, beyond the reach of any further royalties.

Happidrome was a much-loved radio comedy series in which Harry Korris, as Mr Lovejoy, played the manager of an imaginary theatre in the north of England. Robbie Vincent played the callboy, Ramsbottom, and Cecil Frederick was the long-suffering stage manager, Enoch. The show enjoyed the same level of popularity as *It's That Man Again* with Tommy Handley, Deryck Guyler and Jack Train. Through the Overseas Broadcasting Service, which represented the Admiralty, the War Office and the Air Ministry, *Happidrome* was heard in places as far flung as Aden,

Lusaka, Lahore and Nassau. Harry Korris, who wrote the script, was once delighted by a letter from an old lady requesting the chorus to sing a little louder next week as the batteries on her wireless were running down. The chorus, which still evoked smiles fifty years later, went:

> We three in Happidrome
> Working for the BBC
> Ramsbottom, Enoch and me
> We're North Country comics
> Who bring you a tonic
> BUT JUST LET ME TELL YOU . . .

This was Enoch's catchphrase. It always led into a joke. The live show toured Britain until 1944, when it was promptly revived as *The New Happidrome*. It was also turned into a musical comedy film, largely a vehicle for Jack Buchanan, in 1943. Hutch appears in a stagey setting to sing a cheery, upbeat number, 'Take the World Exactly as You Find It', with florid accompaniment, and a more conventional ballad, 'You Are My Love Song'. Stills and publicity material for the film furnished Joan with more cuttings for her scrapbook featuring Hutch – and, much to his jealous disgust, for another scrapbook devoted to Jack Buchanan.

The producer Robert Nesbitt adapted the show and staged it at the Prince of Wales Theatre in Piccadilly in 1942. It was a revue, and Hutch, its biggest star, attracted fulsome notices; one of them included the strange phrase, 'His personality came over the footlights and engulfed us all like a benediction.' Korris, Vincent and Frederick were, of course, constants; and the show was joined on occasion by guest artists including Two-Ton Tessie O'Shea; Evelyn 'Boo' Laye; Wilson, Keppel and Betty; some gifted musical clowns, the Cairoli Brothers; and a Free French comedian, Sherkot.[11] Proceeds from the show went to local charities such as Blackpool's Tanks for Attack Drive, Liverpool's League of Welldoers, Leeds Jewish Charities or Lady Cripps's United Aid to China Fund in London. Eliciting his support at a performance, one charity organiser wrote to Hutch, 'You may wish to know that some very high personages will be present, and that the show will be well covered by the Press.' Some fund-raising methods have not changed.

Hutch greatly liked the North Country comics. At Swansea they played golf most afternoons, with children skipping school to watch them. When Hutch took Korris to a luxurious hotel, expecting to impress him, Korris laconically said, 'What, no dart board?', echoing the 'Chad' signs then chalked on walls nation-wide, showing a little head with a big nose, looking over a wall and saying, 'Wot, no cigarettes?' – or other wartime deprivation. Korris and Hutch each carried printed cards which read, 'CIVIL DEFENCE. The man who hands you this card is an AIR RAID WARDEN. DO NOT BE AFRAID. Lie down on the floor and do exactly what he tells you.'

Hutch continued to attract a self-replenishing stream of girls. In the middle of the war, his most frequent companion in Liverpool was a vicar's daughter, a pretty actress called Violet Davies, who was happy to be known as 'Hutch's whore'. She first saw him at the Empire Theatre in 1942, in *Happidrome*. What with clothes rationing and service uniforms, it was not always easy for young women to match the modish standards Hutch continued to expect of them, even in wartime. He solved this problem by providing them with props for the duration of the date. When he took out a Wren in Portsmouth, his chauffeur picked her up, and there was a fur coat in the car for her to wear for the evening.

Clothes rationing inconvenienced Hutch too. The materials for new clothes were not available, so he had to make do with his existing wardrobe. Moreover, cigarettes and alcohol were in erratic supply, and petrol was rationed except for work-related journeys. Still, he managed to get around.

Hutch was often in trouble for chasing other men's women. The more out of bounds they were, and the less they encouraged him, the keener he was to surmount the challenge. In 1943, on tour in Colwyn Bay in Wales, Hutch laid amative siege to the fiancée of a local doctor. When the doctor told him to stay away, Hutch paid no attention and ended up with a bloody nose.

Some of Hutch's more soppily sentimental songs were banned by the BBC's Anti-Slush Committee, part of a move to stiffen the national spine with martial airs while firmly discouraging the trembling upper lip. Trimming his sails accordingly, Hutch made an appearance with Ella and Leslie on the sleeve of a war propaganda song, 'This Is Worth Fighting For'. Hutch delivers its highly patriotic message in a stentorian style that evokes the famous recruiting poster of Kitchener saying 'Your King and Country Need YOU'.

Despite a twice-nightly stage schedule and frequent cabaret performances into the small hours, Hutch also fulfilled numerous lunchtime engagements. Typical of these was a concert at Port Sunlight in Cheshire, where he received hearty welcome from 7,000 employees of Lever Brothers. A Parlophone representative got caught up in the slipstream of audience fervour after a concert in Hayes, and afterwards wrote to Hutch, 'What an appalling mass of girls; I hardly recovered from the terrific onslaught afterwards, and think most of my ribs must have been broken!' Far from sharing this jaundiced view, Hutch greatly enjoyed much of the adulation; and photographs show him festooned with fans and looking relaxed and gratified. Among his huge audiences were many girls keen to make closer contact in the future, who bombarded Hutch with letters like this: 'My friend and I have plucked up courage to write this letter requesting a personally signed photo EACH of yourself. Please don't think we are being rather forward, but as YOU probably know, a girl MUST try all means to gain her own ends. From two devoted admirers, Elsie and Winnie.' He answered swiftly and efficiently with signed photographs; and to those that pressingly suggested meetings, he sent a short letter of regret that his schedule did not permit him to enjoy himself as much as he would like.

Towards young fans, Hutch was always generous with his time. In one typical instance, a schoolboy watched Hutch rehearse the song 'Island in the Sun' at the Palace Theatre, Reading, in 1944. Hutch asked him backstage, saying, 'You have no need to call me "sir". Just ask the manager to bring you round later on.' The boy spent some twenty minutes with Hutch, who described 'the beauty of his childhood in the West Indies' and arranged for him to sit in the wings during his performance.

Hutch was delighted to receive a letter from C. B. Cochran in February 1943, inviting him to play 'an eminent part' in 'a big show on Wednesday, June 16th, in aid of TocH, which creates new clubs worldwide for men and women of the United Nations Forces . . .'[12] In a letter to Hutch's agent, Cochran wrote, 'The Show . . . is to be called "70 Years of Song". Their Majesties will be present; Prime Ministers and the Ambassadors of the United

Nations are taking part. In short, it will be a terrific affair . . . I should like Hutch to play an important part in it. Should it mean the sacrifice of a week's engagement, a fee can be arranged.' The venue was the Royal Albert Hall, and Cochran was in his element. He described it in his autobiography *A Showman Looks On*:

> I had had this experience before, notably with my Mammoth Cabaret of pre-war days in aid of the Actors' Benevolent Fund and, during this war, with my Big Circus and Fair in aid of the Yugoslav Relief Society. Success in each case was due largely, if not wholly, to the popularity of the entertainments on their merits . . . Here was the idea. A programme of ever-popular songs and tunes, differing widely in artistic and technical merit, yet alike in possessing that inexplicable elemental appeal to the popular taste of the song.

The publicity material described the event as 'a costume cavalcade of tunes whistled by the butcher's boy; played on barrel organs, and by town and military bands; heard in music halls and concert halls from 1870 to the present era of the BBC, with Geraldo's Concert Orchestra augmented by Celebrity Instrumentalists and Many Singing Stars'. The publisher Walter Hutchinson printed and distributed 50,000 copies of a book called *70 Years of Song*. Max Beerbohm wrote the foreword, and there were contributions from Noël Coward and James Agate, among many others. Apart from royalty and various political and diplomatic figures, the Albert Hall was to be packed with prominent socialites. Most of them well known to Hutch, they included the Mountbattens, Lady Emerald Cunard, Lady Charles Cavendish (Adele Astaire), Lady Diana Cooper, Mrs Reginald Fellowes and the Duchess of Westminster.

The first half featured music from 1872 to 1916: excerpts from Gilbert and Sullivan, the can-can, songs by Leslie Stuart (an Englishman who wrote for musical comedy and minstrel shows), Elgar's 'Land of Hope and Glory', highlights from *The Arcadians*, *The Quaker Girl* and *Miss Hook of Holland* (old musical comedies). Then 'Jazz arrives in the person of Hutch': in Cochran's words, 'As the orchestra played the waltz, Hutch walked on, sat at the piano and started to play; Geraldo stops dead, Geraldo looks at Hutch, Hutch plays "Alexander's Ragtime Band", and the whole orchestra joins in. There was a black-out.' Next, a 200-strong chorus let rip with a Great War medley: 'Tipperary', 'Hello, Hello, Who's Your Lady Friend?', 'We Don't Want to Lose You', 'Who Were You with Last Night?' and 'Pack Up Your Troubles'. Ivor Novello played and sang his own first great hit, 'Keep the Home Fires Burning'; and the first half ended with the Albert Hall resounding to a magnificent performance of 'Jerusalem'. 'The audience staggered under all they had seen and heard,' Cochran commented. The royal box received him kindly in the interval.

This accolade did not prevent Cochran from being nervous about the second half, containing songs from 1916 to 1943, because the cast had only rehearsed to the first-half finale. 'How long would it run? Would the people know their exits and entrances? It was all in the lap of the gods.' The second half started with a further burst of Great War songs. Georges Rex, 'a real French soldier', sang 'Madelon'; and George Robey and Violet Loraine sang 'If You Were the Only Girl in the World'. Cochran thought 'they had not aged a day since they drew all the boys on leave to the Alhambra. It was the greatest success of the evening.' There were songs from the talkies with a children's chorus; Tessie O'Shea belted out 'Some of These Days'; Adelaide Hall sang 'I'm a Little Blackbird'; and Edythe Baker played variations on 'My Heart Stood Still'. When Hutch reappeared to perform 'What Is This Thing Called Love?', Phyllis Stanley danced to it in the manner of Tilly Losch, and Cochran delighted in 'another big Pavilion reproduction' from his triumphant 1928 revue *This Year of Grace*. Evelyn Laye, Mary Ellis and Noël Coward rounded off the 1930s; and Vera Lynn, Doris Hare and others weighed in with wartime hits including 'We'll Meet Again' and 'There'll Be Blue Birds Over the White Cliffs of Dover'. Then Hutch thundered out 'Begin the Beguine' before mood and tempo switched to what Cochran called 'the hottest exposition of jitterbugging I have seen off the screen in England'; Eva Turner sang 'Poor Butterfly'; and there was a final roof-raising blast of 'Land of Hope and Glory'. Cochran recounted that 'the vast audience, who, in this memorable evening had run the gamut of pretty nearly all the emotions, was deeply stirred'.

Hutch appeared in the show more than any other solo artist. As well as being a great tribute of esteem and affection, this also recognised the diversity of his talents and the musical contribution he had made since arriving in Britain nearly twenty years before.

He kept several copies of the programme, and some reviews: 'A magnificent and historic show'; 'Stupendous'. A *Times* leader pontificated:

> The pudding was so stuffed with plums that nobody could have gone away with the feeling that particular favourites had been overlooked – here was a measure packed full and running over with the kind of emotion that has nothing mawkish in it . . . *70 Years of Song* kept to a note which managed to combine nostalgia for the past with hope for the future.[13]

For Cochran, it was his last success for three financially straitened years while 'the doodlebugs and V2s came and went and Europe was once more invaded'.[14]

For Hutch, it was the highlight of an eventful year. Other variety stars, such as George Formby and Flanagan and Allen, had great wartime hits, but Hutch continued to be better known for prewar songs. His appeal was romantic and escapist, and, as 'This Is Worth Fighting For' showed, his talent was unsuited to jingoism. In 1944, the BBC producer of *Palestine Half Hour* reflected this by inviting Hutch to play 'a nice medley – songs you have done in the past, and by which they all remember you. A few that come to mind are "These Foolish Things", "Body and Soul", "Smoke Gets in Your Eyes" and "The Best Things in Life Are Free".'

By mid-1945, Hutch was touring with Ted Ray and Nat Jackley in a new comedy show by Tom Arnold, *We'll Be Seeing You*. With the unconditional surrender of the Germans to the Allies on 6 May, the show was renamed *Victory Variety*. In the autumn, Hutch appeared in a charity concert at the Usher Hall, Edinburgh, with a comedy duo, Chic Murray and Maidie. Murray's biographer writes that Hutch, who topped the bill, chatted to Murray as if he was an old friend; this show of warmth would have been far less likely before the war, when Hutch was notoriously aloof.

By this time, friends and a few fans noticed that, with the cumulative strains of war getting to him, Hutch was drinking too much. Their evidence suggests he started as a binge drinker, with the binges gradually increasing to absorb most of his waking hours. His weight increased, his eyes sank into his ballooning cheeks and his physique, like his on-stage persona, tipped into caricature. As a character in one of Elizabeth Bowen's wartime stories says,

'Whatever you are these days, you are rather more so. That's one thing I've discovered with this war.'[15]

Once, when Hutch was appearing at the Glasgow Empire, a member of the audience saw Hutch, at the start of the second house, being 'virtually carried' by two large men; but the quality of his performance a little later was in no way impaired. Joan Skillington, whose Cotswolds skating party had made her a Hutch fan, asked her husband to take her to see Hutch perform in variety in Derby in September 1945. Her husband said, 'You wouldn't like it. He's an awful old drunk nowadays.' But she insisted, and they went to:

> a rather scruffy music hall. A vulgar comedian, a roll on the drums – and Hutch! A big fat sweating dark brown man tightly stuffed into a crumpled silk dinner jacket, with a red carnation, attended by a few sleazy 'girls', women of an uncertain age. But he sat down and began to play and the old magic was there and I was back in my teens when I had learned of romance simply from recorded sound. I shall always be grateful to him.

Having not seen Hutch for five years, Bill Pilkington paged him through newspaper advertisements, and arranged to meet him in Shaftesbury Avenue late in 1945.

> He looked jowly and grey; he had put on a lot of weight – his neck bulged over his collar – and he had lost his air of immaculate dressing. Something was missing. He asked how I was. I said, 'I survive, as you see, but I have 27 wounds and have had a pretty bloody war in intelligence.'
> 'A chestful of medals and they won't pay you any money?'
> I admitted getting a DCM.
> 'Congratulations! My God, I envy you that,' he almost shouted.
> 'You never know your luck, Leslie!' I tried to cheer him up.
> 'I have never had any recognition,' he said bitterly.

Towards the end of the war, there was a propaganda catch phrase on the home front, 'What have you done to relieve boredom?' Hutch could have given a very comprehensive and positive answer: he worked hard throughout the war, diverting hundreds of thousands of people nationwide, often spontaneously and without pay on top of an already gruelling schedule. He was angry that his efforts were never publicly honoured. He felt cheated and passed over, and believed that his colour caused his rejection; but the cause had more to do with his relationship with Edwina. Some said that Hutch had been lily-livered in not going abroad with ENSA. This was an unjust taunt, given Hitler's attitude to blacks: if Hutch had been taken prisoner, he probably would not have survived. Anyway, he had tried to enlist twice, but was turned down.

A letter from a Newcastle fan gives a fair appreciation of Hutch's war effort:

Women went weak at the knees over him. While we had to admit his undoubted talent, us lads regarded him as affected. He reminded me of Charles Laughton as Captain Bligh, when he said with such haughtiness, 'Oh, the things I do for England!' Hutch was like that. Gave you the impression that he was thinking, 'Whatever am I doing playing for this rabble?' Conceit? You've never seen anything like it! Yet, looking back, I admire him. He was one of a few talented artistes who gave of their talent and time, when this country was on its knees. I love him now. Hitler was just across the Channel. Our army had been flung into the sea. We had nothing. Little in the way of food or clothing. London was burning . . . People were brave. It WAS our finest hour.

Hutch and people like him gave of their very best. Morale was very important. You needed a song or a joke. You could only have a concert if it was for charity, that's why there were a lot of them. It was a time for good songs and Hutch sung some lovely ones. He transported us out of our world and into another where tomorrow would be better. He was having an affair with Lady Mountbatten. I saw them together once. Whatever they say, she gave of her best as well. She cared for the poor, the hungry, the dispossessed and the evacuees. A fine lady. Let's hope they enjoyed each other, God bless them.

The war was a cusp of change, both politically and socially. Postwar austerity did not favour Hutch: the variety halls in which he had become a national figure would soon echo to the bark of the bingo caller and the clatter of the bowling alley; and cinema and

television would swiftly supersede the intimacy of the live performance. Hutch suffered these upheavals painfully, and his slow
decline over the next seven years ended in disappearance, until his
return in the mid-1950s to a very different entertainment scene.
Even so, over half a century later, numerous people still recalled
with pride, affection and admiration, the way in which Hutch and
others entertained brightened dark days, revived spirits and shared
their perils in that time of war.

Chapter Nine

Out of Fashion
1946–1953

That winter was the very lowest period of my life, but always there was the one thing that keeps the hardest-pressed entertainer going. Today or any day that 'phone may ring and bring good news.

Ethel Waters

V E Day, Victory in Europe Day, had set off a burst of euphoria throughout Britain, but it was short-lived. Demobilisation took far longer than expected. Rationing continued, and some commodities were in shorter supply than ever: bread, for instance, was rationed for the first time in 1947 and a roll at a restaurant meal counted as a whole course. And, although the lights had gone on again, people slowly began to realise that the country had ceased to be a world-class power. Income tax stayed at around its wartime level of 45–50 per cent; surtax on larger incomes was much higher; and death duties, by which 80 per cent of a person's property was confiscated at their death, significantly diminished the whole way of life of many of Hutch's cabaret patrons. This high taxation aimed to redistribute wealth in such a way that working–class people, the bulk of Hutch's variety audience, would enjoy a great increase in their standard of living. And so they did: every year, while members of the old ruling classes sold or subdivided their large houses and dispensed with their staff of domestic servants, more and more working-class families owned a refrigerator, a washing machine, a television set and a car. The upper class, feeling themselves to be the new poor, loathed the Attlee administration; they described their troubles as the 'Second Battle of Britain', and relied on Elsa Maxwell and other American visitors for electric torches, hot-water bottles, hams, corsets known as 'two-way stretches' and other commodities to lighten the age of austerity. The working class said, 'It's our turn now.'

In this social upheaval, Hutch's fortunes slowly declined. After 1945, his reviews and publicity diminished to a trickle, and his HMV record contract ended in November 1948. Hutch later claimed that all this was due to 'a complete metamorphosis in the business'.[1] There was some truth in this, as Hutch's café-society style was out of step with the rigours and aspirations of postwar Britain – as his agent bluntly said, 'In 1949, he lost his appeal' – but his problems were due less to external pressures than to personal failings. His drinking was now out of control, and stress from performance and heavy smoking had combined to infect his throat and harm his vocal chords. He was very overweight, and complained of high blood pressure and a poor liver. And he was very concerned about his finances. Although he continued to earn a fair amount throughout this downturn, which lasted from 1949 to 1953, his income had fallen and Hutch, as self-indulgent as ever, was incapable of making the necessary cuts. He would send himself roses when the audience could not be counted on to do so. An advertisement in the *Performer* in 1946 stated, 'Artists please note. No impersonations of "Hutch" (Leslie A. Hutchinson) are permitted without obtaining approval and permission.' What control Hutch thought he could exercise over his mimics is open to conjecture; that the advertisement was an index of a rise in self-doubt is certain.

Billed as 'The Millionaire of Melody' or 'Your Favourite British Radio and Recording Star', Hutch was still busy in variety, but he was no longer always top of the bill, and the shows were visiting more remote places. As his moments of triumph declined, the incidence of temperamental outbursts rose. Typical was a band call one Monday morning at the Tivoli Theatre, Hull, in 1949. When the orchestra arrived for the three-hour rehearsal, Hutch's band books, containing thirty-six songs, were already on their chairs. He practised with the orchestra for two hours, and eventually chose some six songs to perform. With only one hour's rehearsal time, the other seven acts, mostly acrobats and comics, underperformed, received only lukewarm applause, and feared for Hutch's reception at the hands of so sluggish a provincial audience. In the event, a fellow artiste, Sydney Shaw, recalled, 'He went on in the closing spot and, to our astonishment, *paralysed* them. For thirty minutes! The crowd cheered and screamed for more, while Hutch beamed and mopped his brow. We all crept away to our dressing rooms somewhat abashed.' This must have boosted his flagging ego; likewise, the florid doggerel that continued to pour in from his fans. This acrostic is typical:

> H stands for handsome on that we agree
> U for understanding we know he must be
> T is for tender when he sings high and low
> C stands for charming a thing we do know
> H comes again at the end of his name
> One that's well known for variety fame

Another adoring verse lists his hits. It names only one post–1939 hit, 'Bless You', a happy, catchy song Hutch clearly enjoyed performing.

In February 1948, Hutch had told a journalist that he was off 'on my first holiday since 1939. I am going to France and then to Switzerland.' In fact, he was about to pay his third visit to a clinic, Mas Aya in Glion sur Montreux, for treatment. In a letter requesting musical arrangements from England, René Schmassmann, a fellow patient who ran an orchestra in Basel, said that Hutch would have to return for new treatment if he got 'fat again'. At the end of February, Hutch wrote to Joan:

> My sweetie, Here at last is my hideout. If you remember, I have been here before . . . You would not believe it if you saw me now. I have lost a *stone* and am looking extremely well. So slim. I shall return early in March. I have no money left. I shall be at the George V about the 4th March en route.

The letter came from the Val-Mont Clinique Médicale, also in Glion, which, after several changes of management, still survives as a clinic in the late 1990s. It is a luxurious Alpine retreat with huge grounds, a lake and sweeping mountain views. When Hutch went there, the way of life would have changed little from that described by Thomas Mann in *The Magic Mountain* and by Scott Fitzgerald in *Tender Is the Night*: people would still have dressed for dinner, and still taken slow cautious walks, exchanging almost imperceptible bows and nods with congenial inmates in mutual assurance of each other's anonymity. Today they dry out in a blaze of publicity, but in those days the stars kept their personal problems and weaknesses to themselves. Hutch may also have seen strength in his secrecy. He hated to appear vulnerable to anyone, even Joan; and, while he needed her to know where he was, he did not always tell her why he was there.

Fourteen months later, Hutch was back in the clinic for two weeks. 'Sweetie,' ran a letter to Joan, 'The weather has been delightful. I didn't write at first as I was on a strict diet and resting in bed for 66 out of 72 hours. But the result . . . My God. You have never seen anything like it.' The clinic offered relief from '*maladies d'estomac: gastrites, ulcères gastro-duodénaux: de l'intestin: entérites, colites; du foie: de la vésicule biliaire; diabète, goutte obésité. Affections du coeur et de la circulation: hypertension, angine de poitrine, maladies des reins et des voies urinaires. Troubles nerveux: cures de repos et de convalescence.*' The exact purpose of Hutch's treatment, apart from '*maigrissement*', is not known. He was suffering from a combination of maladies rooted in overindulgence. In the clinic's brochure he has heavily underlined this note: '*Les affections tuberculeuses pulmonaires et toutes autres maladies contagieuses sont exclués.*' In view of his father's final illness, the possibility of tuberculosis may have been his greatest fear.

At other times, when Hutch was not feeling flush, he would visit a clinic in Lower Beeding in Sussex several times, and probably others. He was fast approaching fifty, and worried about getting old as well as about his mental and physical health. Yet he made little attempt to curb his drinking in the late 1940s. The musician Don Johnson, who often saw him in the Eagle in Clifton Road and the Chippenham in Shirland Road, recalled, 'Hutch was always sozzled and amidst a circle of rowdy drunk Irishmen in those places.'

After the Swiss rest cure, Hutch was sufficiently restored to tackle a weekly half-hour radio series, *Hutch's Song Album*, featuring numbers from the 1930s to the present day. It lasted four weeks from mid-March to mid-April. Like many people at the time, especially those in the entertainment business, Hutch struck an elegiac note in his linking commentary invoking the prewar years as a golden age, a paradise beyond regain. He regretted the loss of carefree, leisurely days when there was scope for true romance, and blamed those who, in their blind pursuit of power, had deceived the world and left it a sadder but not wiser place. The series attracted high acclaim, notably from the *Sound Magazine* critic who declared it to be 'one of the greatest ever shows in the history of BBC presentations. The listening millions, both at home and abroad, will treasure precious memories evoked in the *Song Album* of this most famous gentleman.'

The show was conceived by Sydney Grace, assistant to Hutch's agent Charles Tucker. Tucker went back home to America just before the war, and returned in 1946. He had an impressive portfolio of variety stars – they included Max Wall, Cyril Fletcher, Alfred Marks, Beryl Reid and Julie Andrews – and sent big-name shows on nationwide tours. (He went into semi-retirement long before he finally left the business in 1964; and died, aged 85, in 1978.) In 1949 Sydney Grace took up the reins of the agency, and handled most of Hutch's business. Grace found him 'charming and no trouble to attend to and [he] was a great host. He taught me to make a champagne cocktail.' Grace made way in 1952 for Terry Miller, who took a more jaundiced view of Hutch:

> Not an easy man, he was eccentric and too grand. Our office was above a cigar shop in Piccadilly, where the all-night Boots is now, and Hutch would never come up for contracts and a chat, but insisted that papers be brought down to him. He had lady chauffeurs by then. Hutch had ups and downs like Max Wall. He was an anachronism, who put himself on a pedestal. The Blue Angel paid chicken feed. Hutch was tricky. He often made separate deals which broke his contract in later years, but I tolerated it because the man needed the money.

Miller's attitude is not surprising. After Tucker, Hutch treated his agents as servitors. Tucker had cultivated a grand style, knew everyone in the business, was asked everywhere and had much to teach a willing Hutch at the start of his career in England. His successors rejected this expansive, old-fashioned demeanour in favour of a hard-nosed business approach. Hutch resented this, and dealt with them peremptorily, as he dealt with his bank manager and his accountant. By this time, he was convinced that he knew best and that these functionaries, while necessary, provided little true support. He let them infer that, if he were less important and busy, he could do their jobs much better himself.

Miller continued to make some arrangements for Hutch for the rest of Hutch's life, but in 1954 Hutch wrote to the BBC, saying that all future negotiations should be conducted with a freelance agent, Emlyn Griffiths. In some ways Griffiths was an improvement on Miller. Leslie Berens remembered him as 'a tall businessman, a real gent in a brown tweed suit. He was good for Hutch and more to his liking.' Another friend said, 'He was a swanky sort of socialite, who knew Hutch's clients.'

Of all the wilderness years between 1946 and 1953, when Hutch embarked on a comeback, 1948 is the most typical in its combination of professional reverses, minor successes and desperate attempts to halt the downward spiral. A major setback was the end of his contract with HMV. An internal memorandum dated 3 December 1947 struck an ominous note: 'We need an orchestra accompanying Hutch. The reason for this is that we are trying to make Hutch records more interesting and appealing to the public.' The company then moved his recordings from the magenta label to the more expensive plum label as a way of ensuring low sales – giving a pretext for terminating the contract. This happened in November 1948, and Hutch did not make another record until September 1954. Among his last recordings were 'I May Be Wrong but I Think You're Wonderful', an old song that had been resuscitated by the release of versions by Dinah Shore and Hoagy Carmichael. Hutch also recorded 'Nice to Know You Care' in a way fondly remembered by its composer, Norman Newell; and Bill Ward, another songwriter, wrote to thank Hutch for performing 'My Heart and I' in a *Workers' Playtime* broadcast.

During the summer, Hutch entertained at Butlin's Holiday Camp at Skegness, a venue he would have considered far beneath him in the 1930s. When staying at a local hotel, he flourished his gold cigarette case in which his initials were set in diamonds, and told a fellow artiste, Tom Corbett, that Lady Mountbatten had given it to him. 'He was so arrogant, ordering treble brandies and boasting about his sexual prowess.'

Hutch also performed in a summer show at Oxford, where he befriended the son of a waiter at the Randolph Hotel. 'Every night, after his show, he sat with us and we talked about everything. He was a nice, down-to-earth bloke, and quite unlike his theatrical image of an artiste who associated with royalty and Mayfair society. He told me about his race-horse, and I was lucky enough to give him a winner at Ascot that week. He left me a fiver with my father at the end of the week.' The race-horse was Kabul, the gelding in which Hutch had a share. Some well-known jockeys, including Gordon Richards, rode him, and he was placed several times but never won an important race. Kabul was a passport to private enclosures, owners' bars and other places Hutch enjoyed; a *folie de grandeur* he could ill afford.

The same summer, Hutch went to New York. Had it been possible, he would probably have stayed there. He may have been invited to entertain at a function or looking for work; the Duchess of Windsor is said to have been to hear him in New York in the summer of 1948.[2] It seems likely that he chiefly wanted to escape from the rigours of postwar Britain to a country materially untouched by the war; and, more specifically, to revisit Harlem, the scene of his first triumphs. The Rajmata of Jaipur, then the Maharanee, recalled that she and her husband Jai met Hutch in Duke Ellington's apartment. 'It was my impression that he was staying there, and that they were great friends.'

There is no trace of this trip in Hutch's papers and no stamp in his passport. His British passports, while chronologically complete, do not record all his other travels either, and he may somehow have had an American passport too.

Back in England, Hutch fell back into the old routine of variety and cabaret. At the Ipswich Hippodrome, he again showed the admirable sang-froid he had displayed during raids in the war. When an electrical fault caused a fire in the balcony, Peter Cavanagh, a mimic, abandoned his usual opening to do Robb Wilton's fireman sketch; next came Hutch singing 'I Don't Want to Set the World on Fire'; and the fire brigade rounded off the show by extinguishing the blaze to roars of applause.

On the radio Hutch joined forces with Terry-Thomas in *To Town with Terry*, a mixture of records, live music and facetious badinage. Recordings of the programme in October 1948 show the great rapport between them: at times they make each other laugh so much that they can barely follow the script. They were introduced as 'The double act that might have been – the Teeth and the Handkerchief'; they repeatedly call each other 'old man', and engage in a crossfire of Greyfriars-style insults: 'Leslie Hanky-Panky Hutchinson, you beastly, rotten cad.'

The couple also appeared in a film released that autumn, *The Brass Monkey*, also known as *Lucky Mascot*; it was based on the successful talent-spotting show on radio, *Carroll Levis's Discoveries*, a variant of *Opportunity Knocks*. In it, a radio singer played by Carole Landis thwarts the theft of a valuable Buddhist sculpture. Other performers were Herbert Lom, Ernest Thesiger and Avril Angers, who remembered that Hutch recorded his songs in a garage on a freezing day, which explains the dragon's-breath effect during his performance. Otherwise, he looks portly, scruffy and unworthy of his polished image.

Terry-Thomas engineered Hutch's cameo role in *The Brass Monkey*. Having been helped by Hutch early in his career, Thomas often reciprocated. In 1949, a producer rejected an appearance by Hutch in one of Thomas's shows. This prompted Thomas to intervene: a BBC internal memo reads, 'Terry-Thomas just phoned me to ask if I would reconsider this decision, pointing out that he can do a very successful double act with Hutch. This is a stunt they performed in a radio programme some time ago, which was, I believe, very successful.'[3]

In his first autobiography, *Filling the Gap*, Thomas wrote that Hutch came to Paris to a nightclub where Thomas was appearing. 'And I got him to the mike. He stood, I repeat stood, at the mike and sang "La Vie en Rose" and, despite the fact that he was completely unknown to the audience, was received with just as much enthusiasm as if he were playing to his parishioners at Quaglino's.' Thomas may have thought Hutch came specifically to see him, but he was probably en route for the clinic in Switzerland. An amiable, rather naive man, Thomas believed that 'Another nice thing about Hutch is there aren't any chips on his shoulder. As nearly everybody in the profession, white or coloured, goes round with a ruddy great log, it makes a jolly nice change.' This shows Hutch's ability to be the sort of man Thomas wanted him to be, while Thomas turned a blind eye to the racism Hutch had to deal with. For example, Ernie Wise once overheard a guest leaving a party say to Hutch, 'Goodnight, Sambo.'

Two song lyrics written by Hutch also illustrate his capacity to meet people's expectations of him while completely denying what he really thought. During a short run at the Nightingale in Berkeley Square, later the Colony Room, in December 1948, Hutch sang:

> At the Nightingale I sing to you
> Though no nightingale I bring to you
> A song or two that I like very much
> With the old familiar touch.
>
> The Nightingale at the BBC
> Is the only one that doesn't imitate me
> Not that I mind very much.
> Yours very sincerely Hutch.

The other song, also part of his late-1940s repertoire, went:

> It's a wonderful world after all
> What does it matter if we're rich or poor
> It's a wonderful world after all.
> If you've a friend who will knock on your door
> It's a wonderful world after all.
>
> We may have our heartaches, we may have our cares,
> But if we have friendship, we're all millionaires
> So let us be friendly in all our affairs
> It's a wonderful world after all.

While it was a show-business convention to conclude an act with a turn that showed the performer had a heart under his carapace of knowing cynicism – even maestros of misanthropy like Max Miller and Max Wall signed off with sententiously sugary numbers – these lyrics plumb depths of banality and facility, which are hard to reconcile with someone of Hutch's considerable intelligence. Although he could improvise brilliantly, Hutch – through lack of confidence and application – wrote virtually no words or music for himself. By the 1950s, he employed several writers to provide filler jokes and topical lyrics.

Despite a barrage of good-luck telegrams – one, from Charles Tucker, read 'I know you are going to do a good job and hope that this will be a long run for you' – Hutch only appeared for a few weeks at the Nightingale. However, it was a well-paid assignment, more than £250 a week, at a prestigious club frequented by film stars such as Jean Simmons, Stewart Granger, Elizabeth Taylor and Michael Wilding. Bert Ambrose, the bandleader, also featured there with a twenty-two-piece band, and was himself paid £500, nearly twice Hutch's rate. The proprietor of the Nightingale was Eustace Hoey, an entrepreneur in the wine trade. Its membership was by invitation, and largely comprised young but not necessarily affluent aristocrats. They had to pay 15 shillings for entry, and, under the new Licensing Act, bring bottles from home for which they paid corkage tantamount to the original price; the alternative was to order drink in advance from Hoey's wine store and pay twice the over-the-counter price. A woman employee, then eighteen, was shocked by Hoey – 'debauched, hugely fat, with a string of dirty jokes' – and far preferred Hutch: 'He, at least, was jovial and friendly and respectful.' The drummer in Ambrose's band, Norman Burns, was less impressed: 'There were lots of frustrated white ladies with a fetish for blacks hanging round the club. People used to call out requests for Hutch to sing. I thought him dandified and twee. In Australia, where I now live, they'd say he was too much up himself.'

Two sons were born to Hutch in 1948. The first was Gerald, who later changed his name to Alexander. Listening to his records at the age of fifteen had made his mother, Margaret, from an aristocratic Catholic family, 'crazy' about Hutch. She found him 'madly attractive' and, strangely, thought he physically resembled another tireless womaniser, the film star Leslie Howard. 'He was very conceited, but I had a crush on him for twenty years from 1935 to 1955 and pursued him relentlessly in hotels and dressing rooms. I was determined to sleep with him. I used to join him wherever he was playing, often up north, and sometimes he stayed with me in London.' Margaret was also determined to have a child by Hutch. She was working at the Foreign Office, and when her pregnancy started to show, she invented an excuse to take some leave, and went to stay with a woman in Clacton, Essex, for the rest of her confinement. She told no one about the child, and soon found that she could not cope with the reality. The boy was eventually adopted. 'Once he knew that no one was going to be cross with him about it', Hutch was pleased.

When he was fifteen, Gerald saw Hutch on television and somehow immediately recognised him as his father. He never met Hutch, but he identifies with his mother's family. When he became a priest, he invited his mother and her sisters to the ordination ceremony. He is an excellent linguist, and has taught classical music. As Margaret said, 'Hutch would have been proud of such a clever, holy, good boy.'

The mother of the second boy was called Mary. When she was sixteen she got to know Hutch, and she lived with him from time to time from 1937 to his death in 1969. During the war, when Ella and Leslie were evacuated, Mary became a nurse at St Mary's, Paddington and moved next door to Hutch's house in Steeles Road. Previously she had worked in show business. Although Mary always forbade him to reveal his paternity, her son, Chris, knew his father slightly. In the 1950s, when he met him in Soho, Hutch used to behave as though their relationship was clandestine – which must have been bewildering and distressing for a young boy. Chris followed his parents into show business in 1973, and is now a singer. In an interview in the *Stage*, he said, 'I don't use any of his act, but I'm sure he would be delighted to know that his songs are very much part of mine.'[4] Because he wanted to honour Hutch with love and acceptance, he has changed his name to Hutchinson, and thereby established an identity denied him in his father's lifetime. Over the years he has met many of his father's colleagues, including Max Miller, Tommy Trinder and Arthur Askey. He lives in Sussex with his wife Kay.

In 1953, Mary had another son by Hutch, Graham, who became a schoolteacher.[5]

Hutch may well have gone on to father a further child in 1949. Bloom Clare went with her husband Alan, a jazz pianist, and Jack Jackson, a bandleader and pioneer disc jockey, and his wife, to see Hutch in variety in Bournemouth. When they went backstage, Hutch, toting an open bottle of brandy, tore past them; behind him was a man with a knife in his hand, who was, in turn, pursued by the stage doorman. After a scuffle, the doorman disarmed the furious man. 'Apparently,' said Bloom, 'Hutch had got his fourteen-year-old daughter in the family way, and Hutch had to pay him off.'

Increasingly discernible in Hutch at this time is a tendency to
confer himself as a favour on his material and his audiences.
Although a cover version of Vaughan Monroe's 'Red Roses for
a Blue Lady' was his big hit in 1949, he disliked the song.
According to Brian Johnson, the cricket commentator, 'He used
to hate it. Too silly for him. He would mock it cynically, and we
made up rude versions of it together. He was great fun.'

As a habitué of the Dorchester, Hutch offered to entertain at the
staff dance free of charge. In an affectionate note of thanks dated 18
March 1949, Sir Malcolm McAlpine, whose family owned the
hotel, wrote, 'There is no other artist who could have given them
as much pleasure as you did.'

After his visit to the clinic in Switzerland in 1949, Hutch sang
the 'Harry Lime Theme' on Henry Hall's *Guest Night* and then
embarked on a nationwide tour. He wrote to Joan, enclosing
'more cuttings I know you love to read. Bored stiff, but I can do
nothing about it. Singing extremely well. Love, Leslie.' Ironically,
one of the cuttings read, 'Hutch, as touchingly modest as ever, was
given a warm reception by the audience at the Empire, Nottingham.' The style of performance they enjoyed is well evoked in a
letter written by Max Wall in January 1950, asking Hutch to
feature one of his songs:

> I can already hear you – firstly the announcement that it was
> written by that Great Comedian and Actor, Max Wall, then the
> quiet introduction, and the lovely Reading of that First Chorus,
> then an Out-of-this-world piano arrangement – and Bang, into
> the Smashing slightly drawn-out finish, making that last note
> wait for the perfect timing that only Hutch can give – Now will
> you sing it?

There is no evidence that Hutch ever performed the song, 'Baby's
Smile', but he and Wall continued to be great friends.

In the summer, Hutch toured Ireland and later went to Jersey in
Gala Variety, a production by Harold Fielding, who remembered
him as 'a great showman and a charming man'. In the programme
of this show, Hutch mentions his medical training in America for
the first time in public.

A high point in 1950 for Hutch, as a West Indian cricket
aficionado, was the West Indies' victory over the English team

at Lord's. A well-known improviser of calypsos, Lord Kitchener, led a happy, hip-swinging train of Caribbeans round and round the hallowed turf. To them and their fellow West Indians nationwide, the triumph was far more than a sporting success. The Caribbeans had bettered their masters at their own game on their own ground with grace, style and great good humour; and, if eyebrows were raised in the Long Room, so much the better. Hutch was proud, and celebrated with the best of them. For a time, it must have distracted him from the slow but inexorable decline in his fortunes.

Earlier in the year, he had got caught in the slipstream of a divorce scandal involving Lady Gunter and his old friend Frisco, who had been singing and running nightclubs in Paris and London since the 1920s. The press added, 'Hutch, coloured pianist and singer, known at the Milroy and other London night spots for his magnificent conducting of West Indian dances, was usually seen in the late afternoon at Frisco's with a beautiful English blonde. She took off later for America. Lady Iris Mountbatten, daughter of the Earl of Carisbrooke, took drinks with an Austrian woman friend with Hutch and other near-celebrities.'[6] Even two years earlier, Hutch would never have been referred to as a 'near-celebrity'.

Eric Braun, a journalist then writing a column for the *Show Business and Sporting Review*, met him at the bar of the Nottingham Empire, and found him 'overweight and drunk. He had too much make-up on and weird greenish eyelids. He was dismissive and grand and unfriendly.' Around this time, misuse of maquillage contributed to Hutch being booed off the stage at Cardiff by some miners yelling, 'Get off, you poofter!' A year later, a man aggressively heckled Hutch on a *Workers' Playtime* broadcast; Hutch gave an arrogant riposte, and was roundly booed.

In his early days in variety, before he had sufficiently broadened his cabaret turn, Hutch had misjudged a Manchester audience by complimenting them on being 'sweet'. Now, Hutch was failing to adjust his persona to radical changes in the rapidly dying genre. Up to the end of the war, people looked up to entertainers such as Hutch, who dressed and sounded like their 'betters', holding them in the same sort of esteem as professionals such as doctors and accountants. After the war, the artist had to abandon his *de haut en bas* attitude and operate on the same level as his public. Dave Lee, a pianist and one of the founders of Jazz FM, later said:

Entertainers had to look like one of us, mate, sing badly, don't
sing any high-class stuff, don't pronounce the words proper – it
became a requirement that the artist identified with his audience.
Even in sound studios, Steinway pianos were being wrecked to
get a plunkety-plunk sound like Russ Conway. Hutch was an
anachronism. No one after the war could have gone on the air
and sung Cole Porter.

Hutch continued to do exactly that, of course, but much less
frequently. Radio was still the major home entertainment but
television was catching up fast and by the end of the decade, most
of the venues had changed their use. They were already mounting
seedily coy strip shows such as *Don't Point, It's Nude* and *Halt! Who
Goes Bare?*; and many halls were soon echoing to the shouts of
bingo callers, the pounding of pop groups or the drawn-out
rumble of ten-pin bowling. The variety shows that survived
featured a new generation of stars – Tony Hancock, Jimmy
Edwards, Bob Monkhouse, Spike Milligan, Michael Bentine
and Harry Secombe – some of whom survived into the 1990s.
Many of the better shows came from independent producers such
as Donald Clive and Joe Waxman, who seldom toured more than
one show at a time.

In 1954, Hutch featured in Waxman's 'all-coloured' musical
New York to New Orleans at the Tivoli, Aberdeen, and other
theatres. This show was far superior to most of the assignments to
which Hutch was now reduced. Fewer and lesser jobs included
entertaining at police stag nights and out-of-town nightclubs, at
weddings, parties and balls that rarely raised a mention in gossip
columns or magazines like the *Tatler*. In public and on stage,
however, he still kept up his brio and panache. The singer Benny
Lee remembered him disembarking from the Isle of Wight ferry
en route for a Sunday concert: Hutch, wearing a panama and a
short-sleeved shirt, greeted Lee effusively with an 'Of course I
know you, dear boy' although he hardly did; then, gesturing
towards his traps, he shouted, 'Steward, take these bags ashore' as
though he were leaving a luxury liner at Port Said. A fan, Edward
Phelps, recalled seeing Hutch in the early 1950s at the old Theatre
Royal, Portsmouth, playing to 'a noisy audience of sailors and
their tarts . . . he milked "Ebb Tide" for all it was worth . . . his
voice throbbing round the smoke-filled auditorium. He was

enormously fat, elephantine, but he held the theatre in the palm of his hand.' Appearing at a club opening in Manchester, Hutch had a drink with a female fan in the interval. During the second part of the show, his audience ate and drank noisily so Hutch told them to be quiet, adding that he wanted to sing to his fan, the only member of the audience who actually wanted to listen and enjoy his work.

Although his fan mail was diminished, women from all walks of life continued to shore up his confidence by writing to say how marvellous he was. Hutch kept some of these letters, one of which, in beautiful copperplate, reads:

> You are my one and only delight, so you can imagine the joy I feel when I see you appearing again. Nothing on earth is more lovely than your sweet music . . . Above all, I want you to take care of your dear self. You are so very rare and precious. You are much too modest these days. I suppose it is because you are even greater than ever now. Sweet Prince, thank you for returning to your people in that loveliest of realms, your own melody.
>   Yours very sincerely,
>   Irene W. Howes (Miss)

In 1952, Hutch's mail was swollen by an influx of requests, via J. Walter Thompson, the advertising agency, to play particular numbers on a Radio Luxembourg programme, *Stars of the Evening*, which featured Hutch as a solo artist on Friday evenings. Sponsored by Rowntrees – 'Remember Dairy Box for centres, centres, centres' – the programme gave Hutch exposure needed all the more since the loss of his recording contract in 1948.

At this time, Hutch had one of his less likely liaisons. The object of his affections was Elisabeth Lutyens, daughter of Sir Edwin Lutyens, the architect. Lutyens, only six years younger than Hutch, was separated from her husband. She was one of the first British composers to adopt the twelve-tone system; and, as her autobiography *A Goldfish Bowl* shows, she was an uncompromisingly intellectual and independent woman, who, unusually for any flame of Hutch's, subsequently earned a niche in the women's liberation pantheon. They may have met at the Colony Room in Dean Street, Soho, an establishment that, unlike pubs at that time, was licensed to sell liquor in the afternoon; they certainly used the club as a regular trysting place for the duration of their brief relationship, and they drank a lot.

In the early 1950s, Hutch was also playing occasionally, albeit for no financial reward, on Sunday evenings at a house in Glebe Place, Chelsea. Here, another nightclub pianist, Marc Anthony, held open house for a largely gay circle of friends and acquaintances. Hutch had known Anthony since the 1920s through Joan. All three often went out together, and when Hutch was not available, Anthony became Joan's walker. Anthony was at the heart of an impressive gay coterie; and, wholly at ease with his homosexuality, he must have cut an exhilarating dash in the drab, homophobic 1950s. At the time, Anthony played piano at the Festival Club near the Coliseum; later he appeared at the Spanish Garden in Mayfair. On occasions, Hutch met him in Paris; and in 1962 they spent time together in Penang, Malaysia.

Hutch's friendship with Anthony, which may or may not have been consummated, was one of his few lasting relationships with homosexuals: because of his bisexuality, he switched from one gender to another as fancy took him; and, at country-house weekends, would excoriate 'pansies' before taking the train back to London to spend the night with a male lover. It follows that his gay liaisons were much simpler than his heterosexual affairs. They were either playful flirtations with other flamboyant exotics or pragmatic casting-couch sessions with contemporary or older men from whom he wanted something.

Like many an Englishman in search of illicit sex, Hutch often went to Paris. There he spent his time with gay American intellectuals like James Baldwin and Richard Wright. Both were resident in France since the 1940s, though Baldwin would return to the USA following the success of his second novel, *Giovanni's Room*, in 1956. They felt far more strongly than Hutch about the way their colour had denied them opportunities at home, and Baldwin introduced Hutch to his militantly gay friends. Hutch was always more relaxed about his gay activities when abroad. The young writers loved his company, and he felt flattered by their attention; he would tell them anecdotes and play the piano.

Hutch's finances were shaky, even though he could still demand large sums. A pay slip from the Empire, Brixton, in 1953 shows that for a week's variety work, Hutch received about £175 of gross takings of some £1,000. Of that £175, Charles Tucker took a 10 per cent agency fee, and as a member of the touring company, Hutch had to make a contribution of 17.5 per cent to its expenses for promotion, transport and such. Sometimes he earned different sums on each night of the week, according to the size of the audience: in one instance, £35 and £73 for the first and second houses on Monday rose to £115 and £214 on Saturday. In the provinces, Hutch received less: his pay for a week at the Palace, Hull, in the same year was about £135.

Although handsomely rewarded by the standards of the time – the national average annual salary was £650 – Hutch was not earning regular money; and, like most freelances, he was experiencing difficulties with the Inland Revenue. In reply to what must have been a bombardment of anxious and, quite possibly, patronising telephone calls from Hutch, his accountant, Stanley Gorrie, wrote:

> Now, Leslie, one thing you have to remember is that worry will get you nowhere, so just carry on in your usual way, and let me do the worrying for you. Above all, you must not think that just because I happen to be away or not available each time you 'phone that I do not have that personal interest in your problems – don't forget, we are all in the same boat nowadays, and in an effort to keep things swimming, I am having to tear all over the place myself.

Despite a significant drop in his earnings since 1948, Hutch still had to sustain an opulent appearance for his public; and this necessity, on its own, would have generated financial problems. On top of that, there were outstanding bills from clinics ('I think it would be about time to pay me. Hoping that I won't have too long to wait or have to pass the matter to the police') and regular payments to Ella; to Grenada; and to Mary to help maintain his two sons by her, Chris and Graham. And, as ever, Hutch was incapable of facing up to the reality of having to reduce his outgoings to match his straitened circumstances.

One minor call on his resources had been the annual £20 fee for his daughter Leslie's law course at the London School of Economics. Like her father, however, Leslie did not complete her degree, pulling out after two years in 1947 on the grounds of ill health.

Hutch had passionately wished to see his daughter qualify as a lawyer, and put considerable pressure on her, but to no avail. They became further disenchanted with each other in the early 1950s when, to Hutch's horror, Leslie fell for a Jamaican nightclub proprietor called Tony. When they married in Cambridge in 1954, he execrated Tony as a 'lowdown nigger'. This violent expression shows Hutch's deep disappointment in Leslie for choosing to marry someone who, in Hutch's view, did not reflect her upbringing. He never grasped the paradox that Leslie was reflecting her upbringing by marrying someone of whom he violently disapproved – and who, in fact, bore a strong resemblance in many ways to Hutch. From that time on, father and daughter were estranged. The marriage was unsettled, all the same, and many years after Hutch's death, they divorced.

In March 1953, Hutch returned from performing in Belfast to discuss his appalling financial situation with his accountants. They tried to impress on him that money did not grow on trees, but this was a futile endeavour because, for many spendthrifts, it appears to do exactly that. This was certainly true of Hutch. Frequently, when his situation seemed beyond recovery, his finances looked up without any particular effort from him. Late 1953 was such a time. A brusque letter from his agent, the abrasive Terry Miller, told him that Quaglino's wanted him back for 'four weeks with an option for the fifth week. The times will be 11.30 pm in the upstairs room, and midnight downstairs. You will receive £175 per week.'

Chapter Ten

Back in Mayfair
1954–1960

Is it just the way I sing a popular refrain?
Or is it that my character is still without a stain?
Or is it just because they think I'm tied here with a chain?
That people say that Quag's belongs to me?

C omeback attempts kindle a strange mixture of hopes, fears
and schadenfreude in newspapers and their readers. On the
surface, they wish the fallen idol a triumphant return to his
former status; at the same time, they want him to be incapable of
adapting his act to new audiences, and to see him consign
himself to the dustbin of show-business history – as Tony
Hancock did with his catastrophic solo turn at the Royal Festival
Hall in 1966.

Hutch had always been emblematic of prewar luxury and
leisure, so the success of his comeback would partly hinge on
whether Britain as a whole had made enough of a postwar recovery
to provide the conditions and the mood within which Hutch
flourished. Even if the country was back on its feet, would he seem
irretrievably passé to the new generation of socialites? A prewar
relic at best tinged with a fading glow of nostalgic appeal? No
wonder Hutch was more apprehensive than usual when he started
his engagement at Quaglino's in December 1953. 'Hutch was

more nervous than a rabbit,' reported the *Sunday Graphic* of his
opening night. 'The dabs with the white handkerchief became
more frenzied as he sang a selection of the latest songs. People
listened politely, but rapture was rationed. Only when he tinkled
into the saucy verses of Noël Coward's "Let's Do It" did the
temperature rise.'[1]

Despite this tepid review, Hutch became the comeback entertainer of 1954. Quaglino's extended his contract from five to
fourteen weeks; and early in the run, royal patronage confirmed
and boosted his triumph. Princess Margaret, the Duchess of Kent
and the Windsors all came, the Duchess of Windsor being per-
ceptibly moved by Hutch's revival of the 1927 hit 'My Heart
Stood Still'. She also demanded so many encores of 'Let's Do It'
that Hutch ran out of words and desperately improvised, 'The
French do it, the Dutch do it, and people listening to Hutch do it.'
Both Windsors rocked with laughter. Just before one o'clock, they
danced to 'This Is My Lovely Day'; and as they left, the Duke
murmured to his old protégé, 'It's just like old times. Thank you.'[2]
After the run, the *Variety* critic from New York admiringly
summed up:

> He became the idol of the smart set, the place was patronised by
> royalty and turnaway business was recorded for most of the run.
> Hutch is a savvy performer who writes most of his own material
> and is renowned for his parodies. He has two strong entries for
> this category, one entitled 'Wish You Had Hair' and the other
> introducing new lyrics to 'Bewitched'. There is an indigo streak
> running through most of his songs, but always embellished with
> sophisticated wit. A standard fave is his omnibus version of 'Let's
> Do It', which always comes as a request number and has been
> allowed to grow and grow until it takes up almost half his act.
> The audience apparently cannot have too much of it.

Passing years served only to increase the Duchess of Windsor's
enthusiasm for 'Let's Do It'. One woman observed her applauding
Hutch after seventy-one verses and inciting him, 'One more for
me, Hutch. We know *you* can do it!'

Variety's assertion that Hutch wrote most of his words was, of
course, incorrect. From now until the end of his life, he continued
to write odd extra verses for 'Let's Do It', but most of his material

was assembled by a team comprising Cardew Robinson, John
Hurst and David Heneker.[3] Cardew 'the Cad' Robinson, who
appeared in variety as a knowing overgrown schoolboy, was also a
popular after-dinner speaker. He had been a friend of Hutch since
the 1930s. John Hurst was a variety fan and a seasoned scriptwriter
for other cabaret stars, among them Hermione Baddeley, Beryl
Reid and Nicholas Parsons. Through Hutch, Hurst met David
Heneker, who was then playing the piano at the Embassy Club in
Bond Street. Heneker had written several songs, including one of
Hutch's hits, 'There Goes My Dream'; he went on to compose a
number of successful musicals, including *Jorrocks*, *Half a Sixpence*
and *Charlie Girl*. At the Embassy Club, Hutch and Heneker used to
perform 'Let's Do It' as a duet, taking turns to sing the lines. They
egged each other on in various ways, and were said to conceal the
libidinous wives of irate husbands under their piano. They were so
often together at the Embassy that they were briefly known as the
'Two H's'. At the time, Heneker was living in St James's, and when
he came cycling home from Bond Street – St James's was then a
two-way street – in the small hours, the guard at St James's Palace
had standing orders to halt the traffic so that Colonel Heneker
could turn right across the street without stopping; because if he
did stop, he invariably fell off.

Among Hutch's papers, there are ten pages of extra lyrics for
'Let's Do It'. As usually happens when cabaret material is transferred to the printed page, the words appear ponderous and
without wit; even more so, if the topical references have long
receded into obscurity. However, some of them effectively convey
the mood of the times, and, at the very least, form intriguing
footnotes to social history:

> Sweet milkmaids sitting on stools do it,
> That's when the milk shows a loss.
> Prizewinning bulls do it,
> They can put it across.
> Farmers financed on a grant do it,
> Landgirls go peculiar if they can't do it . . .
> Let's do it, let's fall in love.
>
> Snails do it. Grubs do it.
> Convicts who've escaped from Wormwood Scrubs do it.

Every Scots lad and lass does it.
Fanny Craddock on a medium gas does it.
In one line, Tiller Girls do it,
They do it just for kicks.
Stately Dukes and Lords do it,
But they charge two and six.
Nureyev with one leap does it,
Sooty says that even Sweep does it.[4]
Let's do it, let's fall in love.

In one variation, Hutch referred to the revue team of Michael
Flanders and Donald Swann, then appearing in their own show *At
the Drop of Another Hat* – 'Two chaps the whole world applauds do
it/At the drop of another hat' – and Flanders and Swann
reciprocated rather more wittily by mentioning Hutch in their
'Song of Reproduction' about developments in hi-fi: 'With true
control at a single touch/You can make Caruso sound like
Hutch.' Hutch also sang new lyrics to 'A Nightingale Sang in
Berkeley Square', 'These Foolish Things' and 'You're the Top'
which, while amusing enough at the time, now seem painfully
laboured. John Hurst, who updated 'You're the Top' and provided rugger-club numbers like 'The Girl Who Wouldn't Take It
Lying Down', also wrote specifically for Hutch the point song
'Quag's Belongs to Me'.[5]

Is it just the way I sing a popular refrain?
Or is it that my character is still without a stain?
Or is it just because they think I'm tied here with a chain?
That people say that Quag's belongs to me?

Is it that I'm resident – whatever that might be?
Or is it that I'll still be here in 1963?
Or is it wishful thinking and they'll hope to get in free?
That people say that Quag's belongs to me?

Is it my piano or the rhythm that I find?
(I can also play the tambourine)
Or is it just the fact that I'm rather inclined
To begin with the beguine?

Is it that my enemies are getting on my track?
Do they think I bought the place when things were getting
    slack,
And, now it's on its feet again, they want to buy it back?
And that's the only reason why I keep on coming back.
A handsome profit there would be
If only Quag's belonged to me.

Hurst remembered Hutch to have been 'the most difficult task-
master ever! (Perhaps "perfectionist" would be fairer.) Every word,
virtually every comma, was discussed and deliberated over – but he
eventually performed it and, as he introduced me to all the lords
and ladies who had thronged to his opening night, I shall never
forget him saying to me, "John, we're making history tonight!"'
   Hutch also expanded his repertoire during the 1950s by performing songs from the Broadway musicals that invaded the West
End from 1946 onwards. These included *Oklahoma!*, *Carousel*,
South Pacific and *The King and I*, all by Rodgers and Hammerstein;
Kiss Me, Kate and *Can-Can* by Cole Porter; *Paint Your Wagon* and
My Fair Lady by Lerner and Loewe; Gershwin's *Porgy and Bess*,
Loesser's *Guys and Dolls* and Bernstein's *West Side Story*. Other new
songs included a slight but charming song, 'Too Many Martinis',
written by the film actress Anne de Nys, the mother of Virginia
McKenna. She was also a cabaret performer, and often appeared at
the Allegro. 'Hutch was a poppet and a very fine pianist,' she
remembered. 'I was delighted when he recorded "Too Many
Martinis", which he sang every night at Quag's.' The song was
especially well suited to Hutch since it projected an image of a
romantic, impulsive man living for the moment:

> No wonder we left what was left of the party
> And skipped off to dinner alone
> No wonder we played with fire and delayed
> That lovely taxi journey home.
>
> Too many martinis
> We forgot at the time
> No wonder our eyes told us wonderful lies
> No wonder the night seemed sublime
> Too many martinis, sweetheart.

Many of the naughty jokes he used as fillers seem tame now, but a
few of them, like this limerick, were surprisingly blue:

> At a smart wedding in Bicester
> The bride's mother said as she kissed her
> Here's very good luck
> He's a jolly good chap
> He's done me and your brother and sister.

Some of his patter was feeble – 'In 1952, I studied chemistry, and
was voted the boy most likely to explode' – and Hutch was such a
poor raconteur that he often had to extemporise to regain the
attention of an audience alienated by a stream of bad material badly
delivered; this he did very well. Hutch also brought all his old
panache and professionalism to overcoming the many difficulties of
performing in cabaret. Although it retained all its prewar elegance
– red divans, glinting ceiling of gold and mother-of-pearl, walls of
saffron and glass – Quaglino's was a long, narrow, awkward space,
and Hutch had to perform on a dais in the middle and look both
ways. But he made the venue look ideal, and handled with smooth
good humour a notoriously challenging roomful: the society
clientele toying with chicken in aspic as debutantes and their
verbose escorts prattled and giggled. Although his playing was
sometimes slaphappy, his voice and diction were as commanding as
ever, and he had the poise and authority to quell laughter at source
and rivet the attention of his audience – some of whom complained that Hutch himself was apt to flirt by 'talking all the time he
was playing'.

'I learned my technique in the best of all schools,' Hutch
explained, 'when, as a nineteen-year-old student, Poulsen brought
me to the Café de Paris. To succeed in cabaret, you must, frankly,
have personality and social sense. You must know how to make
people listen. You must be of them. It takes years.'[6] Apart from
this curious revision of his career – at nineteen, Hutch was a
medical student in America, and he was twenty-eight when he
first met Poulsen – Hutch was now looking back with regained
aplomb on a distinguished, if interrupted, career in cabaret. He
even had enough confidence to tell the press about his mysterious
absence, albeit in a bowdlerised way: 'For two years, I refused to
sing. My voice was tired, cracked, uncertain. I decided to gamble

on a long rest. So I turned down engagements, went to Switzerland to recuperate, watched cricket at Lord's – and dodged the
West End like the plague. After the rest, my vocal chords are
stronger than they've ever been.'[7] In a franker interview, Hutch
told the interviewer he had taken time off for a long rest in a
country sanatorium. When he came back to London, he found he
had lost his touch. Bookings were few, and business was slow.

> I suppose you could say that I retired for a time. I could have
> worked, of course. I could have gone on a long variety tour and
> earned between eight and ten thousand pounds that year. But I
> was fed up with touring, tired of provincial hotels. I wanted to
> work in London, and be near my home and the theatres and my
> friends. So I just bided my time, took life easy and waited for
> offers.
>
> When Emlyn Griffiths mentioned a job at Quaglino's, I said,
> 'They don't want me in cabaret, Emlyn, they like the sultry
> Continental-type songstress type nowadays. My stuff's not for
> them.'

As the interviewer archly added, 'How wrong he was!'[8]

Off stage, Hutch was back to his old self. John Hurst and his wife
used to have Hutch to stay at their home in Beckenham, southeast
London:

> The bathroom would be awash, where he had flopped around
> like a hippo. He was a great exhibitionist. When we were due to
> lunch or dine together, he would enter a restaurant, scan the
> menu and say, 'I don't think so', and walk out. The waiters used
> to grin. At the end of the meal, he always went through the bill
> with a fine-tooth comb and paid with a sigh. Then he would
> buy us both £5 cigars. I had a great regard for him.

The return of confidence signalled an upturn in Hutch's love life.
Like most men who feel they have failed, he had been unsociable
and disinclined to embark on affairs during his years off, but now
he had a number of brief liaisons. One slightly longer-lasting affair
was with Diana, who had run away from her rich, upper-class
brewing family to live with a boxer turned theatrical producer. She
was handsome, dressed well, subsisted on earnings from small

acting roles, and was on the fringe of the Quaglino's set. At the time, she was in her mid-fifties and, with dark eyes and hair, had a look of Hedy Lamarr. She was said to 'enjoy power and kinky sex', and boasted of her 'raunchy liaison with Hutch in her Walton Street flat'.

Hutch's social life also flourished. At the annual rag of the Green Room, a club then regarded as the show-business equivalent of the Garrick, a committee member was appointed 'Rag-Picker'; his role was to select a team to entertain the very exacting audience of fellow professionals. Hutch was asked to perform for the last twenty minutes of the first half. Hubert Gregg, an actor who presented nostalgic radio shows such as *Square Deal*, remembered the evening: 'He did forty-five minutes, and then we all went back to my flat, and he played until five in the morning. Jack Hylton was with us, and *The King and I* was current because Hutch was singing "Hello, Young Lovers". '

During Hutch's run at Quaglino's, James Mason came from Hollywood to England to make *The Man Between*, a pallid attempt by the film director Carol Reed to repeat his success with *The Third Man*. Mason went to hear Hutch six times in two weeks. During the first visit, he sent a waiter over with a note: 'Hutch, you are still the greatest cabaret artist in the world. May I play your records in my BBC disc-jockey programme?' The radio series, *Music with Mason*, had started on 25 May, but Hutch was unable to contribute recent recordings because he had not made any since 1948. Mason promptly paid a small independent company, Oriole, to produce seven 78-rpm records, and played them on his programme. Within weeks, they were selling well and attracting good reviews. Larger record companies soon expressed an interest in Hutch, and by the end of 1954 he was signed up with Decca. 'I owe my comeback to James Mason,' Hutch later said. 'I'll never be able to thank him enough.'

Elizabeth II was crowned in Westminster Abbey on 2 June 1953, and Hutch appeared in the BBC's first radio programme for the Coronation, *Commonwealth Gala*, broadcast from the London Palladium. 'A truly magnificent performance' read a special Coronation-issue telegram from a fan, one of many who sent Hutch congratulatory messages on his first comeback performance for a wider radio audience. By the autumn, he was featuring on

Hutch the performer.

Princess Marina, 1934.

Wendy in 1938.

Hutch in 1937.

5. Miss DORRIE DENE
Comedienne
At the Piano - MR. REG. LINDO

6. THE MARCELLE TRIO
Adagio Dancers

7. THE CONDOS BROTHERS
The World's Greatest Tap Dancers

8. "HUTCH" (Mr. Leslie Hutchinson)
Entertainer
(By kind permission of the Management of the Empress Rooms)

Tea and Coffee served in the Auditorium on Request.

A B.B.C. STUDIO ON THE
HIPPODROME STAGE
DURING

RADIO WEEK!

Do you wonder, as you listen to a radio entertainment, just what happens in the studio? Next week you will know! The scene for the second half of next week's show will be a B.B.C. studio, and the artistes will "do their stuff" exactly as they would do it "on the air." We say "exactly," but since those arch conspirators, Messrs Clapham and Dwyer will be in charge of the studio, we had better not v___ for anything! However, book early and see the show as the B.B.C. wo_____ not) produce it.

"HUTCH"

Leslie Hutchinson does what dozens of other artistes are doing to-day. He entertains at the piano—but he entertains as no other artiste can do. His voice and piano-playing have a unique quality which is personal to himself alone. He can croon a Southern ditty with an urgent grief hitherto unknown, and then dart away into a frantic and brilliant rendering of the latest syncopated rythm. "Hutch" comes to the music halls after years of success in London, Paris and New York, and Coventry will be one of the first towns to see him.

HAIG
AND
ESCO

will be quarrelsome—
but friendly.

CLAPHAM

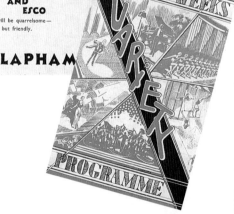

Hutch chooses a beauty queen.

Virginia Keiley with
James Mason in *Fanny
By Gaslight*, 1944.

Marina, Duchess of Kent chatting to Lady Louis Mountbatten, 1941.

Violet in Liverpool.

Hutch in the Cotswolds, 1940.

Hutch and onlookers.

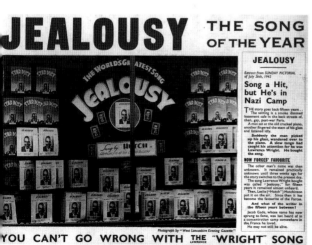

Hutch at the races,
circa 1950.

Mary, mother of
Chris and Graham.

Chris and Graham.

late-evening radio programmes that sought to create 'a nightclub at
your fireside'. For this purpose, a BBC studio was temporarily
named the Golden Slipper, the White Cockatoo or Club Piccadilly, and Edmundo Ros or some other prominent bandleader
introduced a series of guests. Hutch continued to appear on these
and other radio shows for the rest of the 1950s – royal disapproval
had not only evaporated after the war, but he was back in the
family's good books.

Hutch was also returning to his inconsistent, temperamental
ways. On a Coronation Tour of the Moss Empires, he topped a bill
with, at the bottom, the comedians Charlie Drake and Dick
Emery. 'We were very much in awe of Hutch,' remembered
Drake.

> He doubled the New Cross Empire with the Ritz and got
> accolades from both audiences every night – the southeast
> Cockneys loved him. The top of the bill usually closes the
> second half, but Hutch was the penultimate act, so he could be
> driven to the Ritz on time to do a late cabaret. Me and Dick
> Emery did the end. It depended on Hutch's mood how long his
> act lasted. If the oysters had been good at Scott's that day, he
> might do forty-five minutes. A bad day and it would be two
> songs and off. I never knew what Hutch would end on. I was on
> tippy-toes. There was always a ponderous silence after applause
> before he started the next number. One night, I got it wrong and
> came haring on, dressed as a boxing referee, shouting, 'Ladies
> and gentlemen, the next heavyweight champion of the world,
> Dick Emery!' The man was still at the piano. The audience
> rocked with laughter, but Hutch was unamused.

Drake later tried to apologise: ' "You see, sir, I was waiting for you
to finish, sir." Hutch looked aloof, but not unkind. "I have no
intention of ever finishing, my boy." ' Drake thought of him as 'a
black Noël Coward – a great star'.

In a *Radio Times* interview on 25 October, Hutch attributed his
enduring success to:

> sincerity . . . There is such a thing as pure sentiment. No other
> instrument in the world records insincerity so clearly as a
> microphone does. Frankly, my conscience would not let me

sing a number unless I felt it was *right*. I can't bring myself to sing
an unintelligent lyric. The lyric matters tremendously – it may
make all the difference between a song being simple or stupid,
and simple and charming. An intelligent lyric strikes a mood or
compels you to see a vivid picture in your mind. Something that
is not only a rhyme, but has a thought behind it. If lyrics are not
to sound banal, they must be interpreted with unadulterated
sincerity.

Hutch then illustrated his point by playing 'Room 504' and 'A
Nightingale Sang in Berkeley Square'. Like most practised liars,
Hutch was probably deceiving himself as much as he was misleading
the interviewer. Most of the songs he sang were markedly inferior to
the two Maschwitz titles he played. But, like a seasoned professional,
he had to play and sing them as though he believed in every word.
Unconsciously, his audience trusted him not to laugh behind their
backs at material they took seriously: to show them what James
Agate called his 'tongue-in-cheek virtuosity' would have been
disastrous. Not that it was wholly indiscernible to the practised
ear: in the mid-1950s, a critic who knew Hutch of old wrote:

> He still sings with the same passionate insincerity, his crinkly hair
> is as black as ever and his well-mopped brow little wrinkled. He
> tells an old story more for form than for originality, his French is
> the kind the English understand, he throws in an esoteric joke
> for the county and some cynical, man-of-the-world bawdry for
> everybody. His success can be judged by the fact that last night's
> vintage thirties audience had brought along their grown-up
> children, and although he overran his time by half-an-hour no-
> one seemed to notice.

Once again, Hutch was often playing at private parties in London.
Hostesses of charity balls, debutante dances, annual dinners and
other society functions clamoured for his cabaret act just as they
had thirty years before. They and their guests clapped and cheered
him to the echo, and he sat up 'as perky as a Pekinese'.[10] The writer
Nell Dunn recalled:

> To a v. v. defiant debutante of a kind in 1954, Hutch was by far
> the most interesting moment at those dances. He was interesting

because he created a sexual atmosphere. After dancing to his singing, you fell in love, albeit briefly, and ran out into the garden for some wonderful kissing. It was as if he gave permission for all those chirpy young women to become sensual.

Work was pouring in from all directions, and sometimes Hutch had to turn down large and remunerative offers. In September 1953, a show in Australia, *Take It from Me*, was foundering because its star, Joy Nicholls, had gone into hospital. 'Only a top-class singing star will save the situation – and, even across the world, showmen know that Hutch still has the stuff.'[11] One weekend, the desperate producers conducted a cable auction for 'Old Hutch, who must be feeling mighty pleased with himself'. Hutch rejected the overture. He had only just returned to the British show-business scene, and to leave it again for an extended tour would have been risky; anyway, he was enjoying himself too much.

On tour, Hutch was conducting himself with turkey-cock professionalism. The Beverly Sisters, Teddy, Babs and Joyce, a close-harmony group in the mould of the American Andrews Sisters, were several times on the same bill as Hutch at theatres in Manchester, Leeds and Liverpool. They describe him as 'an enormous star', who paid meticulous attention to the lighting plot – 'he loved reds and blues' – and the way in which the curtains were draped. He preferred to play on a white piano, and insisted on supervising its exact position. The 'Bevs' had 'never met a coloured man before', and were impressed by 'his ability to charm an audience . . . [his] beguiling voice like honey . . . and the women always waiting for him backstage'. To them, he seemed 'a very cool customer, stylish, calm and arrogant'. As pretty blonde teenage girls, the Bevs:

> turned heads wherever we were. We thought we were the cat's miaow. Everyone was running after us. Hutch used to come to our dressing room like everyone else, and we thought he must want to invite one of us out. But eventually we realised that he was just after our young blond male pianist – who, incidentally, didn't respond. We were *so* surprised he didn't chase *us*![12]

Around this time, Hutch's gay leanings seem to have been more to the fore. During a short summer break in Majorca, he wrote to

Joan, 'Sun, sea and sand heavenly' and added, 'Who is this boy? He's driving me mad,' referring to a current relationship, which Joan apparently condoned. Now that Hutch was successful again and happier with life, he was getting on better with her. He gave her a number of presents, including a beautiful bag from Burlington Arcade, and wished her 'the loveliest luck'.

On the variety stage, he looked increasingly epicene, sporting a jacket lined with startling red silk, and wearing rings on every finger; he also had, clamped round his left wrist, the gold bracelet engraved 'Edwina' that Bill Pilkington noted in the late 1930s. He would never have worn such lavish trappings in the more intimate context of cabaret.

In February 1954, Hutch briefly left Quaglino's for the Colony Club, until recently the Nightingale, in Berkeley Square. Before he started the month-long Colony engagement, his agent, Emlyn Griffiths, asked him to make his special lighting requirements known there, 'so that the entire new system may suit your purpose perfectly'. Only a year before, Hutch would have had to settle for the existing arrangements.

Hutch returned in November for another season at Quaglino's, which was now synonymous with Hutch's name. Many of his ex-lovers came to see him. On the opening night, the audience included both the Duchess of Argyll and Lady Ursula Vernon, formally Ursula Filmer-Sankey. Before the war, the Duchess of Argyll had often seen Hutch in nightclubs, and in old age she remembered him as 'a special and lovely man' In the 1960s, she took great delight in going to the Blue Angel to hear him parody her exploits. Café society was a small world, and remembering his relationships with figures from the past, who once again were part of his life, must have ruffled even Hutch's sang-froid at times. But he sounded unperturbed: 'They heard me sing during their first season as debutantes, and now they attend my first nights just to hear me again.'

Quite a few titled or rich old men (for example, Lord Northesk, and the Maharajah of Burdwan) and former BYTs took their sons or daughters, when they were in their late teens, to meet Hutch. As he appeared publicly in intimate settings such as nightclubs, this was easy to do. Showing their children that Hutch was a friend or acquaintance of theirs was an attempt to bridge the generation gap, and served to expose a side of them that was rarely evident. It made it easier thereafter to chat as equals about tricky subjects like sex and girlfriends or boyfriends, perhaps with parallels from their own past and a confidential anecdote about Hutch's long-standing affair with Edwina. For the sons and daughters, Hutch embodied the adult sophistication to which they aspired.

It seems odd now that parents could turn the music and idols of their own youth into a rite of passage for their children rather than trying to understand what the teenagers were listening to. But a youth culture barely existed in this milieu then or previously, although the next decade would see it in the ascendant.

The pianist Simon Becker used to impress his girlfriends by taking them to Quaglino's, where he, in turn, was much impressed by Hutch's piano playing: 'He was an ebullient character and a great stride aficionado. His playing was pure Waller, but with the marked absence of the sustaining or loud pedal, which was how Waller got his swing. Hutch's style was much more subdued and delicate.' Becker saw Hutch every night, and then took him to watch other pianists in action. Although Hutch looked 'big and formidable at the low-backed upright' at the Allegro, an annexe to Quaglino's that aimed at a younger clientele, other musicians found him very approachable.[13] However, with Hutch, an upturn in his fortunes rarely coincided with an access of generosity; rather the reverse. When Billy Milton, his fellow café-society pianist from the 1920s, came to Quaglino's to sell him a song, Hutch rejected the song, treated him like an office boy and reduced him to tears of humiliation. When Hutch was up, he often refused to help a man who was down; this was also an instance of gay rivalry at its bitchiest. And Hutch professed to feel some discontent despite his revived success: 'Here I am, still bashing away.' Fats Waller and Cole Porter had both been unknown when Hutch first met them, and *they* were now household names.

'Quag's and the Allegro have become Hutch's spiritual homes,' a journalist announced. 'If ever a plaque should be put up, it is there. For the places brought back Hutch. And Hutch brought back the places. I like the combination. And so do the patrons.'[14]

In early December, Hutch made an auspicious debut on the Decca label in a new format: 'Softly, into the affections of millions interested in discs there creeps the pocket wonder – EP . . . the seven-inch, featherlight, unbreakable record.'[15] The record played at 45 rpm and had two tracks on each side. Hutch chose two songs

from Cole Porter's *Can-Can*: 'I Love Paris' and 'It's All Right by Me'.
Hutch also featured on a 10-inch LP (long-playing) record, which
played at 33⅓ rpm and had four tracks on each side. *The Tatler*
hailed it as that year's 'ideal Christmas present'.[16]

New Year's Eve found a benign Hutch presiding over festivities
at Quaglino's. Paul Tanfield's Diary in the *Daily Mail* reported:

> Cars parked two-deep on each side of the streets leading out of
> Piccadilly; a samba crocodile (evening dress, paper hats) criss-
> crossing out into the street from the normally staid Quaglino's;
> Haymarket, Regent Street crowds giving taxi-drivers the sort of
> headache they must have had on VE Day . . . Ebullient, hard-
> working and so apt for the job, Hutch has appeared so often at
> that restaurant (bookings are being made well into next year!)
> that one regular suggested he should be made a director. I bet
> he'd do well at it.

For most of the time, Hutch exuded an opulent self-possession
which, to some, was offensive. One of his Hampstead neighbours
remembered him making measured progress down Steeles Road to
catch a taxi for the West End. 'As he sat down in his cab, he would
open the window and throw out a bunch of small coins, and
children would scrabble for them. Somehow this suited his stately
gait, though it did have rather a condescending air.'[17]

Even without the agent's description of his client as 'the new
Hutch, streamlined and jet-propelled', the BBC would probably
have been swift to book him. He appeared in a radio show called
All My Eye and Kitty Bluett, also featuring Stanley Baxter, Terry
Scott and Patricia Hayes. Kitty Bluett was an Australian actress who
played 'Ted Ray's Radio Wife' in the long-running radio series
Ray's a Laugh. The setting for the Bluett show was an imaginary
hotel where Kitty was the manageress and Hutch the bartender.

Hutch also made various appearances on television. He was not a
success in either *We Got Rhythm*, billed as 'TV's first coloured
show', or *Starlight*. In the first, 'his nerves were obvious', the *Daily
Sketch* reported, and on the second, the *Liverpool Echo* critic
commented, 'After watching his odd performance last night, I
can only suggest that, in his case, sound is a better medium than
vision.'[18] On the Max Wall TV series in April 1956, Hutch sang a
new song, 'You Above All', and was paid 50 guineas. A review of

his performance described him equivocally as 'the velvet-fog voice'.[19] Wall's turn with Hutch predictably reverted to their old double act with Wall subverting at every turn Hutch's romantic interlude at the piano.

Like many other performers who shine on the stage, in cabaret and on radio, but are uneasy in front of cameras, Hutch rarely did himself justice on television or in films. He also had health problems. In June 1955, the press had reported that 'throat trouble' had forced 'the sepia singer' to take a month's break. Pain in his hands was diagnosed as arthritis. And Margaret, a lover of long standing who first met Hutch in the 1930s, was sitting with him while he was having supper one day, when he had a seizure from high blood pressure. It was time for a change of pace.

Chapter Eleven

Indian Summer
1955–1960

The bottoms were coming up, my dear, and the tops were coming down.

Princess Sita of Kapurthala

Hutch went to India for the first few months of every year from 1955 to 1960, with the exception of 1959. Despite the rioting, massacres and diasporas attendant on partition and independence, some people still lived lives of extraordinary luxury, and Hutch warmed to the thought of adventures away from the English winter. He would enjoy the company of numerous old friends in India, where, among the circles in which he wanted to move, he was already an established celebrity.

One of Hutch's fellow cabaret stars from the 1920s, Mischa de la Motte, had introduced Hutch to J. K. Robert of the East and West Agency, the sole agent for Maxim's at the Great Eastern Hotel, Calcutta.[1] Robert first wrote to Hutch in the summer of 1954, with warnings about the weather and oddly ambiguous references to money. 'I would not like you to come out here and suffer . . . I know that my offer is far below your present earnings, but if you would like a change and . . . to see India, then I give you the opportunity to do so and earn a good deal of money.' The deal deliberately prevented Hutch's agent, Emlyn Griffiths, taking his rightful percentage.

In February 1955, Hutch sent a letter from Calcutta to Lawrence Wright which Wright, keen both to boost a client and fill space, quoted at length in his column in the *Weekly Sporting Review*. So much was he enjoying himself, Hutch wrote, that he had decided to make 'this Maxim's spot an annual trip. It's good for my health – and for my pocket. Already, I've rebooked for 1956.' Maxim's – 'one of the swankiest clubs in the East', where Hutch was 'packing them in' – was doing very well from putting British stars in its cabaret shows; and, in India, in general, there was 'a terrific demand for British singers, bands and cabaret acts – with fares paid both ways and very good salaries'. As so often with Hutch, this was hyperbole. In fact, he got a modest £125 per week; half the tourist-class fare from Calcutta back to England together with a £75 allowance for costume and music; and half the amount charged for excess baggage.

Hutch proved so popular that his contract was extended, and in the event his first sejour in Calcutta lasted five months, from mid-January to mid-June. The Great Eastern was one of the most opulent hotels in Calcutta; and Maxim's, its 'speciality restaurant', had a ceiling hung with crystal chandeliers that tinkled in sympathy with Hutch's high notes. Hutch topped a strangely heterogeneous bill that comprised Carl Ames, a British harpist; Les Kirdalls, a dance and acrobatic duo who wore masks; Lyn and Lys, Egyptian novelty dancers; and, from Hungary, Paul Beregi and Kalman Gidali's Continentals, billed as 'the most talented orchestra ever to come to India'. In typical Indian style, Hutch's performances lasted far longer than scheduled, often up to an hour and a half. One witness, Dan Gillies, said that, as Maxim's was relatively small, these long-drawn-out cabarets reduced bar profits; this accounts for the shift, for Hutch's subsequent engagements, to the Grand Hotel where the dining room was much larger.

In a letter to Joan dated 15 January, Hutch wrote that, while he had been too hot to wear his pyjama trousers, 'the weather is really divine. I went to Calcutta Races and won some money as well. The whole thing is very weird for the moment. The people are walking about in lovely saris on the one hand – then suddenly you see some with lots and lots of cloth between their legs. I can't honestly tell which is which! (Christ!)' This disingenuous confusion was central to his social life in Calcutta, and Joan had long lent a sympathetic ear to Hutch's confidences about his homosexual adventures; these did not worry her, particularly when they happened abroad, and, like many who love philanderers, she had sensibly decided not to imagine too much. Meanwhile, he was at least confiding in her.

Hutch's social life flourished. Old friends invited him to their houses and palaces, and the *Sunday Empire News* archly speculated that 'Hutch, who was such a success on his Indian tour, may have to visit a gunsmith. For the Maharajah of Jaipur's idea of expressing gratitude to a crooner, has been to invite him for a tiger hunt. Hutch's friends say that he has a meditative look as he plays the piano at Quaglino's just now.' Many of those who saw Hutch in Calcutta also went to see him in London at Quaglino's, thus reinforcing his Indian friendships and making them a strong factor in his life in the mid- and late 1950s. Two of those friends were Biki and Tiki Oberoi, the sons of Mohan Singh Oberoi, who bought the Grand Hotel in Calcutta in 1938. It soon became the flagship of the Oberoi chain of hotels in Southeast Asia.

In August, the Oberois' travel agents booked Hutch's passage on the P & O ship *Himalaya* to Bombay so that he could open at the Grand before Christmas. While Biki confirmed these arrangements by businesslike telegram, the less formal, more affectionate Tiki told Hutch by letter of his impending marriage on 15 July 1956:

> My fiancée, Lila Naidu, is a very sweet girl. I am sure you will like her as she plays the piano beautifully and speaks French perfectly, but not of course with that wide range of words which you assimilated on the Left Bank . . . I have told Lila all about you, so you will have much to live up to, or live down. By the way, as I hear you're doing so well in London, nothing less than 22ct. gold will do for our wedding present, and don't forget that Cartier's closes at 5 pm.

Just before he left London, Hutch gave a glibly condescending interview to the *Daily Sketch*. 'I always take my piano when I go to India. You would be surprised at the shortage in that part of the world. I go for a two months' rest, stay at the maharajah's palace in Kashmir, and plan to attend polo matches and race meetings.'

When the interviewer asked, 'Why choose India?', Hutch replied, 'You can always get a good cup of tea there.'[2] In fact, due to Hutch's careful nurture of his clientele, India had chosen him.

Hutch relished the sea voyages there and back. The *Himalaya* provided a generous, stately way of life with comprehensive menus and sedulous service rarely found on land after the Second World War. Hutch was a celebrity and first-class passenger: although his contract allowed only for tourist class, he arranged with P & O to make up the difference by giving performances during the voyage. By day, he sat on the sun deck, inscribing stiff, elaborately beribboned Christmas cards emblazoned on the front with the P & O coat of arms and opening to show a handsome photograph of the *Himalaya*. In the evenings, Hutch often gave impromptu cabarets in the suites of various passengers, having first coerced the purser into moving his baby grand: 'Could you possibly give me a hand with the piano, dear boy?' At these performances, Hutch, as ever, sang specially written choruses of 'Let's Do It':

> People in planes, so they say, do it
> Though they prefer it on earth
> Some on the P & O do it
> Can his lordship get you a berth?
> They say that shy young Parsees do it
> And even old Marwaris in dhotis do it
> Let's all do it . . .

On one of the voyages, Hutch travelled with the Australian cricket team. He 'got along great guns' with the team, and spent hours chatting with them. One evening he gave them a concert on the pool deck. It was presented by one of the cricketers, Ian Johnson, and relayed by Tannoy. Hutch had in 1956 been made an honorary member of the Cross Arrows Cricket Club, which was normally limited to staff of the Marylebone Cricket Club. Sponsored by an old friend and perennial man about town, John Gardiner, Hutch, who had supported cricket at Lord's since his arrival in England in 1927, was delighted to be included. He wore with great panache the club tie and blazer – both were blue and featured crossed arrows in gold – and told a reporter that he played 'opening bat'.

Possibly because of J. K. Robert's contacts there, Hutch, on arriving in India en route for Delhi or Calcutta, usually performed for a night or so in Bombay. In 1956, his guest appearance in Jack Voyantzsis's Other Room prompted waggish coverage in the local papers. Reports claimed that he 'was a tremendous hit with the gals' and had said, as he 'slid through Bombay, "I Can't Give You Anything but Love, Baby" '. Another touched on the Edwina connection: 'Most of you will have read about him as a prominent entertainer, who built himself a prominent place in London society following Lady Mountbatten's invitation to perform in London, after she had been thrilled by one of his Paris recitals – he has lived in London entertaining its elite since then.'[3]

Hutch usually played at the Taj Mahal Hotel, a gigantic late-Victorian pile, white with red domes, which, in Aldous Huxley's words, 'combines the style of the South Kensington Natural History Museum with that of an Indian pavilion at an International Exhibition'.[4] Placed to absorb visitors of all races arriving by liner, it had long been acclaimed as the equal of world-famous hotels such as Raffles in Singapore, Shepheard's in Cairo and the Peninsula, Hong Kong. With its bizarre suites, complete with rooms for staff, it still has an air of grandeur and considerable eccentricity.

As ever, Hutch unobtrusively acknowledged friends and celebrities in the course of his performance. Silloo Mody of Bombay remembered him behind a black grand at the Taj, raising his hand in greeting, quietly saying 'Hello, there', and deftly switching into her favourite tune. One night, in mid-cabaret, Hutch saw a cockroach approaching him across the floor. 'I hated the thought of killing it, I don't believe in killing, but luckily it changed direction and I changed key and continued.'

Hutch found much to distress him in India. To his own surprise, he was disgusted by the abyss between rich and poor, and by the passivity and inertia that he thought prevented the masses from making any attempt to better their lot. On the street, as an obvious foreigner, he felt exposed and ill at ease. In fact, a friend said he was so light-skinned that he could pass for Indian and was far less conspicuous than he believed. Nonetheless, he retreated behind closed doors and became a pampered, caged exotic, able to relax only when he was with people he already knew. His concern for his health may well have contributed to this withdrawal.

Delhi provided a therapeutic oasis of calm, a chance for Hutch to play himself in before he tackled the challenges and excesses of Calcutta. As one of Hutch's fellow performers said, Delhi was 'quite different from Calcutta, more low-key, more discreet, more private'. Hutch featured in the Tavern at the Hotel Imperial, in the Oberoi chain, which, despite its vast lawns and soaring palms, lacks the Taj's quirky distinction or the glamour of the Grand in Calcutta. He also played at another Oberoi hotel, Maiden's. In the 1940s the Vicereine, Lady Wavell, had held charity shows there; but by the mid-1950s its audiences were relatively provincial, comprising government officials, minor diplomats, senior officers and a scatter of businessmen and their wives. One evening, this worthy assembly was enlivened by the appearance of Errol Flynn, who had come to hear Hutch. Everyone recognised him and gave him an enthusiastic welcome.

A friend and employee of the Oberois, Lawrence Pratt, recalled that Hutch stayed in a room behind the reception desk, on the ground floor of the Imperial. 'After his show, we all went to Biki's fabulous flat at Maiden's. Biki used to tell him that he couldn't come if he didn't play, but he loved playing for us. His gold-plated cigarette case was much in evidence.' Despite embarrassment at going out and being 'black in the local shops', Hutch and Pratt 'used to go to the Connaught Circle every day . . . and drink huge glasses of fresh orange juice in the street'.

In the autumn, the socialites of India moved east to Calcutta and, in particular, the Grand, for a season that officially lasted from 15 November to 15 January, but often stretched well into February or even March. The Maharajahs of Cooch Behar and Burdwan stayed in their cavernous and columned city palaces, but every night they went to Prince's, the rarefied nightclub at the Grand, or to Firpo's, the 300 Club or Maxim's at the Great Eastern, to meet their friends and enjoy the cabaret. Scions of other royal houses took sumptuous suites at the Grand;[5] they included Jodhpur, Dumraon, Kashmir, Bhopal, Pataudi and Jamnagar. The dashing Jai of Jaipur was married to Ayesha of Cooch Behar, who, as the Maharani Gayatri Devi, was ranked as one of the most beautiful women in the world. By day, this coterie went to the races and played or watched polo. The Oberois' official historian described this doomed world:

The rustle of silk, the starch of the shirt, the lustre of the pearl of great price and rubies the size of pigeon's eggs. The charmed spell was still to be broken by wealth tax, death duties, socialism and the de-recognition of the maharajahs . . . The post-war boom had allowed the Indian Government to be generous with the release of foreign exchange for hotels and restaurants, and not only chefs, but bands and nightclub acts, could be imported with ease. They may not have been the top drawer of that European season, but they were very good. And, sometimes, the best. The Great Hutch, the celebrated black entertainer, the toast of London and rumoured to be the lover of the Duchess of Kent, played and sang at Prince's, his baritone belting out 'Hey There, You with the Stars in Your Eyes' or 'Let's Do It', sending the audience into ecstatic raptures. Later came the equally trumpeted Duke Ellington . . .[6]

In Calcutta, years afterwards, Hutch's old friends and their children spoke of him with a proprietary affection – 'You remember old Hutch? Of *course* you do!'

In strident contrast to the gentler promotional techniques of Delhi, Hutch's engagement at the Grand Hotel's two nightclubs – the hugely exclusive Prince's and the less prestigious Scheherezade, outside in the Winter Garden – were prefaced by an explosion of costly publicity. Photographs of Hutch beamed down from key poster sites in the city; and he smiled up from table mats, coasters, flyers and newspapers. Even the *Statesman*, the subcontinent's most sombre paper, carried a huge advertisement on 6 January 1956: 'Grand Hotel, the social centre of Calcutta, are proud to present nightly the Calcutta success HUTCH, chosen one of the top twenty cabaret acts in London during 1955 – "Hutch . . . his songs can hold a room in nostalgia's grip for an hour".' With the run under way, coverage became even more extravagant: 'More popular than ever, Hutch held an audience of 800 people spellbound on Saturday night.'

Hermione Baddeley, who was performing in Calcutta at the same time, fared less well: while Hutch's contract was extended, hers was abruptly cut short – because, according to another performer, she was often very drunk. On 7 February 1956, Hutch wrote a complacent letter to Joan:

By now, Hermione Baddeley is back in London. She was the biggest tragedy India has ever seen. Dire flop. Business has been fantastic for January, Wednesday at Scheherezade over 500 people and, at Prince's, 350, never been known . . . I am still puzzled. Can't tell the men from the women, especially at night and when it's a little chilly. They all wrap up. Bastards.[7]

Comments on the weather, the habits of the locals, the rise in prices, his continuous success and his exalted audiences, the glittering people in his audiences, recur time and again in the letters Hutch wrote during his visits to India. A letter to Joan, written from the Grand on 8 April 1957, is typical:

It is very hot here, 96 degrees, but of course my suite is air-conditioned. The opening night was brilliant. Everybody returned to Prince's apparently. I am told they do not come when I am not here. Scandal galore, but it would take reams to tell it . . . There was one serious thunderstorm with rain. In about five minutes, water entered the door of the hotel. You could not get out, such is the drama and lack of system here. The Indians spit just the same as ever and pick their noses and roll the findings in their fingers – dirty bastards. In one party on the second night, there were the maharajahs of Cooch Behar, Jaipur and Burdwan with their maharanis at one table. But Calcutta is changing and is so expensive . . . 10/6d for a medium-size bottle of whisky . . . What's new in London? I miss the Adams trial.[8]

Apart from rare concerts at 11 a.m., Hutch slept all morning, and then went out to long lunches with friends before going to the races or watching polo. After a long siesta, he would be at the piano for the cocktail, dance and floor show at Prince's, finishing at 3 or 4 a.m. after a long dinner–dance–cabaret routine at the Scheherezade. A Calcutta businessman recalled that the charges at Prince's 'escalated as the night went on. From 10 till 12, it cost two rupees for a chotapeg [i.e. small] whisky; from 12 to 2, three rupees; from 2 until 6 a.m., they charged six rupees for the same drink. The musicians were not allowed to stop until the last person had left the dance floor. Prince's was for boxwallahs, no riff-raff.' To this businessman, Hutch was 'just the piano-player, a sort of servant'. To Hutch, the businessman was typical of the parvenus he encountered everywhere, people to be treated correctly but kept at arm's length; increasingly, they were the bane of his life.

Ellis Joshua, usually known as Josh, was the manager of the Grand in the 1950s, having started there in 1942 after his family was evacuated from Rangoon. He planned the themed nights which, every Saturday during the season, filled Prince's with celebrities. Josh understood Hutch well, and indulged him at every turn:

> He was moody, selfish, vain, unpredictable and affectionate. We gave him a suite at the Grand, where he was treated very well. He always dressed immaculately. He took infinite care, and often asked my advice about which tie with which shirt, but he was just making me feel good. He always knew. He never got up before lunchtime. Every year he came he was drinking a bit more than the last. I would bring him on about 11.30, when the 'after-picture' crowd had arrived.
>
> When I left the Grand to go to Trinca's, Hutch missed me. He was very upset and came and played there, which was against his contract. But he did it for me. He sang risqué stuff . . . Hutch didn't mix with the local Calcutta crowd or other entertainers; his friends were the top tea crowd at Williamson Magor, the elite with money who spent it.[24]

Pat Williamson, the focal point of the group with which Hutch was most intimate, had inherited a leading tea company, Williamson and Magor, founded in 1816. He was a rich, flamboyant, devious and insecure man, sometimes described as the last of the nabobs. He was also brave and resourceful: in 1935, when there was an earthquake in Bihar, he piloted himself to the area and organised help; he won a Military Cross in the war; and in 1962, when the Chinese invaded the north bank of the Assam and put many families to flight, Williamson bribed the remaining men to stay and arranged for the evacuation of their women and children. He owned a yacht, *Merry Dancer*, which was moored in England at Plymouth or Cowes, and was often brought to meet him and his friends at Le Touquet, Deauville or the Riviera. Although the group used to stay at hotels, they used to eat and drink on board.

During the mid- to late 1950s, Hutch often joined Williamson's parties in Europe to watch racing and polo and gamble – but only a little. Williamson, as a steward of the Turf Club in Calcutta, was not a betting man, and under his aegis, Hutch would have restrained himself. In India, he was also sometimes present when Williamson's leisurely motorcade used to proceed up-country – with frequent stops for gin and tonic or brandy on tables with white linen cloths, glass and silver – to his house in Darjeeling, where he lived in expansive, old-fashioned style. A friend, B. M. Khaitan, remembered Williamson's group gathering at his house at 2 Penn Road, Calcutta. 'Pat used to say, with a fanfare for his pet celebrity, "Hutch has come", and in Hutch would walk, arrogant like a prince, walking on his toes. He had a violet smoking jacket with black satin frogging of which he was very proud.' Khaitan, who had first met Hutch in 1954 with William-son at Quaglino's, found him 'really introvert and secretive'. And, like most of Hutch's Indian friends, he gently deplored his valetudinarianism. When elaborate arrangements were made to extricate Hutch from the Grand so that he could join a midweek beach party at Pouri, Hutch muffled himself in his bathrobe, huddled under his sunshade and never swam, saying, 'My throat will get bad. I'm a singer. I look after my assets.' Another time, he went to an open-air concert featuring Cliff Richard, where he shivered and put a handkerchief over his head; he also evinced his 'paranoid fear of big crowds which reduced him to a quivering jelly'.[9]

Vina Lindsay, who was brought up in Calcutta, had more positive recollections of both Williamson – 'a smooth gent . . . generous in every way' – and Hutch, who was 'very genial and good company. Nothing was too much trouble; however tired he was, he would play and sing for us. He became one of the more attractive pieces of furniture around during the Season.' William-son and Hutch had much in common. Both drank heavily and both, when drunk, could be deeply unpleasant. Pearson Surita recalled that Williamson 'started with Campari at breakfast, and was a very nasty drunk. He was not a nightbird and did not dance. When drunk, which was all the time, he couldn't stand up, let alone dance. He also had a horrible temper.' He could be 'vicious in business if crossed and there were no second chances if you let him down'. At this stage in his life, Williamson was so incapacitated by drink and so impulsive in his ways that his company would have gone broke had an efficient young colleague not stepped in to save it.

Pat Williamson was homosexual, and looked disconcertingly like the actor and comic Kenneth Williams. Hutch was certainly his lover, and probably also that of the Maharajah of Burdwan, a vast man, who had his suits made in Savile Row in the hope they would make him look more svelte. Burdwan was a zamindar, meaning from a princely family but not a proper prince; in his own words, from 'a top family, but not a royal family'. In relative terms, the Burdwans were arrivistes, having emerged from the Punjab only three hundred years earlier. Unlike true princes, they had been elevated by the British for services rendered; and were regarded by many as collaborators – not least because they took the British side in the Indian Mutiny in 1857. The difference between a real prince and a zamindar is similar to that between a hereditary baronet and a man who has been knighted. Gun salutes reflected the hierarchy: the Nizam of Hyderabad, like the Viceroy, rated thirty-one; Cooch Behar, eleven; but Burdwan, none. Like Hutch and Williamson, Burdwan was introspective but kind to those he liked. As formal education and qualifications were thought to be necessary only for wage slaves, Burdwan, who would never have to earn his living, was educated at home. He spoke three Indian languages, and could recite long stretches of both Shakespeare and Sanskrit. After the First World War, his father changed his mind and sent Burdwan's younger brother off to college.

Burdwan was pompous and clever. He verbally abused his wife, and referred to her in public as the 'hooded cobra'. However, Hutch liked her, and used to go to the palace in Alipur in Calcutta to chat and drink tea with her. There were then 600 acres surrounding this massive palace, which is now a filthy, crumbling – if still impressive – ruin with most of its land sold for development. So dilapidated are the inner courtyards that they were chosen as the setting for the slum scenes in the film *City of Joy* in the early 1990s. Burdwan's grandson, a graduate of Exeter University, has renovated some of the rooms, which he hires out for weddings and other events.

Burdwan's youngest son, Danny, recalled that his father only visited Burdwan 'as little as fourteen days a year' and, after 1954, never returned. This was because, after sixteen generations of

Burdwans had ruled there, Burdwan lost the election in 1952, largely because he regarded the constituency as his kingdom by right and refused to canvass for votes. 'We went out with our heads up,' he said, 'and we should now stay away.' Danny said, 'When he lost his kingdom, my father lost his soul, his *raison d'être*, his identity – it was like death.' When the viceroy asked him 'What do you think you are now?', Burdwan answered, 'Indian by birth, English by education, Scotch by absorption.' Danny remembered his father as 'patriarchal and traditional . . . precise, punctual and formal', although apt to wake him on his return at dawn by bawling across the echoing lake in front of the palace, 'Love Is a Many-Splendoured Thing', a favourite learned from Hutch.

After his banishment, Burdwan was less happy but more approachable and entertaining. He had always been a frequent visitor to Europe, and regarded London as a home from home 'just like going to Delhi. Other places like Greece, France and the US, now they *were* abroad.' He grumbled bitterly that the authorities forbade him to take his servants on his travels; and in 1955, in the Savoy, complained that he had been forced for the first time in his life to tie his own shoelaces. His brother Mehtab used to say, 'I have only two shirts, but I have five people to put them on and take them off me. Why should I care how many I have?'

Burdwan knew Hutch from the 1930s. When they met him in the Berkeley in the early 1950s, his eldest son Henry thought, 'It was obvious that they were old friends. I had heard from my father that Hutch had been Lady Mountbatten's lover. I also remember him and Hutch roaring with laughter about her relationship with Nehru and gossiping about his present impotence. They seemed very well informed.' Hutch also revealed that his own liaison with Edwina still intermittently continued at that time.

Whenever Burdwan turned up at Prince's, Hutch sang one of two contradictory signature tunes: either 'A Bird in the Hand Is Better Than Two in Burdwan' or 'A Bird in the Burdwan Is Worth Two on the Maidan', the Maidan being an open, grassy space where Calcatians parade, play games and mount exhibitions and festivals. The Maharajah invariably rocked with laughter. Like Hutch and Williamson, Burdwan drank heavily to avoid having to think and talk honestly; and, again like his two friends, he was an ambiguous, proud, spoiled introvert who made merry to sustain a public façade. The Williamson clique was regarded by many as 'profligate and degenerate in a well-brought-up sort of way; what you might call Hooray Henrys with culture'. They formed a drinking club called the Fourteen Apostles, which, after dwindling to only two members in 1992 – Pearson Surita and Burdwan's brother Mehtab – is now defunct.

Although they were fairly discreet, the trio were odd enough to generate gossip. Their closeness ended after only three years, in 1959, when Hutch failed to answer Williamson and Burdwan's joint summons to board the *Merry Dancer* at Monte Carlo because he was drunk and depressed. On his last trip to Calcutta, in 1960, he did not contact any of the group. For a time, however, they were all three close friends; triangular friendships are always hazardous, and it is probable that the relationship was too intimate to last long, and erupted in a terminal row. Furthermore, Hutch no longer had the energy to evince bonhomie he did not feel; and, knowing that the modus vivendi of the two men would in time push him to a point of collapse, he may also have relinquished their company in a rare attempt to discipline himself. In his acute financial difficulties, he may also have found it impossible to tolerate the company of people with boundless wealth; indeed, given his momentary awareness of global inequality, he may even have come to despise their lives of carefree privilege.

Hutch's other friends in Calcutta included Pearson Surita and his brother Ivan, both of whom were sometimes part of the Williamson–Burdwan nexus. Also homosexual, Pearson was a regular sports commentator for All-India Radio and, one season, for the BBC, as a guest commentator for an Indian test series in England. He was a competent pianist and in 1954 had played the organ at Peter Heneker's wedding. Hutch also saw something of the Maharajah of Cooch Behar, whom he knew well from Quaglino's, but away from the Williamson set. Hutch had known Cooch Behar's mother well in Paris and London in the 1920s and 1930s, when she was a great friend of Tallulah Bankhead. Cooch Behar's aide-de-camp Khaddju Mama remembered Hutch coming to the Maharajah's house, Woodlands: 'A nice man, good-looking and a perfect gentleman with lovely manners and a soft voice . . . a top pianist . . . the bosom friend of my friend. They were very fond of each other [and] played all day sometimes. They had nothing else to do. Cooch Behar loved jazz and anything jazzy. He was knowledgeable, too.' Hutch also cultivated the maharajahs of Jaipur, Kashmir and Baroda.

Boris Lissanovitch, the proprietor of the 300 Club (its name was a self-deprecating reference to the 400 in Leicester Square) where people went to after Prince's, was another friend. Years before, he had danced with Diaghilev's ballet company, his body painted as a cobra. Pearson Surita recalled Lissanovitch as 'everybody's favourite, a great drinker and a friend of the King of Nepal, where he died'. On his nights off, Hutch often went to the 300, where he 'gently perambulated around the floor with Lady Mary Herbert, the wife of the Governor of Bengal'. Along with the other guests, he was continually plied by Lissanovitch with a steady flow of canapés including pâté de foie gras, accompanied by vintage champagne.

Hutch made common cause with the proprietor of another nightclub, the Golden Slipper, a small, seedy first-floor retreat packed with jockeys and stable lads unable to qualify for the 300. A resourceful lecher, Dadi Mazda, tempted likely conquests to his flat, where he sat them in a cleverly positioned swing so he could see up their skirts. Hutch spent time with Peter Sarter and his wife Lilian. Promoted as 'a celebrated dance couple', they came from Budapest, and had 'set Calcutta on fire' with their routine before the war. They usually appeared on the same bill as Hutch at Prince's; and Peter Sarter, as well as being a performer, was also the 'artistic director' of the programme and the choreographer of a revue, *Romance*, which began nightly at eleven. Before Hutch started his act, he occasionally handed Sarter a flat platinum watch glinting with diamonds, with a loud whisper, 'It was from Edwina; look after it for me, will you, dear boy?' Sarter was unimpressed: 'Hutch loved himself very much and was very conceited – a real *grand seigneur*. He was very elegant and smelt very good [and] always chose from the à la carte menu . . . He was vain and dyed his hair. He used to say "My voice is growing with my age", which was not true.' Sarter also recalled a tall Englishwoman, who called Hutch 'Maestro', going to his room. When the management asked Sarter to choreograph a dance sequence to synchronise with Hutch performing 'Night and Day' and 'Begin the Beguine', Hutch vetoed the idea outright as he did not want to share the limelight with anyone. 'He never cooperated with me.'

Biki Oberoi, brother of the lighter-hearted Tiki, tempered similar views of Hutch with more positive comments: 'Hutch came out late in 1958 because his wife had died. That was the first and last we heard of her. He hinted that every girl in London had been in love with him. He was a great name-dropper, but he did know the Indian maharajahs well.' Oberoi admired Hutch's swift wit, 'but he was vain and he sulked. He liked to tease others but took umbrage himself very fast.' By now, he frequently stood on his dignity and expected the deference due to a star and friend of royalty.

Peter Heneker had fonder memories. Having known Hutch since childhood as a great friend of his father, David, Heneker was now a member of the sizable expatriate enclave in Calcutta. He recalled Hutch coming to lunch on Sunday – 'well, brandy with lunch on the side' – and playing variations on Fats Waller's 'Honeysuckle Rose' 'for half an hour without repetition'. 'He always struck me as an egocentric man, not really selfish. He exuded professionalism, loyalty and honesty. I remember his pained surprise that my father had once deliberately avoided paying for a train ticket; he hated that. I remember him as a kind man.'

When Hutch returned to Calcutta for February and March in 1960, the Grand billed him as 'the West Indies' brilliant contribution to the world' and – possibly a jibe from Biki Oberoi – 'the popular short snorter himself'. With the Williamson connection severed and the Season almost over, this was an uneventful engagement. The jaunty letters he wrote to Joan conceal any disappointment. One describes flying by jet:

Unbelievable . . . yet it has its teething troubles . . . via Rome, where it was pissing, more than 1,000 miles to Cairo in under 2 hours doing 612 miles per hour. You go so fast there is no vibration at all. Then, of course, a little technical trouble . . . I was stuck in the bloody thing like a prisoner – you cannot move in transit in Cairo – for 8 hours, not able to lie down. Arrived eventually in Calcutta one day late. God, I was tired and my back was breaking. But the sun was hot. I soon got into tropical

clothes – heavenly feeling . . . Sorry, duckie! At the Red Cross
Ball opening, there were about 1,000 people in the garden, open
air, who screamed their reception after about 3 years [sic].

He continues briefly on a euphoric note – 'Every bearer, every
clerk, every waiter grinned their approval of my return. Ever since,
business has been phenomenal' – before griping:

Then, in the light of day, I looked once more at Calcutta. I
walked round some of the places I knew. The horrible urination
smells, the spitting – the continual gathering in the throat before
expectorating and praying that it doesn't land on you. The drive
from the airport was a veritable nightmare. The grey-black
dhotis they wear. The oblivious nose-probing, the blowing
from the nose with two fingers and wiping it on their clothes.
Truthfully, I am pleased about the weather – but for anything
else, Calcutta is one big bore. I miss you too, very much, my
brainless wonder.

Clearly, Hutch was distancing himself from India by focusing on
superficial faults.

Towards the end of the visit, another letter to Joan touches on,
and possibly exaggerates, his continuing acclaim – 'My success here
is unbounded' – after mentioning 'a painful attack of fibrositis,
mainly due I think to the chilly air-conditioning. Have had to have
deep ray. Slowly going away. I think I might arrive the latter part of
March.'

The long-term influence of India on Hutch was slight and
largely sartorial. His friendship with Cooch Behar persisted, and
they continued to meet in London; either on their own or joined
by English and Indian friends. When entertaining in London,
Hutch often wore jodhpur coats acquired in Calcutta with shining
shalwani buttons. He also took to acknowledging the applause of
his audiences in both variety and cabaret by using the traditional
Calcatian obeisance, the namaste, a complex gesture which signifies
greeting, forgiveness, obedience or valediction. Many remembered
him clasping his hands in prayer or blessing and the slight inclination of his thickening waist; then, the Buddha-like smile which
made his eyes disappear into his bloated cheeks as he straightened
up to respond to acclaim from another part of the room.

But to a friend he said, 'Don't go to India. It'll break your heart. They believe their karma is never to advance. The people treat each other like animals.'

Chapter Twelve

The Sweet Smell
1956–1959

Il lupo perde il pelo non vizio.
(The wolf may lose his skin but not his vice.)

Some time after the death of Group Captain Peter Townsend in October 1955, Princess Margaret was briefly close to Hutch. People believed at the time that Establishment pressures had forced her to give up the possibility of marrying Townsend – a commoner, equerry to her father and sixteen years her senior – because he was a divorcé. Her much-loved father, George VI, who had died in 1952, had known what it was like to be born second; as a result, he had spoiled her; and now, at twenty-six, she was beautiful, fragile and lonely. Lord Beaverbrook had created a mildly raffish party-girl image of Margaret in his papers, and much of the rest of the popular press had followed suit. Some said this was a hangover from the abdication crisis when Beaverbrook backed the Duke of Windsor, a continuation of a perverse grudge against the royal family which most frequently manifested itself in astringent comments on the Mountbattens. Hutch, at fifty-six, was funny, tender, still glamorous and reassuring. Margaret, like her

H U T C H

mother, had always had a faiblesse for those involved in the performing arts; indeed, she was something of a performer herself, a mimic, a singer and a pianist. During 1956, as well as seeing Hutch, she spent a lot of time with Danny Kaye.[1]

Early in 1956, Tom Eggerdon, a past president of Variety, was working for a second-hand car dealer, a personable young Italian called Joe, in the East End of London. Joe was having a desultory affair with a girl working in a chemist's shop in Golders Green. One day she gave him an antique fob watch and told him it was a royal heirloom, originally owned by Queen Mary. As it was too valuable to wear, Joe put it in his safe. A few days later, a Mrs Turnbull rang to tell him that the watch had, in fact, been stolen from its owner, who urgently wanted it back. Joe, who was now courting his future wife, did not want any trouble, so he agreed to return it – and asked Tom Eggerdon to act as his go-between.

Eggerdon arranged to meet Mrs Turnbull at a pub, the Mason's Arms, and insisted on the owner providing proof of possession. A rugby-playing boxer was asked to be in the pub as his bodyguard, but Mrs Turnbull changed the venue at the last minute.

When Eggerdon arrived, 'There was a black gentleman wearing dark glasses, who looked a bit daft, sitting at the bar, who introduced himself as "Leslie Hutchinson." Eggerdon had seen Hutch many times. After two drinks and an anodyne exchange about show business, Hutch said, 'We have a little bit of business to transact. I will prove to you that I am the owner, but you must never breathe a word about the contents of this letter.' He then showed Eggerdon:

a letter from Princess Margaret, which had obviously accompanied her gift to him. I handed over this exquisite ruby and diamond watch and made him sign for it. He ordered a bottle of champagne, and I was mysteriously landed with the bill. We shared a taxi. I dropped him off in Bayswater. I gave Joe the receipt and told him who the watch belonged to. Joe's girlfriend had been two-timing him with Hutch, and was also a thief. He was not best pleased.

Johnny Wise, a musician, was writing songs for Lawrence Wright. He had been introduced to Hutch by Hutch's song-plugger friend Ted Morgan, and had written a song called 'You Above All', a deliberately commercial number suited to a 'big voice'. Back from India in April and still suffering jet lag, Hutch had played through some fifty songs sent him by various publishers to await his return. 'You Above All' appealed to him, and he went round to Wright's agency to discuss it with Wise. Wise recalled that before Hutch left, he telephoned Princess Margaret for half an hour, and 'made sure I knew who he was talking to'.

In Wise's view, Hutch put 'showmanship first and musicianship second'. He added, 'Max Wall was later to use a version of this song called "Used Above All" in his imitation of Hutch. He was as aware as I was that Hutch was over the top singing this song.'

Hutch kept three or four newspaper photographs of Princess Margaret among his private papers. Farcically, he sometimes wore a false moustache when he accompanied her to weekend house parties; Bill Pilkington registered this with baffled amusement when he met them together at the house of some of his relatives. Others saw him dancing and chatting to her between sets at the Colony: 'Princess Margaret would wait through his performance to dance and talk to him, and they obviously loved each other's company. He was a big man, but he danced like an angel.' Pilkington also noticed that Hutch manoeuvred himself to be near the Princess at public engagements: he used to bow and smile as they met; and, when they shook hands, they did so for ten seconds. While Pilkington himself had some reservations about Margaret, he said Hutch was invariably enthusiastic about her.

The Manchester Daily Dispatch, on the 27th of April 1955, mentioned that when Hutch opened again at Quaglino's the Duchess of Kent took Princess Margaret to hear him.

In an interview in July 1956, Hutch presented himself as a complacent and very willing darling of high society:

He's the deb's delight – and he says he's always 39. Hutch might have read my thoughts. 'When you were a teenager, I was top of the bill. I'm *still* top of the bill. I've had my ties and sleeves torn off by admirers. If my arms weren't permanently fixed, they would have had those, too . . . Today, I am *always* 39. I am *proud* to be a Society entertainer. I think I am probably the last. Records, radio and television interest me little. I *like* entertaining society. Dukes and duchesses, lords and ladies – all are my admirers . . . Rarely do you see me on the variety halls today,

though I *can* top the bill, and I *do* like playing to big audiences.
It's just that I *like* playing for Society.'[2]

The *Daily Express* gossip column headed 'William Hickey' provides a perfect illustration: 'As Princess Alexandra left Quaglino's,
so the Duke of Kent entered. She asked Hutch to play "Night and
Day". When Hutch started his "Let's Do It" routine, Julian
Tennant, as anyone would have long ago, shouted, "Let's have
the vulgar versions". And Hutch obliged.' Tennant and his wife
Miranda were good friends of both Hutch and David Heneker.
The couple were intelligent, attractive, rich, well-connected,
generous – and very loyal fans. They were just the sort of friends
Hutch liked to make in the younger generation, and he sometimes
spent weekends with them in the country; as far as they knew, they
were his only great friends. Their cousin Colin Tennant, now Lord
Glenconner, had asked Hutch to play at his wedding at St
Margaret's, Westminster, but the church council forbade it.

Opinion was divided over Hutch. Roger Longrigg, a writer,
found him 'like a lion radiating sexual conceit. He wasn't just a
legendary success with women, he was a pest. He had such
irritating, affected mannerisms. At Quaglino's, he kept mopping
his brow and pressing his palms together at the end of a song, like a
fancy mandarin.' Others, including the author, playwright and film
producer Wolf Mankowitz, at whose parties Hutch often played,
were more enthusiastic about him:

He was a good mate. A public personality in a private world. He
projected a very delicately balanced public persona, which was
almost a comic persona. He was a flaneur, a camp version of
himself when a romantic singer in the twenties. He sweated
enormously and behaved as though he suffered – it seemed a real
nuisance to him to sing the songs he sang. He had a great
following, and I always enjoyed his performances. He was
evidently bisexual, a multiple personality and a very clever fellow.
Hutch moved in that weird world of nightclubs at 3 a.m. He gave
it reality because he did not really exist in any other.

The man recalled by Adrian Foley, a pianist and broadcaster, presaged
the latterday Hutch. In the course of a three-year weekly series on
Radio Luxembourg, Foley did a thirteen-week stint with him.

It was a time when sweet music was what sold, and Teddy
Holmes at Chappell's wanted Hutch to sing 'Nature Boy'.
Hutch was a caricature of himself then, and I remember him
at 9 a.m. recording dates in his big vicuña coat, wielding a throat
spray and moaning 'I feel dreadful' and then banging away at the
piano. He had become a very uneven performer. He was still a
good musician, but had been more sensitive to atmosphere in his
younger days. He was miles better with the right amount of
Scotch and pretty girls hanging round his Steinway after midnight. He invaded the room with his huge personality. He loved
extraordinary chords but he spoiled it all by turning to assembled
worshippers and saying aloud, 'Christ, aren't I wonderful?' Just
like Peter Pan crowing, 'Oh, the cleverness of me!'

Quaglino's was flexible over Hutch's contract. By July 1956, he
was also appearing at the Colony, presumably between his first and
second set at Quaglino's. Harry Morris, who was proprietor of the
Studio Club during the war, ran the Colony as a restaurant which,
from the moment the cabaret started at eleven, discreetly turned
into a nightclub without hostesses. As well as Hutch, Lance
Percival and Edmundo Ros sometimes provided cabaret; once
it was over, Morris dimmed the lights and the band played for
dancing until 2.30 a.m. Princess Margaret and her set were often
there. Back at Quaglino's, Hutch performed for royalty en masse
when the Duke of Beaufort invited him to perform privately for
the Queen, the Queen Mother and other members of the royal
family. The occasion was a dinner for the British team which had
won a number of equestrian events at the Stockholm Olympics. At
dinner, Hutch said he would include in 'Let's Do It' a verse about
Prince Philip's recent fall at polo, but the Duke firmly censored it.
Hutch substituted a verse about learning to ride in the Blues, the
Royal Horse Guards, and was gratified to hear a bray of ducal
laughter.

Several newspapers commented that Hutch, in a misconceived
effort to move with the times, was making his lyrics a shade too
blue. The influential *Performer* was crushing:

It is always sad to see a legend die . . . What makes it sadder is
that Hutch, once the maestro of sophisticated schmaltz . . . is
committing professional hari-kari. Instead of singing the haunt-

ing, nostalgic numbers which made him famous, he is singing
smutty lyrics, some so full of sexual innuendoes that, the night I
heard him, one woman walked out . . . so I give him a word of
friendly advice. Clean up your act, Leslie, and give the customers
more of that old black magic.[3]

Until the mid–1950s, London night life perpetuated the traditions
of the 1930s: evening dress was usually mandatory, and dancing
girls were fairly discreetly dressed. In the second half of the decade,
the code relaxed and there were many changes: the 400 ceased to
insist on dinner jackets; the Café de Paris, so long a gilded showcase
for top cabaret, became a replica of a suburban palais de danse; and
in January 1958 the Savoy announced that it would stage no more
cabaret until further notice. Many clubs were now retreats for
entrepreneurs using their expense accounts to entertain clients.
The host usually doubled as a comic who, as the night wore into
the small hours, made increasingly risqué jokes and treated his
clientele as though he was running a particularly tart group-therapy
session. Al Burnett at the Stork Room, the generously moustached
Harry Meadows at the Embassy and Rico Dajou at the Don Juan
were all masters of this abrasive genre, but they had their counter-
parts at Eve's Club, the Astor, the Latin Quarter, Winston's,
Churchill's and Murray's. The last-named was the club where,
in 1961, Christine Keeler met Mandy Rice-Davies; like the rest of
the small and rather ragged chorus line, both girls were got up,
Folies Bergères-style, in tights, nodding plumes and judiciously
positioned spangles, a provocative style that was also part of the
new order. The more stately clubs that catered only for supper and
dancing, such as the Milroy, the Edmundo Ros Club and the
Society, were survivors from a bygone era, and doomed shortly to
make way for upper-class discos like the Saddle Room and
Sibylla's.

In 1956, Hutch and Viera, the 'Continental Songstress', between them performed most of the cabaret at Quaglino's. But, far
from confining himself there and at the Colony, Hutch was doing
the rounds. Lew Lane, a friend and theatrical agent, often went
with Hutch on his nocturnal peregrinations.

A routine evening would start at the Dorchester bar at about
8.30. Hutch always bought the drinks there. Professionally, he

needed to be seen around town in the flow of things. Then we
would go to the bar of the Milroy, and out to dinner. We used to
go to the Pheasantry Club, where Mario Casani, who had come
from the Monseigneur, served us flaming kebabs on a sword.
Hutch played at the 21 Club, Churchill's, the Gargoyle at Meard
Street in Soho, the Copacabana and Eve's Club, where we used
to see Prince Philip and Milford Haven chasing chorus girls.

Many people remember Hutch at the Blue Angel at 14 Berkeley
Street, just round the corner from the Colony in Berkeley Square.
It was so named because the owner, Max Setty, was a friend of
Marlene Dietrich, who had gained international stardom by the
film *The Blue Angel* in 1930. She gave her blessing to the name in
1955, when she was starring at the old Café de Paris and he was
starting up the club. She also agreed to the use of a larger-than-life
still from the film. Placed behind the bar, this showed Dietrich
sitting on a barrel, wearing a tutu and a silver topper, suspenders at
full stretch as her hands interlace round the knee of her raised left
leg.

According to Leslie Berens, 'The cabaret room was on the left.
The place had been built by a mad Russian. There were trees
painted on a fence which ran along the passage. The whole thing
looked like a wood. At the back of the stage were loos and a
kitchen. Lance Percival, David Frost (later famous as a TV presenter), the composer and pianist Richard Stilgoe and the entertainer Ned Sherrin employed there, too.' Lance Percival was
paid £25 for a six-day week there working ten weeks at a stretch.
His recollections complement those of Berens: a receptionist and,
to the right, a sitting-out area which later was also used for
gambling; to the left, a long room with chairs, tables, a lattice
screen, a cramped dancing area and just space for 'the Benny
Morgan Trio'. The place was always packed when Hutch was
there. His piano would disappear under a snowstorm of slips of
paper with requests; and when he had finished, he used to sit and
hold court in the lobby. Percival particularly admired his 'tremendous capacity for drink' and his 'beautiful dinner jacket, bluer than
navy blue, with large satin-faced lapels'.

Beryl Bryden, the self-styled 'Queen of the Blues', sang there in
the late 1950s. She remembered the Blue Angel as:

The haunt of BYTs, Guards officers and debs – brainless, wealthy, jolly socialites having a good time. Max Setty, who ran it, had been a used-car salesman. He was shady, but nice and quite fair. There was some scandal about his brother's murder.[4] Noel Harrison acted as master of ceremonies, announcing the acts and playing the guitar. Dave Allen was in cabaret there, too. Hutch was a bit aloof, he was a legend. He played a mini–piano there, and every night there would be new lyrics to 'Let's Do It'. His material was saucy, not blue.

Noel Harrison remembered Hutch coming on from Quaglino's at the end of the evening. One night, Noel's father, Rex Harrison, dropped in after playing Professor Higgins in *My Fair Lady* at Drury Lane. Hutch enjoyed singing parodies of songs from the show, and after he had delivered a pointed send-up of 'On the Street Where You Live', one of his big numbers from the show – 'I have often strolled down Park Lane before/But I never saw it look like Salisbury Plain before/Not a tart in sight . . .' – Harrison angrily walked out. Confronted by much more provocation, Nora Docker, Hutch's old friend from the Café de Paris, where she had been a hostess alongside Merle Oberon, showed great equanimity. To the tune of 'Clementine', Hutch at the Blue Angel used to sing:

> Down Park Lane in a Daimler
> Leaning back on zebra hide
> That old shocker
> Nora Docker
> With Sir Bernard by her side.[5]

Richard Stilgoe said that Hutch was 'very grand, and been everywhere and done everything'. As a pianist himself, he was 'thrilled that Hutch still made such a wonderful sound'; and he admired 'the way he accompanied himself as though he was separate as a pianist from the singer'. Stilgoe remembered the Kray brothers and other criminals coming in, gangsters being thought 'amusing' by society at the time. He also recalled that, owing to a quirk in the licensing laws, 'You could only drink if you ate, and all there was to eat were some very old cheese sandwiches. People ordered them and left them.'

Because the Blue Angel was remarkably cheap for a nightclub in a prime West End site, it attracted a rich variety of itinerant topers after hours. One habitué remembered, 'We used to go there very late, after playing rugger and drinking in pubs. Then, nine-tenths to the wind, we would adjourn anywhere which was open that served drink. The Blue Angel cost £3 a year for membership, and I then earned £2 a week.' He added, 'My dad used to say that Hutch used to procure girls for him and his friends at parties after the Blue Angel'; tacky functions along the lines of those which Hutch used to arrange for Cole Porter in the 1920s.

After he had fulfilled his cabaret obligations, Hutch used to be driven about the West End in a Bentley Continental drophead as he made up his mind where and with whom to while away the rest of night. The huge elegant man in the huge elegant car, restlessly plying from one nightspot to another like some landbound Flying Dutchman, was one of the small-hours sights of Mayfair in the mid-1950s. He often chose Churchill's, a club where he also occasionally worked. For some of the time, he sat alone, but when people offered him drinks at the bar, he accepted; and, as the night wore on, he became increasingly drunk and boastful, flashing the signet ring Edwina had given him, with her coat of arms on the inside. Most or all his audience would have heard the story many times before – the hard core that stays on at nightclubs after half past two rarely changes – and would have been dismayed at Hutch's insistence on telling it time after time. In the late 1940s, the club had had a flash gilt-and-plush chic, but in the mid-50s it was fairly seedy, and by the end of the decade it was 'full of tarts'. Hostesses stalked among the tables, encouraging customers to give them champagne; and, for cabaret, there were turns by has-beens or coming stars like Ronnie Corbett and Danny La Rue. 'Hutch was like Liberace,' La Rue said, 'very flamboyant and definitely charismatic with an enormous presence. I admired his elegance as a black man.'[6] Laurette Boston, whose mother was half-English and half-Sierra Leonian, was the resident singer there for nearly twelve years. 'If Hutch had been working at the Berkeley, he would come in after his cabaret; we didn't shut till 4 a.m. He knew Danny well, and used to talk to clients more than to other musicians.' Eartha Kitt, a friend of Bricktop's, also entertained there, and, with encouragement from Hutch, added Cole Porter numbers to her repertoire. She and Hutch are thought to have had a relationship at this time.

A similar sort of club, Winston's, was another of Hutch's late-night staging posts. Peter Charlesworth, a theatrical agent, remembered him there. He admired Hutch as an entertainer – 'a riveting act . . . style . . . and loads of class' – but disliked the man: 'He was still a potent name, but was pretentious and had a highly inflated opinion of himself. He was very close to the royals at that time. He wore a silk dressing gown in his dressing room, and a touch of make-up always. He was effete. He was a user and not a pleasant man. He propositioned young white women all the time.'

Hutch filled his afternoons watching cricket or going to the races, usually at courses near London. While his Bentley drophead and chauffeur languished in the car-parks at Sandown, Kempton, Alexandra Palace or further afield at Lingfield or Brighton, Hutch would glow expansively in the members' enclosure. 'Everyone knew and liked him and called him Leslie. He was part of the scenery . . . He was always done up like the best man at a wedding. Hutch lost great sums of money at the races. He took too many tips from the trainers and jockeys that he knew.' And a *Picture Post* photograph of Hutch in October 1955 shows him, burnished and black-tied, among fellow members of the newly revived National Sporting Club, all set to watch a boxing match in the Banqueting Room of the Café Royal. He looks a thoroughly established man in a near-Establishment setting.

Around this time, a woman called Anne Marie Swent, who worked for UNESCO in Paris, revived a relationship with Hutch that had flickered on and off since 1928. To reignite it, Anne Marie sent Hutch some snaps of her house in Montparnasse: one showed the drawing room, the chimney piece adorned with photos of Hutch; another showed herself at the piano in the music room. In one of several letters, part French, part English, she writes:

I am a born artist and like to show off, in front of other people and in front of myself. Why not? It gives me the illusion of living a life full of events, that in reality never take place for good. I am an eternal 'fugitive', hungry after all that is bright, full of music and warmth, but shrinking away every time when life, with its brutal and intense sensuality, stands in front of me,

claims me and tries to involve me in its course. I suppose you to
be of the same sort of nature. I think work and duty are the only
things in life to rely on, all the rest is just a play: nothing to
remain after, nothing to be created of. 'Love is like a cigarette',
an inscription I read on a box in your home. This is true: tout
s'en va en fumée, rien de tangible, rien de ferme. Self-control is
the quality I most appreciate in Englishmen. So that I am trying
to be English in your respect, for the time being, and hope to
succeed.

They also conducted a political dialogue in their letters. Hutch
wrote to her of 'the Indian problems and the social and cultural
implications of colonial policy in Asian countries'. She had studied
sociology, economics and politics, and felt passionately about
'unilateral justice worldwide'. She was a disciple of Paul Robeson,
whom she described as 'the wonderful fighter, whose name will be
written in glowing letters in the history of civilisation and struggle
for freedom and justice', an encomium with which Hutch can
hardly have been entirely pleased. They discussed Nasser's likely
motives over Suez. They fervently agreed that, despite the horrific
aftermath, Indian independence and partition had given people a
far better chance in life than they would ever have had under a
foreign culture, language and way of life.
    Hutch's experiences in India and his friendship with Anne
Marie, whom he used as a sounding board, seem to have prompted
him, relatively late in life, to think about world politics, a subject he
had previously avoided. Just being well informed about international events was no longer enough; he began to analyse his own
observations. Before, such thinking had seemed too inflammatory
for a black man in what was still regarded as a white country. Hutch
had a conservative clientele and a deep dislike of confrontation. But
staying in Paris with James Baldwin, Richard Wright and other
hardline literary blacks had touched off in him real curiosity about
what other people were doing beyond the narrow horizons of café
society. Slowly and deeply, Hutch came to realise that he had
cultivated rich libertines and fools – at the cost of starving his mind.
It is also possible that he wanted to show Anne Marie that he could
be every bit as committed as his old friend and rival Robeson. His
friendship with Anne Marie Swent became 'a little relaxation
together, maybe once or twice a year. Cela nous ferait du bien,

n'est-ce pas?' In the early 1960s, he told a recording colleague that
he still went to Paris to see her.

The press once more announced that Hutch was thinking of
launching his own West End restaurant, but as before, the backers
withdrew and the plan was laid to rest. Instead, the autumn of 1956
saw the return of Hutch's glory days in variety. In a long, rather
breathless review of his performance at the Finsbury Park Empire,
the critic for the *Record Mirror* charted each stage of Hutch's
performance from his entry – 'hands held in front, pressed together
at the fingertips, as if he were about to conduct a prayer meeting.
His expression is part serious, part obsequious, part quizzical' –
through a virtuoso series of changes in mood and tempo to 'Hutch
perspiring somewhat and preparing to dab his forehead with that
celebrated handkerchief as the curtains close'. The review ends,
'And, above all, he varies his volume from ingratiating whispering
to the most glorious hammy declamation . . . no matter how much
competition he gets from new arrivals, he'll never have to wave
that white handkerchief.' At £225 a week, Hutch was still
excellent value on stage.

   Hutch's cabaret schedule too was almost as hectic as before the
war. He was still attracting capacity crowds at both Quaglino's and
the Allegro despite strong competition: Hermione Gingold and
Carl Brisson were starring at the Café de Paris, and Lena Horne was
in cabaret at the Savoy. (Horne was also staying at the hotel, having
refused to perform unless the hotel relaxed its colour bar.) Hutch
played for two months at the Mayfair Hotel in Berkeley Street, also
providing cabaret on occasion at the Dorchester. Les Brown, the
guitar player in Albert Marland's band at the Mayfair, remembered
that because of petrol shortages during the Suez crisis, the management axed Hutch's cabaret. Marland's band sometimes accompanied Hutch, and Brown used to produce a wolf-whistle effect on
his electric guitar for 'C'est Magnifique' and 'I Love Paris'. He
admired Hutch's piano playing 'though his style was a bit dated.
Still, Albert Marland was even more dated, so they got along well.'
On New Year's Eve, Hutch finished his turn at the Mayfair, ran up
the street, around the corner and arrived panting at his second
piano at the Cascade Restaurant.

   In March 1957, Hutch was photographed at Heathrow, travelling on the same flight as Aneurin Bevan, then Labour's Chief

Spokesman for Foreign Affairs. Hutch was on a five-week cabaret
tour, starting in Calcutta; Bevan was off on a tour of the Far East,
first stopping in Delhi with Nehru. They exchanged compliments:
'Said Bevan of Hutch, "I certainly like his style as an entertainer."
Said Hutch of Nye, "I like his direct, forceful approach. I follow his
speeches with interest." ' Hutch was right to be ambiguous: first,
because, in the 1950s, entertainers, like prewar servants, were not
expected to be politically aware; and second, because the Conservative and Labour parties were far further apart in the 1950s than
they are today, political feelings ran correspondingly higher: had he
endorsed Bevan, Hutch's cabaret audiences would not have forgiven him; had he opposed him, his variety audiences would have
taken offence.

Confirming his return to favour at this time is the high press
coverage of Hutch's more minor activities. The day before the
Bevan story, a magazine called the *Indicator* had run a feature on
tipping. The norm ranged from one to five shillings. At one
extreme, Lord Rothschild, realising that a previously untipped
liftman in his office had completed twenty years' service, gave the
man tuppence. On the other hand, 'some people tip stupidly.
Probably entertainers like Hutch, the singer, who gives £1, and
Gracie Fields, who gives £1 (plus £1 each to the engine-driver,
fireman and guard) feel that this is useful expenditure on publicity.'

Back from India, Hutch was at Quaglino's for a month, making
sure to mention the names of famous old friends in the audience so
that the room could applaud their visit:

> Thanks to the Revenue
> Noël is allowed back in town;
> All this, and Tallulah too
> London is quite upside down.

Hutch also appeared in an all-black radio series, *The Music Box*,
broadcast every other Friday for twelve weeks on the BBC's
Light Programme. His co-star was the singer and actress Bertice
Reading. She found Hutch 'debonair, there aren't men like him
around any more, debonair men have disappeared. I had an
inkling he was gay when I first saw him, but bisexual certainly.
He was a gorgeous hunk of a man, you felt he was playing to
you personally.'

In the summer, Hutch could often be found sitting at the American Bar at the Embassy Club and prompting David Heneker, still the pianist there, with the words of old songs; when he joined Heneker in 'Let's Do It', the compere, the diminutive but stentorian-voiced Davy Kaye, was unable to stop them.

In September, Hutch joined Max Miller at the top of the bill at Reading's Palace Theatre of Varieties, then celebrating its fiftieth anniversary. Since 1907, prices for seats had risen between four to six times: the gods, from fourpence to two shillings; and the best seats, from one and fivepence to six shillings. On free afternoons Hutch went racing at Newbury; and everyone went to parties on Max Miller's boat moored at Henley. Possibly because he was a last-minute inclusion and technical rehearsals were skimped, Hutch had to cope with a runaway microphone during a recording. With a lazy arm and a loose screw, it slid slowly but surely away from him down the steep rake of the stage. Still playing the piano, Hutch stood up to lean towards the retreating microphone and sing 'Speak Low, My Heart'. A technician rescued him just in time. The cricket commentator Brian Johnson witnessed the near-disaster, and afterwards had a good laugh about it with Hutch. An employee at the theatre recalled that Hutch 'always had a lady friend around. He was a little on the stout side by then, but he didn't change much. The Palace was on the way out with half-empty houses normally. But on this special occasion, it was packed out.'

Hutch next performed for two weeks at the Palace, Chelsea, and at the Metropolitan, the 'Met', in the Edgware Road, accompanied at both theatres by a small orchestra; his billing read, 'The Welcome Return of HUTCH, The Fabulous Star'. When Miranda Tennant took her mother to see him at the Palace, she shouted a request to him from the darkness of the auditorium. 'Certainly, Miranda,' said Hutch, recognising her voice at once, 'you shall have it!'

By early 1958, Hutch was 'well on his way to his 5000th cabaret performance'.[8] A second LP appeared, *Hutch Again*. This included the wistful elegy to a broken marriage 'Dinner for One Please, James', written in 1935 by the British songwriter Michael Carr.

On 1 April 1958, Ella died, aged sixty-three. She died as she had lived, almost unknown to the outside world. Hutch told newspaper reporters:

The old lady was a fine woman. We were married 30 years. She was Anglo-Chinese. I had been to Lincoln for a day at the races. I returned to the house in Hampstead, put the key in the door, and shouted, 'Hello, there'. But there was no answer. The night she died, I was appearing at the Colony Restaurant. My doctor gave me an injection and insisted I should carry on with the show. I did. The restaurant was full and the applause warm and there were many laughs. But I don't remember much of that evening. She lived quietly far from the spotlight.[9]

She was certainly buried out of the spotlight – and far from her husband. Her completely unmarked grave in the vast Hampstead cemetery shares a grassy space with three other bodies. The burial cost £12. It was a shockingly poor return for all that Ella had done for Hutch: for all her goodness and her tireless, un-complaining efforts to please everyone; despite all her difficulties with Hutch, she had always looked after him; she had been a devoted grandmother to her daughter's children; she had asked for nothing in return, and was not much disappointed.

It is impossible to determine what precipitated Hutch's sudden return to depression, relative penury and drinking too much. His diary for 1958 and early 1959 reads as though all were well: engagements at the Dorchester, the Coconut Grove, the Colony, the Blue Angel and the Satire, a new venture in St James's. Hutch was hiring Daimlers for the weekend; having lunch with barristers at the Temple; spending afternoons at Lord's and evenings at cocktails in Belgravia. Shortly after a Grand National week en-gagement at the Royal Restaurant, Liverpool, Hutch was back at the clinic at Montreux. In mid-April, he wrote to Joan:

I have nearly finished this gruelling course. I didn't realise that it was two years since I was here, so you see it was doubly difficult. I stayed in bed for four days and had every test made. Adhering strictly to orders, I have so far lost 12 lbs. Heavens, I do look different. You know I was in pretty poor shape before I left London. I was beginning to be worried because the sleeping capsules were refusing to work. My liver has completely 'gone away' and the B/P is now 150/90 – wonderful. I'm afraid that from here onwards I must and will only have grills, salads etc.

That makes it much easier for you – you little bastard. I do look
and feel so much better. Now back to work and earn money to
pay Income Tax. By the way, prices have shot up here, everything has been completely renovated.

Back in London, Hutch was asked to the first night of Cole Porter's
Aladdin with a script by the humorous writer S. J. Perelman. It was
a musical of little charm with a substandard score, a lacklustre
swansong to a brilliant career. Porter had had a leg amputated the
year before, and was in a parlous state as he approached his
seventieth birthday, but he came to London for the opening.
At Quaglino's, he listened with a smile on his face as Hutch sang
twenty-two verses of 'Let's Do It'.

In mid-July, Hutch played at the Café Roma in Alassio, in
northwest Italy, near the French border. A disaffected letter to Joan
read: 'Went on a yacht the other day, that was pleasant. Plenty of
palms, plenty of flowers, but very common. Food very much
below par. I defy you to get a beefsteak forever. Very gossipy and
bitchy, because it's small. Audience in shirtsleeves. Miss you.' Two
weeks later, his situation was even worse: 'You are a bastard, you
don't write . . . The men here have foul breath, and the women
don't shave under their arms – so I have a GRAND time. The
"thing" is slipping again and causing great discomfort [a reference
to a scrotal truss]. What is going to happen to me this winter? You
don't miss me one bit.'

Later that summer, 1959, the black militant leader Malcolm X lent
his flat in Harlem to a Pakistani student, Eqbal Ahmed, who was
embarking on Persian studies at Columbia University; and Ahmed
later asked a fellow student, Firuz Berenzian, to join him. Malcolm
X had told Ahmed that the apartment had belonged to James
Baldwin, and that a friend of Baldwin's was already in residence.
The friend turned out to be a middle-aged man – stocky and often
drunk – who 'had known Jim in Paris'. The students admired the
way he played the grand piano, and called him Hutch or Hutchie.
When they could spare the time, they sat and chatted to him in the
evenings. He stayed about four months.

In the 1990s, Ahmed immediately recognised Hutch from a
photograph. He remembered that Hutch, whenever he could,
borrowed money which the students could ill spare at the time. He

drank a lot of whisky and boasted about going to bed with Lady Mountbatten. 'Never anybody else, just her.' (Edwina had a mild stroke that year and was to die early in 1960.) Ahmed sometimes saw Hutch 'transform himself into a true gent' by renting a tuxedo and a Cadillac:

> for parties downtown . . . He was keen to meet Robert Moses, then Commissioner of New York City . . . the greatest impresario of the twentieth century, a big power broker. He renovated Carnegie Hall and the Lincoln Center. The son of a bitch didn't call him back, but Hutch doggedly claimed friendship, asking rather wistfully, 'I wonder if Bob will be at the party?'

Ahmed found Hutch a good storyteller. He particularly admired his description of ants building a nest and mating.

> He had grown up outside near a beach, and had an obsession with shells. He remembered all the different types of shells in his village. He used to meet Duke Ellington who was trying to help him.[10] I saw them together in a restaurant. He told us that Leonard Bernstein wanted him to work with him. Bill and Rosie Styron knew him, too.

Hutch may have been seeking work in Harlem, the scene of his early triumphs, or he may have gone there chiefly to get away from his worries, his women and distintegrating career. If so, the escape attempt failed. Hutch was back in London in time for the release of *Treasure of San Teresa*, a British film in which he had a small role as a piano player. The film, about an American secret-service agent finding Nazi loot in a Czech convent, had an international cast that included Eddie Constantine and Christopher Lee, and was one of the first to be directed by the Canadian Alvin Rakoff. *Variety* described it as 'a routine meller [melodrama] which might make a useful second feature in average houses. But it rarely sparks to life, is pulled down by an unimaginative script and only flickers into real action at the end.' It certainly did nothing for Hutch's career.

The 1950s were over. Although he was used to evading reality, Hutch must have known that he had left it too late to make any radical changes in his circumstances, and that the ruts of his life were deep and set until his end. Still, he always tried to avoid responsibilities, and when they weighed too heavily on him, he would go abroad whenever he could.

Chapter Thirteen

Clinging On Abroad
1960–1966

Free from love's illusion, my heart is my own, I travel alone.

Noël Coward

In July 1960, Hutch began an intimate liaison which was to last until 1967. A young society fan, whose parents were great friends of Hutch and Joan, commissioned a portrait of Hutch from an amateur artist called Jill. At first she worked from a photograph, but once she met Hutch, they immediately embarked on an affair. Jill was twenty-three at the time. She had trained as a nurse, been on the stage and had a child. Although she often stayed at his house in Steeles Road, they never lived together; the relationship followed the usual pattern of Hutch's more lengthy affairs: sporadic bursts of intense passion between long gaps. Jill's account of life with Hutch confirms his high-handed treatment of Joan – 'very rude, always issuing her with streams of instructions' – and the discrepancy between the accumulated squalor at Steeles Road and Hutch's personal elegance: 'The house was filthy and chaotic with lots of newspapers and rubbish lying around . . . There were silver ornaments everywhere and Art Deco lamps. It was rather a creepy place.'

Like most of Hutch's girlfriends, she was expected to be a willing valet: 'I used to dye his hair for him, be invited to admire his slim ankles, massage his neck and shoulders and help him tie his cummerbunds. I also used to iron his dress shirts, fifteen at a time.' Jill also contributed to the house – 'pheasants and flowers from the country' – and arranged short holidays. 'The three of us [the third was Jill's daughter] went to Snape in Suffolk, where she and I stayed in a rented cottage, and Hutch stayed in a local hotel overlooking the sea. He used to swim like a porpoise in the turbulent sea, making no concession to the freezing cold.' This was in sharp contrast to India, where, because he was working, he had been too concerned about his health to swim or get out of bed before noon. 'He got up each morning at 9.30, had breakfast in his dressing gown, made phone calls and went off to drink in bars near Shaftesbury Avenue. He would have lunch somewhere, then go racing or watch cricket or visit the Old Bailey, then to drinks, dinner and finally to work. He bought the newspapers nightly and read them until 3 a.m.' And work, of course, was where Hutch came into his own:

> I used to accompany him to Quaglino's, the Blue Angel, the Dorchester and the Savoy. It was an upmarket life. His performances at Quaglino's were the best – his brilliant topical puns and asides switched on a rich young crowd, who pressed him with questions on current affairs and relished his quick repartee. He loved the songs and their words. I think some part of him believed in their romance. His timing was superb, and he brought freshness to each performance – he never sounded jaded.

The BBC producer Dennis Main Wilson saw Hutch at the Blue Angel and was pleasantly surprised. A memo to his boss reads:

> Hutch was top of the bill . . . and . . . as great a showman as he ever was. True, his voice is not quite so virile as it used to be, but it makes no difference, he covers it superbly. He got an ovation from the audience (the house was full) who would not let him go at the end of his act. The surprising thing was that the audience was composed almost entirely of the younger set in the twenties. If you are still toying with the idea of a half-hour show

with artists who are strong enough for a single, but not strong enough for a series, may I suggest that Hutch would be one for the list?

Hutch's other preoccupations seem unchanged since the early 1930s: Jill went with him to watch boxing in Brighton, and to see justice done at the Old Bailey; he delighted in performing at the Long Room at Lord's, and in various London prisons; he impressed Jill with his knowledge of racing and his circle of friends – 'I met Learie Constantine [captain of the West Indies cricket team] with him and [the film star] Laurence Harvey. He often met Turner Layton' – and he took her to first nights of plays. Above all, he demanded total, almost subservient loyalty to himself: 'Once at the Savoy, he insisted, 'Always look at *me*. So I did. I also called him "sir". He liked that.'

Jill saw more of Hutch than many of his earlier girlfriends did, because, for all his name-dropping and still-impressive contacts, the socialites who enjoyed his cabaret performances no longer asked him for weekends or dinner in their homes. Hutch felt bitter about being dropped, and shared his feelings with Jill, who filled the vacuum they had left. But she was much more to him than a receptacle for his rancour or a young, biddable escort. He derived much strength and comfort from their relationship, and a tape of them singing duets to Hutch's piano accompaniment demonstrates the warmth of their feelings towards each other.

About this time, Philip Harben, Britain's first 'TV chef', acknowledged that he had learned a lot from Hutch's culinary expertise. In an undated press clipping, Harben – a burly, bearded man who always wore a butcher's apron – said that, while on a provincial tour together, 'him singing, me making soufflés', they dined together after the show at a drab hotel. 'He looked at the menu, sent for the chef and gave him minute instructions as to what to do and how to do it. I just sat back! He knew far more than I did about how to get a good meal out of a mediocre kitchen. I lacked both his genius and his experience.'

Hutch returned to the Swiss clinic in March 1961. His latest problem was insomnia – 'sleeping or trying to is the very devil,' he wrote in a letter to Joan, adding that he had celebrated his birthday 'quietly, because no-one knows, but I prefer that to the hypocritical grins and good wishes. NO drinking for a while, funny, but I don't feel like it.' Back in London and opening at the Colony, Hutch was greeted by an 'ecstatic reception'. He told a journalist, 'I just haven't allowed modern times to overtake me. I have lost pounds and pounds on my cure – very expensively – but gained a new voice. I can sing and sing and sing without strain now. Of course my shirts don't fit me any more.'[1]

In a feature on Hutch's life, a French journalist was impressed: '*M Hutchinson parle l'anglais, le français, l'espagnol et le hindi. Il a étudié le Droit, et il écrit.*'[2] This was the usual brazen melange of truth and wishful thinking. Hutch had long been saying that he had reached the age when it was time to write his memoirs. But he put off the task. A friend, David Browne, said the Palace had asked him not to. 'He was very royal family in those days and constantly invited to entertain at Buck House. He was an honourable man.' But that was in 1957. There is some correspondence, dating from 1962, with a publicist who promised newspaper serialisation of the book. Hutch talked and wrote to a friend in Australia, saying he would be glad to be abroad when it came out because he did not want to 'be around to deal with the embarrassment'. In 1965, he told the press that he had almost finished writing the book, and that it would be long and revealing.[3] Later in the year, he claimed that it would be published in 1966. There was no trace of the book in his papers. He liked the idea of producing a sensational autobiography, but writing it would have been an unthinkably arduous task. On 25 July 1980, eleven years after his death, Joan wrote to a Dutch record collector that 'he was only just commencing writing the book, when, unhappily, he became too ill to continue'. If Hutch had had the persistence to write the book, and if he had been capable of disentangling fact from fiction, the book would indeed have been an embarrassment to him and many others.

In July 1961, Hutch sang at the Room at the Top in Ilford. He claimed it was 'a wonderful new club',[4] but would have disdained to appear there in his prime. By August, he was at the Hungaria; and, by October, back at the Blue Angel.

When he was about ten, Nigel Dempster, the social columnist for the *Daily Mail*, had met Hutch in Calcutta where Dempster's father was managing director of the Indian Copper Company: 'He became a friend of my parents when he was performing at the Grand Hotel.' About ten years later, Dempster came to London, and often saw Hutch at debutante dances. His memories of Hutch at this time suggest a man set in his ways and opinions, of reduced energy and means, but still leading a grand, if limited, life:

> My mother used to lunch with him at the old Caprice, where Hutch had his own table. He also [had] tea with her about once a fortnight at her club. I [went] racing with him at Sandown, where he was well known to everyone; racing was a small, cliquey world in those days. Hutch took enormous care of himself. He was a tremendous snob, and very proud of his associations. He didn't regard himself as black. He was entirely content in his domain where everyone recognised him and greeted him. Piccadilly, Berkeley Square and St James's formed the borders of his little kingdom in Mayfair. In the '60s, he seemed older than he was . . . he looked like a silverback gorilla.

In the autumn Hutch announced on a radio show, *The Commonwealth of Song*, that he was going to Australia. He told reporters that he was about to sail for Melbourne and Sydney and that it was his 'first ever visit there . . . I shall be away for five months. I have some wonderful introductions. I'm also looking forward to eating my first Christmas dinner in the sun.'[5] Once again, P & O did him proud, and he reciprocated by entertaining in the ballroom several times. A passenger taught him the words of 'Waltzing Matilda' so he could write parodies of it. To Joan he wrote on 3 November 1961:

> The weather is now truly heavenly. The Bay of Biscay crossing was the smoothest ever. I feel sure I shall benefit from this trip which I sorely needed. A fucking awful crowd of old bastards aboard except for one Yorkshire man, who on the first day kept walking around me and finally stopped and said, 'I wondered if you were going to recognise me from the club at Skipton when you played that Christmas three years ago.' 'Eh bah gum,' I said. We drank whisky, the brandy, then lagers, then back to spirits. By then, we were sitting in the ballroom listening to the band (??? Gawd) and, after one or two more tots, his head bent over and [he] fell fast asleep. I pissed off then.

As soon as Hutch arrived in Melbourne, he started rehearsing for *The Golden Days*, a revue at the Tivoli Theatre to mark its sixtieth anniversary. The press gave both the show and Hutch good reviews: 'It is the singingest and most consistently enjoyable show seen there for a long time . . . the star, Leslie Hutchinson, is perhaps a more subdued Hutch than some may remember – those characteristic asides are missing – but still a polished and accomplished singer of songs at the piano. His distinctive offbeat accompaniments are a joy to hear.'[6] In a postscript to a letter to Joan, Hutch explained that the 'more subdued' meant not performing cabaret songs. He was put out that there were too few people in the audience who knew him well enough to give him the adulatory welcome he felt was his due. He told the tour manager, Frank Duffy, that he was very nervous, and far preferred to work in nightclubs where he could see familiar faces in the audience.

Two letters to Joan casually delegate responsibility for 31 Steeles Road to her: 'My house has never been lived in properly during the 25 years or so that I have lived in it. The rooms have never been furnished, and only a certain number have ever been used. I have been most unhappy there. I leave the whole matter to you, Joanie dear, entirely your pigeon. I hope it doesn't catch fire with cigarettes in bed', and, in the second letter: 'Now that you have kindly offered to run the house, and make a bit of extra money by letting, there is no need to send on letters to me. Gas, electricity, water etc. are all paid up to date.' The first letter is positive about Australia – 'It is very hot here. I have arrived safely and I must say at once that the people in the theatre and the shops have been embarrassingly kind. I have an ear for dialects so I am trying to get used to the accent' – but the second is more complaining: 'I am staying in a flat. It is very expensive . . . it is horribly lonely here. Were it not for the Melbourne Cricket Club, I don't know what I'd do . . . . Aren't you lucky to be in England for Christmas?'

On Christmas Day, Joan sent Hutch a telegram, 'Turkey arrived from Priory Dunbar and lots of cards. Any instructions? Merry Christmas. Love Joan.' He replied, 'Keep cards use turkey invite Macintyres merry Xmas Leslie.' Further grumbles followed in a letter dated 1 February 1962, just before the show moved: 'I came for the sun and I'm getting my fair share, but I never bargained for the humidity, the hot dry sultry north winds and the fucking flies.

You have to spit them out. They get in your ears, eyes, nose, hair, eyelids, everywhere. I go to Sydney with the show until 20th April.'

After the relative failure of Melbourne, Hutch was more successful in Sydney, where Frank Duffy found him unrelaxed and secretive, a 'hardened pro . . . who dressed to impress . . . with a pleasant and dignified demeanour . . . very eloquent in his speech'. His 'creeping lack of confidence' could be 'devastating', and Duffy noticed that he frequently flourished his Edwina-inscribed cigarette case. 'He was originally supposed to close the show, since he was top of the bill, but was relegated to closing the first half. It didn't do much for his delicate ego. He didn't like it at all.' As Hutch wanted unqualified admiration from Joan, not sympathy for failure, he did not mention this matter in his letters to her. Indeed, by the time he wrote again on 6 March, he was cheerful and assertive, and gave a quick sketch of Sydney:

> a sprawling uncharted city. Kings Cross is the Piccadilly of it . . . Hungarian, Czech, Yiddish, Italian, Greek and Ustrylian (as pronounced), every language under the sun. Narrow dirty streets with pools of left-over rain. I've seen the Bridge and some of the beaches. Restless, continuous surf with the sharks sometimes swimming in it. Constant look-outs plus air-patrol are main-tained – sharks are sighted, an unholy siren is blared and everybody scampers. Some not so fortunate. The opening was excellent. More like London. I made a speech and intro-duced the Old-Time Aussies in the Boxes. There is no social life to speak of. Australians are very touchy about their country. If you are giving a radio or television interview, for Christ's sake, praise it, otherwise you're out. But they are getting to the point when they want to know what's wrong with Australian artists – most stars are always being imported from overseas. I will sell the house, I think, and get a studio flat where I can have the piano. How can I thank you enough for all you are doing?

In Sydney, Hutch caught up with a popular entertainer from Trinidad, Winifred Atwell. A classically trained pianist, Atwell made her name by playing a piano acoustically doctored to make a slightly jangly, echoing sound. After scoring hits with synthetic ragtime and boogie numbers, she produced piano medleys. A few years later, when the Beatles and the Rolling Stones put her type of music out of fashion, she and her husband, Lew Levisohn, would emigrate to Australia. Levisohn helped Hutch to supplement his income by entertaining at private parties in Sydney.

As Hutch could not leave Australia until his income-tax position was sorted out, he departed much later than planned, flying on 7 May to Singapore to perform at the Goodwood Hotel until the 21st. The press reported that:

> he had a tremendous ovation – plus five encores – in a packed house at Goodwood Park Hotel's Arundel Room. Once he got going, Hutch found no difficulty in persuading the audience to join him in several sing-song sessions. Hutch, who had been engaged to appear for ten days, took to his piano 20 minutes late. 'I don't start singing until everyone's finished eating', the hefty, cigar-smoking gagman said, 'Might spoil their grub'. Hutch cleared his first and most difficult hurdle – creating a party kind of atmosphere – from the word 'Go'. Every vocal number that followed – 'Love is a Many Splendoured Thing and 'Smoke Gets in Your Eyes' – was sung in a style all his own, the Hutch style. His repertoire of gag songs and double entendre numbers was also limitless.[7]

Hutch wrote triumphant letters to Joan:

> I've had a few receptions in my life – but [here] they must have been 'starved of sophistication'. They shouted and applauded for over an hour . . . Singapore has gone mad. No tables to be had, and don't they like to talk about that. These bastards do nothing but meet for cocktails or a dinner party every night. As Noël Coward said, when he surveyed the motley sun-burnt crowd, 'Now I know why there is such a shortage of servants in Kensington.' Isn't that heaven?

Hutch also commented on the entrance to the hotel – 'quite unbelievable . . . floodlit every night'; adding that 'there are thousands of Chinese here'; and that he 'had lunch with the Sultan of Johore [sic] today. What a bore! I think he suffers from gout.'[8]

While at the Goodwood, Hutch was offered two weeks' work

for £1,000 at another luxurious establishment, the Merlin Hotel, Kuala Lumpur. A fan from Glasgow, Joy Gillespie, remembered that Hutch was 'unimpressed by some members of his audience, Rita Hayworth and her then boyfriend Gary Merrill held hands and talked throughout his performance; Hutch put that down to their disdain for a coloured artiste. We went back again on Saturday night. He was marvellous.' A local pressman was more perceptive and more critical.

> Hutch was introduced at a private party in the Harlequin Restaurant – not as Hutch, the singer, not as Hutch, the pianist, but as Hutch, the raconteur. And the guests who surrounded him, delighted by his witty anecdotes, charmed by his sophisticated turn of phrase, mesmerised by his elaborate gestures, had the satisfaction of knowing that the only facet of this many-splendoured personality that had eluded them was Hutch, the identity. For Hutch is like that. He talks a lot, but tells you little. You chased through the labyrinth of words with a butterfly net, hoping for the one exotic trophy, the slip of the tongue that will provide the clue to the real Hutch. But it never comes. Hutch is much too clever to be caught. He spins his smokescreens of personal magnetism and then slips quietly away, whole and completely untouched. His first impressions of Malaysia? Hutch grew suddenly tense. His features took on a touch of awe, of drama. 'I've never been so close to the jungle. I looked out of my bedroom window, saw all that luxuriant growth and suddenly felt I must penetrate its mysteries.' Of the 24-carat-gold buttons on his high-necked 'tutup' jacket – 'The engravings are in Urdu, and they are supposed to be terribly, terribly old. But of course I wouldn't know what they say.'[9]

The last comment was meant to imply that he knew all along, but would never deign to let on. He was playing the inscrutable sage, the benign man of mystery. Small wonder some found him a know-all and a windbag. But the cashier at the Merlin, S. K. Saw, who used to watch him sitting daily at the same table in the Bamboo Grill, thought that while outwardly happy, he 'always seemed to be inwardly sad'.

By the time he joined the SS *Chusan* at Penang on 11 June, Hutch had once again persuaded P & O to give him a first-class passage in exchange for entertaining on the ship. Predictably, the company fell short of Hutch's standards. In a letter to Joan, he complains of:

> the most loud, big-arsed and big-fronted Americans I have ever seen. The styles and the feet, the spectacles and the settling of world problems by them, have provided me with the biggest laughs ever. One woman, looking like Hermione Gingold's mother and twice as ugly (impossible!) makes an entrance with a new head creation, morning, noon and late at night.

In his next letter, ingratiating himself with Joan, Hutch ordered his homecoming menu:

> Darling, Did you really think I meant you to run out of the house just like that without chatting and having a meal and seeing and hearing all that you've done? I couldn't be such a sod, even though you have called me worse than that sometimes. I have not touched FRESH FOOD for months; it's all been deep frozen. I would like you to get a milk-fed chicken to split down the centre and grill. Then, with that, fresh asparagus or cauliflower au gratin. That would be for dinner about 8 o'clock, Tuesday. So will you ring me about 3 o'clock Tuesday, please, having bought the food in the morning. There is a lot to discuss. I have been away a long time. I cannot thank you enough, dear Joan. Ever, Leslie.[10]

Joan must have run out of tolerance for Hutch's demands. Busy with her own concerns and never domestically inclined, she had unwillingly agreed to deal with months of dreary renovations and other problems to maintain 31 Steeles Road conditional on doing it independently, in her own way – only for Hutch to undermine her every effort. For example, Hutch wrote on 30 May berating Joan for failing to have the pillars round the front door fixed, and for not being more resolute in choosing builders to do the work. ('Joanie, you silly. You must have some sort of brain.') And now, on his return, he wanted her out of the house so that he could invite other lovers there. She briefly imagined herself immune to his charm. He had exploited and hurt her too much, and now it was time to leave. In the event, she welcomed

him back warmly, perhaps more than ever his devoted slave and
prisoner.

For Hutch, Joan's devotion was, at close quarters, irritating. He
found it hard to reciprocate her affection; and, when she accompanied him anywhere, she did not, now she was in her fifties, elicit
the envious admiration of other men – whereas Jill, who was half
her age, did, a factor that meant more to Hutch than ever, because
women were always accessories to his vanity.

At Quaglino's (and, soon after, at the Blue Angel) Hutch's friends
and society fans welcomed him back in style.

> A packed room greeted Hutch, just back from eight months in
> Australia, which seems to have done him no harm at all, and his
> personality is just as expansive as ever and his wit unimpaired. To
> show that he had been keeping up with the times, the maestro
> kicks off with 'Sail Away' (the title song of Noël Coward's newly
> opened musical), but his faithful followers soon demand the old
> favourites, some romantic, some saucy, and heading the list is, of
> course, 'Let's Do It'.[11]

At this time, Hutch appeared as a guest star on *My Friends, the
Dankworths* (the reed player and bandleader Johnny Dankworth
and his wife, the singer Cleo Laine), a radio programme recorded at
the Tempo Club. Hutch's two songs sound confident but overblown; and, his voice, during a brief interview, sounds pompous.
In July, Hutch entertained the Earl of Home, then Foreign
Secretary, and various distinguished cricketing cronies at the Cross
Arrows dinner in the Long Room at Lord's, a date after his own
heart. Far less to his liking were stints in October at the Ambassadors Club, Birmingham; and, even more abhorrent, in November,
at La Bamba Club at the Imperial Hotel, Darlington – 'How can
people live here? This emporium is on the main street with very
heavy traffic – huge trailers etc. My only consolation is the public
. . . they are really quite intelligent.' Hutch took on these assignments because his weekly pay at Quaglino's had been reduced to
only £150 – possibly Hutch was now less of a draw or Quaglino's,
in general, was doing less well – whereas provincial nightclubs such
as the Ambassadors paid £175.

An out-of-town booking Hutch thoroughly enjoyed – because

it delivered a young, Quaglino's-like audience – was the Rum Hole in Somerset, owned by John Hannam. Hannam remembered him as 'a nice old boy, a great trouper. He'd do two cabarets a night for four days. He used to stay in the motel which adjoined the restaurant/nightclub, and used to douse his pillow with perfume.' It was unclear for whom he was dousing his pillow until a candidate emerged from the autobiography of Richard Eyre, director of the National Theatre and, later, the Royal Opera:

After my expulsion from school, I became a barman and wine waiter in a restaurant in Somerset, and I continued to work there intermittently during my university years. The restaurant where I worked had been started on the cusp of a social revolution; outside London, it was rare then to find a restaurant that wasn't in a hotel, and as surprising as snow in the Sahara to find one that had cabaret and stayed open until one o'clock. They served modestly ambitious food and presented stars of the dying London cabaret circuit – Noel Harrison, who sang about the 'Windmills of the Mind'; Cy Grant, to whose Othello I was later to play Third Cypriot; Los Valdemosas, a Majorcan singing group to whom I lost my first four weeks' wages in a game of poker; and conjurors, charlatans, crooners and undergraduate wits. The most memorable of the performers was a man whose name no-one who is under forty-five would recognise. He was the authentic voice of post-war supper clubs like Quaglino's, Les Ambassadeurs, The Stork, names tinged with raffish but faded elegance. Hutch was black, romantic, effortlessly elegant: he sang with a touching grace and the ease and charm of Dooley Wilson in *Casablanca*. Hutch's song was 'This Is a Lovely Way to Spend an Evening', and he sang it with an air of weary melancholy, which may have had something to do with having had to sing the same song for thirty or so years but may have had as much to do with the way that women fell in love with him when he sang it. My girlfriend, who was French and a waitress in the restaurant, was no exception and he treated her with a practised courtesy and tenderness that I regarded with undis-guised envy. 'Don't worry, young man,' he said, 'I won't be around much longer.' He died soon after and I missed him as much as she did.[12]

Early in 1963, Hutch fired off two telegrams from Birmingham to Joan: 'It had to come sometime be brave love Leslie' and 'Provident Law think due see bank urgent love Leslie.' Whatever the problems behind this particular crisis, Hutch thought he had to sell the house as soon as possible to raise funds. In August, he took the less drastic course of selling most of the northern part of the large garden to his neighbours for £700. As a result, the garden of number 31 is now a strange shape.

To get away from these perplexities, Hutch opted, yet again, to spend the first few months of the year abroad, this time in Kenya. In December 1962, a letter from 'Aubrey', with the RAF in Singapore, assured him that 'Nairobi is 5,500 feet above sea level, and the air has a certain champagne quality . . . it may be this that makes the inhabitants leap in and out of bed with each other's wives!' The people of Nairobi, Aubrey thought, were 'more sophisticated than those in Singapore'.

One of Aubrey's friends, Diana Howard-Williams – 'ball of fire, very efficient, knows everyone' – wrote in January, predicting Hutch would have 'a great reception'. She then unwittingly lists the components of the sort of audience Hutch most dreaded: 'Nairobi is a funny place, people are inclined to "sit on their hands" . . . I believe Ron [Ron Partridge, the proprietor of the Equator Club] has already given you a picture of what the club is like . . . some of the younger members may not know who you are, unless they have been around in London recently. However,' striking a note of blithe reassurance, 'the sophisticated types will of course remember you well.' She concludes with some insultingly obvious hints: 'I think your normal type of song will go down like a bomb.[13] The smoochy, slightly risqué material is always popular. I think a tip worth remembering is that if you add a couple of verses with local topical material (these would have to be carefully vetted so as not to upset local personalities) into 'Let's Do It', it would be a riot.'

In the 1960s, time moved more slowly in Nairobi than in Britain. Most of Hutch's audience lived on large coffee and tea estates or huge dairy farms or in ample suburban villas. Nairobi was the social focus and commercial centre which people from up-country visited once a week. Its wide streets were lined with oleander, jacaranda and flame trees. The climate was sunny and cool, money went much further and domestic servants and labourers were abundant and cheap. Mostly for these reasons, a large community of British people thrived there; a small number of them indulged themselves in ways that would have been less acceptable at home – the gay community and the remnants of the raffish aristocratic set associated with Happy Valley.

The day after Hutch arrived, the local Nairobi newspaper, the *Daily Nation*, quoted Ron Partridge as saying, 'It's costing me more than £1,000 for the deal, but it's worth it. I've been a fan ever since I saw him on the halls more than 20 years ago. Bringing him to the Equator Club has been my greatest ambition.' Hutch wrote to Joan from the New Avenue Hotel, Delamere Avenue, Nairobi:

> You must be having a rotten time. I am so helpless – there is nothing I can do from this distance, except give instructions. The general picture is peculiar – better to tell you when I see you. The proprietor has really gone out of his way to be affable and charming – slightly queer for African boys. A very nice place, nicely run – paid £45 excess baggage, mainly for music. They [the 'excellent African band'] can't read it. I went nearly mad, trying to teach them note for note. I have been to several dinners because there is fuck-all else to do. They are bored with each other's company, so any celebrity who arrives, is collared a few times.[14]

The *Daily Nation* reviewed Hutch's performance with praise too qualified to please him:

> A living legend . . . the plump, extrovert purveyor of haunting romantic songs . . . to we slightly older Britons, Hutch, like the Dean of Canterbury and Noël Coward, has always been with us. We have only to hear that voice with its odd mixture of gravel and molasses singing 'Begin the Beguine', to fall again under the spell of a man who epitomises a slightly dated West End sophistication. Hutch is still the complete professional, immaculately dressed, still debonair, with a string of quotable, carefully rehearsed 'asides' . . . Will he appeal to the young? Yes, if only because they will rarely have an opportunity to see such professional expertise again in their young lives. And, by comparison, seeing Hutch might at least enable them to judge the rawness of the current wave of pop singers.[15]

The last sentence referred to Cliff Richard, who was also appearing in Nairobi to great acclaim. When asked what he thought of the clean-cut teen idol, Hutch damned him with faint praise: 'I think he's very handsome.'[16] He referred more directly to declining standards – this time, of his fans – in an interview in the *Sunday Post*: 'In earlier days, I was known as "lover boy". Women used to come to the front row and faint, but in those days, they used to arrive in Rolls-Royces, not sweaters.'[17]

Also in Nairobi were Rock Hudson and Sidney Poitier, taking time off from filming *Uhuru*. Juanita Carberry took the film stars to see Hutch at the Equator. To her great embarrassment, Poitier was refused entry: 'It was a great disgrace. Rock Hudson was such a thug, Sidney Poitier was so nice. I felt awful.'[18] The receptionist at the Equator also recalled Burt Lancaster and Joan Crawford coming to the club. Thirty years later, Pamela Kikumi, who performed as the 'Tantalising Tassel-Tosser' at a nearby club, remembered Hutch as a great draw.

In the afternoons, Hutch went racing with Micky Migdoll, who as a fifteen-year-old had played drums for him at Pops nightclub in Soho Square. Migdoll, now the owner of two race horses, took him to the members' enclosure at Ngong racecourse, 'where visiting cabaret star Hutch could hardly be missed'.[19]

In late February, Hutch set off on safari and photographed lions. His next stop was Mombasa, on the coast. He was booked to perform at the Oceanic Hotel, where Mr Lakhia, who was still the owner in 1992, recalled Hutch as 'an excellent pianist, who pleased everybody'. On a postcard of the beach, Hutch told Joan that the white sand and warm water reminded him of 'the island'.

Hutch went on to the Punch Bowl Hotel, Greendale, Salisbury – now the Red Fox, Harare – which, he wrote to Jill:

I hated. Particularly discovering lots of people that I knew in London. Everyone in Rhodesia is shit-scared of the political situation . . . Look at your map, and you'll see that I am now in the Depths of Central Africa – the area bordered by Tanganyka [sic] and Uganda with the Congo on the other side. All troubled areas . . . Everything is deadly middle-class and can be very isolated socially. Teeming with Scots (obvious settlers) who are worried sick as to how the political situation will turn out. The air is full of foreboding and ominous in outlook. The audience in this place is amazingly alert, scores having seen and heard me in London and, for that matter, England. Again the band, except the pianist, cannot read . . .

Hutch almost invariably disparaged his backing bands. His improvisations made it difficult for them to stick to an arrangement, and typically he blamed them for the resulting confusion. His attitude reduced their confidence and made them more prone to mistakes. He put down his women in the same way; his letters and postcards often address Joan as 'Silly' and Jill as 'Stupid'. That way, he did not have to take their demands seriously or accept any criticism himself.

If Hutch hated Salisbury, Salisbury loved him. The local paper reported that:

a great entertainer held a packed audience under his formidable spell. Hutch played, sang and joked his way to a tumultuous reception . . . He has as much to offer the new generation as he did the one that made him famous. Encore followed encore; but, with admirable timing, he finished on a nostalgic medley and a fiery burst of 'I Could Have Danced All Night'. Hutch could have played and sung all night if he had wanted to. A memorable evening, indeed.[20]

On his return from Africa, Hutch took general stock of himself, and found that having to keep solvent by going abroad for much of the year was fast becoming as much of a strain as provincial tours of Britain. He was getting too old to live out of a suitcase. On the other hand, he experienced almost more stress if he stayed at 31 Steeles Road, which required a daunting number of repairs before it went on the market.

Hutch plunged into the usual round of cabaret dates, and accepted an offer to entertain on the *Mauretania* for a three-week cruise starting on 24 March 1964. Two days after sailing, he wrote a typically put-upon letter to Jill:

This ship is painted a sickly jungle green, madly irregular in the planning of rooms. All heavy wooden furniture and above or below she has NO stabilisers. Some of the motley crowd of passengers have not left their cabins, for with the slightest sea it rolls somewhat. A woman dropped dead in front of the purser's office just before departure and had to be taken ashore in a coffin. What a beginning! Lord Goddard is on board, if that is any good. I am having great difficulty with my throat aggravated by this chill. I hope it yields to treatment shortly. The pianos, for these shows, are behind huge pillars, part of the ship and cannot be moved, so the passengers can hardly see me. Such fun! Never mind, I shall stick it for our sakes.

Two of the other contributors to the on-board cabaret were already known to Hutch. Peter Cox, a drummer, had accompanied him at the Ambassadors, Birmingham, and been duly humiliated by Hutch: 'He used to stop with a loud sigh and groan, "The drummer can't do this right, we'll all have to do it again." ' Dreading a repetition, Cox was surprised to find that Hutch was pleased to see him again and satisfied with his drumming – although he was typically critical of the other musicians. Hutch told him that Cole Porter 'had taught him all his tunes personally'. Cox found Hutch 'a bit lame', and unwilling 'to spend time with anyone who did not know what he had been . . . I ended up quite liking the old bugger.'

The second was Larry Adler, the virtuoso harmonica player. He had known Hutch for some time, but took a more astringent view: 'I never felt that Hutch was a natural performer. He was too affected and effeminate for me to relax and enjoy his act. He was latently homosexual, bitter and difficult.' Hutch became increasingly camp as he got older. His upbringing in Grenada had taught him to despise homosexuality, and he always preferred himself as a lover of women. So it is not surprising that his homosexual affairs seem to have been fraught with spite and self-punishment, either direct or projected onto his partner; hence the sado-masochistic tendencies which only rarely featured in his relations with women.

For many years, even Hutch's appetite for unthinking adulation had been fully satisfied; but, as this was no longer the case, he put on an air of cosmopolitan condescension to show his superiority to those around him. Now puffy and overweight, he was more vain and self-obsessed than ever; but he must have known that his worldly-wise manner disguised a lack of maturity. The squalor at Steeles Road, the letters from accountants and other demands confronted him with his inadequacies, with aspects of himself which he avoided at every opportunity. Hence, in part, the trips abroad and, away from home, his extreme fastidiousness. Hutch at this time outwardly presented himself as a diffident ambassador from a golden era, gamely seeking to brighten an increasingly grey world – indeed, one reporter took him at face value and commented, 'He hid behind his sunglasses: a man from a slower, surer, sweeter, more tuneful world.'[21] Self-dramatising as ever, Hutch once described himself to his friend Bill Pilkington as 'the darkest angel that Gabriel ever had'.

Michael Thornton, then the *Daily Express* drama critic, went to the Society Restaurant in Jermyn Street in April to see Jessie Matthews in cabaret.

> She packed the place out night after night, largely due to her restored publicity value as the BBC's new Mrs Dale in the radio serial. At the next table was a rather portly gentleman with greying hair. I did not recognise him. As Jessie made her entrance, however, to 'My Heart Stood Still', her eyes lit up as she caught sight of my neighbour, and, with a delighted smile, she blew him a kiss which he returned.

At the end of her first set, Matthews announced Hutch's presence to the audience – 'I had no idea he was coming' – to 'huge applause which Hutch acknowledged by standing up and blowing a kiss round the room'. She then told the audience that Hutch had played the piano when she first recorded 'My Heart Stood Still', and left the stage to sing the song directly to Hutch at his now spotlit table. 'During the second refrain, she pushed the mike towards him and they completed it as a duet. It was an inexpressibly moving moment. At the end, everyone in the room stood up to applaud them both.' When Hutch, Matthews and Thornton talked together after the show, Hutch said he had especially wanted to see Matthews's return to the West End after over thirty years' absence. Thornton described the reunion as 'touchingly affectionate'; and when Hutch died, Matthews told Thornton, 'There will never be another like him. He personified the carefree charm of those years before the war.'

Hutch himself entertained at the Society in the early 1960s. One habitué recalled, 'Women all wore little black dresses, short white mink jackets, long satin gloves and pearls. It used to be *the* place to go. It was expensive and sophisticated. You went down a big wide staircase, and Hutch would greet you with a smile at the bottom.'

In May 1964, Hutch started rehearsing for his TV drama debut, a Play of the Week called *A Really Good Jazz Piano*. It starred two Broadway actors, Brian Davies and Stuart Damon, and a Swedish-German actress and cabaret singer, Astrid Frank. The theme was loneliness. The director, Peter Sasdy, recalled that, as a Hungarian, he had not known anything about Hutch, but had cast him in the role of Sid, a 48-year-old jazz pianist, because he was 'black and popular . . . could play the piano and maybe act a bit'.

Having met Hutch at Quaglino's, Sasdy took him to the Gay Hussar, a famous Hungarian restaurant in Soho. As he had long been a solo act, Hutch demurred at having to learn lines, but Sasdy insisted that the other actors needed cues, and that improvisation was out of the question. 'He looked very worried. I looked after him and so did all the cast. He got on well with everyone [and] created an ambience because he was a huge, important presence. He was very professional [and] cared about getting it right and doing it well. I liked his jokes, too.'

Hutch was equally impressed by Sasdy. In a *TV Times* interview, he said, 'I like acting very much indeed, but I'd no idea what it involved. It is intensely hard work. But I can't praise Peter Sasdy too highly. He's given me a taste for it.'

In the play, Hutch said, 'this fellow comes up to me and says, "Can you play 'Stardust'?" So I tell him, "I wouldn't be in this business very long if I couldn't!"' He also sang 'Sweet Lorraine'. 'There's a lot of things in this play which reflect my own life,' he commented. 'For one thing, I play a nightclub entertainer. For another . . . I'm American, which is what people here often think.'[22]

Because of the 1964 general election, which swept the Labour Party into government for the first time since its defeat in 1951, the screening of the play was postponed. When it was finally broadcast on 26 October, the reviewers panned it but were polite about Hutch's performance. His agent Terry Miller wrote to congratulate him: 'For a first effort I thought you did an excellent job of work. The variations in your style of acting for each of the segments you were in were perfect, and your final part of the play was beautifully done.' But Hutch was not offered other parts.

Hutch's name rated a mention in Sandy Wilson's musical pastiche of the 1930s, *Divorce Me, Darling* (a follow-up to *The Boyfriend*), which opened in the West End that year. In the scene, three erstwhile flappers had to guess the identity of a mystery cabaret star who was shortly to appear. The first suggested Maurice Chevalier; the second, Florence Desmond; while the third and most strident, played by Maria Charles, delivered a cockatoo screech of 'Hutch!' evoking roars of laughter and applause from the audience. The word 'Hutch' was a potent symbol of the 1930s, readily recognised even by a largely young audience. When Sandy Wilson met Hutch, he noticed, like so many people, the urgently ostentatious way in which Hutch brandished Edwina's cigarette case.

In July, Hutch was providing cabaret at the Dog and Partridge at Swinscoe, Derbyshire. The proprietor, George Gage, once a flamboyant chef at the Savoy, had known Hutch for years; he was later jailed for smuggling gold from Holland. Hutch did not enjoy working there. He seemed perpetually tired – a common symptom of liver trouble – and disliked his audience, a racy set whose indifference to his performance prompted Hutch to say, 'Aren't the young so passionate about everything?'

There were compensations. He went to a famous pub at Ashbourne, the Green Man, where he got to know Tom Webster, a sporting cartoonist who worked for the *Daily Mail*. He reminisced to Webster about life in the Caribbean and his marriage to Ella in Brooklyn, also telling him that he was still a close friend of Elizabeth, the Queen Mother. Another friend, Humphrey Scott-Moncrieff, lent one of his Rolls-Royces to Hutch during his visit.

But the shortcomings of the Dog and Partridge assignment were nothing compared with the privations and humiliations attendant on his next job in Athens that autumn. Michael Sullivan of the Bernard Delfont Agency, representing the Auberge Tatoi, offered a three-month contract, with an option for three more, at £500 per month. In his letter he described the venue as 'one of the most beautiful auberges in the world, which is very much a hobby for Mr Vernikos, the manager, who has other business concerns'. Hutch needed the work badly as he had promised to pay off his overdraft, and the income-tax authorities were after him.

Everything went wrong. For a start, Hutch found the Greeks unappealing and un-European, and their language impenetrable.

> All I do is get up and listen to the Greek servants screaming at each other in the kitchen below me. I get up and take the autobus into Athens or beg a lift. It is not quite me. I sit in a café and wait for the English newspapers. I sometimes have an Ouzo and return to the Auberge. The breakfast of two hard-boiled eggs come like rocks. I could easily knock the waitress out with them. The Greeks eat like pigs. They bring their heads down to the plate, and do not lift their forks to their mouths. Noisy fuckers. The absolute boredom drives me mad. Everything is written in Greek. You don't know where you are. Vernikos has a dreary wife, a cheerful mistress, who is a danseuse at the Opera House, and many little girls on the side, aged 14 to 16.[23]

After a seemingly successful opening with all Greek society present, Hutch found the job to be a let-down. Most of his repertoire was lost on the Greeks. 'The press were extraordinarily kind, calling me "The Darling of Royalty". Very snobbish here. The French songs go well, and I have to learn some Greek ones because "Let's Do It" is Greek to them! It is no fun playing here. I am just like a pianist in a bar. No status here at all.'

Moreover, there were 'misunderstandings' over money. First, the contract had not specified that Hutch was to be paid in sterling, and the bank charges for conversion from drachma seemed extortionate. At first Vernikos provided him with money to spend locally, but stopped when Hutch vehemently complained that he was not being properly paid. He then bombarded Jill, Joan and Terry Miller with an increasingly desperate series of letters, telegrams and telephone calls.

Michael Sullivan took his client's part, insisting that Hutch was being 'unreasonable and petty', until Vernikos broke off communications with him. At that point Sullivan backed down, and Hutch went to the local police. By Christmas, the money problems were resolved, and Sullivan was in full agreement with Hutch and Miller that it had been 'a disgusting situation'. On 28 December Hutch wrote a short, sour note to Joan: 'I hope you had a nice Xmas. I didn't have any Xmas pudding and the turkey was luke-warm. They don't believe too much in the spirit of Xmas here. I will take a little time to recuperate from all this.'

The Athens debacle rounded off a bad year for Hutch: alongside his more immediate concerns, he was depressed by Cole Porter's death, the Labour government and the news that the Chinese could now make the atom bomb.

Back in London in January 1965, Hutch had a card from his daughter Leslie, announcing the birth of his third grandchild, Gae, almost seven months earlier, in July. The previous two were another daughter, Romaine, and a son, Neil. Hutch, too, was still adding to his family. After a miscarriage in late 1964, Jill bore him a daughter, Emma, probably his last outside child, on 25 April. Hutch was quick to express financial concern. Three days later, he wrote that 'there was never any question of shirking responsibility. Let us just say that under present conditions the emotional stir is nerve-racking . . . I wonder sometimes if I am capable of having any feeling after the buffeting I have taken in this world.'

In March, Hutch was playing at the 69 Club in Newcastle, a tawdry joint where people could go on drinking when the pubs shut. It was an appalling place but it paid £175 a week, and Hutch needed work wherever it was offered: the Westminster Bank had paid his tax bill with the stern proviso that he must sell his house, and if it was not sold within three months, he had to clear his overdraft from another source. At the 69 and comparable venues, Hutch was unable to set up a rapport with his audience; and, without a warm appreciative response, he felt isolated and desolate. At any age, he would have found this situation hard to handle, but at sixty-five he was totally incapable of coping. Worse still, he was now impotent. He sought to combat this by proposing to Jill, but she declined. She had worked hard for Hutch for very little return, and did not think that marriage would change anything. Her refusal only added to Hutch's insecurities.

Performing at the Dorchester, Hutch started wearing a Beatle wig. Beatlemania was at its height and the media had little time for anyone bucking the trend. The changes the Beatles brought about, not only in popular music but also in British society and attitudes, were sweeping Hutch into a backwater of irrelevance. A saddening photo of Hutch in the wig, dandling a guitar, and about to leave for a tour of Northern clubs, appeared in the *Evening Standard*. 'It makes me look quite ridiculous,' he said, 'but I am playing for laughs these days.' As ever, he exaggerated his earnings:

Hutch at a wedding at
St Margaret's, Westminster with
David and Gwenol Heneker.

Princess Margaret at
twenty-five, August 1955.

Princess Margaret visits St George's, Grenada, 1955.

Hutch in the 1950s, by Baron.

Hutch in India.

Hutch and Aneurin Bevan, off to
India, 1956.

Hutch in India.

Hutch with Joan at the Blue Angel.

Emma, born 1965.

Jill, mother of
Emma, 1960s.

Hutch in Australia, 1962.

Hutch at the Burford Bridge
Hotel, 1967.

Hutch, late 1960s.

The audiences are tougher, but the money is as good as anything you get in the West End. I can still get my £300 a week and meals up there. I must keep working if only to keep myself in clean handkerchiefs. My laundry bills are astronomical. I'm fighting fifty and it's fighting back. I don't mind discussing money or even my love life. But be kind enough to stop harping on at my age. It spoils the illusion, dear boy.[24]

When Hutch was interviewed at the Piccadilly Club in Manchester, he impressed a reporter by ordering drinks in Spanish. While laudatory, the piece lets us see Hutch's diminishing confidence.

From the audience, this coffee-skinned mountain of a man with the ironic eye gets absolute attention. And I witnessed something rare in the hard-bitten nightclub world . . . applause at rehearsal time. Not just polite claps, but shouts. The applause even came from dancing girls and waiters. Hutch is nothing if not a perfectionist. He will worry at a number and give of his best at a mere band call, as few other performers do. Yet, surprisingly, he has never lost his taste for compliments. They mean more to him than any performer I have ever met. His new radio series has given him a great lift. 'I'm a hyper-sensitive man, and it's done me the world of good.'[25]

The radio series, *Piano Parade*, comprised six programmes in which Hutch played and sang himself, and also acted as linkman introducing a variety of other pianists. Surviving recordings show that Hutch thoroughly enjoyed the series. Pat Hamshere, a long-standing fan with a bulging file of Hutch cuttings, got tickets from the BBC so that, even though there was no studio audience, she and her two elder children could attend the recording at the Camden Theatre, Mornington Crescent, NW1. She also kept in regular contact with Hutch. 'I was an ordinary housewife. I used to wheel the pram down to the local callbox at noon every Tuesday and ring him. I did it for years and he always seemed interested in the minute details of my domestic life.' This may have been because he was incapable of visualising such a life for himself; and in any case her views were typical of a sector of his clients. Hutch thrived on admiration at arm's length, with no involvement.

Hutch suggested to the BBC producer of the series, Frank Hooper, that he would like to play a more dominant role in *Piano Parade*. Hooper responded in a letter to Hutch at the end of the series:

> Just a short note to thank you for your strong part in the programme and always coming up trumps. We have been working all the way in the same direction and we both know that it has been worthwhile. For my part, it has confirmed in me again that the first ideas are generally the right ones and that one's energies should be devoted to pulling that off rather than looking over one's shoulder for further consideration; the end-product in this way is honest, consistent and uncompromising, which the listener respects and takes to.

Otherwise, the times were moving too fast for Hutch. In November he appeared again at the Blue Angel. At an interview there, Hutch, recently returned from working in clubs in the Midlands and the North, growled, 'Things are very very changed. The kids think they are sexy and kinky. But, quite honestly, they seem to be plain dirty. Their hair, their fingernails . . . the young things of the thirties would have knocked strips off them.'[26] The mixed metaphor is an index of the bewilderment Hutch felt when confronted by the postwar generation. As for Hutch himself, Bill Shand Kydd remembered him in the mid-1960s at the Blue Angel as 'a sorry sight, with his make-up running, and he always had boys with them. They were all younger, and we all knew he was "ambi". He used to go off with them when he finished at the Blue Angel. But, having said that, he also had an affair with our cook, Joanna.'

Hutch was still capable of behaving in an extravagant, imperious way. At some point in the mid-1960s, John Chilton, the jazz trumpeter and writer, was musical director of one of the medium-successful beat groups, the Swinging Blue Jeans. The group played at a club in Wales where Hutch had featured the previous week – though it is hard to imagine that the same audience would have been equally diverted by the two entertainments. Hutch had left his hat behind by mistake, and the manager had written to ask whether he would like it back. Hutch loftily answered that he had plenty of hats and did not need it. 'Knowing of my interest in

'30s musicians,' said Chilton, 'the Swinging Blue Jeans gave it to me. It didn't fit, but I kept it as a souvenir, and it sometimes served as a trumpet mute.'

In a more expansive, even supplicatory, mood, Hutch embraced Hubert Gregg, the actor and radio presenter of vintage records, on the first night of David Heneker's musical *Charlie Girl* in December 1965. ' "Hubert's my benefactor," he boomed and hugged me. I was playing a lot of his music on my programme (*Square Deal*) at the time, and we were all hoping that he would land a recording contract again.'

With less work in the evenings, Hutch was getting up earlier to spend even more time at the Old Bailey, indulging his interest in crime, ritual and oratory. These visits also reinforced his entirely specious claims to legal qualifications, and brought him into contact with people whose company he relished – barristers, judges, crime reporters and police. Robert Woods, a retired policeman, remembered Hutch as a much respected figure, large, benign and wreathed in Bandit aftershave.

> He used to hand out chocolates and boiled sweets. Although the body of the court was strictly for vital witnesses and relatives of the accused, we always found a place for Hutch. He was so popular with everybody, and never once did he have to queue up for space in the public galleries. He repaired to the pub called the Magpie and Stump, over the road, with the crime reporters.

Woods recalled Hutch being hugely amused when, shortly after the abolition of corporal punishment, a man was found guilty of bestiality with a sheep. 'Sir Gerald Dodson was sitting . . . and at the end of the case, he sent him down, saying, "I only wish I could give you the cat as well." '

George Glenton, once chief crime reporter for the *News Chronicle*, recalled:

> Hutch knew all the staff at the Old Bailey. He often arrived with a smart woman on his arm, who was instructed not to speak. He knew the judges well, and they knew him. The Sheriff and Lord Mayor would join the judge and Hutch for lunch on occasion. Hutch was broke and had become a back number, but not to the

judges and barristers. He was their generation. I asked him to
dine as my guest at a dinner to mark the sixtieth year of the
Central Criminal Court. It was held at Cutler's Hall and he
insisted on singing for his supper without a fee. He just moved to
the piano and sang everything we remembered. We all knew the
words. All the judges and famous Fleet Street reporters and their
wives sang their hearts out. He seemed inexhaustible. It was a
delightful and memorable occasion.

Hutch was especially gratified when black defendants were
harshly punished. Just as he sang what he thought people wanted
to hear, so also did he say what he felt was expected of him,
especially on racial issues. Racism, steadily rising in Britain since
the Notting Hill riots in 1957, was now widespread, and there
was talk of the supposed need to repatriate blacks. Hutch,
typically, told several people that he wanted to return to
Grenada; indeed, that he had always meant to go home. This
seems most unlikely, as there was now no one there for him. In
the mid-1950s, he had sold the house in Gouyave for £725,
frequently complaining at the low price. As he did not expect to
see her again, he had also cut his allowance to his ferocious
cousin Wyomi, despite his distantly related lawyer telling him
that she was ill and had bad debts. Had his financial position
become irretrievably calamitous, he might, as a last resort, have
gone back; but he probably pretended an ambition to return in
order to preempt hurtful comments that blacks, including him,
should be on their way. Such remarks came from the roughest
people he had ever met in his professional life: by his lights, they
were social inferiors.

By contrast, some of his old associates saw Hutch as they
thought he saw himself – 'as an honorary white man'. For much
of his life, Hutch equated being white with success; for him, being
white was a state of mind, and, if he *thought* white, the prejudices
of whites would not turn against him. He was dismayed by the
influx of West Indians in the 1950s and 1960s, and blamed them
for a variety of social problems. Before that, he had been enraged
by the English assumption that he was American, but that was
preferable to being associated with 'bus conductors and lavatory
cleaners'. He thought of himself as a British citizen; yet, for all his
panache, he always lived with the insecurities and uncertainties of

an alien. He aimed to be accepted in England as the end-product of his wishful thinking – and not as just another talented black, which is all he ever was to most white British people, however sophisticated.

As he got older, Hutch, like many people, became more at odds with the world around him. Although his age marched with the century, he was now out of step with it. Age also brought increasing isolation and, with it, lessening confidence in the solidarity and continuity of human relationships. In *The Fire Next Time*, James Baldwin wrote, 'Most Negroes cannot risk assuming that the humanity of white people is more real to them than their colour.' Hutch had taken this risk, and he now realised he might have made a mistake. Because of his anomalous situation, Hutch allied himself with other outsiders.

None of them was more bizarre than Richard Blake Brown. A near contemporary, just two years younger than Hutch, Blake Brown was the chaplain at Horfield Prison, near Bristol. Hutch met him when giving performances in the prison, and immediately warmed to this camp, erudite, upper-class eccentric. In his eulogy at Blake Brown's funeral, Bishop Mervyn Stockwood, a close friend and once his boss, said, 'Richard once caused grave offence by serving gin at Communion. It was impossible to be responsible for him. He made me laugh more than anyone else in my life.'

Blake Brown's letters to Hutch are extravagantly arch. Started appropriately on April Fool's Day 1964, the correspondence was on stiff, expensive paper embossed with bright-red copperplate capitals that read, in the top right corner, FROM THE CHAPLAIN, HER MAJESTY'S PRISON, BRISTOL 7; and, across the left, WOULD YOU PLEASE WRITE RATHER THAN TELEPHONE. Blake Brown wrote in a vast, florid cursive, occasionally upside down, using black and red inks alternately, and garnished the letter with drawings and press cuttings. The letter says, 'I offer you four Sundays to come and lunch with me at the Grand Spa and entertain my mischievous flock from 2.45 to 3.45 in your inimitably RICH way! Are these possible for YOU, dear Sir? RSVPee. Would you be an ARCHANGEL and write your reply as soon as possible . . . Ever yours, Richard.' Another reads:

My dear Leslie, How DELIGHTFUL to have a pretty postcard from you in Athens! VERY MANY THANKS . . . I took 48 hours off lunching at Vast Navy Establishments, one of which I had myself been Chaplain of from 1944 to 1947. Here is an extract from my notorious talk to WRENS OVER FORTY, that used to have the most splendid results!! Many a Wren is now a great-grandmother through my cautious counsels . . . On the whole, I am in fairly rude health, thank you; but, at the moment, am too busy to come to Lovely London – All happy wishes from Irrepressible Richard.[27]

Hutch soon went to visit Bristol and did so often for the rest of his life. Blake Brown was always appreciative. On 30 May 1964 he wrote:

I can't really describe how much your visit was loved and appreciated. I think every time you come, you grow better in voice and your LOVELY manners are always so enjoyed by my mischievous men. It was a huge SUCCESS; and of course I myself always so much enjoy your company. I have referred to my records, and find that today was your FOURTH visit. Your new SLIMNESS of figure is astounding; you look a new person altogether; and I can only congratulate you on your rediscovered YOUTH!! But are not you and I altogether AGELESS? Thank you so deeply for coming here today. You are – as always – a TONIC! . . . Which reminds me I have just had a couple of Gins and Italians . . . Always gratefully yours, Richard.

The prisoners liked Blake Brown very much and vividly recalled his friendship with Hutch. 'These concerts were entirely free of charge, and much enjoyed by us all,' a former inmate remembered. 'We were entertained for two solid hours on each occasion with songs and anecdotes and jokes. Hutch was a sympathetic and caring man as well as a great entertainer.' Another prisoner said:

Richard Blake Brown was a very colourful character who used to dress in amazing clothes. He wrote books in the '20s and '30s and then went back to the church. Hutch was a great friend of his, and often came down from London at week-ends. They got pissed together. Hutch sang us the Beatles song 'Yesterday', but ironically, joking about his age. He told us that Hoagy Carmichael had said to him that, when he sang

'Georgia on My Mind', he was talking about a girl and not the place. Hutch was a lovely guy. Perhaps I should just mention that his friendship with Blake Brown was not platonic.

His letters often ask for photos of Hutch to add to his collection. They also include obscene verses, of which this is a mild example:

Two dear old ladies live next door: one is 92, the other only 88; the other day, they both did some pavement-spadework on their path: so I began the following delicate poem:
> 'Ladies of ninety are scraping their FRONTS
> What else could they do the silly old DEARS?'
Is it not nicely phrased?

Blake Brown and Hutch enjoyed meeting for lunch in gourmet restaurants in the West Country, where the former proved a lavish host. He also provided the entrée to another world where Hutch could forget his pressing concerns, and where people were in far more trouble than he was. Furthermore, Blake Brown was good-looking, well born, well off, ostentatious and a figure of scandal: the fact that he was a prison chaplain suggests that he had disgraced himself in some more elevated role in the Church of England. He was also generous-spirited, energetic and happy in his work – all traits that heartened Hutch, who also enjoyed his cranky religiosity.

When in the West Country, Hutch sometimes entertained at Colston Hall or Arno's Country Club. At the latter, Hutch never tipped the staff; and in retaliation they used to play games with his hat in the cloakroom, not knowing that poverty had constrained him to break a lifetime's habit of lavish tipping.

Hutch had been performing for incarcerated men regularly since the late 1930s, possibly for longer. He often visited prisoners at Wormwood Scrubs in west London, among other places, bringing them chocolate and cigarettes; he also corresponded with them. It is possible that he may himself have been threatened with a sentence or briefly been in prison during his time in Harlem. Hutch was brought up to respect authority and the fitness of punishment. He was also fascinated by the processes of the law, and what prompted people to commit crimes. During his lifetime, when motives for prison-visiting went unquestioned, he was widely applauded for his good works; and he clearly brought much cheer to many convicts, relieving their suffering and restoring their self-respect – at least temporarily. But, given his character – his private misery, bitterness and confusion – his motives may not have been entirely altruistic. As an outsider, Hutch felt part of the establishment when he entertained at police and judicial functions, and perhaps even more so in prisons, when he could feel superior to his mostly white audience. And they were always so grateful and uncritical; indeed, the ultimate in captive audiences.

One of the women whom Hutch took to the Old Bailey, where he insisted she be silent, was called Collie. Collie had adored him since the 1930s, and later became a friend to both Hutch and Joan, devoting time and money to their joint needs. Collie remembered that when she first met him, her father took Hutch to lunch and warned him, 'My daughter has a pash on you, and if she's any trouble, send her back in a taxi. C.O.D.' As in the Cole Porter song, Hutch was true to Joan 'in his fashion', she observed. She also thought the words of another Porter song, 'More Than You Know', were applicable to Hutch's feelings for Joan:

> There's nothing I can do about it
> Loving may be all I can give . . .
> If you got tired and said goodbye
> I'd miss you so, more than you'd ever know.

In the positive sense, Collie patronised Hutch during the 1960s. She gave him a watch conditional on his returning it to her one day, which he probably failed to do. She also gave him £100, and paid for some private recordings he made for her in a Denman Street sound studio. After telling her gruffly that she 'was either silly or had too much money', Hutch recorded 'Someone to Watch Over Me', 'As Time Goes By', 'Stay as Sweet as You Are' and a louche number called 'I Remember Tillie'. She sold them, and they were eventually donated to the National Sound Archive in Kensington.

Collie adored Hutch, but she had no illusions about him: 'He was a naughty boy, who sometimes acted like a shit, because he had adopted English aristocratic amorality. He simply did not feel himself accountable to anyone and hated to be challenged. "I don't think what I do is wrong", he would say. But he would say that, wouldn't he?'

As ever, those who knew him less well had unqualified praise for him. Dick Gaby, then secretary of the Cross Arrows, a loyal friend for years, said, 'I used to meet him regularly in front of the Tavern, by the clock tower. He was adored by everyone at Lord's. He was always a very modest, charming fellow and sang us marvellous songs. I remember a rude one about pigeons on the pitch. I used to go off to nightclubs with him after dinner' Almost to the end of his life, Hutch provided the cabaret for the Cross Arrows annual cricket dinners, always performing impenetrably esoteric variations on 'Let's Do It'.

In February 1966, Hutch went to perform near Weston-super-Mare at the Webbington Country Club, once the home of the banker Henry Tiarks, father of one of the most publicised debutantes of the 1950s. Transferring previous ownership of the house from father to daughter, Hutch wrote to Joan, 'Poor Henrietta Tiarks' house is now a gambling joint plus a striptease joint with me added. In the ballroom where I appear, there is a very long bar which has draught beer (shame) right next to brandy and champagne. I survive.' Just as many a theatre was now a bingo hall, so had many of Hutch's friends and acquaintances been forced to abandon large houses which were now converted for other uses. This phenomenon depressed Hutch, who saw it as yet another example of the collapse of the world in which he had prospered. He was also often mortified by audiences talking through his performances, treating them as mere background music. He rarely erupted at this lack of respect but once, over Christmas 1966, during a two-week stint at the Peacock Club, Streatham, he sang 'Begin the Beguine'; and, when a woman started talking, he shocked the audience by shouting, 'Oh, shut up!'

Hutch was desperate for a lucrative stint, preferably abroad away from the cold grey English spring. And sure enough. Anthony Ross, manager of the Mandarin Hotel, Hong Kong, offered him four weeks at the Button Club for £300 per week together with food, accommodation and return flight; his predecessors included Max Bygraves and Dickie Henderson. Ross's assistant Maggie

Christiansen recalled how surprised she had been to find, on looking through Foster's Agency List, that Hutch was still alive.

After receiving the offer, Hutch wrote to Ross to ask if the Mandarin had any bathrooms. Ross exploded to Christiansen, 'What on earth does he think this place is? A flop house?' Hutch was still extremely wary after the bad time he'd had in Greece.

Christiansen remembered that Hutch was so drunk on arrival that she had to have him carried out of the plane, avoiding waiting pressmen, and laid across the back seat of the hotel Rolls-Royce. 'After that flaky start, he behaved beautifully throughout his stay.' She thought he had 'a good time' in Hong Kong, and that his 'pianistic ability had not failed him, but he was always losing his glasses. He told me that Edwina Mountbatten had always wanted him. He talked about her quite a bit, but made it sound as though he had had enough of her. He said that he'd had more women than I'd had hot dinners. I believed him.' Christiansen looked after Hutch with adoring care during his stay, and made a scrapbook of his Hong Kong cuttings which survived among his papers.

As a fast-moving financial and trading city, Hong Kong with its soaring skyscrapers was far livelier than the other colonial outposts where Hutch had played. It had an extensive and wealthy British community, mostly resident on the Peak. Unlike the aristocrats and farmers of Nairobi, the British in Hong Kong tended to be in business or the services. They welcomed Hutch's visit, as did a significant number of English-educated Chinese.

Once at the Button Club, named after the button on the top of a mandarin's hat, Hutch asked for the piano to be raised 18 inches above the orchestra. The first night proved to be a triumph. His audience was discerning and appreciative, and gave Hutch a standing ovation when he sang 'Love Is a Many-Splendoured Thing', a declamatory, sentimental number that was now almost another theme song.[28]

In a four-column review, the *China Mail* described Hutch as:

timeless, like the songs he presents. Still a giant after four decades in the topsy-turvy world of entertainment . . . Since Saturday's reassuring opening (he was called back twice and did an extra 15 minutes) he has played to capacity houses. The 60 minutes go quickly. Except for the traditional pauses to take his handkerchief and wipe his brow or lips, Hutch goes at a cracking pace, song

and joke coming hard and fast. At times, it is difficult to keep up
with the comedy and satire – Hutch's delivery is exceptionally
quick – and occasionally mumbled. But it's instant fun . . .
Talent which stands the test of time and trends is the real talent –
the heart of show business. And Hutch has real heart . . . But it
was good to see him nervous as he entered the Button Supper
Club. He was worried. Hutch, it was obvious, still feels he has to
prove himself with a new audience.[29]

The *Hong Kong Standard* was equally enthusiastic, comparing the
speed of the act, 'fast-paced yet smooth', to 'riding on a jet-stream'.
The paper found his timing 'impeccable', and that 'his rich baritone
. . . reached the upper scales without breaking'. The only mildly
critical note was struck in a radio review by a musician who noted
that the backing group caused Hutch some annoyance at times.

His old agent, Charles Tucker, in a rare return to his desk, wrote
that he was delighted by Hutch's 'good write-up', and suggested a
permanent job at the New Colony Club; in fact a refurbished
version of the old Colony Club in Berkeley Square. Tucker closed
with congratulations on Hutch's weight loss, probably a tactful
warning that Hutch should drink less: '. . . try and keep it down. It
requires a lot of will-power and, with a proper diet, you can
probably take off another 10 or 15 lbs.'

Hutch wrote to Jill:

I motored to a spot called Aberdeen where you dine in the
middle of the river on a huge barge. It was most kind of Mr S
from India (who is dying of the usual liver complaint) to offer me
such hospitality. He does speak in a very loud bogus American
voice which tends to grate and annoy. A fascinating thing was to
see the house in which the famous film 'Love is a Many
Splendoured Thing' was made. Hong Kong is weird and
unusual, but frankly too far from you, and you? You're on
holiday and most frustrating. Do you feel you would like to
come here for a week? The hotel is marvellous – quite luxurious.
It could be such fun.

On the next day, 11 April, Hutch wrote to Joan, offering her no
such invitation, but reassuring her that the riots in Kowloon were
no danger to him. (The riots were in support of the Cultural

Revolution, led by Mao Zedong, which was in full swing in mainland China.) Interviewed on radio, Hutch talked about his wartime experiences in the black-out, and disparaged modern pop music: 'There is no melody – that is the tragedy today. It has an exciting beat – rat a tat tat – but that is all.'[30]

Well promoted by the Mandarin – posters and advertisements showed Hutch smiling under the line 'One of the all-time greats in show business, the inimitable Hutch' – the engagement was successful enough to be extended by four nights to 10 May. The last night was a party for the 'full house who paid tribute to this famous entertainer'; an audience that Hutch delighted with these closing words: 'I shall never forget this wonderful interlude in my life. This city has been very kind to me and I enjoyed every moment of my stay. It is nice to go home, but life will never be quite the same again after Hong Kong.'[31]

Indeed, life at home was to prove very different. In Hong Kong Hutch had for the last time enjoyed acclaim on a prewar scale.

Chapter Fourteen

The Darkness Deepens
1967–1969

Oh pass not by their grave without one thought
Whose relics here recline
Grief for the dead, not virtue, will reprove.

Plaque in the Anglican church, Gouyave

In England, the most acceptable job on offer was a season at a Lyons-owned family restaurant called Showboat on the corner of Northumberland Avenue, just off Trafalgar Square. Hutch, there to attract a superior clientele, was paid his lowest fee so far, £40 a week. Lew Lane remembered that Hutch 'had to perform in the corner because he was too unsteady on his feet to make centre stage'. Showboat, in Lane's view, 'was like a holiday camp in the West End' with family parties and raucous anniversaries, complete with flashing cameras and birthday cakes; Hutch attracted 'the old variety crowd . . . and some nights were full, busy and fun, if you liked that sort of thing'. One of his most loyal fans, Pat Hamshere, noted that 'Hutch didn't smile. He didn't bow. He didn't look at his audience. He never used his handkerchief. It was just as though he gave up on his act in such a place. He sang most of the old favourites, and added "Climb Every Mountain".' The song was from the Rodgers and Hammerstein musical *The Sound of Music*; the highly successful film version had been released the previous year, 1965. Right to the end of his career Hutch continued to add to his repertoire.

Sir Peter Saunders and Colin Brown of Decca formed equally jaundiced views of the job. Saunders recalled that no one made 'any fuss' over Hutch, 'and the worst part was that, when pop singers came on, the audience was silent for them'. Brown remembered that Hutch went on about nine o'clock at night, and:

> Showboat was never packed out. Hutch was very overweight and did sweat a lot. He went into his shell. He drank rum and Coke. Once evening we fed the pigeons together and Hutch stood in Trafalgar Square sadly reminiscing about the old theatres and buildings which had now gone. He loved them. They had been his home for years and had glamorised his life. He was a lost figure. He used to hang around the Paddington area and pick up very young boys and girls in his last years.

Hutch's old friends Harold and Leslie Berens agreed that he had been 'into the god-forbids', apt cockney rhyming slang for 'kids'. Harold confirmed this squalid fact only after speaking to a number of friends and old police contacts: 'No question, that's what he did. God help him.'

Fortunately, Hutch was also appearing at the Blue Angel, where he felt more at home. In June he sang along with Annie Ross on *Radio Dance Orchestra*, rendering 'Hello, Dolly' and, inevitably, 'Let's Do It'. Ross recalled him as 'frightfully elegant and grand with a red carnation of course. He was more English than the English. He was extremely impatient with his age and everything to do with the 1960s, but charming to me.'

Early in January 1967 Hutch sold 31 Steeles Road for £13,037; some £10,000 went to pay off his Westminster Bank loan, leaving a modest £3,000 in his current account. He moved into a small ground-floor flat close by at 9 Eton Hall, Eton College Road, NW3.

The less work there was, the more agents Hutch used. One of the least official of this burgeoning group, Dave Mitchell of the eponymous company, 'representing attractions the world over', communicated in an urgent street-trader style that contrasts strangely with Charles Tucker's patrician approach:

Hope this finds you well and that Bournemouth remembers you [this refers to an engagement with a fat fee at the Winter Gardens].

I have a suggestion re some One Night Venues open Sunday to Sat – one show nightly at each joint – some good, others Lousy Working Mans Clubs. They offer, which is their best for the seven days including encores (if any) £200. This would be for any week you wish. I tried for more lolly but they shook their heads like Russians.[1] Liverpool suggestion didn't come off. They want Poppers and Crutch huggers, male and female, the un-talented types who are getting big money. However let me know re above suggestion.

April found Hutch at a successful new venue, the White Hart at Sonning-on-Thames, Berkshire, where he entertained the sort of audiences he liked, and lived in some comfort. But most of the venues where Hutch now performed were far less salubrious than the White Hart and the Winter Gardens. Typical were the 69 Club in Newcastle, well paid but as soul-destroying as ever, and a 'seedy' club in Sunderland, Weatherall's, where Hutch appeared:

ill at ease. Within ten minutes, he departed from his programme, and invited the audience to call out anything they wanted to hear. I called for 'Room 504', and got it. He never faltered and sung every word with the clear diction . . . always associated with his style. He seemed to have finished with all the little gimmicks which we once knew. There was no mopping of the brow with a white hanky. But we loved him, and he responded to that affection.[2]

Yet another agent, Keith Salberg, had to prompt Hutch several times before he signed his name and provided photographs and biographical details for a booking on the Dunfermline restaurant circuit during August. A couple who saw him on that tour – paying three pounds, six shillings and sixpence for a dinner dance for two including cabaret – remembered Hutch being 'not very steady on his feet' and the small restaurant being 'not full, maybe only thirty people were there'.

By now, Hutch was both emotionally and physically unstable. In early October he was treated for pneumonia at St John and St

Elizabeth Hospital, St John's Wood, and later he was moved to
Gordon Hospital, Vauxhall Bridge Road. Jill wrote from the
country, where she was struggling with financial difficulties. Since
she had refused Hutch's offer of marriage, they had, contrary to her
expectations, drifted apart. Her awkward letter struck a plaintive
note: 'My dear Sir, My resources, being stretched as they are in so
many directions, do not extend to sending you flowers or such
dainties as the more financially attentive of your friends can
provide. But if words as good wishes may blossom and comfort
you, such are mine to you.'

Joanna, the Shand Kydds' cook, kept up a daily stream of
interminable letters, assuring Hutch of her devotion. In the pre-
ceding few months, she had spent most of her time off from her
domestic jobs to be with him. Now she brought him farm eggs and
other treats, but these attentions served only to exasperate Hutch:
whenever Joanna thanked him for demeaning himself to spend
time with her, he brutally dismissed her gratitude. After a lifetime
of carefully pigeonholing his intimates, he was now subject to a
stream of comings and goings over which he could assert no
control. There were a number of unfortunate encounters in the
hospital corridors, which hugely embarrassed Hutch. He vented his
frustration on poor Joanna. He was furious that she kept turning up
without an invitation and invading his life, and was so angry with
her that the connection ceased, although she did take the day off to
attend his memorial service.

These importunities aside, Hutch was spoiled during his stay in
hospital. Friends, agents, fans and show-business contacts – the
Henekers, Chappells and the regulars of the press room at the Old
Bailey were typical of his well-wishers – sent him baskets of fruit
and delicacies, usually from Fortnum and Mason, as well as letters
and cards, many with ribald notes on his chances of getting off with
the nurses. He rested as much as possible, took antibiotics, and was
discharged in early December.

At Christmas, he was surprised to be invited to Blenheim by the
Duke of Marlborough, who gave him some elegant hand-
embroidered slippers.

On 25 January 1968, Hutch started on his traditional winter break.
This time he returned, after five years, to Kenya to perform at the
Topaz Grill, Nairobi, part of the New Avenue Hotel, for a

relatively modest £150 per week. Emlyn Griffiths paved the way meticulously, ensuring that the hotel manager met Hutch at the airport, and smoothed his passage through immigration.

Hutch got the usual kind of good notice in the *East African Standard* ('veteran entertainer . . . the years fell away as he got into 'his stride'), though the critic noticed Hutch 'occasionally faltering over the words, but carrying it off with an insouciance all his own'.[3] On other nights, this failing became distressingly obvious; he also had problems keeping his balance.

Still, a Kenyan singer, Sal Davis, thought, 'He was great. I've seen him singing in London, and, man, he's still a fantastic performer.'[4]

Among other other old friends of Hutch's, Joan Vyvyan was now resident in Nairobi. She wrote him a hugely evocative letter of welcome:

> Dear wonderful Hutch. We old squares – eight of us – will be chez vous tonight at the Topaz. It is not Ciro's, nor the Embassy with the Martineaus, nor the Starlight Roof at the Waldorf, but we all remember the Blue Lantern at Ham Yard and Edwina at Broadlands, and the Du Mauriers at Fowey and Betty Chester and Cole and Noel and Irving Berlin. Please will you sing 'What Is This Thing Called Love?' [Vyvyan thoughtfully enclosed the words] and something modern, i.e. 'Strangers in the Night', but not that bloody 'Yellow Submarine'!

After the adulation and warm weather, Hutch returned to London, feeling stronger and more cheerful. Joan (who had found a part-time job at the Ideal Home Exhibition) had stocked his flat before his return, ordered new headed notepaper and made sure that the porter mended the bath drain. These and other domestic concerns had been detailed in her ill-written letters to Hutch, together with the information that she was 'taking yeast tablets to build my strength up!!' She still kept her own flat but was spending more time with Hutch now that he had more use for her again.

In March 1968, Joan Bakewell interviewed Hutch on *Late Night Line-Up*, an upmarket news and arts programme on BBC2, to celebrate his birthday. He sang 'More Than You Know' and 'These Foolish Things'. He performed sporadically at his usual haunts in London and the provinces. One night he lurched into the Trattoo, a fashionable Italian restaurant in Kensington. The

Burtons (Richard Burton and Elizabeth Taylor) and the Snow-
dons (Princess Margaret and her husband) were dining there, and
his old friend Alan Clare was at the piano. In an upsurge of
maudlin, drink-fuelled anger, Hutch loudly berated the two
couples: 'All my old friends, surely you miss me as I do you?
But what do you care? Or is it time for an old man to go home?'
Shambling, shaky and still muttering, he left the Trattoo, leaving
in his wake a swell of incredulous comment that drowned the
sound of the piano.

Ignoring his doctors' advice to live a quieter life, Hutch often
accepted invitations from the younger generation. In particular, he
often met Mark Sykes, a raffish young socialite, to drink at Ruby
Lloyd's Maisonette Club in Shepherd Market, or dine at Rico
Dajou's Casanova Club off Piccadilly. Although unaware of his
poor health, Sykes knew about his financial straits as Hutch often
referred to the 'beautiful jewellery and cigarette cases decorated
with rubies and diamonds which . . . he often popped if he had had
a bad run of luck gambling'. One day Sykes:

> together with Hutch, Jackie Baroda and Bhayya Cooch Behar,[5]
> went to the Star in Knightsbridge, a noted haunt for homo-
> sexuals. The pub was run by a Mr Paddy Kennedy, a cantan-
> kerous, drunken and exceptionally foul-mouthed Irishman, who
> was a great favourite with all of us. He fixed us with a baleful
> red-rimmed eye as we tumbled up the stairs; and when we asked
> him what we could have to eat, he shouted, 'Roast missionary,
> you black bastards! And don't tie your fucking camels to the pub
> railings!' Even Hutch's treacly voice was silenced as we rocked
> with laughter.

Sykes recalled that Hutch's skin became darker as he grew older,
'almost a blue-black, and he dyed his hair, of course. I thought he
had retired long before.'

Hutch also spent more afternoons at the Colony Room, the bar
presided over by the squat, saturnine Muriel Belcher and her
cheerfully abusive lieutenant Ian Board. Here he met the painter
Francis Bacon, the photographer John Deacon, the writer and pub
owner Dan Farson, the artists' model Henrietta Moraes and the
journalist Jeffrey Bernard.

Hutch fell ill again in November and was admitted to New End Hospital with high blood pressure. He had been due to record two LPs the following weekend. His 'secretary', probably Joan, told the press that she had no idea what was wrong with him; he had just complained of feeling unwell; but David Heneker remembered Joan telling him that Hutch had fallen out of bed and she had been unable to move him.

The press reports triggered a good deal of fan mail. As well as old friends, people who had only glancingly met Hutch wrote with grateful memories of him in variety or cabaret, urging him to get well again. A few were very touching:

> You were very kind to me 35 years ago. I was then a small child in a pram. You used to come down to the riding stables, but you never passed by without giving me pennies for sweets. My mother used to tell me how clever you were on the piano, and whenever I hear your name, my mind travels back all those years, when I know we were very poor and your pennies meant a lot to me. God bless you, and make you well soon.[6]

Hutch caught a chill in hospital, but antibiotics cleared it up, and he left after four weeks with a low-protein diet sheet. He briefly followed this regime but, averse to nagging from others and incapable of self-discipline, he soon reverted to his old ways. An affair with a new girlfriend – 'young, blonde and beautiful' – lasted only a few months, but raised his spirits: Hutch much enjoyed taking her racing and showing her off to such people as his old friend from India, Lawrence Pratt. He also went on performing, despite creeping arthritis in his fingers.

Before Christmas, Joan joined the temporary sales staff at John Lewis in Oxford Street.

For the first few months of 1969, Hutch appeared to be his old self. In March he went back to hospital for a check-up, but quickly emerged. He performed again at the White Hart during the summer from time to time and was well received there. He went to a number of cricket matches, and especially revelled in the MCC–West Indies match at Lord's in June.

Hutch worked occasionally until three months before his death. He seemed to his public and most of his friends to be as expansive and entertaining as ever; still listening out for new tunes to add to his repertoire, still making topical references in his linking patter. To them, he was a survivor who stayed infectiously cheerful, an unsinkable show-business phenomenon. They were unaware of his chronic misery, his introspective bitterness and loneliness. In fact, he was a sadly diminished, prematurely aged figure: his energy – both emotional and physical – was running out, and his horizons were narrowing fast. He now wished only for the companionship of those who cherished and loved him unconditionally.

His last engagement was at a private party at the Metropole Hotel, Brighton; a fitting final venue, since he had spent many happy times there over the past forty years. Harold Berens offered him a job with him in a variety show later that summer, but Hutch turned it down because he wanted to be remembered as he had been.

In July, Hutch was back in the Royal Free Hospital. He was 'extremely grumpy and the nurses were fed up with him'. The doctors' report read: 'His chronic disabilities resulted from long continued hypertension, chronic failure of kidney function and a recurring failure of cerebral function which caused varying degrees of dementia.' He went home for a few days, and was nursed night and day by male nurses from a private agency. On 7 August he collapsed unconscious in the middle of the night, and was readmitted to hospital. Three days later, he had an epileptiform fit; a respiratory infection developed; and, on Monday 18 August he died, aged sixty-nine, of 'overwhelming pneumonia', having been mortally ill for some eight weeks. This was hardly the quick death for which he had so fervently hoped. He died intestate, leaving £1,949, which went to his daughter Leslie.

The funeral was on the following Friday, 22 August, at St John-at-Hampstead. His brother Ivan attended with Joan and Leslie. The service was subdued, and the two hymns were 'Praise my soul, the king of heaven' and the stagey Victorian dirge 'Abide with me', 'perhaps the most inspiring and comforting hymn that's ever been written,' Hutch once said, 'one that I first learned to love in that little church in Grenada'.[7] Among other organisations, the BBC, the MCC, Quaglino's and the Dorchester sent wreaths.

The small attendance, only forty-two mourners, was the result of Hutch's having lost touch with many of his friends; others saw the announcement of his death but did not know how to find out about the funeral arrangements. Among those who turned up were David Heneker, Marc Anthony, Adelaide Hall, Turner Layton, Maggie Christiansen and the actor Kenneth More. Collie gave lunch to Joan, Leslie and Ivan, but didn't accompany them to the funeral because she sensed that Joan preferred her not to go. Jill stayed away, because she feared that a press report of her presence might compromise her position as a teacher at a Roman Catholic convent. However, her parents went. So too did Mary, together with her and Hutch's sons Chris and Graham. Leslie told all three to leave. They were hurt, but they stayed.

Hutch was buried just inside the east gate of Highgate cemetery (in 1991 Joan was buried nearby). J. H. Kenyon, the undertakers, told the cemetery authorities that Lord Mountbatten had tele-phoned, offering to pay for Hutch's grave. It is impossible to know the motives behind this extraordinary gesture: Mountbatten may have wished posthumously to humiliate the rival who had caused him so much anguish; he may have wanted to ensure an appro-priate resting place for Edwina's love; he may even have wished to express his own liking for Hutch – the three feelings are by no means mutually exclusive.

Hutch's many obituaries would have delighted him. He rated two columns, illustrated by a photograph, in *The Times*, then unassailably the paper of the Establishment. It concluded:

> Hutchinson was an extremely civilised man as well as an extremely able piano entertainer. Charm, technique and tact made a spectacular approach to the keyboard and everything forceful and blatant completely foreign to his style. He was the ideal artist for the relaxed hour after dinner, with an unusual gift for convincing large audiences that they had dined well and were sitting at ease in opulent surroundings.[8]

Hutch's life encompassed many of the century's upheavals in society, in race relations, music and entertainment. He had used his talents to become English society's pet exotic, the living definition of a certain type of mildly decadent small-hours sophis-tication. His last record, a posthumous release, should never have been issued. Called *The Magic That Is Hutch*, it sadly belies its title: Hutch's heart simply was not in it; his voice is thin and weak, his piano playing hesitant and lacklustre. Better turn to almost any of the other 400 songs he recorded, to get some idea of how Hutch served his public by reflecting their own most aspiring concepts of wit and high romance. His oeuvre is proof of hard work, intelligence, energy and style. His singing nearly always showed that he had fully understood, felt and, often, lived the lyrics; beneath the carefully enunciated delivery, there is dramatic, pulsing emotion. His piano playing, poised, elegant and meticulous, is a constant joy. Unwittingly, as both singer and player, he created a genre; and without his pervasive influence, succeeding generations of cabaret performers would have sounded very different.

Since his death, Hutch fans have kept his memory alive. In 1996, his grey, faux-marbled Bluthner piano was sold in Manchester for £10,000. Some people old enough to remember Hutch meet at intervals to play his records and discuss tiny details of his interpretations of this or that song. They search for his 78s in specialist music shops, in mail-order catalogues, flea markets and car-boot sales. They plague the presenters of nostalgic radio programmes with requests for his records. And there is at least one instance of a fan asking for his music to be played at her funeral. As well as his countless conquests, many total strangers made him their focus of adoration and excitement; for them, he was an idol who offered a notional escape route from the daily round to glamour and romance. There are still granny flats and bed-sitters in retirement homes that are decorated with photographs of Hutch, signed programmes, albums of yellowing cuttings, neat columns of 78s and, with luck, acknowledgements of their fan letters. There is also a Web site dedicated to Hutch – www.tales.ndirect.co.uk/ HUTCH.html – maintained by a former sexton at Highgate cemetery.

At Christmas 1969, a man visiting his parents' grave showed a weeping woman where Hutch was buried. She told him that she had been Hutch's mistress for eighteen years, and that when he had first played for her, he had sung 'I Get Along Without You Very Well'. Even now, in the late 1990s, one of the cemetery guides, who had known Hutch in India, frequently leads visitors to his grave, which is rarely without fresh flowers.

Memorial notices used to appear every year in several newspapers. Now only the *Stage*, on the date of Hutch's death,
invariably regrets his passing and assures him of eternal admiration
'Till the stars forget to shine'.

AFTERWORD

Initially, it was hard to find out anything about Hutch. David Heneker, pianist, composer and family friend, invited me to lunch in 1988 to tell me that Hutch had asked him to write a book about his life. David felt he was now too old to do it. I told him that my generation did not know or care about Hutch, so I definitely wouldn't take on such a task, but I would hunt for material and then find someone else to do it. Three months later we met again and I admitted that I was hooked. The fact that I could find out so little tantalised and held me. All I then knew of Hutch was that I had heard his music intermittently since I was a child.

Hutch was not a very private person, as he wished others to believe, but rather an imaginative liar who kept his family, friends and lovers apart, so that they were unable to share his life and draw collective conclusions. His long affair with Edwina Mountbatten caused enough trouble for powerful people to wish to consign him to nonpersonship. Most of the existing biographical notes on cassettes and LPs turned out to be untrue, invented out of frustration. Several more august biographers had given up the task before I started, because so little information was available.

It was chance that Hutch had lived or toured in places that I knew – the West Indies, New York, Paris, Venice, Turkey, London, India, Nairobi. I asked friends to help me with my quest as I travelled and unravelled. I fell in love with Hutch's singing and playing, and, through them, his perfectionism, originality and intelligence. I read contemporary accounts of the people and places that Hutch knew, I scoured newspaper, theatrical and music archives, contacted old-time theatrical agents, variety performers, musicians, record-company technicians, radio people and socialites, and I wrote to newspapers requesting help from readers in the UK and abroad. Many people, including some of Hutch's children, responded – they announced themselves like characters in a play, in turn, as though deliberately summoned to help me with the jigsaw. They met each other for the first time.

Leslie, Hutch's first-born (1926) and only legitimate child, did not want to meet me. Gordon (1928) and I had dinner in Liverpool and chatted about his life, and as we talked I noted his long fingers and the broad span of his hands. When Hutch was in Liverpool in 1932 or 1933, performing at the Empire or the Shakespeare, his mother, Frances, took Gordon to see Hutch. Gordon remembers sitting in the wings during Hutch's performance, and then being patted on the head by this big black man. Frances never told Gordon why, in a family of four, he was the only black child, nor did he himself ever enquire; but, when she died in 1961, she left a brown envelope marked 'Gordon', empty but for a photograph of Hutch. Today Gordon is a calm, content man who himself sings well, has a devoted wife and six children – four boys and two girls – who are exceptionally musical. The youngest is called Leslie.

Gabrielle (born 1930) had a stern, unloving upbringing in a nursing home in Sidcup, Kent, owned by Miss Markes, the midwife who delivered her. Miss Markes did not feel she had to express affection for the charges she was paid to bring up, and made frequent references to the 'bad blood' she believed to be inherent in Gabrielle.

Gabrielle married an Indian engineer, had three daughters, divorced, studied law and anthropology, and retired recently as an education officer in the Health Visitors Association.

She had gone to Ireland to try to contact her mother through her ex-husband, but he denied all knowledge of her and sent her away. In 1993, she saw a brief story in the *Daily Telegraph* about my research and rang me. Soon after, she came to stay and we started investigating her papers. By ringing the house in Ireland and several adoption agencies, Gabrielle got in touch with the fellow officer's wife who, at a meeting in London, told her about the circumstances of her birth and her mother. Gabrielle later met her mother Elisabeth's second daughter, who said she did not know her mother well. In the 1970s Gabrielle had looked up another half-sister, Hutch's daughter Leslie. She said that she had not known her father well.

Gabrielle travels worldwide and is an open, energetic woman

with confidence and panache who has embraced both the research and her new relatives as easily as her grandsons.

Chris was born in 1948 and is a gentle, musical man with justifiably ambivalent memories of his father, 'part blame, part pride', but is slowly re-examining his view of him. His brother Graham arrived in 1953. Gerald, who changed his name to Alexander, was also born in 1948. He wrote me a kind letter explaining why he would rather I did not write the book.

Emma, the last of the known brood, arrived in 1965. She is warm, lively, funny and clever with a Hispanic beauty. She composes songs, sings solo and has recorded with a group, Sweet Soul Sisters. A few years ago, wondering whether to give up her job and become a singer, she consulted a medium, who told her that her father 'will not give you advice. He says that his heart is shrivelled like a walnut.' Emma and her mother, Jill, were amused at Hutch's lasting self-concern, but found it sad that he had so far proved unable to revert to a happier, more stable state of mind in the spirit realm.

In 1997 Emma married an American actor, William Taylor, who has also been a boxer and a musician, and they settled in Los Angeles. The same medium said that this development made Hutch feel that he had more in common with Emma than he thought, and that he now wished to communicate with her urgently. Emma is currently disinclined to talk to him again.

Research into Hutch's performances in Halifax produced an anonymous letter saying, 'Yes I remember Hutch appearing at the Palace Theatre, Halifax, around 1935–1937 when I was in my teens. It was local knowledge that an attractive young lady by the name of [. . .] became pregnant by him during his stay at the White Swan Hotel, Princess Street.'

Attempts to contact 'the young lady' resulted in three telephone calls on the same evening from herself, her daughter and her granddaughter. The woman said, 'I did go and see him but I never knew him well.' Her daughter said, 'Then why won't she tell me who my father was? I'm not at all black, but who knows?' And her granddaughter said, 'So, we will at last discover . . .'

The outcome was that the mother finally told the daughter who her father was – and he was not Hutch.

It is not at all likely that each of Hutch's children is known to me, now or probably ever. I heard strong rumours of the existence of at least three others and there may be some who will never themselves know who their father was.

When Hutch left Grenada, life continued there for all the other family members. It was to be a long time before he sent money home. His father's sister Miss Carrie is remembered there as 'kinda tall, stern, light-skinned and a real little old maid'. Herbie Hyacinth, the elder adopted boy, cared for her in her old age, when she had to lie prone all day. She used to hide the money that Leslie sent her in her bosom, said Stressman Thomas, a neighbour in Gouyave.

Wyomi, Hutch's cousin, became a musician and lived in Maracaibo and Caracas. She often visited Leon Hutchinson, Hutch's half-brother, in Trinidad. Wyomi became a cross that Hutch bore out of guilt, not affection. He disliked her tough negotiations over the shop, house and land, but it took him forty years even to reduce the allowance he sent her. Wyomi was eighty-six when she died in 1971.

Earl Duprey, the younger adopted boy, worked in the shop too and eventually inherited the business on George's death. He looked after the family land nearby at Moran as well. He visited Ivan in London in the 1970s after Hutch's death. His wife still lives in Gouyave.

Leon, Hutch's elder half-brother, completed his studies at Meharry in Nashville and became a successful dentist in Trinidad. He donated a scholarship to their local school. Villagers in Gouyave still remember a day when he returned to the shop to accuse his father of not supporting him well when he was a student.

Leon later had trouble with his own outside child, a part-Indian boy who stole from him and twice burned down his business premises. He married a half-German and half-English woman who was accused of being a spy during the war, and they later divorced. Leon had a son called Leonard, who was born in Panama in 1911. Leonard has two daughters. He plays the piano, sings and composes songs; he lives in New York.

George, the younger half-brother, became the blacksmith in nearby Dougalstown. He was a strong, stupid man who received little attention from the family. He remained poor and lived in labourer's quarters. Meals were sometimes sent to him by kindly villagers. He died aged fifty-four.

When I quizzed my friends and their more exalted connections, it seemed as though every one of them knew some society woman who had had an affair with Hutch. Some shamefacedly admitted that their mothers had succumbed to his charms, often adding aunts and cousins too and recalling 'how much nanny had disapproved'. Sometimes reaction to his name was violent.and evasive enough to be equivalent to the frankest admission.

Of the many lovers and friends mentioned in the book, almost all are now dead. This story was only just accessible in the last decade and it was an adventure to discover it. I went to Grenada to talk to villagers and friends of his, to Istanbul to understand life there in the 1920s, then to India to discover how Hutch spent his time in the winters of the 1950s and soon after to Nairobi, where he spent two long periods entertaining in the 1960s. One of Hutch's daughters, Gabrielle, went to New York with her daughter Poweena to explore leads there for me, and I commissioned research from a journalist in Paris.

Then Joan died intestate in 1991. She had lived intermittently with Hutch from 1928 until his death in 1969. She was known to David Heneker, but did not want to discuss Leslie Hutchinson with me then or ever. Anything that remained of his possessions, if not with his daughter, must surely have been left in her care on his death. Just so! I ran alongside the negotiations of several sets of lawyers and watched claimants come and go, and, just as I was about to give up hope, the Crown appointed genealogists to determine the heir to Joan's estate. Rosemary Jill Casson Lewis of New Zealand decided she wanted nothing to do with the effects of her unknown cousin's black lover. She directed that they should be given to me, the obsessional woman who did.

One day I collected a carload of battered suitcases. They contained several thousand press cuttings, letters, diaries, passports, hundreds of photos, Hutch's own collection of his records, posters and memorabilia. They took months to sort through. I was glad that I had done the groundwork and had some clues in place to piece together Hutch's life from this chaotic treasure trove.

It has been my intention not to expose the living to publicity. I have limited details of their lives and used only given names deliberately to frustrate anyone who might wish to find them. Over a decade now they have come to trust me, have helped me greatly, and understandably do not wish to have their privacy further invaded. The few exceptions have been denied their publicity-seeking wishes!

Now in 1999 when David Heneker is ninety-three, his friend Hutch would be ninety-nine. David is one of the very few of his contemporaries who are still alive. The magic of Hutch's music is less transient than his life; new compilations appear annually. David has kept his promise, and I have fulfilled my own to him.

Hutch's life is charted in many of its complexities, and its legends are explored. To his many children, friends and lovers, I can only say that I have written as I found and could have had no idea at the start what I would discover. Hutch has taught, shocked, inspired, healed and extended me. While many people have helped me research, in the curious ways of myriad coincidence of acquaintance and memories, the story has written itself. Hutch has been present, though ambiguously collusive, throughout an unfolding process which continues. He could not know of many of the reverberations and consequences of the impressions that he made and there is much still that remains scattered, obscured or interred.

Charlotte Breese
London 1999

APPENDIX

It is impossible to reconcile the authorised and the unauthorised biographies of the Mountbattens. Philip Ziegler, the biographer of Mountbatten, recommended Janet Morgan to the Mountbatten family as a biographer for Edwina. In her book *Edwina* (Harper-Collins, 1991), Morgan writes that Hutch was one of Edwina's favourite entertainers in London in 1923. This is incorrect, as Hutch was still in America. Another, equally baffling passage, ascribed to an entry in Edwina's diary, says that 'Hutch, the ugly but dextrous black pianist, played in Marjorie's [Brecknock, her cousin's] drawing room'. Even Hutch's most fervent detractors recognised his good looks, and many considered him beautiful. After her description of the court case, Morgan writes:

> Some biographers assumed that, if Robeson was not her paramour, some other black man must have been. Edwina had given a silver cigarette case, affectionately inscribed to Hutch the pianist, who had played at Brook House parties for nothing; it must have been him. This is piffle – but people wanted to believe that their prejudices were being violated and that the King and Queen, representing purity, had put a stop to it. The effects of the story were ineradicable for years.

Not so: the 'silver cigarette case' was gold, and Hutch used to hand the case round and leave it around open so that people could read the loving inscription on the inside. When I spoke to Morgan in 1991 before her book came out, she said, 'Hutch, like Robeson, was not her type. She liked tall, Anglo-Saxon, good-looking public-school boys.' In other words, Edwina only fancied men like her husband. Again, not so: given the time, Edwina was surprisingly colour blind; anyway, colour aside, Hutch precisely meets Morgan's requirements: he was lean, tall and handsome;

clever, talented and famous. Morgan also told me repeatedly that there was no one still living to confirm whether or not Edwina and Hutch had had an affair. She also told me that the Mountbattens would never let me see Edwina's private papers.

When Morgan's book came out, the *Sunday Times* of 7 July 1991 summarised its critical reception. 'The problem, several reviewers decided, lay with the involvement of Lady Mountbatten's daughters in the book, which, it was thought, Morgan had repaid with excessive tact.' In a *Sunday Telegraph* interview, Minette Marrin discussed with Morgan how she had discovered that Lady Mountbatten found sex tedious. The story had come from a Mountbatten daughter who had been told by her father who had been told by one of his wife's lovers – a curious provenance revealed in conversation but not in the book. This stance was reversed by the Mountbatten daughters soon afterwards on television. 'Self-restraint and discretion are virtues in a friend or in Jane Austen,' wrote Marrin, 'but not necessarily in a biographer.' Lynn Barber in the *Independent* was more barbed. 'The limitations of authorised biography are occasionally transparent. Crucial questions are fudged . . . Perhaps it was indeed Hutch, who played at her parties? Janet Morgan covers the subject with the air of one treading on eggshells.'

A former girlfriend of Hutch wrote:

> I wonder if you heard the BBC Kaleidoscope programme and discussion of the book? It was so funny. A group of earnest commentators all armed with white-wash brushes doing their best to clean up Edwina's image. I don't think she would have liked it a bit. She was a lot more honest and brave than they are. Of course, Hutch never spoke of her to me, and I'm quite sure she never heard about me from him. In Liverpool all the time, I had no idea of such an illustrious rival! But I am sure, had we known, we would have wished each other the best of him.

It was rare indeed for Edwina to come across people from Hutch's world in her own and socially that would normally have been unlikely, but as a patron of music and the theatre, she was occasionally entertained in great state by these artistes. On one such occasion, Bill Pilkington was placed next to her at dinner and rather boldly reminded her that he had seen her collecting Hutch from the theatre one night in her car. Edwina smiled collusively and nodded her head – thus she acknowledged that their affair was an open secret, well known to their friends for years.

The Mountbatten daughters seek to obscure three aspects of their parents: their mother's physical relationships with 'men of colour'; her perjury; and both their parents' bisexuality. While I did not seek definitive proof of any of these, all three are evident from existing research in other books and from people I have interviewed. I have provided irrefutable evidence that Edwina lied in court, and admitted doing so; and that she had a long affair with Hutch. As for Lord Mountbatten's bisexuality, many of those I interviewed were convinced of it. When he was Supreme Allied Commander in Southeast Asia, several officers boasted of their liaisons with him. A naval friend came across him on an island, when he was serving in Malta, nude in flagrante with another officer. And in the 1960s Jackie Cryer, the daughter of Hutch's producer at the BBC, used to watch Mountbatten entering a male brothel from Grosvenor Mews. There was also a *Private Eye* libel case about Mountbatten's bisexuality (outcome unsuccessful). These and other stories that refer to Mountbatten's sexual proclivities have been consistently denied by their family.

If they are unspoken and not formally acknowledged, then even authorised biographers can meet with constraints. These seem to have applied not only to Janet Morgan but also to Philip Ziegler, whose otherwise excellent biography of Mountbatten insists that his subject was not bisexual. In fact, both Mountbatten and his wife did sometimes express their bisexuality, and it is hard to concede Ziegler's and Morgan's ignorance of this: one way to rewrite history has always been to lie by omission. Some of their contemporaries have often suggested to me that, once Mountbatten had come to terms with Edwina's infidelity and, in particular, her affair with Hutch, he found Hutch just as attractive as she did, and embarked on an emotional form of triolism.

As for Edwina's affairs with 'men of colour', the Hutch and Robeson stories surely confirm that she did. I met one of Patricia Mountbatten's godsons who told me that when he mentioned Edwina and Hutch 'she laughed out loud.' It is possible that research into her 'black period' in Harlem in 1934 might provide further names. Typically, both Ziegler and Morgan deny that Edwina ever had a physical affair with Nehru. Henry Burdwan remembered that, when in Calcutta in the 1950s, Hutch used to hear that Edwina's relationship with Nehru was 'complicated by his then reputed impotence'. At this news, Burdwan's father, who was 'very well informed' and had known Edwina and Hutch in London for years, used to roar with laughter. Many people in India believed in Nehru's affair with Edwina, and those still surviving (time of writing, 1998) provide the evidence of their own eyes. Furthermore, every year from 1950 until her death in 1960, she went to see Nehru in Delhi whenever she could; and he sometimes visited her in England. While I accept that the impotence gossip is unproven, I find it strange of Morgan to insist that Edwina and Nehru conducted an exclusively affectionate and spiritual relationship. I was also sad to find that, despite her love and admiration for Nehru, Edwina's sexual greed impelled her to continue her affair with Hutch. All else aside, given Edwina's character and physical needs, it is far more likely than not that she had a fully consummated affair with Nehru. Richard Hough agrees:

> Considering the nature of the relationship between these two highly emotional and sensitive people, it is impossible to believe that it did not extend to the physical level. This is of small importance compared with the fact that the great majority of people in India at the time believed that it did, and only a small number of those who knew them, believe that it did not . . . Certainly, Mountbatten himself knew that they were lovers. He was proud of the fact, unlike Edwina's sister who deplored the relationship and hated Nehru for the rest of his life as a result.

Cartier-Bresson took a remarkable photograph of Nehru and Edwina shrieking with intimate laughter on the steps of Government House, while Mountbatten looks haughtily in the other direction. Significantly, it is absent from both Ziegler's and Morgan's books.

Many people, including both Burdwan and Hutch, believed that Nehru was impotent. This makes sense of Janet Morgan's claim that his relationship with Edwina was platonic: as an authorised biographer, she would seek to negate a relationship that was not consummated. For the first time in her life, Edwina had fallen in love with a man for whom she felt boundless respect; her love for him was unconditional and idealistic, and it was deeply ironic that, unlike her numerous other lovers, he was unable to make love to her in the conventional way; for all that, whatever alternatives they devised seem to have afforded satisfaction of a sort. There were many stories in Delhi and Kashmir of servants finding them in bed together. Indians were also simultaneously amused, amazed and shocked both at Edwina's flagrantly affectionate behaviour to Nehru in public and at the way the relationship was uneasily condoned by Mountbatten. They now refuse to join in any attempt to gloss over the affair.

Finally, Nigel Nicolson related a story to illustrate the accident-prone character of the hostess Sibyl Colefax:

> She took me one evening to watch a newsreel of the departure from Delhi of two of her closest friends, the Mountbattens, at the end of his viceregal term. They were seen off at the airport by Jawaharlal Nehru. As the plane took off, Sibyl said to me, 'But what they *didn't* show was that Edwina at the last moment kissed Nehru full on the lips, which deeply shocked Indian feelings, undoing all the good that Dickie had done.' The woman sitting immediately in front of us, turned and said, 'Hullo, Sibyl.' It was Edwina Mountbatten, and sitting beside her was her husband. They had come incognito to the cinema to watch themselves. There was little doubt that they had heard what Sibyl said. I whispered to her, 'Would you like to leave?' 'I think we'd better,' she replied. We left.

NOTES

Quotes are from the author's own interviews and correspondence when not otherwise stated.

Chapter One:
A West Indian Upbringing 1900–1916

1. *Before the Sunset* by Eileen Gentle (a Grenadian), privately printed in Toronto
2. Georgie Gibbs and Joseph Benjamin, interview, Gouyave, February 1991
3. *Glasgow Evening Citizen*, 27.3.1935

Chapter Two:
Harlem Stride 1916–1924

1. His name was James Ethelbert Fleming. He 'passed for white' and owned a block of apartments mostly tenanted by Grenadians. Source: Mavis and Marissa Fleming, interviews by Gabrielle Hutchinson Markes, New York, summer 1993.
2. Eslanda Robeson, quoted in *When Harlem Was in Vogue* by David Levering Lewis
3. Louis Armstrong in his book *Swing That Music*
4. *Desert Island Discs*, BBC Radio 1959. Leslie also gave consistent and vivid accounts of his life in various publications, notably the magazine *Australian Women's Weekly*, 17.1.1962.
5. Charlie Johnson (1891–1959) was a bandleader, trombone and piano player. He led a band at Small's Paradise, a club in Harlem, 1934–38. In his own view, he provided Duke Ellington with lively competition.
6. Quoted in Smith (ed.), *Jazz: The Essential Companion*
7. *Music on My Mind* by Willie the Lion Smith with G. Hoefer
8. Quoted by Hyacinth Curtis Robinson interviewed by Val Wilmer, New York, 12.11.1992
9. *Bricktop* by Jim Haskins

10. *The Black Blocks of Manhattan* by Konrad Bascovici
11. *Variety*, May 1926
12. *When Harlem Was in Vogue* by David Levering Lewis, p. 183.
13. Quoted in *Terrible Honesty* by Ann Douglas
14. *This Magic Wilderness* by Robert Hunt. Thanks to C. Eames, Okefenokee Regional Library, Waycross, Georgia.
15. Anonymous article in the *Evening Standard*, London, 1969, just after Hutch's death
16. *Negro Life in New York's Harlem* by Wallace Thurman (Holderman and Julius, Kansas City, n.d.)

Chapter Three:
I Love Paris 1924–1927

1. Princess Beatriz, now Princess Torlonia, Queen Ena of Spain's daughter, interview by Viscountess Hambleden, Rome, 1995
2. Quoted in *Ena: England's Spanish Queen* by Gerald Noel
3. *Era*, London, 1931
4. *Chicago Defender*, 9.12.1922
5. Alberta Hunter in *Amsterdam News*, quoted in *Alberta Hunter* by Frank C. Taylor and Gerald Cook
6. *The Big Sea* by Langston Hughes
7. *Paris Was Yesterday 1925–1929* by Janet Flanner
8. *The Big Sea* by Langston Hughes
9. *Being Geniuses Together* by Robert McAlmon and Kay Boyle, p. 286. Boyle is describing a visit to Bricktop's in 1928.
10. Fred Allen quoted in *Tallulah* by Leftrey L. Carver
11. *Funny Years with the Famous and Infamous* by Milton Berle
12. Quoted in *Bricktop* by Jim Haskins
13. Quoted in *Capote*, a biography by Gerald Clarke
14. *Bricktop* by Jim Haskins. When Tallulah was in the play *The Marriage* in London, her co-star Cathleen Nesbitt used to feed her baby son during breaks in rehearsals. Tallulah gave him expensive presents from the White House, a rarefied baby-clothes shop in Bond Street, gave up her dressing room for the feeds – 'I couldn't bear the thought of that divine baby going upstairs for his meals' – and was fascinated by the sight of the baby pulling and sucking. Source: *Tallulah, Darling of the Gods* by Kieran Tunney.
15. Marcel Proust described Princess Violette Murat as being 'more like a truffle than a violet'. In later life she retired to the docks in Toulon, where she lived in an abandoned submarine and smoked opium. Source: *Paris Was Yesterday* by Janet Flanner.
16. Quoted in *Jazz Away from Home* by Chris Goddard
17. Quoted in *Red, Hot and Rich!* by David Grafton, as are all other quotes in this paragraph

18. *Red, Hot and Rich!* by David Grafton
19. *Cole Porter* by William McBrien, p. 63
20. Radio magazine in the 1960s, among Hutch's papers. Undated (most of his cuttings were unidentified and undated).
21. *Australian Women's Weekly*, 17.1.1962
22. *The Autobiography of Alice B. Toklas* by Gertrude Stein (Penguin, 1989)
23. *Europe at Play* by E. H. Tattersall
24. *Red, Hot and Rich!* by David Grafton
25. *Expatriate Paris* by Arlen J. Hansen
26. 'Love for Sale' was first performed by a trio of white girls in the Cole Porter musical *The New Yorkers*. This was thought so shocking that the setting was shifted to Harlem, and, on the recommendation of Irving Berlin, the song was given to Elizabeth Welch to sing solo. Source: Ned Sherrin.
27. *Edwina Mountbatten: A Life of Her Own* by Janet Morgan
28. *Eminent Churchillians* by Andrew Roberts
29. Married Sir Walter Gibbons in 1913, divorced in 1929
30. *Art World*, January–March 1928
31. *A Moveable Feast* by Ernest Hemingway

Chapter Four:
London at Last 1927–1930

1. *Tatler*, 1926 (otherwise undated), among Hutch's papers
2. *As You Were* (autobiography) by Douglas Byng
3. *Over My Shoulder* (autobiography) by Jessie Matthews
4. Michael Thornton, biographer of Jessie Matthews, recalls that in the late 1950s, a BBC gramophone librarian found a chip in the BBC's only copy of the record. So he asked Sir Peter Saunders, the West End impresario, if the BBC could borrow and tape his copy. Sir Peter agreed but only if the BBC insured it for £500. With characteristic meanness, the BBC refused. Thornton has been offered £2,500 for his own original copy.
5. According to the programme, J. B. Hastings was the conductor until 1929, so Irving was the musical director, not the conductor
6. An indication of how powerful Edwina's influence was in the world of entertainment is evident in connection with 'The Man I Love' by George Gershwin, which flopped in the USA until Edwina heard it and launched it in London, according to *Edwina Mountbatten* by Janet Morgan. Edwina evidently suggested that Hutch promote it too.
7. Norman Hackforth (interviewed for this book) was Noël Coward's accompanist for many years. He was also the 'Mystery Voice' on the long-running radio programme *Twenty Questions*.
8. Serge Lifar was a leading dancer with Diaghilev's Ballets Russes
9. *As You Were* by Douglas Byng
10. Quoted in *The Song of the Hawk* by John Chilton

11. *The Age of Illusion* by Ronald Blythe
12. Iris Mountbatten was the daughter of Lord Carisbrooke, Queen Ena's brother, and a cousin of Lord Louis Mountbatten. A bridesmaid at the Duke of Kent's marriage to Princess Marina, Iris was also a friend of Hutch's.
13. Coward was often critical of those less adept than himself at aping the upper classes. 'When Robert Stephens starred in a revival of *Private Lives*, Noël said Stephens was "incapable of handling a cigarette case".' Source: Tim Leon.
14. The figure 400, as applied to an elite, derives from the number of coattails Mrs John Jacob Astor could squeeze into the ballroom of the Astor mansion on Fifth Avenue, New York, in the late 1850s. In London in the 1920s, it became the number of people 'who really mattered'; it was also the name of a famous nightclub in Leicester Square.
15. *The Weeping and the Laughter* by Viva King. This book shares its title with a novel by Noel Barber (cited in Chapter Five) and with an autobiography by J. Maclaren-Ross. The phrase comes from a poem by Ernest Dowson.
16. David Herbert, second son of the Earl of Pembroke, was a ubiquitous gay socialite. Telephone interviews to Tangier 1990–93.
17. *The Diaries of Evelyn Waugh*, edited by Michael Davie (Little, Brown, 1976)
18. Note in *Evelyn Waugh* by Selina Hastings
19. Honor Henderson, née Kylsant, had married Gavin Henderson, later Lord Faringdon, earlier in 1927. The marriage was annulled in 1931.
20. This is the conjecture of Martin Stannard in his biography of Evelyn Waugh. Waugh's son Auberon thinks Chokey may have been based on Paul Robeson, but Waugh's diaries make it clear that Waugh did not meet Robeson properly before 1930.

Chapter Five:
London After Dark 1927–1930

1. *Aly* by Leonard Slater
2. Quoted in *Paul Robeson* by Martin Bauml Duberman
3. *As Wonderful as All That?* by Henry Crowder
4. Quoted in *Jazz Cleopatra* by Phyllis Rose
5. Information is loosely based on Jeff Green's article in *New Community*, vol. XIII, No. 3, Spring 1987, entitled 'High Society and Black Entertainers in the 1920s and 1930s'
6. Quoted in *Alberta Hunter* by Frank C. Taylor and Gerald Cook
7. The four dots are unexplained in Bruce Kellner's edition of Van Vechten's letters: the qualifying 'some' precludes his wife Ella; 'tart' is a possibility

8. *Sunday Chronicle*, 5.2.1929
9. *The Mistinguett Legend* by David Bret
10. *Daily Sketch*, 11.12.1929. Early in 1926, Loelia Ponsonby met her future husband for the first time at the Embassy Club. The evening continued at the Café de Paris and, at two o'clock when the club closed down, the Duke swept a party of twenty or so back to his house near Berkeley Square. There, the future duchess found a band preparing to play and 'Hutch, the coloured singer, whom everyone wanted at their parties. He used to croon things like "These Foolish Things" which made us feel wonderfully sentimental.' From *Grace and Favour* by Loelia, Duchess of Westminster.
11. Dougie Byng, Edythe Baker and Evelyn Laye were founder members of the Kind Dragon in 1927. Some say that it was not in Ham Yard, off Windmill Street, W1, but in Garrick Yard, St Martin's Lane.
12. In 1944, when John Gardiner was in Kuchin, a Japanese prisoner-of-war camp, he wrote *A Guide for Gourmets*, an exhaustive guide to London night life of all kinds in the 1930s and 1940s, which has provided much useful material for this book.
13. *Vogue*, December 1930. Claire Luce was an American who later starred in the West End, playing the Ginger Rogers role in *Gay Divorce* at the Palace Theatre in 1933.
14. Julian Vedey was a drummer who founded and edited *Rhythm*, a technical magazine for drummers and banjo players, first published in 1927
15. The *Traveller*, Boston, Mass., 7.9.1930
16. For example at the Argyle Theatre, Birkenhead, 2.12.1929
17. *Daily Chronicle*, 26.4.1930
18. She inspired the eccentric hotelier Lottie Crump in Evelyn Waugh's novel *Vile Bodies*. Rosa never spoke to Waugh again. She was presented with the Cavendish Hotel by Edward VII, and her life was the basis of a TV series, *The Duchess of Duke Street*, shown in the 1970s.
19. Anton Dolin, born in 1904, christened Sydney Francis Patrick Chippendall Healey-Kay, was one of the great Russian choreographer Diaghilev's British finds. Like Alicia Markova, previously Lilian Alicia Marks, another Diaghilev discovery, Dolin changed his name and pretended to be Russian to make himself acceptable to the public as a ballet dancer. Both Dolin and Markova, when they could not find work in ballet, turned to variety. In 1933 they appeared together in a Jack Buchanan revue; and, having formed the Markova–Dolin Company, they appeared in the pantomime *Mother Goose* with Florence Desmond and George Lacy in 1935. In 1944, they appeared on Broadway in *The Seven Lively Arts*, dancing to 'Easy to Love' by Cole Porter, who was largely responsible for the score. Many found Dolin to be conceited, self-centred and short-tempered.
20. *Daily Sketch*, 15.8.1930
21. Quoted in *Merle* by Roy Higham and Charles Moseley

22. In *The Lives of Beryl Markham* by Errol Trzebinski, the author describes Beryl Markham's involvement with the Prince of Wales and the Duke of Gloucester. In 1929 the Markhams threatened to cite the latter in a divorce case and 'instructed Rollo (well-known divorce lawyer of the period) who went to the Palace. Said they had two days to settle. Duke settled a large sum on Beryl.' Source of quote: James Fox, 'African High Flyer', *Observer* colour supplement, 30.9.1984.

Chapter Six:
From Revue to Variety 1931–1938

1. *Evening Standard*, 31.3.1931
2. *Daily Sketch*, 12.3.1931
3. Michael Arlen (1895–1956) was a popular writer of Armenian descent, who wrote numerous novels and short stories based on life in Mayfair. The best known is *The Green Hat* (1924), said to be based on Arlen's affair with Nancy Cunard. It was filmed with Greta Garbo and John Gilbert. The *Melody Maker* writer is comparing one *déraciné* with another.
4. *The Star*, 17.11.1931
5. *Era*, 13.8.1932
6. Lord Ashley had picked his new wife, Sylvia Hawkes, out of the chorus line of *The Whole Town's Talking*. They would get divorced in 1935 when she was cited in Douglas Fairbanks's divorce from Mary Pickford; she then became Lady Stanley of Alderley; next, she married Clark Gable; and she ended as the wife of Prince Dimitri Djordjadze. She also had an affair with Hutch.
7. At this time, the couple should correctly be called Lord and Lady Louis Mountbatten. When in 1947 he became an earl and Edwina a countess, Lord and Lady Mountbatten became the correct nomenclature. Many English and American press reports ignore this distinction. I have not corrected them: hence the many inconsistencies.
8. News of Edward VIII and Mrs Simpson was published by the British press at that point only because of the clamorous American press and a misunderstood remark made by Dr Blunt, the bishop of Bradford, who stated at a diocesan conference that he wished the King 'would show more positive evidence of his awareness of the needs for Divine Guidance', meaning only that he wanted him to set a good example and attend church regularly.
9. Rosemary d'Avigdor Goldsmid was the original source of this story, and in the author's hearing she rang three contemporaries who confirmed that 'everyone knew it was true'
10. *Edwina* by Richard Hough
11. Quoted in *Paul Robeson* by Martin Bauml Duberman

12. Ibid.
13. Married to Bobby Cunningham-Reid, and then to Lord Delamere
14. Clipping from the *Independent* sent by a Hutch fan, undated, 1990s. By 1926 Lord Louis had faced the reality of his marriage and started a long affair with Yola Letellier, a former Paris model who inspired Colette to write *Gigi*.
15. *Daily Sketch*, 31.5.1932. Later the same year, during the notorious trial over the custody of Gloria's daughter, known as little Gloria, the Palace refused to let Nada go to America to clear her name when she was publicly accused of having had a lesbian relationship in the south of France with Gloria Vanderbilt, which, the prosecution averred, made her an unfit mother. Source: *Little Gloria Happy at Last* by Barbara Goldsmith.
16. Unauthorised biographers include Richard Hough, Gavin Lambert and Charles Higham and Roy Moseley – details of their books appear elsewhere in these notes and in the bibliography. In *Wallis*, Charles Higham states that 'Edwina Mountbatten found consolation in an odd assortment of partners, including the famous black nightclub pianist Leslie "Hutch" Hutchinson'. Richard Hough refers to 'hints and innuendoes about "dark-skinned gentlemen" . . . one of them was Leslie Hutchinson, the immensely popular nightclub singer and pianist . . . [he] was often bidden (for a fat fee) to private parties, including those held at Brook House. Edwina was extremely fond of Hutch, and did not attempt to conceal her affection.' Gavin Lambert in his biography of the film star Norma Shearer, and Gloria Vanderbilt in her autobiography, also accept the relationship.
17. Letter to the *Evening Standard* from Leslie Jackson, Willesden, north-west, London, 21.10.1983
18. Arthur Dodds heard this from John Burnaby of Light Entertainment, son of Dave Burnaby of the Co-optimists. John Burnaby was a society pianist. The Grenadian group mentioned in Chapter One and also separately Peter Charlesworth, theatrical agent, met Edwina Mount-batten backstage in Hutch's dressing room.
19. Zaza Peters, born Sarah Prentice in Glasgow, now Zaza Geldray. She appeared at the Palm Beach nightclub in Frith Street 1938–40 and later, when the club moved to Wardour Street in 1941. Interviewed by Val Wilmer, Highgate, 3.8.1991 and 9.9.1991.
20. Patricia Varley, singer, interview, Denville Hall, 1991, and later also by Tom Eggerdon, 1993
21. Hutch left this watch to Leslie Macdonnell, who was once manager of Harry and Sid Roy and succeeded Val Parnell as the manager of the Moss Empire theatre chain. Macdonnell presented the watch to Johnnie Riscoe, theatrical agent, who told me the story in 1995.
22. Van Straten's niece has the diary. Sandy Forbes of the BBC had seen it and the disc jockey Alan Dell confirmed this story, which was told me at the Coda Club, London, in 1993.

23. According to Mike Craig in *Callboy*, a posthumous tribute. Later, Max Wall was ostracised after his divorce and subsequent marriage to a Miss England in the mid-1950s. This is sympathetically described by Larry Adler in his autobiography *Ain't Misbehavin'*. In the late 1970s, Wall made a comeback with a series of one-man shows. He also starred in Shakespeare and Beckett and, most improbably, as a garage hand in the TV soap opera *Crossroads*.
24. *Housewives' Choice* by George Elrick
25. My cousin Cicely Lancaster remembered Hutch coming to lunch and playing the piano in the 1930s
26. Nina Mae McKinney from South Carolina, a friend of Hutch, first came to London with *Blackbirds* in 1928. Her film career reached its zenith when she starred with Paul Robeson in *Sanders of the River* in 1935. That year she announced to the press that she was making a film in England with Hutch, but the project never materialised.

Chapter Seven:
Touring and Climbing 1931–1938

1. Bill Pilkington, many interviews. Hutch earned his £500 a week in a country where 88 per cent of the population had incomes of less than £250 a year, around £5 a week; 31 per cent earned around £125 a year. At the upper end, some 2,000 people each enjoyed annual incomes that averaged £43,500 a year.
2. *Daily Sketch*, 26.10.1933
3. Peter Machin, *Glasgow Evening Citizen*, 28.11.1933
4. Moreton and Kaye took over from the first two Tiger-Ragamuffins, Monia Liter and Stanley Black
5. *Manchester Evening Chronicle*, 25.4.1933
6. *Bromley and Kentish Times*, 25.9.1936
7. *Paignton Observer*, 24.8.1938
8. Article entitled 'This Music Hall Business' by Patrick Campbell in the *Bournemouth Times and Directory*, 27.5.1932
9. *Daily Sketch*, 14.3.1935
10. *Daily Mirror*, 9.5.1935
11. *Sunday Express*, 8.1.1935
12. *The Gramophone*, February 1935
13. *Variety News*, 7.3.1935
14. The cigarette case is now in the possession of Mrs Lewes in New Zealand
15. BBC, 18.12.1936
16. Eric Maschwitz, interviewed in the *Sunday Dispatch*, 8.12.1957
17. Robert Cushman, *Independent on Sunday*, 9.10.1994

18. *Sunday Referee*, 8.3.1938
19. *Daily Herald*, 21.10.1936
20. Ann Penn, *Liverpool Evening Express*, 19.3.1936
21. *Radio Pictorial*, 8.1.1937
22. *Musical Trades Review*, September 1937
23. Undated 1960s interview among Hutch's papers
24. Quoted in *Cole Porter* by William McBrien, p. 212
25. Harold Berens, a Jewish comedian, was successful in the 1940s and 1950s. He performed with ENSA during the war and acted on stage and film, but was best known for his radio shows. He appeared on four Royal Variety Shows, and his catch phrase was 'Wot a geezer!' All quotes are from the author's interviews.
26. Cockney rhyming slang: Bristol City, titty
27. Hyacinth Curtis Robinson, interviewed by Val Wilmer, New York, 12.11.1992
28. *Princess Marina, Her Life and Times* by Stella King
29. *Princess Marina* by Sophia Watson
30. *Daily Mail*, 4.9.1998
31. *Princess Marina* by Grace Ellison
32. *The Duchess of Kent* by Jennifer Ellis
33. David Firmin, interviews 1991 and 1996. Other material about Hutch's affair with Princess Marina was offered by the following: a couple of double-barrelled debutantes from 1938 (*The Last Season of Peace* by Angela Lambert); ex-King Rat Bert Needham; Sir Peter Saunders; Alfred Black; three members of the public; and Bill Pilkington, with whom Hutch discussed his affection for her.

Chapter Eight:
Reserved Occupation 1939–1945

1. *Performer*, 6.10.1938
2. *Sunday Times*, 8.1.1939
3. *Westminster at War* by William Sansom. Douglas Byng also escaped the mayhem as he was due at the Café de Paris that night but was delayed at an ENSA meeting. Source: Patrick Newley of the *Stage*.
4. *Birmingham Gazette*, 19.9.1939; *Birmingham Post*, 19.9.1939
5. *Caterer and Hotel-Keeper*, 3.11.1939
6. *Bootle Times*, 3.11.1939
7. Sir Adrian Boult conducted the BBC Symphony Orchestra from 1930 to 1950
8. The *Performer*, 22.2.1940, critically cited him as the biggest tipper in the entertainment world
9. Manchester newspaper clipping, undated, among Hutch's papers
10. *Chronicle and Echo*, Northampton, 12.11.1940

11. The Free French identified with the Allies while the Vichy French accepted occupation by the Axis powers

12. TocH stands for Talbot House. It was founded by an army chaplain, the Reverend Studdert Kennedy in 1915; it is a cross between the YMCA and the NAAFI. The United Nations was a synonym for the Allied Forces, not the UN which was founded in 1945.

13. Quoted (undated) in *A Showman Looks On* by Charles Cochran

14. *The Cochran Story* by Charles Graves

15. A woman called 'Pink May' in 'The Demon Lover' by Elizabeth Bowen

Chapter Nine:
Out of Fashion 1946–1953

1. Radio interview in Hong Kong 1966

2. H.E. Ambassador John Pringle, then the Duke of Windsor's aide-de-camp, escorted her to hear Hutch perform. Both were visiting from the Bahamas.

3. BBC memo from Pat Hillyard, then head of Light Entertainment, dated 13.12.1949

4. The *Stage*, 13.9.1990. This apparently contradictory statement only makes sense if the words 'act' and 'songs' are emphasised.

5. Mary and Graham have declined to be interviewed for this book; hence the lack of information about both of them.

6. A cutting from an Australian publication called *Truth*, dated 29.1.1950 and headlined 'Negro in Divorce Suit – Mayfairs Fowlyard Society A-Twitter'. The article concludes:

> A big increase in Britain's negro population since the war is presenting authorities with a serious problem. People do not take kindly to the sight of big buck niggers, in all shades from black to brindle, dancing cheek to cheek with English girls in halls all over London. Already there have been a number of brawls and police fear even more serious repercussions . . . The more decadent of the English aristocracy and upper classes couldn't get away in Australia with what they do in London. What they regard as being smart, most Australians see as being revolting.

Chapter Ten:
Back in Mayfair 1954–1960

1. *Sunday Graphic*, 20.12.1953

2. *Daily Sketch*, 3.12.1953

3. David Heneker MBE, born 1906, became a colonel and after the war played the piano in pubs and bars until offered the job of pianist-cum-

host at the Embassy Club, Old Bond Street. As well as his big hit musical *Half a Sixpence*, his credits include *Make Me an Offer*, *Expresso Bongo*, *Phil the Fluter*, *Peg* and *The Biograph Girl*. He gave me many interviews, supplemented by letters, between 1989 and 1999.

 4. Sooty and Sweep were TV glove puppets; the puppeteer was Harry Corbett

 5. The title was a variant of *London Belongs to Me*, a successful postwar novel by Norman Collins

 6. *Daily Mail*, 5.6.1954

 7. *Ibid.*

 8. *Weekly Sporting Review*, 9.10.1953

 9. *Evening News*, 28.4.1955

10. *Evening News*, 5.4.1954

11. *Sunday Pictorial*, 20.9.1953. Joy Nicholls, a gifted Australian, had only recently pulled out of the BBC radio show that had made her a star, *Take It from Here*, to marry and return home. She was replaced on *TIFH* by June Whitfield and Alma Cogan.

12. All three Beverlys on different extensions, telephone interview 1991

13. Simon Becker, interview 1997. He is now pianist and host at the Pizza on the Park, Knightsbridge, one of the few venues in London in the 1990s that field both international and homegrown cabaret performers.

14. *Daily Sketch*, 20.4.1955

15. *Daily Sketch*, 6.12.1954

16. *Tatler*, 22.12.1954. The record was Parlophone GEP 8505, which was one of several reissues of prewar titles brought out by EMI riding on the back of his revival.

17. *Variety*, New York, 22.6.1955

18. *Daily Sketch*, 10.9.1955; *Liverpool Echo*, undated

19. *Eastern Evening News*, Norwich, 27.4.1956

Chapter Eleven:
Indian Summer 1955–1960

 1. Mischa de la Motte 'entertained in four voices and burlesqued a mad soprano singing the 'Jewel Song' from Faust'. Source: *As You Were*, Douglas Byng's autobiography. Robert had been the male half of the dance duo Marianne and Roberts (sic), well known in prewar Europe.

 2. *Daily Sketch*, 19.2.1955

 3. Undated press clippings among Hutch's papers

 4. *Jesting Pilate* by Aldous Huxley

 5. The suites are still in existence, but Prince's has made way for a substantial car park, evidence of the venue's great size

 6. *To a Grand Design* by Bachi Karkaria, a book commissioned and published by the Oberois

7. Hutch uses 'bastards' as a dated term of usually slightly exasperated affection; it is not one of opprobrium, nor, in this case, racism

8. Dr Bodkin Adams, an Eastbourne GP, was charged at the Old Bailey in 1957 with persuading some of his rich, elderly female patients to leave him handsome bequests, and then giving them lethal doses of medicine. Due to a legal technicality – key witnesses, three women who had nursed the old ladies, were found to have spoken among themselves about the case prior to giving evidence – the case was dismissed.

9. Pearson Surita, several interviews, Calcutta, 1992. He was a regular sports commentator on All-India Radio and a competent jazz pianist himself who played the organ for Peter Heneker's wedding in Calcutta in 1954. Peter said of Pearson that he 'probably introduced Hutch to some of the more interesting entertainments Calcutta had to offer'.

Chapter Twelve:
The Sweet Smell 1956–1959

1. *The Secret Life of Danny Kaye* by Michael Freedland
2. *Daily Herald*, 7.7.1956
3. The *Performer*, 23.9.1956
4. Stanley Setty, a Warwick Street car dealer, was murdered in the mid-1950s by a contract killer, Donald Hume, who cut up the corpse and disposed of it by hiring an aeroplane and dropping the pieces over the Essex marshes. The evidence against Hume was only circumstantial, and he was acquitted. Soon after, he made legal history by confessing his guilt for a huge sum to the *Sunday Pictorial*, knowing that British justice protected him from being tried twice for the same crime. He was found guilty of another murder, and died in prison in Switzerland.
5. Sir Bernard Docker was chairman of BSA – British Small Arms – which also was the prime producer of motorbikes. David Browne knew this verse (telephone interview, California, 1991).
6. *From Drags to Riches* by Danny La Rue
7. *Daily Express*, 24.3.1957
8. *What's On* 7.3.1958
9. *News of the World*, 7.4.1958
10. Although Hutch had spent time with Ellington a decade earlier and in Calcutta and previously in London and Paris, neither Duke's sister Ruth Boatwright nor his son Mercer Ellington had ever met Hutch or heard Duke speak of him. Stanley Dance, a record producer and biographer of Duke, met Hutch with Duke, but could not remember when. Baldwin's brother and other friends did not know Hutch. Baldwin's biographer David Leeming never met him either, but remembered Baldwin mentioning Hutch. 'I think their relationship flourished in the years before I met Baldwin. I worked for him from 1963 to 1967.' But

Eqbal Ahmed, now a professor, certainly met Hutch in New York that summer.

Chapter Thirteen:
Clinging On Abroad 1960–1966

1. *Evening Standard*, 11.4.1961
2. *Le Sportif – Paris*, 27.5.1961
3. *News of the World*, 9.11.1965
4. *Daily Herald*, 25.7.1961
5. *Evening News*, 1.11.1961
6. Australian newspaper, unidentified, undated cutting among Hutch's papers
7. Newspaper cutting from Singapore, undated, unidentified
8. Hutch's letter to Joan dated 17.5.1962
9. Interview in unidentified Kuala Lumpur newspaper, undated
10. Hutch's letters on board ship to Joan dated 11.6.1962 and 18.6.1962
11. *Stage and Television Today*, undated
12. *Utopia and Other Places* by Richard Eyre
13. Meaning, of course, to be a great success, although the American usage of 'bomb' means the opposite
14. Hutch's letter to Joan dated 11.2.1963. Hutch was right about Partridge's sexual predilections: when he left the Equator, he ran a restaurant in Lamu where liaisons with Arab boys exposed him to blackmail. He was locally known as 'Akiba', meaning 'savings' or 'moneybags', and also as Bwana Kiko, 'Mr Pipe', a name he inherited from another officer who smoked – Partridge didn't. I met his last partner, Mzee Juma, from the Maragoli tribe. He had been Partridge's driver in Lamu.
15. *Daily Nation*, 22.1.1963. Hutch's predecessor at the Equator Club was none other than Viera, the 'Continental Songstress', with whom he had alternated at Quaglino's.
16. Hutch would have been irritated to know that although he remembered the media comparing him to Hutch, Cliff Richard was unaware that Hutch was in Nairobi at the same time. Letter from Sir Cliff Richard dated 29.6.1993.
17. *Sunday Post*, 10.2.1963
18. Juanita Carberry, telephone interview, London, 15.2.1993. As a child she had been one of the key witnesses at Sir Jock Delves-Broughton's trial for the murder of Lord Erroll in 1940.
19. *Sunday Post*, 10.2.1963
20. *Sunday Mail*, Salisbury (now Harare), undated
21. Manchester newspaper, undated
22. *TV Times* interview with Hutch, 30.10.1964

23. Hutch's letter to Joan dated 21.10.1964
24. *Evening Standard*, 26.6.1965
25. *Evening News*, 17.7.1965
26. *News of the World*, 9.11.1965
27. Richard Blake Brown's letter to Hutch dated 23.11.1964
28. *Love Is a Many-Splendoured Thing* was also a film, made in 1955, starring Jennifer Jones and William Holden, based on a sentimental novel by Han Suyin. Set during the Korean War, it concerns the ultimately tragic romance between a Eurasian doctor and a hard-bitten war correspondent. It remained popular for years largely because of its theme tune, much played by Hutch and many others. Music by Sammy Fain; words by Paul Francis Webster.
29. *China Mail*, 15.4.1966. The *Hong Kong Standard* article is undated.
30. Recording of a radio programme broadcast from the Mandarin called 'A Date with a 78', introduced by Richard Bulmer, featuring songs and an interview of Hutch. Found among Hutch's belongings.
31. *China Mail Leisureguide*, interview entitled 'Hutch at his last show', undated

Chapter Fourteen:
The Darkness Deepens 1967–1969

1. This refers to the Russian foreign minister Molotov who, during negotiations after the Second World War, invariably vetoed every proposal. The letter, on paper stamped lopsidedly with Dave Mitchell's address in Great Newport Street, London WC2, is dated 'Dec 10th'; found among Hutch's papers.
2. Charles Dallas, letter, 7.9.1993
3. *East African Standard*, 31.1.1968
4. Sal Davis, article signed by JMR, another undated clipping. Sal Davis was a stage name for Salim Abdullah, son of the late Shariff Abdullah, a well-respected member of the Arab community in Mombasa.
5. These were Hutch's old friends the maharajahs of Baroda and Cooch Behar
6. Pat Bennett of Brighton, letter to Hutch dated 17.11.1968
7. *Desert Island Discs*, BBC Radio, 1959
8. *The Times*, 19.8.1969

SELECT BIBLIOGRAPHY

Acton, Harold. *Memoirs of an Aesthete*. Methuen, 1948

Acton, Harold. *More Memoirs of an Aesthete*. Hamish Hamilton, 1986

Acton, Harold. *Nancy Mitford*. Hamish Hamilton, 1975

Adler, Larry. *Ain't Misbehavin'* (autobiography). Collins, 1984

Agate, James. *The Contemporary Theatre, 1927*. Chapman and Hall, 1926

Agate, James. *A Shorter Ego*. George Harrap, 1946

Aldrich, Richard Stoddard. *Gertrude Lawrence as Mrs A*. Readers Book Club, 1956

Amstell, Billy. *Don't Fuss Mr Ambrose*. Spellmount, 1986

Anderson, Jervis. *Harlem: The Great Black Way 1900–1950*. Orbis Publishing, 1982

Ansen, Arlen J. *Expatriate Paris*. Arcade Publishing, Little, Brown, 1990

Arlen, Michael. *The Green Hat*. Collins, 1924

Armstrong, H. C. *Grey Wolf*. Arthur Barker, 1932

Armstrong, Louis. *Swing That Music*. Longmans Green, New York, 1936

Astor, Michael. *Tribal Feeling*. John Murray, 1964

Baddeley, Hermione. *The Unsinkable Hermione Baddeley*. Collins, 1984

Baldwin, James. *Another Country*. Michael Joseph, 1963

Baldwin, James. *The Fire Next Time*. Modern Library, 1995

Barber, Noel. *The Natives Were Friendly . . . So We Stayed the Night*. Macmillan, 1977

Barber, Noel. *The Weeping and the Laughter*. Hodder and Stoughton, 1988

Barrow, Andrew. *Gossip*. Hamish Hamilton, 1978

Bascovici, Konrad. *The Black Blocks of Manhattan*. Harpers, 1924

Beaton, Cecil. *Diaries 1922–1939: The Wandering Years*. Weidenfeld and Nicolson, 1961

Beaumont, Binkie. *Richard Huggett*. Hodder and Stoughton, 1989

Bechet, Sidney. *Treat It Gentle*. Cassell, 1960

Bennett, Richard. *A Picture of the Twenties*. Vista Books, 1961

Berendt, Joachim E. *The Jazz Book*. Granada, 1983

Bergreen, Laurence. *Louis Armstrong*. HarperCollins, 1998

Berle, Milton. *Funny Years with the Famous and Infamous*, McGraw Hill Book Co., New York, 1988

Bevan, Ian. *Top of the Bill*. Frederick Muller, 1952

Blair, Lionel. *Stage-struck*. Weidenfeld and Nicolson, 1985

Blake Brown, Richard. *The Apology of a Young Ex-Parson*. Duckworth, 1932

Blake Brown, Richard. *Yet Trouble Came*. Cassell, 1957

Blume, Mary. *Cote d'Azur: Inventing the French Riviera*. Thames and Hudson, 1992

Blythe, Ronald. *The Age of Illusion*. Hamish Hamilton, 1963

Booth, Mark. *Camp*. Quartet, 1983

Botham, Noel. *Margaret: The Untold Story*. Blake, 1994

Bowen, Elizabeth. *The Demon Lover*. Jonathan Cape, 1947

Bradford, Sarah. *George VI*. Weidenfeld and Nicolson, 1989

Bret, David. *The Mistinguett Legend*. Robson Books, 1990

Brown, Claude. *Manchild in a Promised Land*. Signet, 1965

Bruccoli, Matthew J. *Some Sort of Epic Grandeur: A Biography of Scott Fitzgerald*. Hodder and Stoughton, 1981

Bryan, J. III, and Charles J. V. Murphy. *The Windsor Story*. Pitman Press, 1979

Buckle, Richard. *In Search of Diaghilev*. Sidgwick and Jackson, 1955

Buckley, Gail Lumet. *The Hornes: The Story of Lena Horne and Her Family*. Weidenfeld and Nicolson, 1987

Bygraves, Max. *I Wanna Tell You a Funny Story*. Robson Books, 1992

Byng, Douglas. *As You Were*. Duckworth, 1970

Carpenter, Humphrey. *The Brideshead Generation*. Weidenfeld and Nicolson, 1989

Carrick, Peter. *A Tribute to Fred Astaire*. Robert Hale, 1984

Carver, Jeffrey L. *Tallulah: A Bio-biography of Tallulah Bankhead*. Greenwood Press, New York, 1991

Castle, Charles. *The Duchess Who Dared: The Life of Margaret, Duchess of Argyll*. Sidgwick and Jackson, 1994

Castle, Charles. *Noel*. W. H. Allen, 1972

Castle, Charles. *Oliver Messel*. Thames and Hudson, 1986

Charmley, John. *Duff Cooper*. Weidenfeld and Nicolson, 1986

Charters, James, *This Must Be the Place*. *Memoirs of Jimmie the Barman* as told to Morrill Cody. Lee Furman, New York, 1937

Charters, Samuel, and Kunstadt, Leonard. *Jazz: A History of the New York Scene*. Da Capo, New York, 1984

Chevalier, Maurice, *With Love*. Cassell, 1960

Chilton, John. *The Song of the Hawk*. Quartet, 1990

Chilton, John. *Who's Who of Jazz: Storyville to Swing Street*. Papermac, 1989

Chisholm, Anne. *Nancy Cunard*. Sidgwick and Jackson, 1979

Clarke, Donald, ed. *The Penguin Encyclopedia of Popular Music*, 1989

Clarke, Gerald. *Capote*. Simon and Schuster, New York, 1991

Cleeve, Brian. *1938: A World Vanishing*. Buchan and Enright, 1982

Clunn, Harold P. *The Face of Paris*. Spring Books, n.d.

Cochran, Charles B. *Cock-A-Doodle-Doo* (autobiography). J. M. Dent, 1941

Cochran, Charles B. *I Had Almost Forgotten . . .* (autobiography). Hutchinson, 1932

Cochran, Charles B. *Secrets of a Showman*. Morrison and Gibb, 1925

Cochran, Charles B. *A Showman Looks On* (autobiography). J. M. Dent, 1945

Cochrane, Peggy, *We Said It with Music*. New Horizon, 1980

Cockburn, Claud. *In Time of Trouble*. Rupert Hart-Davis, 1956

Cockburn, Patricia. *Figure of Eight*. Chatto and Windus, 1985

Collier, James L. *Louis Armstrong*. Michael Joseph, 1984

Cooper, Diana. *The Light of Common Day*. Rupert Hart Davis, 1956

Cooper, Duff. *Old Men Forget*. Rupert Hart-Davis, 1956

Cooper, Artemis, ed. *A Durable Fire: The Letters of Duff and Diana Cooper, 1913–1950*. Collins, 1983

Courtneidge, Cicely. *Cicely*. Hutchinson, 1953

Coward, Noël. *Cavalcade*. William Heinemann, 1932

Coward, Noël. *The Essential Noël Coward Songbook*. Omnibus Press, 1980

Coward, Noël. *Future Indefinite*. William Heinemann, 1954

Coward, Noël. *The Noël Coward Diaries*. Edited by Graham Payn and Sheridan Morley. Weidenfeld and Nicolson, 1982

Coward, Noël. *Present Indicative: An Autobiography*. Da Capo, New York, 1980

Crawford, Iain. *The Profumo Affair*. White Lodge Books, 1963

Crowder, Henry. *As Wonderful as All That?* unpublished autobiography written in the 1930s with Hugo Speck

Crowther, Bruce, and Pinfold, Mike. *The Jazz Singers: From Ragtime to the New Wave*. Blandford Press, 1986

Cunard, Nancy. *Negro*. Continuum, 1996

Dahl, Linda. *Stormy Weather: The Music and Lives of a Century of Jazzwomen*. Pantheon Books, 1984

Dance, Stanley. *The World of Duke Ellington*. Da Capo, New York, 1977

Darroch, Sandra Jobson. *Ottoline: The Life of Ottoline Morrell*. Cassell, 1976

Davie, Michael, ed. *The Diaries of Evelyn Waugh*. Little, Brown, 1976

Davies, Hunter. *The Grades*. Weidenfeld and Nicolson, 1981

Davis Sammy, Jr, with Jane and Burt Boyar. *Why Me?* Warner Books, 1989

Dawson, Les. *No Tears for a Clown*. Warner Books, 1993

De Courcy, Anne. *1939: The Last Season*. Thames and Hudson, 1989

Desmond, Florence. *Florence Desmond by Herself*. Harrap, 1953

Devi, Gayatri, the Maharani of Jaipur. *The Princess Remembers*. Weidenfeld and Nicolson, 1982

Dexter, Dave. *The Jazz Story*. Da Capo, New York, 1997

Douglas, Ann. *Terrible Honesty: Mongrel Mahattan in the 1920s*. Picador, 1996

Duberman, Martin Bauml. *Paul Robeson*. Bodley Head, 1989

Duncan, Peter. *In Show Business Tonight*. Hutchinson, 1954

Eells, George. *The Life That Late He Led: A Biography of Cole Porter*. G. P. Putnam's Sons, New York, 1967

Ellington, Duke. *Music Is My Mistress*. Da Capo, New York, 1976

Ellis, Jennifer. *The Duchess of Kent*. Odham Books, 1952

Ellis, Vivian. *A Composer's Jubilee*. Chappell Music Ltd, 1982

Ellis, Vivian. *I'm on a See-Saw*. Michael Joseph, 1953

Ellison, Grace. *Princess Marina.* Heinemann, 1934

Ellison, Ralph. *Invisible Man.* Random House, 1947

Elrick, George. *Housewives' Choice.* Mainstream, Edinburgh, 1991

Eyre, Richard. *Utopia and Other Places.* Bloomsbury, 1993

Fielding, Daphne. *The Duchess of Jermyn Street.* Little, Brown, Boston, 1964

Fisher, Clive. *Noël Coward.* Weidenfeld and Nicolson, 1992

Fitch, Noel Riley. *Sylvia Beach and the Lost Generation.* W. W. Norton, New York, 1983

Fitzgerald, F. Scott. *The Great Gatsby.* Penguin, 1950

Fitzgerald, F. Scott. *Tales of the Jazz Age.* Charles Scribner, New York, 1922

Flanner, Janet. *Paris Was Yesterday, 1925–1929.* Viking Press, 1972

Fletcher, Cyril. *Nice One Cyril.* Barrie and Jenkins, 1978

Ford, Hugh. *Published in Paris: A Literary Chronicle of Paris in the 1920s and 1930s.* Macmillan, 1975

Fowler, Gene. *Schnozzola: The Story of Jimmy Durante.* Permabooks, New York, 1953

Freedland, Michael. *Irving Berlin.* Stein and Day, 1974

Freedland, Michael. *Jerome Kern.* Stein and Day, 1981

Freedland, Michael. *The Secret Life of Danny Kaye.* W. H. Allen, 1985

Fryer, Peter. *Staying Power: The History of Black People in England.* Pluto Press, 1984

Gallati, Mario. *Mario at the Caprice.* Hutchinson, 1960

Gammond, Peter, ed. *Duke Ellington: His Life and His Music.* Da Capo, New York, 1977

Gammond, Peter, and Clayton, Peter. *Jazz Companion.* Guinness Publishing, 1986

Gavin, James. *Intimate Nights.* Limelight Editions, New York, 1991

Gentle, Eileen. *Before the Sunset.* Privately printed in Toronto, 1989

Gershwin, Ira. *Lyrics on Several Occasions.* Alfred A. Knopf, New York, 1959

Gielgud, John. *Early Stages.* Macmillan, 1939

Gielgud, John. *John Gielgud.* Sidgwick and Jackson, 1979

Gilbert, Julie Goldsmith. *Ferber: A Biography of Edna Ferber and Her Circle.* Doubleday, 1978

Giles, Sarah. *Fred Astaire: His Friends Talk.* Bloomsbury, 1988

Gill, Brendan. *Cole: A Biographical Essay*, edited by Robert Kimball. Michael Joseph, 1971

Gingold, Hermione. *My Own Unaided Work.* Campfield Press, 1952

Glyn, Anthony. *Elinor Glyn.* Hutchinson, 1955

Goddard, Chris. *Jazz Away from Home.* Paddington Press, 1977

Goffin, Robert. *The Frontiers of Jazz.* Disque Vert, 1920

Goldsmith, Barbara. *Little Gloria Happy at Last.* Macmillan, 1980

Grafton, David. *Red, Hot and Rich! An Oral History of Cole Porter.* Stein and Day, 1987

Graham, Sheila. *The Late Lily Shiel.* W. H. Allen, 1979

Graham, Sheila, and Gerold Frank. *Beloved Infidel.* Cassell, 1958

Graves, Charles. *Champagne and Chandeliers: The Story of the Café de Paris*. Odhams Press, 1958

Graves, Charles. *The Cochran Story*. W. H. Allen, n.d.

Green, Martin. *Children of the Sun: A Narrative of 'Decadence' in England After 1918*. Basic Books, New York, 1976

Gregg, Hubert. *Thanks for the Memory*. Victor Gollancz, 1983

Green, Benny. *Let's Face the Music*. Pavilion Books, 1989

Gunn, Peter. *Harold Acton*. Hamish Hamilton, 1978

Hackforth, Norman. *And the Next Object . . .* Angus Robertson, 1975

Hall, Henry. *Here's to the Next Time*. Odhams Press, 1955

Harding, James, *Cochran*. Methuen, 1988

Harding, James. *Ivor Novello*. W. H. Allen, 1987

Haskins, Jim. *Bricktop*. Atheneum, New York, 1983

Haskins, Jim. *The Cotton Club*. Random House, 1977

Haskins, Jim. *Ella Fitzgerald*. Hodder and Stoughton, 1981

Hastings, Selina. *Evelyn Waugh*. Hamish Hamilton, 1995

Hastings, Selina. *Nancy Mitford*. Hamish Hamilton, 1985

Hemingway, Ernest. *A Moveable Feast*. Jonathan Cape, 1960

Heppner, Sam. *'Cockie'*. Leslie Frewin, 1969

Herbert, David. *Second Son*. Peter Owen, 1973

Heymann, C. David. *Poor Little Rich Girl: The Life and Legend of Barbara Hutton*. Hutchinson, 1985

Higham, Charles. *Wallis: The Secret Lives of the Duchess of Windsor*. Sidgwick and Jackson, 1988

Higham, Charles, and Moseley, Roy. *Merle*. New English Library, 1983

Hoare, Philip. *Noël Coward*. Sinclair Stevenson, 1995

Hoare, Philip. *Serious Pleasures. The Life of Stephen Tennant*. Hamish Hamilton, 1990

Horne, Alistair. *A Bundle from Britain*. Macmillan, 1992

Hough, Richard. *Edwina*. Weidenfeld and Nicolson, 1983

Howard, Jean. *Travels with Cole Porter*. Harry N. Abrams, New York, 1991

Hughes, Langston. *The Big Sea*. Thunder's Mouth Press, New York, 1986

Hunt, Robert. *This Magic Wilderness*, n.p., n.d.

Huxley, Aldous. *Antic Hay*. Chatto and Windus, 1923

Huxley, Aldous. *Jesting Pilate*. Chatto and Windus, 1926

Jablonski, Edward. *Gershwin*. Simon and Schuster, 1988

Jenkins, Alan. *The Twenties*. William Heinemann, 1974

Jewell, Derek. *Duke: A Portrait of Duke Ellington*. W. W. Norton, New York, 1977

Johnson, James Weldon. *Along This Way*. Viking, New York, 1968

Jones, Max. *Talking Jazz*. Macmillan, 1987

Karkaria, Bachi. *To a Grand Design*. The Oberoi Grand, 1988

Katkov, Norman. *The Fabulous Fanny: The Story of Fanny Brice*. Alfred A. Knopf, New York, 1953

Kellner, Bruce. *Letters of Carl Van Vechten*. Yale University Press, 1989

Kendall, Henry. *I Remember Romano's*. Macdonald, 1960

Kennedy, Ludovic. *On My Way to the Club*. Collins, 1989

Kimball, Robert, and Alfred Simon. *The Gershwins*. Atheneum, New York, 1973

Kimball, Robert, ed. *Music and Lyrics of Cole Porter: A Treasury of Cole Porter*. Random House and Chappell, New York, n.d.

King, Stella. *Princess Marina: Her Life and Times*. Cassell, 1969

King, Viva. *The Weeping and the Laughter*, Macdonald and Janes, 1976

Kirkeby, Ed. *Aint Misbehavin': The Story of Fats Waller*. Da Capo, New York, 1975

Kobal, John. *Gotta Sing, Gotta Dance*. Hamlyn, 1970

Korda, Michael. *Queenie*. Collins, 1985

La Rue, Danny, with Howard Elson. *From Drags to Riches* Viking, 1987

Lambert, Angela. *1939: The Last Season of Peace*. Weidenfeld and Nicolson, 1989

Lambert, Gavin. *Norma Shearer*. Hodder and Stoughton, 1990

Lambton, Antony. *The Mountbattens*. Constable, 1989

Lancaster, Osbert. *With an Eye to the Future*. John Murray, 1968

Lanchester, Elsa. *Elsa Lanchester Herself*. Michael Joseph, 1983

Langley Simmons, *Dawn: A Blithe Spirit*. Arthur Barker, 1983

Latimer-Smith, John, ed. *Jazz: The Essential Companion*. Paladin, 1987

Laye, Evelyn. *Boo to My Friends*. Hurst and Blackett, 1958

Lehmann, Rosamond. *Album*. Chatto and Windus, 1985

Leonard, Maurice. *Markova the Legend*. Hodder and Stoughton, 1990

Lerner, Alan Jay. *The Musical Theatre*. Collins, 1986

Lesley, Cole. *The Life of Noël Coward*. Jonathan Cape, 1976

Lewis, David Levering. *When Harlem Was in Vogue*. OUP, 1989

Lillie, Bea. *Every Other Inch a Lady*. W. H. Allen, 1973

Lovell, Mary S. *Straight on Till Morning: The Biography of Beryl Markham*. Hutchinson, 1987

Loy, Myrna, and James Kotsilibas-Davis. *Myrna Loy: Being and Becoming*. Alfred A. Knopf, New York, 1987

Lynn, Vera. *Vocal Refrain*, W. H. Allen, 1975

Lynn, Vera, with Robin Cross. *We'll Meet Again: A Personal and Social Memory of World War Two*. Sidgwick and Jackson, 1989

Lyons, Len. *The Great Jazz Pianists*. Da Capo, New York, 1983

Lyttleton, Humphrey. *The Best of Jazz: Basin Street to Harlem 1917–1930*, Taplinger, 1982

Lyttleton, Humphrey. *Second Chorus*. MacGibbon and Kee, 1958

McAlmon, Robert, and Kay Boyle. *Being Geniuses Together 1920–1930*. Revised with supplementary chapters by Kay Boyle. Doubleday, 1968

McBrien, William. *Cole Porter: The Definitive Biography*. HarperCollins, 1998

Macleod, Kirsty. *A Talent for Friendship: Sibyl Colefax and Her Circle*. Michael Joseph, 1991

MacQueen Pope, W. *Ivor*. W. H. Allen, 1952

Mander, R., and J. Mitchenson. *Revue*. Peter Davies, 1971.

Mander, R. and J. Mitchenson. *The Theatres of London*. New English Library, 1975

Manley, Michael. *A History of West Indian Cricket*. André Deutsch, 1968

Marbury, Elizabeth. *My Crystal Ball*. Hurst and Blackett, 1924

Margetson, Stella. *The Long Party: High Society in the Twenties and Thirties*. Saxon House, 1974

Marlborough, Laura, Duchess of. *Laughter from a Cloud*. Weidenfeld and Nicolson, 1980

Marshall, Francis. *London West*. The Studio, 1944

Marshall, Michael. *Top Hat and Tails: The Story of Jack Buchanan*. Elm Tree Books, 1978

Marshall, Norman. *The Other Theatre*. John Lehmann, 1947

Martin, Brian P. *The Great Shoots*. David and Charles, 1987

Maschwitz, Eric. *No Chip on My Shoulder*. Herbert Jenkins, 1957

Mason, James. *Before I Forget*. Hamish Hamilton, 1981

Masters, Anthony. *Nancy Astor*. Weidenfeld and Nicolson, 1981

Masters, Anthony. *Rosa Lewis*. Weidenfeld and Nicolson, 1977

Masters, Brian. *Great Hostesses*. Constable, 1982

Matthews, Jessie. *Over My Shoulder* (autobiography, as told to Muriel Burgess). W. H. Allen, 1974

Maugham, Robin. *Escape from the Shadows*. Hodder and Stoughton, 1972

Maugham, Robin. *Somerset and All the Maughams*. Longman, 1975

Maxwell, Elsa. *I Married the World*. Heinemann, 1955

Maxwell, Gilbert. *Helen Morgan: Her Life and Legend*. Hawthorn Books, New York, 1974

Meade, Marion. *What Fresh Hell Is This? A Biography of Dorothy Parker*. Heinemann, 1988

Mellow, James R. *Charmed Circle: Gertrude Stein and Company*. Praeger, New York, 1974

Middleboe, Penelope. *Edith Olivier: From Her Journals 1924–1948*. Weidenfeld and Nicolson, 1989

Mills, John. *Up in the Clouds, Gentlemen Please*. Weidenfeld and Nicolson, 1980

Milton, Billy. *Milton's Paradise Mislaid*. Jupiter, 1976

Mitford, Jessica. *Hons and Rebels*. Quartet, 1978

Mitford, Nancy. *Letters*, edited by Charlotte Mosley. Hodder and Stoughton, 1993

Mitford, Nancy. *A Talent to Annoy. Essays, Journalism and Reviews. 1929–1968*, edited by Charlotte Mosley. OUP, 1986

More, Kenneth. *Happy Go Lucky*. Robert Hale, 1959

Morgan, Janet. *Edwina Mountbatten: A Life of Her Own*. Harper Collins, 1991

Morley, Sheridan. *A Bright Particular Star: A Biography of Gertrude Lawrence*. Pavilion, 1986

Morley, Sheridan. *The Great Stage Stars*. Angus and Robertson, 1986

Morley, Sheridan. *Marlene*. Elm Tree Books, 1976

Morley, Sheridan. *The Other Side of the Moon*. Weidenfeld and Nicolson, 1985

Morley, Sheridan. *A Talent to Amuse*. Heinemann, 1969, revised 1984

Morrow, Ann. *Picnic in a Foreign Land: The Eccentric Lives of the Anglo-Irish*. Grafton, 1989

Mosley, Diana. *A Life of Contrasts*. Hamish Hamilton, 1977

Muggeridge, Malcolm. *Like It Was*. Collins, 1981

Muggeridge, Malcolm. *The Thirties*. Hamish Hamilton, 1940

Neagle, Anna. *AN Says 'There's Always Tomorrow'*. W. H. Allen, 1974

Nichols, Beverly. *The Sweet and Twenties*. Quality Book Club, 1928

Nicolson, Harold. *Diaries and Letters 1930–1964*. Penguin, 1964

Noel, Gerald. *Ena: England's Spanish Queen*. Constable, 1984

O'Connor, Patrick, and Bryan Hammond. *Josephine Baker*. Jonathan Cape, 1988

Ogden, Christopher. *Life of the Party*. Warner Books, 1994

Oliver, Paul. *The Story of the Blues*. Pimlico, 1996

Ottley, Roi. *No Green Pastures*. John Murray, 1952

Owen, Maureen. *The Crazy Gang*. Weidenfeld and Nicolson, 1986

Pakenham, Frank, Earl of Longford. *Five Lives*. Hutchinson, 1964

Panassie, Hugues, and Madeleine Gautier. *Dictionary of Jazz*, The Jazz Book Club, 1959

Parker, John. *King of Fools*. Macdonald, 1988

Parker, John. *Prince Philip*. Sidgwick and Jackson, 1990

Pearson, John. *Façades: Edith, Osbert and Sacheverell Sitwell*. Macmillan, 1978

Petrie, Sir Charles. *King Alfonso XIII*. Chapman and Hall, 1963

Pickford, Mary. *Sunshine and Shadow*. Heinemann, 1956

Quennell, Peter. *The Marble Foot*. Collins, 1976

Rampersad, Arnold. *The Life of Langston Hughes*, vol I; *I Too Sing America*. OUP, 1986

Redhead, Wilfred. *A City on a Hill: St Georges, Grenada*. Privately published 1985

Reid, Beryl. *So Much Love*. Hutchinson, 1984

Roberts, Andrew. *Eminent Churchillians*. Weidenfeld and Nicolson, 1994

Roberts, Cecil. *The Bright Twenties: 1920–1929*. Hodder and Stoughton, 1970

Robyns, Gwen. *Princess Grace*. W. H. Allen, 1976

Rodgers, Richard. *Musical Stages*. Random House, 1975

Rose, Phyllis. *Jazz Cleopatra: A Biography of Josephine Baker*. Doubleday, 1989

Sachs, Harvey. *Arthur Rubinstein*. Orion, 1995

Sansom, William. *Westminster at War*. Faber and Faber, 1948

Saunders, Sir Peter. *The Mousetrap Man*. Collins, 1972

Schwartz, Charles. *Cole Porter*. Da Capo, New York, 1977

Schwartz, Charles. *Gershwin: His Life and Music*. Bobbs-Merrill, New York, 1973

Segal, Ronald. *The Race War*. Jonathan Cape, 1966

Seton, Marie. *Paul Robeson*. Dobson Books, 1958

Shapiro, Nat, and Nat Hentoff. *The Jazz Makers*. Da Capo, New York, 1979

Shaw, Arnold. *The Jazz Age*. OUP, 1987

Sherrin, Ned. *A Small Thing – Like an Earthquake*. Weidenfeld and Nicolson, 1983

Short, Bobby. *Black and White Baby*. Dodd, Mead and Co., New York, 1971

Short, Bobby, with Robert Macintosh. *Saloon Singer*. Clarkson N. Potter, New York, 1995

Silberman, Charles E. *Crisis in Black and White*. Random House, 1964

Slater, Leonard. *Aly: A Biography*. Random House, 1965

Smith, Willie the Lion, with G. Hoefer. *Music on My Mind*. MacGibbon and Kee, 1965

Spain, Nancy. *Why I'm Not a Millionaire*. Hutchinson, 1956

Stannard, Martin. *Evelyn Waugh. The Early Years 1903–1939*. J. M. Dent, 1986

Suyin, Han. *Love Is a Many-Splendoured Thing*. F. A. Thorpe, 1971

Sweeny, Charles. *Sweeny*. Wingham Press, 1990

Sykes, Christopher. *Evelyn Waugh: A Biography*. Collins, 1975

Taki. *High Life*. Viking, 1989

Tattersall, E. H. *Europe at Play*. Heinemann, 1938

Taylor, Frank C., and Gerald Cook. *Alberta Hunter*. McGraw Hill, 1987

Taylor, John Russell. *Dictionary of the Theatre*. Penguin, 1966

Thomas, Howard. *With an Independent Air. Encounters During a Lifetime of Broadcasting*. Weidenfeld and Nicolson, 1977

Thomas, Terry. *Filling the Gap*. Max Parish, 1959

Thomas, Terry, with Terry Daum. *Terry-Thomas Tells Tales*. Robson Books, 1990

Thurman, Wallace. *The Blacker the Berry*. Prentice Hall 1970

Tomkins, Calvin. *Living Well Is the Best Revenge*. Penguin, 1962

Toynbee, Philip. *Friends Apart*. Sidgwick and Jackson, 1954

Trefusis, Violet. *Don't Look Round*. Hutchinson, 1952

Trzebinski, Errol. *The Lives of Beryl Markham*. Heinemann, 1993

Tucker, Sophie, with Dorothy Giles. *Some of These Days*. Doubleday, New York, 1945

Tunney, Kieran. *Tallulah, Darling of the Gods*. Secker and Warburg, 1972

Vanderbilt, Gloria. *Once Upon a Time*. Chatto and Windus, 1985

Vickers, Hugo. *Cecil Beaton*. Weidenfeld and Nicolson, 1985

Wall, Max, with Peter Ford. *The Fool on the Hill*. Quartet, 1975

Waters, Ethel, with Charles Samuels. *His Eye Is on the Sparrow*. W. H. Allen, 1951

Watson, Sophia. *Princess Marina*. Weidenfeld and Nicolson, 1994

Waugh, Evelyn. *Decline and Fall*. Chapman and Hall, 1928

Waugh, Evelyn. *A Handful of Dust*. Chapman and Hall, 1934

Waugh, Evelyn. *Vile Bodies*. Chapman and Hall, 1930

Waugh, Evelyn, and Diana Cooper. *Mr Wu and Mrs Stitch*, letters edited by Artemis Cooper. Hodder and Stoughton, 1991

Weld, Jacqueline Bograd. *Peggy, the Wayward Guggenheim*. Bodley Head, 1986

Westminster, Loelia, Duchess of. *Grace and Favour*. Weidenfeld and Nicolson, 1961

Wildeblood, Peter. *Against the Law*. Weidenfeld and Nicolson, 1955

Williams, Kenneth. *Diaries*, edited by Russell Davies. HarperCollins, 1984

Wilmer, Valerie. *As Serious as Your Life. The Story of the New Jazz*. Pluto Press, 1977

Wilson, Earl. *The Show Business Nobody Knows*. Cowles, 1971

Wilson, Edmund. *The Twenties*. Macmillan, 1975

Wilson, Sandy. *I Could Be Happy*. Michael Joseph, 1975

Wilson, Sandy. *The Roaring Twenties*. Eyre Methuen, 1976

Windsor, The Duchess of. *The Heart Has Its Reasons*. Odhams Press, 1958

Wineapple, Brenda. *Genet: A Biography of Janet Flanner*. HarperCollins, 1990

Winn, Godfrey. *Personality Parade*. Peter Davies, 1937

Woollcott, Alexander. *The Story of Irving Berlin*. Da Capo, New York, 1983

Wright, Richard. *Native Son*. Harper and Row, New York, 1940

Ziegler, Philip. *Diana Cooper*. Hamish Hamilton, 1981

Ziegler, Philip. *King Edward VIII: A Biography*. Alfred A. Knopf, New York, 1991

Ziegler, Philip. *Mountbatten*. Collins, 1985

DISCOGRAPHY

compiled by James H. Moore

Chronological List of All Commercial Recordings Issued Within Hutch's Lifetime

Pathe 021060	Original Charleston (with Ruth Coleman) 10/9/23
Pathe 021061	She Walked Right Up (with Ruth Coleman) 10/9/23
Voc 14688	Graveyard Dream (with Hazel Meyers) 1/10/23
	Low Down Papa (with Hazel Meyers) 1/10/23
Ajax 17058	Good Time Ball/Lost Opportunity Blues –/9/24
	(with Mamie Smit)
Voc X9952	(Because I Love You/Moonlight on the Ganges –/3/27
	(with Opal Cooper)
Voc X9968	Mama's Gone Young/I Wonder What's Become of Joe? –/
	3/27
	(with Opal Cooper)
Bruns 104	Me and My Shadow –/10/27
	When I Discover My Man (with Helen Morgan) –/10/
	27
Bruns 110	Just Like a Butterfly –/10/27
	You Remind Me –/10/27
Bruns 111	Tree in the Park –/10/27
	Where's that Rainbow? –/10/27
Bruns 113	Lazy Weather –/10/27
	If Possibly –/10/27
Bruns 129	Do Do Do –/12/27
	Maybe –/12/27
Bruns 117	The Girlfriend –/12/27
Bruns 125	Do Do Do –/12/27
	Someone to Watch Over Me (piano solos) –/10/27
Bruns 135	My Heart Stood Still –/10/27
	Just a Memory (with Jessie Matthews) –/10/27

Bruns 126	It Takes a Good Woman −/9/27
	I Ain't That Kind of a Baby −/9/27
Bruns 139	I Ain't Got Nobody −/11/27
	Bless Her Little Heart −/11/27
Bruns 142	There's a Trick in Pickin' −/2/28
	Who's That Knocking at My Door? −/2/28
12" 20056	Medley − Hutch plays My Heart Stood Still −/10/27

Parlophone 12"

E 10869	Wake Up and Dream − medley −/4/29
E 11080	Maurice Chevalier − medley −/9/30
E 11262	Hutch − medley 17/11/34
E 11385	Cole Porter − medley 9/11/37

HMV 12"

| C 3194 | Cole Porter − medley −/11/40 |

Parlophone 10"

261	He Loves and She Loves −/1/29
	High Hat −/1/29
R 272	Forever −/12/28
	Happy Days and Lonely Nights −/12/28
R 342	Let's Fall in Love 19/2/29
	Looking at You 1/3/29
R 343	I'm a Gigolo 15/4/29
	What Is This Thing Called Love 15/4/29
R 373	To Know You Is to Love You/You're the Cream −/7/29
R 403	Wake Up Chillun' Wake Up −/7/29
	When I Only Think of You −/9/29
R 416	Huggable, Kissable You −/10/29
	Now I'm in Love −/10/29
R 444	I'm Still Caring −/11/29
	My Sin −/11/29
R 461	I Don't Know How −/11/29
	Thou Swell −/11/29
R 468	Button Up Your Overcoat −/12/29
	I Wanna Be Bad −/12/29
R 469	Ain't Misbehavin' −/12/29
	S'posin −/12/29
R 544	If I Had a Talking Picture of You −/2/30
	Aren't We All −/2/30

R 578	I May be Wrong −/3/30
	Moanin' for You −/3/30
R 591	Little by Little −/4/30
	My Fate Is in Your Hands −/4/30
R 606	Body and Soul −/4/30
	My Heart Is Saying −/4/30
R 617	Cochran's 1930 Revue (2 sides) −/5/30
	Piano solos −/5/30
R 639	The Little Things You Do −/6/30
	With a Song in My Heart −/6/30
R 646	Fond of You −/6/30
	The Wind in the Willows −/6/30
R 695	Handsome Gigolo −/8/30
	There's Danger in Your Eyes −/8/30
R 738	I Love You So Much −/10/30
	You Brought a New Kind of Love −/10/30
R 749	She's My Secret Passion −/10/30
	Song of the Dawn −/10/30
R 760	Falling in Love Again −/11/30
	Without a Song −/11/30
R 774	Always Your Humble Slave −/11/30
	Syncopated Pierrot −/11/30
R 805	My Description of You −/12/30
	Okay Baby −/12/30
R 826	I'll Be Good Because of you −/1/31
	I'm Yours −/1/31
R 835	I'm Just Wearing Out My Heart for You −/2/31
	There's a Religion in Rhythm −/2/32
R 871	Memories of You −/3/31
	Over Night −/3/31
R 879	Blue Without You −/4/31
	Singing a Song to the Stars −/4/31
R 897	Blue Again −/4/31
	Ten Cents a Dance −/4/31
R 908	Half Caste Woman 10/4/31
	Something to Remember You By 10/4/31
R 925	I'm Glad I Waited −/5/31
	Time on My Hands −/5/31
R 937	I Surrender Dear −/6/31
	Fairweather Friend −/6/31
R 962	O Lord, Send Us the Sunshine −/7/31
	River Stay Way From My Door −/7/31
R 1001	Just One More Chance −/10/31
	Nevertheless −/10/31
R 1012	Out of Nowhere −/10/31
	Whistling in the Dark −/10/31

R 3273	Just One More Chance −/10/31
	Out of Nowhere −/10/31
R 1041	When Your Lover Has Gone −/11/31
	Gone −/11/31
R 1083	For You −/11/31
	I'm Through with Love −/11/31
R 1087	Close Your Eyes 13/11/31
	Life Is Just a Bowl of Cherries 13/11/31
R 1126	Guilty −/2/32
	If I Didn't Have You −/2/32
R 1132	Dancing in the Dark −/4/32
	You're Blasé −/4/32
R 1156	You Try Somebody Else −/4/32
	Was It the Moon or Love −/4/32
R 1178	If I Had to Go on Without You −/5/32
	When the Rest of the Crowd Goes Home −/5/32
R 1198	Can't We Talk It Over −/6/32
	Lawd, You Made the Night Too Long −/6/32
R 1214	My Goodbye to You −/6/32
	What a Life −/6/32
R 1228	After All Is Said and Done −/7/32
	What Makes You So Adorable? −/7/32
R 1250	Disappointed in Love −/8/32
	When Work Is Through −/8/32
R 1272	Hummin' to Myself −/9/32
	Troubles Are Like Bubbles −/9/32
R 1285	I Wanna Be Loved −/9/32
	Why Waste Your Tears? −/9/32
R 1296	Shadows on the Window −/9/32
	Happy Go Lucky You −/9/32
R 1304	I'm Wrapped Up in You 10/9/32
	Sing a New Song 10/9/32
R 1350	Nightfall −/10/32
	Say It Isn't So −/10/32
R 1352	Love Me Tonight 13/10/32
	Round the Bend of the Road 13/10/32
R 1371	How Deep Is the Ocean? 12/11/32
	Love Is the Sweetest Thing 12/11/32
R 1381	Goodbye to Love −/12/32
	What Would Happen to Me −/12/32
R 1408	I'll Follow You −/12/32
	Try a Little Tenderness −/12/32
R 1422	Here Lies Love 13/1/33
	What More Can I Ask? 13/1/33
R 1456	Just So You'll Remember −/1/33
	My Darling −/1/33

R 1459	Poor Me, Poor You 16/2/33
	You'll Fall in Love 16/2/33
R 1483	Blue River Roll On –/3/33
	My Love Song –/3/33
R 1504	Maybe I Love You Too Much 8/4/33
	My Wishing Song 8/4/33
R 1525	Stormy Weather 13/5/33
	You've Got Me Crying Again 13/5/33
R 1546	No Thrill at All –/6/33
	You Are Too Beautiful –/6/33
R 1551	It's Best to Forget –/6/33
	One Tiny Tear –/6/33
R 1577	I Cover the Waterfront 13/7/33
	I've Got to Sing a Torch Song 13/7/33
R 1566	I've Got the World on a String –/8/33
	You're Still in My Heart –/8/33
R 1595	Let's Call it a Day –/8/33
	Lover –/8/33
R 1623	Trouble in Paradise 9/9/33
	Lay Your Head on My Shoulder 9/9/33
R 1637	Don't Blame Me –/9/33
	Madamoiselle –/9/33
R 1647	Night and Day 3/10/33
	Dusty Shoes 3/10/33
R 1660	Love Locked Out –/10/33
	Weep No More My Baby –/10/33
R 1691	The Winds in the West 9/11/33
	You Ought to See Sally on Sunday 9/11/33
R 1720	Close Your Eyes 11/12/33
	Did You Ever See a Dream Walking? 11/12/33
R 1747	Dark Clouds 20/1/34
	So Shy 20/1/34
R 1755	Everything I Have Is Yours –/2/34
	It's Only a Paper Moon (piano solos) –/2/34
R 1773	I'll Follow My Search Heart 17/2/34
	This Little Piggie 17/2/34
R 1801	One Morning in May –/3/34
	That's Love –/3/34
R 1818	In Other Words We're Through 18/4/34
	You Have Taken My Heart 18/4/34
R 1831	True –/4/34
	After All You're All I'm After –/4/34
R 1856	As Far as I'm Concerned 22/5/34
	Little Man You've Had a Busy Day 22/5/34
R 1867	Over My Shoulder/
	When You've Got a Little Springtime in Your Heart –/6/34

	The Very Thought of You –/6/34
R 1885	All I Do Is Dream of You –/7/34
	It's All Forgotten Now –/7/34
R 1909	The Ache in My Heart 5/9/34
	For All We Know 5/9/34
R 1922	Isle of Capri –/9/34
	With My Eyes Wide Open I'm Dreaming –/9/34
R 1931	Dreaming a Dream –/10/34
	This Is No Sin –/10/34
R 1950	As I Sit Here 11/10/34
	I Travel Alone 11/10/34
R 1971	I Saw Stars –/12/34
	Smoke Gets in Your Eyes –/12/34
R 2002	I Only Have Eyes for You –1/12/34
	June in January 1/12/34
R 2024	Hands Across the Table 28/12/34
	Wish Me Luck, Kiss Me Goodbye 28/12/34
R 2044	Blue Moon 1/2/35
	You and the Night and the Music 7/2/35
R 2045	Back to Those Happy Days –/2/35
	Maybe I'm Wrong Again –/2/35
R 2056	Down by the River –/3/35
	Because of Once Upon a Time –/3/35
R 2059	Vienna in Spring Time –/3/35
	With All My Heart and Soul –/3/35
R 2060	Love Was a Song –/4/35
	The Bridal Waltz –/4/35
R 2077	If the Moon Turns Green 14/5/35
	Zing Went the Strings of My Heart 14/5/35
R 2085	Anything Goes 17/5/35
	Two Little Babes in the Wood 17/5/35
R 2093	The Leech 12/6/35
	Why Was I Born? 12/6/35
R 2108	Kiss Me Goodnight –/9/35
	Love Is Everywhere –/9/35
R 2109	Wake –/9/35
	Two Tired Eyes –/9/35

Parlophone Magenta reissues

F 233	Murder in the Moonlight –/9/35
	Red Sails in the Sunset –/9/35
F 234	Dream Shadows –/9/35
	I Couldn't Believe My Eyes –/9/35
F 242	Looking at You★

★ F 242 to F 272 are reissues. See original releases for recording dates

	Let's Fall in Love
F 243	What Is This Thing Called Love
	I'm a Gigolo
F 244	The Little Things You Do
	With a Song in My Heart
F 245	The Wind in the Willows
	Fond of You
F 246	Lawd, You Made the Night Too Long
	Can't We Talk It Over
F 247	You Are Too Beautiful
	No Thrill at All
F 248	One Tiny Tear
	It's Best to Forget
F 249	Lover
	Let's Call It a Day
F 250	Dusty Shoes
	My Love Song
F 251	Close Your Eyes
	Did You Ever See a Dream Walking?
F 252	So Shy
	Dark Clouds
F 253	Everything I Have Is Yours
	It's Only a Paper Moon
F 254	This Little Piggy
	I'll Follow My Secret Heart
F 255	One Morning in May
	That's Love
F 256	In Other Words We're Through
	You Have Taken My Heart
F 257	True
	After All You're All I'm After
F 258	As Far as I'm Concerned
	Little Man You've Had a Busy Day
F 259	Over My Shoulder/When You've Got a Little Spring Time in Your Heart
	The Very Thought of You
F 260	All I Do Is Dream of You
	It's All Forgotten Now
F 261	For All We Know
	The Ache In My Heart
F 262	Isle of Capri
	With My Eyes Wide Open I'm Dreaming
F 263	This Is No Sin
	Dreaming a Dream
F 264	As I Sit Here
	I Travel Alone

F 265	I Saw Stars
	Smoke Gets in Your Eyes
F 266	June in January
	I Only Have Eyes for You
F 267	Hands Across the Table
	Wish Me Good Luck, Kiss Me Goodbye
F 268	Blue Moon
	You and the Night and the Music
F 269	Back to Those Happy Days
	Maybe I'm Wrong Again
F 270	Because of Once Upon a Time
	Down by the River
F 271	Vienna in Spring Time
	With All My Heart and Soul
F 272	Love Was a Song
	The Bridal Waltz
F 273	Zing Went the Strings of My Heart 14/5/32
	If the Moon Turns Green 14/5/35
F 274	Anything Goes 17/5/35
	Two Little Babes in the Wood 17/5/35
F 275	The Leech 12/6/35
	Why Was I Born? 12/6/35
F 276	Love Is Everywhere −/9/35
	Kiss Me Goodnight −/9/35
F 277	Wake −/9/35
	Two Tired Eyes −/9/35
F 285	I Feel a Song Coming On 10/10/35
	Whenever I Think of You 10/10/35
F 286	East of the Sun 10/10/35
	My Heart Is Haunted 10/10/35
F 311	Dinner for One, Please James 31/10/35
	Homestead 31/10/35
F 323	In the Dark 31/10/35
	To Call You My Own 31/10/35
F 324	As Long as Our Hearts Are Young 31/10/35
	Sweet Dreams, Sweetheart 31/10/35
F 350	Love Is Like a Cigarette 9/12/35
	The Morning After 9/12/35
F 373	These Foolish Things −/1/36
	Lights Out −/1/36
F 373	These Foolish Things (with orchestra) −/1/36
	Lights Out (with orchestra) −/1/36
F 399	Bird on the Wing 4/2/36
	If I Should Lose You 4/2/36
F 400	When April Comes Again −/3/36
	You Can Always Tell a Jaffa −/3/36

F 420	If You Love Me −/3/36
	My Heart and I −/3/36
F 436	But Where Are You −/3/36
	I'm Building Up to an Awful Let Down
F 444	Gloomy Sunday 2/4/36
	Alone 7/4/36
F 444	Gloomy Sunday 2/4/36
	Wake Up and Sing 2/4/36
F 467	Tormented 7/5/36
	Dream Time 7/5/36
F 493	All My Life 29/5/36
	Where Am I? 29/5/36
F 511	I Nearly Let Love Go Slipping 5/7/36
	Would You 5/7/36
F 529	The Scene Changes −/7/36
	Empty Saddles −/7/36
F 541	When I'm With You −/8/36
	Your Heart and Mine −/8/36
F 552	Cryin' My Heart Out for You −/8/36
	Did I Remember −/8/36
F 553	Lonely Road 28/8/36
	New Heart 28/8/36
F 574	Foolish Heart 3/10/36
	It's a Sin to Tell a Lie 3/10/36
F 586	Does Your Heart Beat for Me −/10/36
	When the Poppies Bloom Again −/10/36
F 604	Miracles Sometimes Happen 6/11/36
	No Regrets 6/11/36
F 620	Did You Mean It? −/11/36
	Front Page News −/11/36
F 644	After Glow −/12/36
	The Way You Look Tonight −/12/36
F 655	Chapel in the Moonlight −/12/36
	There's a Small Hotel −/12/36
F 670	Easy to Love 7/1/37
	I've Got You Under My Skin 7/1/37
F 705	Gone 5/2/37
	I'm Delighted to See You Again 5/2/37
F 740	All Alone in Vienna 4/3/37
	Goodnight My Love 4/3/37
F 752	May I Have the Next Romance with You 10/3/37
	Watching the Stars 10/3/37
F 759	Broken Hearted Clown −/4/37
	I Need You −/4/37
F 790	Tomorrow Is Another Day 10/6/37
	Where Is the Sun? 10/6/37

F 819	Carelessly 12/6/37
	September in the Rain 12/6/37
F 838	They Can't Take That Away from Me 7/7/37
	Where Are You? 7/7/37
F 866	The Greatest Mistake of My Life –/7/37
	In an Old Cathedral Town –/7/37
F 873	On the Avenue (vocal and piano medley, 2 sides) 15/7/37
F 894	I Know Now 1/9/37
	You're Just Looking for Romance 1/9/37
F 895	Moon at Sea 1/9/37
	Let Us Be Sweethearts Over Again 1/9/37
F 915	Singing for You 26/8/37
	Paris Is Not the Same 26/8/37
F 916	That Old Feeling 11/10/37
	Whispers in the Dark 11/10/37
F 917	Goodnight to You All 11/10/37
	Stardust on the Moon 11/10/37
F 947	Moon or No Moon 5/11/37
	Just Remember 5/11/37
F 971	Afraid to Dream 16/11/37
	I Still Love to Kiss You Goodnight 16/11/37
F 989	Blossoms on Broadway 8/12/37
	Remember Me? 8/12/37
F 990	After All These Years 8/12/37
	For Only You 8/12/37
F 1016	My Gypsy Dream Girl 5/1/38
	Please Remember 5/1/38
F 1017	By the Sweat of Your Brow 5/1/38
	A Foggy Day 5/1/38
F 1038	Once in a While 26/1/38
	It's a Long, Long Way to Your Heart 26/1/38
F 1039	The Girl in the Alice Blue Gown 26/1/38
	With You 26/1/38
F 1069	Outside an Old Stage Door –/2/38
	So Many Memories –/2/38
F 1070	Two Dreams Got Together –/3/38
	Souvenir of Love –/3/38
F 1093	So Long Sweetheart –/3/38
	Tears in My Heart –/3/38
F 1094	With a Smile and a Song 6/4/38
	Why Talk About Love 6/4/38
F 1119	Have You Ever Been in Heaven? 11/5/38
	I Can Dream Can't I? 11/5/38
F 1120	In Santa Magherita 11/5/38
	Please Be Kind 11/5/38

F 1143	My Heaven on Earth 14/6/38
	So Little Time 14/6/38
F 1144	Love Walked in 14/6/38
	Weep and You Dance Alone 14/6/38
F 1164	I Won't Tell a Soul 30/6/38
	Two Shadows 30/6/38
F 1165	Says My Heart 30/6/38
	Two Bouquets 30/6/38
F 1188	Meet Me Down in Sunset Valley 20/7/38
	Goodnight Angel, Goodnight 20/7/38
F 1189	My New Song 20/7/38
	Solitude 20/7/38
F 1212	Take Me in Your Arms 30/8/38
	There's Rain in My Eyes 30/8/38
F 1213	Little Lady Make Believe 30/8/38
	Music, Maestro Please 30/8/38
F 1244	It's D'lovely 7/10/38
	Now It Can Be Told 7/10/38
F 1245	I Hadn't Anyone Til You 7/10/38
	The Red Maple Leaves 7/10/38
F 1268	Cinderella Sweetheart 21/10/38
	A Garden in Grenada 21/10/38
F 1269	Change Partners 21/10/38
	I Used to Be Colour Blind 21/10/38
F 1310	Love Makes the World go Round 13/12/38
	When Mother Nature Sings Her Lullaby 13/12/38
F 1311	While a Cigarette Was Burning 13/12/38
	Two Sleepy People 13/12/38
F 1338	If Ever a Heart Was in the Right Place 8/2/39
	This Is the Kiss of Romance 8/2/39
F 1339	There's Something About an Old Love 8/2/39
	They Say 8/2/39
F 1361	Grandma Said 8/2/39
	I Have Eyes 8/2/39
F 1362	Romany 8/2/39
	You Go to My Head 8/2/39
F 1383	Hurry Home 9/3/39
	Thanks for Everything 9/3/39
F 1384	Let's Dream in the Moonlight 9/3/39
	Lonely 9/3/39
F 1412	Deep Purple 5/4/39
	The Masquerade Is Over 5/4/39
F 1413	Let Me Whisper I Love You 5/4/39
	Prelude to a Kiss 5/4/39
F 1443	Begin the Beguine 5/5/39
	I Paid for the Lie That I Told You 5/5/39

F 1444	A Mist Over the Moon 5/5/39
	This Night 5/5/39
F 1463	A New Moon and an Old Serenade 8/6/39
	We've Come a Long Way Together 8/6/39
F 1464	Our Love 8/6/39
	Sing My Heart 8/6/39
F 1476	Life Is Nothing Without Music 8/6/39
	Don't Worry 'Bout Me 8/6/39
F 1485	I Get Along Without You Very Well 6/7/39
	Only When You're in My Arms 6/7/39
F 1486	If I Didn't Care 6/7/39
	My Prayer 6/7/39
F 1512	The Moon Remembered but You Forgot
	Why Begin Again?
F 1513	I Never Knew Heaven Could Speak
	Stairway to the Stars
F 1543	Bon Voyage, Cherie 12/9/39
	There's Danger in the Waltz 12/9/39
F 1544	I'm in Love with the Honourable Mrs So and So 12/9/39
	I Poured My Heart into a Song 12/9/39
F 1555	Begone –/9/39
	Moon Love –/9/39
F 1556	The Day We Meet Again –/9/39
	A Man and His Dream –/9/39
F 1562	Lords of the Air 27/10/39
	Ridin' Home? 27/10/39
F 1570	Later On –/11/39
	This Heart of Mine –/11/39
F 1613	Let's Make Memories Tonight 3/12/39
	Over the Rainbow 3/12/39
F 1614	I'll Remember 3/12/39
	Somewhere in France with You 3/12/39
F 1628	Faithful Forever 29/12/39
	Goodnight My Beautiful 29/12/39
F 1629	There Goes My Dream 29/12/39
	Where or When 29/12/39
F 1665	A Small Café by Notre Dame 8/2/40
	It's a Lovely Day Tomorrow 8/2/40
F 1666	I'll Pray for You 8/2/40
	Rosita 8/2/40
F 1687	When You Wish Upon a Star/The Old Music Box –/3/40
	A Kiss in the Dark –/3/40
F 1688	Careless 2/3/40
	I Cried for You 2/3/40
F 1713	Don't Make Me Laugh 30/3/40
	I Forgot the Little Things 30/3/40

F 1714	Indian Summer 30/3/40
	You Made Me Care 30/3/40
F 1736	A Nightingale Sang in Berkley Square 7/5/40
	Shake Down the Stars 7/5/40
F 1737	If I Should Fall in Love Again 7/5/40
	The Woodpecker Song 7/5/40
BD 847	Begin the Beguine −/5/40
	I've Got My Eyes on You −/5/40
BD 850	Fools Rush In 8/6/40
	I'll Never Fail You 8/6/40
BD 851	Imagination −/7/40
	They Call Me a Dreamer −/7/40
BD 856	I Can't Love You Anymore −/7/40
	I'll Be Waiting −/7/40
BD 863	I'm Stepping Out with a Memory Tonight 22/8/40
	Mist on the River 22/8/40
BD 872	All the Things You Are 27/9/40
	Love Stay in My Heart 27/9/40
BD 875	I'll Never Smile Again 10/10/40
	The Nearness of You 10/10/40
BD 882	All Over the Place 4/11/40
	They'll Come Another Day 4/11/40
BD 893	My Romance 6/12/40
	You're Breaking My Heart All Over Again 6/12/40
BD 902	The Best Things in Life Are Free 7/1/41
	The Moon Won't Talk 7/1/41
BD 904	Just One of Those Things 30/1/41
	Weep No More 30/1/41
BD 909	Down Ev'ry Street 30/1/41
	Yesterday's Dreams 30/1/41
BD 913	Room 504 28/2/41
	Something to Remember You By 28/2/41
BD 918	The London I Love 21/3/41
	Over the Hill 21/3/41
BD 926	Do I Love You? 2/5/41
	For All That I Care 2/5/41
BD 929	Let There Be Love −/5/41
	It's Always You −/5/41
BD 930	Whispering Grass −/6/41
	The Day It Rained −/6/41
BD 938	There Goes That Song Again −/7/41
	Boa Noite −/7/41
BD 944	This Heart of Mine 25/7/41
	Just a Little Cottage 25/7/41
BD 945	Dolores 27/7/41
	What Do We Care 27/7/41

BD 949	Hearts Don't Lie 2/9/41
	I'll Never Let a Day Pass By 2/9/41
BD 950	Tell Your Troubles to the Breeze 2/9/41
	It Always Rains Before the Rainbow 2/9/41
BD 966	When the Sun Comes Out 8/10/41
	You and I 8/10/41
BD 967	Marie Elena 8/10/41
	Don't Cry, Cherie 8/10/41
BD 971	Yours 31/10/41
	You Stepped out of a Dream 31/10/41
BD 972	I'll Guess I'll Have to Dream the Rest 31/10/41
	I Don't Want to Set the World on Fire 31/10/41
BD 982	That Lovely Weekend –/11/41
	You're in My Arms –/11/41
BD 992	Sand in My Shoes 5/1/42
	Intermezzo 5/1/42
BD 999	I Know Why –/2/42
	Rose and a Prayer –/2/42
BD 1001	Shrine of Saint Cecilia –/3/42
	I'll Always Remember –/3/42
BD 1003	Flamingo 8/4/42
	Daydreaming 8/4/42
BD 1006	Someone's Rocking My Dream Boat 8/4/42
	Absent Minded Moon 8/4/42
BD 1008	Stardust 9/7/42
	Jealousy 9/7/42
BD 1010	Moon Light Cocktail 9/7/42
	If You Haven't Got Dreams 9/7/42
BD 1013	Where in the World 8/8/42
	This Is Worth Fighting for 8/8/42
BD 1019	You Walk By 3/9/42
	Anywhere on Earth Is Heaven 3/9/42
BD 1024	White Christmas 7/10/42
	Only You 7/10/42
BD 1027	Just Around the Corner 2/12/42
	Where the Waters Are Blue 2/12/42
BD 1029	My Devotion 1/12/42
	Every Night About This Time 1/12/42
BD 1030	Serenade in Blue 1/12/42
	Nightingale 1/12/42
BD 1033	Day Break 4/12/42
	Starlight Souvenirs 4/12/42
BD 1038	My Heart and I 2/12/42
	There Are Angels Outside Heaven 2/12/42
BD 1040	You Are My Love Song 2/12/42
	Take the World Exactly as You Find It 2/12/42

BD 1042	Where's My Love 20/4/43
	Letter from Home 20/4/43
BD 1047	Three Dreams 20/4/43
	Romanesca 20/4/43
BD 1049	You'll Never Know 6/7/43
	You'd Be So Nice to Come Home to 6/7/43
BD 1054	You're Lovely to Hold 14/8/43
	You Rhyme with Everything That's Beautiful 14/8/43
BD 1055	Alone with My Dreams 5/9/43
	All or Nothing At All 5/9/43
BD 1060	Pale Hands —/10/43
	You Happen Once in a Life Time —/10/43
BD 1066	We Musn't Say Goodbye 10/11/43
	I Never Mention Her Name 10/11/43
BD 1067	It Can't Be Wrong 1/12/43
	I Have a Vision 1/12/43
BD 1070	My Heart Tells Me 10/1/44
	Hold Back the Dawn 10/1/44
BD 1075	How Sweet You Are 3/2/44
	Kiss Me 3/2/44
BD 1080	All My Life 16/4/44
	An Hour Never Passes 16/4/44
BD 1081	One Love —/5/44
	I Couldn't Sleep a Wink Last Night —/5/44
BD 1083	Don't Ever Leave Me 11/6/44
	I'm Going to Build a Future World 11/6/44
BD 1085	Long Ago and Far Away 25/6/44
	A Lovely Way to Spend an Evening 25/6/44
BD 1087	Sophisticated Lady 11/8/44
	'Till Stars Forget to Shine 11/8/44
BD 1089	I'll Be Seeing You 3/9/44
	Too Much in Love 3/9/44
BD 1091	Do You Believe in Dreams? 3/10/44
	Spring Will Be a Little Late 3/10/44
BD 1094	Time Waits for No One 7/11/44
	It Could Happen to You 7/11/44
BD 1096	Don't You Know I Care? 6/12/44
	No One Else Will Do 6/12/44
BD 1097	Holiday for Strings 4/1/45
	Little Star 4/1/45
BD 1100	While We're Young 29/1/45
	You're So Sweet to Remember 29/1/45
BD 1101	More and More 20/2/45
	I'll Remember April 20/2/45
BD 1102	I Promise You 29/3/45
	In the Middle of Nowhere 29/3/45

BD 1104	I'm Confessin' 11/5/45
	Waiting 11/5/45
BD 1106	You Moved Right In 11/5/45
	I'm Happy in Rags 11/5/45
BD 1108	Dream 7/8/45
	Don't Take Your Love From Me 7/8/45
BD 1110	The Gypsy –/9/45
	There, I've Said It Again –/9/45
BD 1111	I'll Always Be with You 11/10/45
	There's No You 11/10/45
BD 1112	Manana 26/10/45
	Symphony 26/10/45
BD 1116	Rhapsody in Blue
	(selection 2 sides, piano and vocal) 29/11/45
BD 1121	Nancy 3/4/46
	Everybody Knew but Me 3/4/46
BD 1122	I'm So All Alone 24/1/46
	My Heart Is Dancing with You 24/1/46
BD 1124	Promises 1/3/46
	I'm Glad I Waited for You 1/3/46
BD 1129	Wait and See –/4/46
	Seems Like Old Times –/4/46
BD 1133	A Door Will Open 2/5/46
	Amado Mio 2/5/46
BD 1137	Bless You 20/6/46
	Time After Time 20/6/46
BD 1141	Do You Love Me 20/6/46
	All Through the Day 20/6/46
BD 1143	You Keep Coming Back Like a Song 28/8/46
	You Always Hurt the One You Love 28/8/46
BD 1151	'Till Then 8/10/46
	Anyway the Wind Blows 8/10/46
BD 1160	I Keep Forgetting to Remember –/12/46
	Either It's Love or It Isn't –/12/46
BD 1163	La Mer 2/4/47
	That's the Beginning of the End 2/4/47
BD 1170	They Say It's Wonderful 29/5/47
	People Will Say We're in Love 29/5/47
BD 1173	There's Danger Ahead, Beware 1/7/47
	Heart Aches 1/7/47
BD 1181	Peg o' My Heart –/8/47
	Now Is the Hour –/8/47
BD 9611	A Tree in the Meadow 6/12/47
	I Never Loved Anyone 6/12/47
B 9629	But Beautiful –/2/48
	Nice to Know You Care –/2/48

B 9650	You Do –/5/48
	Ask Anyone Who Knows –/5/48
B 9698	It Only Happens When I Dance with You 15/9/48
	Hush-a-bye, Sleep Well 15/9/48
CB 1183	Let's Do It
1954	Too Many Martinis
CB 1185	I Talk to the Trees
1954	Begin the Beguine
CB 1189	On the First Warm Day
1954	Theme Song from the Moulin Rouge
CB 1191	I've Never Been in Love Before
1954	If I Were a Bell
CB 1192	The Bells of Home
1954	The Queen of Everyone's Heart
CB 1217	Remember to Remember Me
1954	Fisherman John
CB 1292	I Live for You
1954	Make Her Mine
F 10388	It's Alright with Me Dec 54
	I Love Paris Dec 54
F 10436	Surprisingly Dec 54
	Wait 'Til April Dec 54

These were the last of Hutch's commercial recordings. He did, however, release an LP in 1957 which contained the following titles:

Side One
1 A Nightingale Sang in Berkeley Square
2 I Cover the Waterfront
3 Dinner for One, Please James
4 I Am Loved
5 Trees
6 The Best Things in Life Are Free

Side Two
1 Bang Goes the Drum
2 You're Nearer
3 Mind If I Make Love to You
4 That Certain Feeling
5 Tenderly
6 You Took Advantage of Me

The original catalogue number is unknown to me, but it was rereleased on the World Record Club label in 1969, presumably as a memorial album. The session was produced by Norman Newell.

Hutch Vinyl,
Cassette and CD issues 1954–1999

Catalogue number
and date

Title

Vinyl

1. no cat. number
   1954

   Hutch in India (8 titles) 10"
   not released in Britain

2. Decca LF 1207
   Dec 1954

   Hutch at the Piano (8 titles) 10"
   with Bob Shardles and his music

3. Conquest (cat. no. not known)
   October 1957
   Cat. no. SH 137 in 1969

   Hutch (12 titles) 12"
   Rereleased on World Record
   Club

4. Morgan MX 7003
   1969

   The Magic of Hutch (10 titles) 12"
   with rhythm accompaniment

5. World Record Club SHB 28
   1975

   Hutch. Leslie Hutchinson at the
   Piano (32 titles) double 12" LP

6. Joy D 269
   1983

   Dance Music of the 1930s
   Leslie Hutchinson. The Magic of
   Hutch (16 titles) 12"
   Recordings from radio broadcasts

7. Decca RFL 38
   1984

   Hutch with a Song in My Heart (18
   titles) includes recording of 'I've
   Got the Feeling I'm Falling.' 1929

8. EMI – EG.260456–1
   1984

   Hutch Moonlight Cocktail
   (20 tracks) 12" 1940–47

9. EMI GX 2550
   1986

   Hutch: The Golden Age of Hutch
   (16 tracks) 12"

10. Saville – SVL 183
    1986
    12" 1930–1935

    You and the Night and the Music
    Leslie A. Hutchinson (20 tracks)

11. Burlington BUR 011

    That Old Feeling (18 tracks) 12"

Cassettes

1. World Record Club TC2 SHB 28
   1975

   Hutch: Leslie A. Hutchinson at the
   Piano (32 titles) double cassette
   (same as double LP SHB 28)

2. Flapper Past 7755
   1989

   The Cream of Hutch (22 tracks)
   Also on CX 9755

3. Pickwick DTO 10298

   Hutch at the Piano. Legendary
   Performances 1936–1938. Double
   cassette (24 tracks)

Compact Discs

1. Academy Sound and Vision
   CD AJA 5084

   Hutch:
   Treasured Memories 1937–1947

1992   Some recordings from air shows. (24 tracks)

2. Conifer CDHD 213   *Hutch Sings Cole Porter, Noël*
1994   *Coward and others*. (25 tracks)
                                               1929–43

INDEX

A Hutch archive which comprises videos of films and newsreels in which he appeared and his own record collection, tapes of rare recordings, photographs and memorabilia are available for study by arrangement with James Moore near Manchester and will eventually be gifted to Mander and Mitchenson Theatre Collection and the National Sound Archive. Please write with enquiries to James Moore, 12 Westminster Drive, Cheadle Hulme, Cheshire SK8 7QX.

A NOTE ON THE TYPE

The text of this book is set in Bembo. The original types
for which were cut by Francesco Griffo for the Venetian
printer Aldus Manutius, and were first used in 1495
for Cardinal Bembo's *De Aetna*. Claude Garamond
(1480–1561) used Bembo as a model and so it became
the forerunner of standard European type for the
following two centuries. Its modern form was designed,
following the original, for Monotype in 1929 and is widely
in use today.